INSIDE AMERICAN EDUCATION

INSIDE AMERICAN EDUCATION

The Decline, the Deception, the Dogmas

THOMAS SOWELL

THE FREE PRESS
A Division of Macmillan, Inc.
New York
Maxwell Macmillan Canada
Toronto
Maxwell Macmillan International
New York   Oxford   Singapore   Sydney

The Free Press
A Division of Macmillan, Inc.
866 Third Avenue, New York, N.Y. 10022

Maxwell Macmillan Canada, Inc.
1200 Eglinton Avenue East
Suite 200
Don Mills, Ontario M3C 3N1

Macmillan, Inc. is part of the Maxwell Communication
Group of Companies.

Printed in the United States of America

printing number
   6 7 8 9 10

Library of Congress Cataloging-in-Publication Data
Sowell, Thomas
 Inside American education: the decline, the deception, the dogmas/
 Thomas Sowell.
  p. cm.
 Includes bibliographical references.
 ISBN 0-02-930330-3
 1. Education—United States—Aims and objectives. 2. Education—United
States—Evaluation. I. Title.
LA210.S65 1993   92-19198
370'.973—dc20   CIP

The author is deeply grateful for permission to quote extensively from copyrighted material published in *The Public Interest* and in these sources:

Los Angeles Magazine. Reprinted with permission from Los Angeles Magazine. Copyright © Los Angeles Magazine. All rights reserved.

The University of Toledo Law Review, Volume 1970. Reprinted by permission of *The University of Toledo Law Review*, Volume 1970.

To

NA LIU

whose dedicated work
helped make this book possible

For the first time in the history of our country, the educational skills of one generation will not surpass, will not equal, will not even approach, those of their parents.

—JOHN COPPERMAN

CONTENTS

PREFACE

LIKE MANY other people, I have long been appalled by the low quality and continuing deterioration of American education. However, after doing the research for this book, I am frankly surprised that the results are not even worse than they are. The incredibly counterproductive fads, fashions, and dogmas of American education—from the kindergarten to the colleges— have yet to take their full toll, in part because all the standards of earlier times have not yet been completely eroded away. But the inevitable retirement of an older generation of teachers and professors must leave the new trends (and their accompanying Newspeak) as the dominant influence on the shaping of education in the generations to come.

Much has been said about how our young people do not meet the academic standards of their peers in other countries with which we compete economically. While this is both true and important, their academic deficiencies are only half the story. All across this country, the school curriculum has been invaded by psychological-conditioning programs which not only take up time sorely needed for intellectual development, but also promote an emotionalized and *anti-intellectual* way of responding to the challenges facing every individual and every society. Worst of all, the psychotherapeutic curriculum systematically undermines the parent-child relationship and the shared values which make a society possible.

Parents who send their children to school with instructions to respect and obey their teachers may be surprised to discover how often these children are sent back home conditioned to disrespect and disobey their parents. While psychological-conditioning programs may not succeed in producing the atomistic society, or the self-sufficient and morally isolated individual which seems to be their ideal, they may nevertheless confuse children who receive very different moral and social messages from school and home. In short, too many American schools are turning out students who are not only intellectually incompetent but also morally confused, emotionally alienated, and socially maladjusted.

At the college and university level, the intrusion of non-intellectual and anti-intellectual material into the curriculum takes more of an ideological, rather than a psychological, form. New courses, new departments, and whole new programs concentrate on leading students to preconceived ideological conclusions, rather than developing the student's ability to analyze issues so as to reach independent conclusions. The particular subject matter of these ideological courses and programs may range from race to the environment or foreign policy, but the general approach is the same, not only in its fundamental anti-intellectualism, but also in its underlying hostility to American society and Western civilization, and the tendentiousness or even dishonesty with which it attempts to indoctrinate. Here again, the danger is not that these methods will succeed in achieving their goals, but that they will undermine or cripple education in the attempt.

Thomas Sowell
Hoover Institution

CHAPTER 1

Decline, Deception, and Dogmas

VIRTUALLY EVERYONE has heard how poorly American students perform, whether compared to foreign students or to American students of a generation ago. What everyone may not know are the specifics of how bad the situation has become, how and why the public has been deceived, or the dogmas and hidden agendas behind it all.

The general decline in educational performance that began in the 1960s encompassed elementary and secondary education, as well as education at the college level. The evidences of this decline include not only results on a variety of objective tests, but also first-hand observations by teachers and professors, and dismaying experiences by employers who have found the end-product seriously lacking. The most widely known decline was in the scores on the Scholastic Aptitude Test (SAT). However, scores also declined on the rival American College Testing Program (ACT) examination, as well as on the Iowa Test of Educational Development,[1] and on a variety of local tests. As of 1991, only 11 percent of the eighth-grade students in California's public schools could solve seventh-grade math problems.[2]

1

Significantly, this era of declining academic performance has also been a period of rising grades. American high schools gave out approximately twice as many C's as A's in 1966, but by 1978 the A's actually exceeded the C's.[3] By 1990, more than one-fifth of all entering freshmen in college averaged A minus or above for their entire high school careers. At private universities, entering freshmen with averages of A minus or above were an absolute majority—54 percent.[4]

Similar grade inflation has become common at the college level. Between 1958 and 1988, the average grade at Dartmouth rose from C to B. More specifically, the Dartmouth student body's grade-point average rose from 2.2 in 1958 to 3.2 in 1988.[5] At the University of Chicago, the once common grade of C constituted only 15 percent of all grades by 1988—yet Chicago's grades are considered "comparatively low" relative to grades at comparable institutions around the country. At Yale, for example, the proportion of grades that were A's never fell below 40 percent during the entire decade of the 1980s.[6] At Smith College, likewise, A's were 40 percent of all grades by the end of the 1980s—a tripling of the proportion of A's over a period of 25 years—and A's and B's combined constituted more than 90 percent of all grades.[7] Rare is the college like Franklin & Marshall, where the student body's grade-point average has remained consistently below B over the years.[8]

Among the factors behind nationwide rises in college grades, in addition to more lenient grading by professors, have been such widespread practices as not recording failing grades on the student's records, allowing students to withdraw from class when a failing grade is impending, and ordinary cheating. Between 1966 and 1988, the proportion of students cheating increased by 78 percent, according to a national survey.[9]

These two trends—grade inflation and declining test scores—are by no means unconnected. Without the systematic deception of parents and the public by rising grades, it is highly unlikely that the decline in performance could have continued so long. The deeper question is—Why? Whose purposes are being served, and whose agendas are being advanced, as American education declines?

PERFORMANCE AND DECEPTION

Perhaps nothing so captures what is wrong with American schools as the results of an international study of 13-year-olds which found that Koreans ranked first in mathematics and Americans last. When asked if they thought they were "good at mathematics," only 23 percent of the Korean youngsters said "yes"—compared to 68 percent of American 13-year-olds.[10] The American educational dogma that students should "feel good about themselves" was a success in its own terms—though not in any other terms. A related educational dogma is that learning must be enjoyable to be effective. However, another international study found that a higher percentage of Japanese twelfth-graders disliked mathematics than did their American counterparts—but the Japanese did much better on mathematics tests.[11]

When nearly one-third of American 17-year-olds do not know that Abraham Lincoln wrote the Emancipation Proclamation, when nearly half do not know who Josef Stalin was, and when about 30 percent could not locate Britain on a map of Europe,[12] then it is clear that American educational deficiencies extend far beyond mathematics. As for trends over time, perhaps the best-known and most revealing statistic is that scores on the Scholastic Aptitude Test (SAT), taken by high school seniors applying for college admissions, began declining in the early 1960s and did not begin to rise again until the early 1980s. This decline was gradual but steady, falling from a composite verbal-and-quantitative score of 980 in 1963 to 890 in 1980 and 1981.[13] Despite a small upturn, the average SAT score has never returned to the level it reached more than a quarter of a century ago. As of 1990, the average combined verbal-math SAT score was 900—10 points above the low of 1980 but still 80 points below the high of 1963.[14] As of 1991, the average verbal SAT score dropped to an all-time low.[15]

Even these data do not capture the full story of educational disaster in American public schools. Members of the educational establishment often try to downplay such evidence by dismissing the importance of mere "facts" acquired by "rote memory." Unfortunately, as we turn from simple knowledge to more complex abilities in reasoning, the full debacle of American education becomes even more painfully clear. An international study of thirteen-year-olds showed that American youngsters fell further and further behind, the more they were required to *think*.

When given science questions on "everyday facts" American youngsters did almost as well as Korean youngsters, answering correctly 96 percent of the time, as compared to 100 percent among the Koreans. But when required to "apply simple principles," a significant gap opened up, as Koreans answered correctly 93 percent of the time and Americans only 78 percent of the time. Going on to a higher level, requiring students to "analyze experiments," Korean youngsters answered correctly 73 percent of the time, while Americans answered correctly only 42 percent of the time. At a still higher level of analysis, where only 33 percent of Korean students could answer correctly, only 12 percent of Americans could answer correctly.[16] In short, while American youngsters could pretty much hold their own at the level of simple facts, the advantage shifted decisively in favor of the Korean youngsters when thinking was involved, becoming more than a two-to-one advantage when more sophisticated levels of reasoning were reached.

Science is not the only field in which American students are lacking in knowledge and—more importantly—in the ability to tie what they know together to form a coherent chain of reasoning. Many American students seem unaware of even the need for such a process. Test scores are only the tip of the iceberg. Professor Diane Ravitch, a scholar specializing in the study of American education, reports that "professors complain about students who arrive at college with strong convictions but not enough knowledge to argue persuasively for their beliefs." As Professor Ravitch concludes: "Having opinions without knowledge is not of much value; not knowing the difference between them is a positive indicator of ignorance."[17] In short, it is not merely that Johnny can't read, or even that Johnny can't think. *Johnny doesn't know what thinking is*, because thinking is so often confused with feeling in many public schools.

Psycho-Therapeutic "Education"

The phrase "I feel" is often used by American students to introduce a conclusion, rather than say "I think," or "I know," much less "I conclude." Unfortunately, "I feel" is often the most accurate term—and is regarded as sufficient by many teachers, as well as students. The net result, as in mathematics, is that many students are confident incompetents, whether discussing social issues, world events, or other subjects. The emphasis is on having students express opinions on issues, and on having those opinions taken seriously (enhancing self-esteem), regardless of whether there is anything behind them. When a reporter who spent months in a Los Angeles high school asked graduating seniors what they had learned, he received this reply from a boy described as "the smartest student in the class":

> I learned that in the Vietnam War, North and South Korea fought against each other, and then there was a truce at the 38th parallel, and that Eisenhower had something to do with it.

The reporter asked:

> Would it bother you to know that the things you learned were wrong?

The answer was:

> Not really. Because what we really learned from Miss Silver was that we were worth listening to, that we could express ourselves and that an adult would listen, even if we were wrong. That's why Miss Silver will always be our favorite teacher. She made us feel like we mattered, like we were important.

The teacher herself saw her role in very similar terms:

> I want to be real in class and be a human being. . . . And I want my students to know that they can be themselves and I'll still listen to them. I want every one of them to have a chance to express himself or herself. Those are my priorities.[18]

Neither this teacher nor this school was unique. A large literature has urged teachers to be non-judgmental, to "humanize" the classroom, to raise the "self-esteem" of students. A leading writer on such matters, the late psychotherapist Carl Rogers, spoke of "helping students to prize themselves, to build their confidence and self-esteem,"[19] of "teachers who are real persons"[20] and who "humanize their classrooms."[21] It was *assumed* that intellectual development would be part of this process.[22] The Los Angeles reporter's observation, however, was that the students he saw "know little in the way of organized thought processes or even basic ways of solving intellectual problems." While the reporter noted the "sincerity or intensity" of the teachers, he nevertheless concluded: "A human being who has not been taught to think clearly is a danger in a free society."[23]

Too many American students learn neither an intellectual process nor a knowledge base, nor acquire habits of study. Writer Mary McCarthy, after a stint on campus as a visiting professor, said that today's college students seemed "almost totally ignorant of the whole period spanned by my life, to say nothing of what happened before."[24] More generally, a Carnegie Foundation survey of faculty members found that 67 percent of the professors reported "a widespread lowering of standards in American higher education," 75 percent characterized their students as "seriously underprepared in basic skills," and 62 percent reported "grade inflation" as a problem at their colleges.[25] Moreover, 55 percent said that undergraduates at their institution "only do enough to get by."[26] Just how little that is may be indicated by the fact that only 33 percent of college students put in 16 or more hours of study per week outside of class in 1985—and this declined to 23 percent by 1988.[27] As of 1966, 52 percent of all college freshmen had checked at least one book out of a library during the preceding year. By 1990, only 27 percent had done so.[28]

Educators and parents are not the only ones dissatisfied with the kinds of students American schools are turning out. A survey of Fortune 500 companies showed that 58 percent complained of the difficulty of finding employees with basic skills.[29] The Chief Executive Officer of Pacific Telesis reported: "Only four out of every 10 candidates for entry-level jobs at Pacific Telesis are able to pass our entry exams, which are based on a seventh-grade level."[30] In 1989, New York Life began airlifting its health insurance claims to Ireland for processing, because American workers made too many mistakes.[31]

Changes over Time

One of the reasons why basics are not learned is that they are not taught—at least not at the same level or with the same emphasis as in the past. For example, the process of making public school textbooks easier to read has been going on so long and so widely that it has even acquired a well-known generic name—"dumbing down." For example, when a well-known history book was revised with an eye toward the high school market, words like "spectacle" and "admired" were eliminated as "difficult."[32]

Some idea of how far this deliberate erosion of standards has gone may be gotten from looking at the once-standard *McGuffey's Readers* from generations ago, or by looking at examinations from that by-gone era. *McGuffey's First Reader*, for example, included diacritical marks to indicate the pronunciation of vowels and the emphasis of syllables.[33] *McGuffey's Third Reader* contained such words as "heath" and "benighted" and asked such questions as "What is this species of composition called?" and "Relate the facts of this dialogue."[34] *McGuffey's Fourth Reader* included selections from Longfellow and Hawthorne, and the *Fifth Reader* from Shakespeare.[35] These were not the textbooks of the elite but of the masses. For the better part of a century, from 1836 to 1920, *McGuffey's Readers* were so widely used that they sold more than 122 million copies—second in sales only to the Bible.[36]

In the early years of the twentieth century, pupils finishing the eighth grade in Kansas had to pass an examination which included spelling such words as "elucidation" and "animosity," defining such terms as "zenith" and "panegyric," as well as diagramming sentences and doing such problems in arithmetic as finding the interest earned on a $900 note, at 8 percent, after 2 years, 2 months, and 6 days.[37] Questions of similar difficulty were asked in geography and history—all in order to get a diploma awarded at the end of the eighth grade. These were not elite prep schools. Often they were one-room school houses in rural Kansas.

EXCUSES FOR FAILURE

The responses of the educational establishment to the academic deficiencies of their students today include (1) secrecy, (2) camouflage, (3) denial, (4) shifting the blame elsewhere, and (5) demanding more money.

"Confidentiality" policies maintain secrecy, while inflated grades and a policy of not recording failing grades help many institutions to camouflage the facts, so that optimistic public statements can effectively deny what is happening. When the facts become so blatant as to overwhelm these defenses, the strategy is simply to shift the blame to some other factor—outside the educational system. These include both social factors and financial resources.

Social Factors

Although educators have been quick to blame the failures of the schools on factors outside the schools, there has been remarkably little critical examination of these claims. It is unquestionably true that the home backgrounds of children influence how well they do in school, and that these backgrounds vary by social class and by race.[38] However, to say that an influence exists is not to say that it explains the particular pattern that we see.

Many have tried to use the changing social mixture of students in American schools and colleges as an explanation of declining test scores. American Federation of Teachers president Albert Shanker used this tactic during a 1986 debate at the University of California at Davis. During the period of falling SAT scores, Shanker said, schools had "discouraged students from dropping out," thereby retaining "more difficult youngsters," whose scores presumably lowered the average.

In reality, however, SAT scores declined *at the top*, not because there were more low scores averaged in. More than 116,000 students scored above 600 on the verbal SAT in 1972 and fewer than 71,000 scored that high ten years later.[39] Between the early 1960s and the early 1980s, median SAT scores dropped at colleges from coast to coast, including the most prestigious institutions. Both verbal and quantitative SAT scores declined at Yale, Princeton, Cal Tech, the University of Chicago, Oberlin, Rice, Brandeis, Carleton, Pomona, Reed, Whitman, and Davidson, for example. The composite score decline was more than 100 points at Brandeis and Reed.[40] As Diane Ravitch put it: "The shrinkage of the top scorers has proceeded steadily since the 1960s and obviously is unrelated to the overall composition of the test group."[41] Obviously— except to the educational establishment.

The false argument that retaining a higher proportion of low-performance students accounts of low average scores is also used to excuse the dismal performance of American students in international comparisons. But virtually all 13-year-olds are in school in all the countries surveyed in international mathematics performance surveys. While some countries have a smaller proportion of their students remain in school to reach the last year of high school than the United States does, Japan has an even higher proportion staying in school to finish than the U.S. does, so selectivity can hardly explain the superior performance of the Japanese.[42] Carnegie Foundation President Ernest L. Boyer has claimed that for "a small percentage of students" at the top, "the American high school provides an outstanding education, perhaps the finest in the world."[43] However, this wholly unsubstantiated statement is contradicted by the results of international tests. The top 5 percent of American high school seniors scored last on algebra and calculus tests administered to the top 5 percent of twelfth-graders from a dozen countries.[44]

While it is undoubtedly true that there are many negative factors at work in many low-income neighborhood schools, especially those in the inner-city ghettos and barrios, that does not automatically explain away the declining academic performances of American schools in general. Black and Hispanic students have lower than average test scores on such examinations as the Scholastic Aptitude Test, but their SAT scores cannot explain the national decline, for Hispanic scores have *risen* during much of the national decline, and black scores have risen still more.[45]

Even in low-income, crime-ridden neighborhoods, Catholic and other private schools have often produced far better academic results than the public schools in the same areas.[46] The public schools' usual attempts to escape comparisons by claiming that Catholic and other private schools have children from higher-income, better-educated families will not work in these particular cases. A Rand Corporation study not only confined its sample of Catholic schools to those in low-income ghetto and barrio neighborhoods in New York, but also included youngsters whose parents did *not* pay to send them to Catholic schools, but whose tuition there was paid by private individuals who wanted to enable an unselected sample of public school children to attend Catholic schools, to see if these unselected youngsters would also do better than those remaining in the public schools. The youngsters who transferred into the Catholic schools did significantly better than their peers who remained in the public schools, even though these transferees from the public school came mostly from single-parent households on welfare and entered the Catholic schools two or more years behind on placement tests, some scoring in the bottom tenth.[47] For that matter, some special public schools located in poor neighborhoods also did much better than most other public schools.[48] In short, better schools produce demonstrably better results, even in the worst neighborhoods.

The serious social problems of many inner city youngsters cannot explain the downward trend of American education in general, nor even fully explain the educational catastrophes in bad neighborhoods. The fervor with which various social problems are seized upon as explanations of American educational deficiencies is not based on any evidence that will stand up under scrutiny. These explanations are only a symptom of the desperate necessity of shoring up the dogma that educational failures could not possibly be the fault of the public school system.

Financial Factors

When all else fails, spokesmen and apologists for the education establishment blame a lack of money—often expressed as a lack of "commitment" by the public or the government—for their problems. The issue is posed as how "serious" the public, or its political leaders, are about "investing" in the education of the next generation. This cleverly turns the tables on critics and loads guilt onto the tax-paying public for the failures of American schools and colleges. Implicit in all this is the wholly unsupported assumption that more money means better education. Neither comparisons among states, comparisons over time, nor international comparisons, lend any credence to this arbitrary (and self-serving) assumption.

States that spend more per pupil in the public schools do not generally have any better educational performance to show for it. The correlation between financial inputs and educational outputs is very weak and shaky. Connecticut, for example, spent more than $4,000 per pupil in 1984 but student test scores were lower than those in Vermont, which spent just under $3,000 per pupil. Rhode Island also spent close to $4,000 per pupil and had the lowest average SAT scores of the three. New York state spent more than $5,000 per pupil that year, finished just barely ahead of Rhode Island, and significantly behind Vermont.[49] One could cite other cases where the more expensively educated students did better but, over all, there is no real evidence to support the claim that more money means better educational quality. More affluent communities are typically better-educated communities, where parents emphasize education to their children, and may be more willing and able to put more money into the local schools. But it is by no means clear that whatever better educational results come out of this combination of circumstances is due to the money. A highly respected Brookings Institution study concluded: "When other relevant factors are taken into account, economic resources are unrelated to student achievement."[50]

One reason why spending has so little effect on educational performance is that most of the money never reaches the classroom. Studies of the Milwaukee and New York City school systems show that less than half the money spent per high school student in New York or per elementary school student in Milwaukee actually reached the school—and less than a third of the total expenditure went to classroom services.[51] Over a period of a quarter of a century, teachers' salaries have been a declining percentage of school budgets,[52] as bureaucracies and other non-instructional costs absorbed the growing sums of money being spent on the educational establishment.

Looking at money input and educational output over time makes the education establishment's claims of inadequate financing look even more ridiculous. The period of declining test scores was also a period when expenditures on education were rising—rising not only in money terms but also in real terms, allowing for inflation. Per-pupil expenditures rose 27 percent in real terms during the decade of the 1970s and 29 percent in real terms during the decade of the 1980s. This was after a huge 58 percent increase in real terms during the decade of the 1960s—which was the very decade when the long decline in performance began. Financial input was not lacking. Educational output was lacking—and still is.

An international look at per-pupil expenditures likewise gives the lie to claims that more money produces better education. Despite claims that money is needed to hire more teachers to relieve "overcrowded classrooms," the United States already has a smaller average class size than a number of countries whose educational achievements are higher. Japan, for example, averages 41 students per class, compared to 26 for the United States. In mathematics, where the performance gap is especially glaring, the average class size in Japan is 43, compared to 20 in the U.S.[54] Within the United States, the ratio of pupils to teachers declined throughout the entire era from the 1960s to the 1980s, when test scores were also declining.[55]

In over-all per-pupil expenditure, the U.S. ranks near the top, even though the performance of its students often ranks at or near the bottom. American elementary and secondary school pupils receive more educational expenditures each than pupils in most Western European countries, more than pupils in Canada, more than 50 percent higher expenditures than in Japan or Australia, and more than twice the per-pupil expenditure in New Zealand.[56] Our schools are already turning out some of the most expensive incompetents anywhere. Making them still more expensive will not change that.

Here too the education establishment has resorted to deception, in order to deny plain facts and claim more money. Instead of comparing real expenditures per pupil in various countries, they compare the percentage of annual national output devoted to education, as "a measure of national effort." Because the United States has the largest national output in the world, the percentage going to education is lower than that in some other countries, though not usually by much.[57] But percentages are not a measure of resources. Existing resources devoted to educating pupils in the United States already exceed what other nations have found sufficient to produce much better results. It is not "national effort" that is lacking. What is lacking is the educational system's ability to deliver results after it has been supplied with ample resources.

Higher Education

At the college level, the claim that more money translates into better education is likewise blatantly fallacious. As increasingly vast sums of money have poured into colleges and universities over the past half-century, one of the most striking results has been that professors have taught fewer and fewer classes, and have done more and more research. When Jacques Barzun wrote his classic *Teacher in America* back in the 1940s, he referred to a typical college professor spending 15 hours a week in the classroom.[58] Today, even half of that time would be considered an excessive teaching load at many institutions. Indeed, 35 percent of today's faculty teach undergraduates only 4 hours a week or less. At research universities, 51 percent of the faculty teach undergraduates only 4 hours or less, and fewer than 10 percent spend as much as 11 hours a week teaching undergraduates.[59] However, more than half of research university faculty spend 11 or more hours per week on research.[60]

College professors, like elementary and high school teachers, often claim that their time in the classroom underestimates how much time they spend on instruction, because it omits the time spent preparing lectures, grading examinations, and the like. For university professors, the teaching of graduate students must be added to their undergraduate teaching load, though graduate seminars often require little or no preparation on the professor's part, when they serve primarily as a forum for the presentation of students' papers. Still, a study of the total time spent on duties relating to instruction showed an average of only about 15 hours a week among faculty at research universities, slightly less than the time spent on re-search—and less than one third of all their weekly working hours, including time spent taking part in various scholarly activities and earning additional money with outside consult-ing, lecturing, or other activities.[61] More money for higher ed-ucation will never mean more teaching—much less better teaching—as long as that money goes into reducing teaching loads and financing more research.

At Harvard, the number of faculty members more than dou-bled between 1952 and 1974, while the undergraduate student population grew by only 14 percent. Yet the number of courses enrolling undergraduates actually *fell* by 28 percent.[62] At the University of Wisconsin, a study found that only about one-fourth of the economics professors taught two courses in the semester surveyed.[63] As long as research competes with teach-ing for the time of professors, throwing more money at colleges and universities is unlikely to improve either the quantity or the quality of education. The amount of money currently being thrown at higher education is already so large that there are literally dozens of institutions receiving more than $100 million each in research and development funds. Johns Hopkins Uni-versity receives more than $500 million.[64] The money it receives in tuition payments is less than one-fifth its annual receipts.[65] In academia, as elsewhere, money talks—and what it says is "research."

It is not only the attraction of research money that lures professors out of the classroom. The spread of the publish-or-perish principle reinforces a drive for research at the expense of teaching. More than three-quarters of all faculty members at four-year academic institutions say that it is difficult for anyone to get tenure in their department without publishing. In research universities, more than 90 percent say so.[66] One symptom of the relative importance given to teaching versus research are the many instances of untenured faculty members who receive teacher-of-the-year awards, only to be told that their contracts will not be renewed. During a recent span of years at M.I.T., three out of four untenured recipients of such awards were denied tenure.

None of this is meant to claim that research is not impor-tant, nor even to assess its relative importance compared to teaching. The point is simply that more money does not translate into more or better education, at the college or university level, any more than elsewhere in the American educational system.

DOGMAS AND AGENDAS

American education is undermined by numerous dogmas and numerous hidden agendas. The dogmas fall into two general categories—dogmas about education and dogmas about the larger society. "Self-esteem," "role models," "diversity," and other buzzwords dominate educational policy—without evidence being either asked or given to substantiate the beliefs they represent. Sweeping beliefs about the general society, or about how life ought to be lived, likewise become prevalent among educators without empirical verification being required. More important, world-saving crusades based on such beliefs have increasingly intruded into the classroom, from kindergarten to college, crowding out the basic skills that American students lack. Some of this represents changing views among educators as to the role of education. Behind much of the world-saving curriculum, however, are the organized efforts of outside interests and movements, determined to get their special messages into the classroom.

For example, a pharmaceutical company which manufactures birth control products supplies thousands of so-called "sex education" kits to high schools.[67] Automobile interests promote driver education.[68] Such commercial interests are joined by psychological experimenters, disarmament advocates, crusaders for world population control, and innumerable other "causes" that invade the classroom to absorb time sorely needed to teach American children to read, write, do mathematics—and to learn to *think* critically, rather than repeat propaganda.

Unfortunately, the educational establishment itself is heavily involved in non-educational issues, fashions, and crusades. A symptom of this mindset can be found in the February 1990 issue of *PTA Today* magazine, published by the National Parent-Teacher Association, featuring articles on (1) diet and cancer; (2) food allergies; (3) radon gas dangers; (4) medicines; (5) vaccination; (6) speech disorders; (7) aging and dying; (8) AIDS;

(9) teenage drivers; (10) corporal punishment and (11) being a hospital patient. Not one article dealt with the educational basics in which American schools are so deficient. Instead, the focus was on matters of personal lifestyle and general world-saving. The largest teacher's union in the country, the National Education Association, likewise often wanders far afield from education, to promote all sorts of ideological crusades. At the N.E.A.'s annual meeting in 1991, for example, delegates passed resolutions on things ranging from nuclear weapons to immigration, housing, highways, environmentalism, and "development of renewable energy resources."[69] These political interests of the education establishment often find their way right into the classroom, as children are given assignments to write letters to public officials, in order to forward such political agendas, whether to urge the President of the United States toward a certain policy on nuclear weapons,[70] or to demand that state legislators appropriate more money for education.[71] It speaks volumes about today's educators that a captive audience of school children would be used in this way.

At the college level, the world-saving agendas are even more blatant, as whole fields and departments have been created to promote particular causes, under such names as "environmental studies," "peace studies," and various racial or ethnic "studies" boosting group images, promoting ideological visions, and often serving as organizing and recruiting centers for political activism.

Much of the politicizing of education during the current era happens to have been done by the political left, and much of the exposure and criticism of it has therefore come from conservatives, but it would be a very serious mistake to think that this issue is basically political. Increasing numbers of honest people of liberal, and even radical, views have likewise been appalled at the prostitution of education for ideological ends. The liberal *Washington Post* for example, has criticized one of the widely-used curriculum guides by saying that it "is not education, it is political indoctrination."[72] The liberal *New Republic* has denounced the ideological version of "multiculturalism" as being "neither multi nor cultural," but instead an attempt to impose "a unanimity of thought on campus."[73] Marxist scholar Eugene Genovese has urged "honest people across the spectrum" to stand up for academic principles and to oppose "the new wave of campus barbarism."[74] In short, the politicization of education is not fundamentally a political issue, but an educational issue.

The educational consequences of ideological indoctrination efforts are likely to be far more serious than the political consequences. The ideologies of young people in schools or in colleges are not set in concrete. Most of the leading conservative figures of our time were once either liberals (like Ronald Reagan and Milton Friedman) or outright radicals (like Friedrich Hayek and Irving Kristol). The politicization of education is unlikely to have as much long run effect on politics as it does on education. It is not the particular goals of ideological zealots which are at issue here, but the damage they are doing to American education while pursuing those goals. The real issue is not political "imbalance," as some conservative critics have claimed, for adding more teachers and professors from the political right, doing what those on the left are doing, would not solve the *educational* problem.

Whether blatant or subtle, brainwashing has become a major, time-consuming activity in American education at all levels. Some zealots have not hesitated to use the traditional brain-washing technique of emotional trauma in the classroom to soften up children for their message. Gruesome and graphic movies on nuclear war, for example, have reduced some school children to tears—after which the teacher makes a pitch for whatever movement claims to reduce such dangers. Another technique is the ambush shock: A seventh-grade teacher in Manhattan, for example, innocently asked her students to discuss their future plans—after which she said: "Haven't any of you realized that in this world with nuclear weapons no one in this class will be alive in the year 2000?"[75]

These are not isolated incidents. Nor is the emotional shock treatment confined to this issue, as we will see in Chapter 3. A whole new social phenomenon known as "affective education" has spread across the country, seeking to re-shape the moral values, personal habits, and social mindsets of American children. Affective education is not to be confused with effective education. Indeed, it is one of many agendas which distract schools from effective education. The emotionalizing of education not only takes time away from intellectual development; it also casts teachers in the role of amateur psychologists, though they are unqualified to gauge the consequences of their manipulations of children's emotions. Beyond that, it is the very antithesis of education.

The purpose of education is to give the student the intellectual tools to analyze, whether verbally or numerically, and to reach conclusions based on logic and evidence. The attempts of schools and colleges to encompass far more than they can handle are an important part of the reason why they are handling education so poorly.

PART ONE

SCHOOLS

CHAPTER 2

Impaired Faculties

No DISCUSSION of American education can be realistic without considering the calibre of the people who teach in the nation's schools. By all indicators—whether objective data or first-hand observations—the intellectual calibre of public school teachers in the United States is shockingly low. While there have been, and continue to be, many schemes designed to raise the qualifications and performance of the teaching profession, the intellectual level of this occupation has, if anything, *declined* in recent times, just as the performance of the students they teach has declined. To understand why innumerable efforts to improve teachers and teaching have failed, it is necessary to understand something about the occupation itself, about the education which prepares people for that occupation, about the kind of people who become teachers, and about the institutions which attempt to educate American children.

THE OCCUPATION

There are well over 2 million school teachers in the United States—more than all the doctors, lawyers, and engineers combined.[1] Their sheer numbers alone mean that there will inevitably be many exceptions to any generalizations made about teachers. However, a number of important generalizations do apply to the great majority of these teachers. For example, public school teaching is an overwhelmingly unionized occupation, an occupation with virtually iron-clad job security, an occupation in which virtually everyone has a degree or degrees, and yet an occupation whose lack of substantive intellectual qualifications is painfully demonstrable.

The National Education Association (NEA) alone has approximately one and a half million members and the American Federation of Teachers (AFT) has more than 600,000 members. Together, they represent the great majority of teachers.[2] Both organizations are highly effective lobbying groups at both the federal and state levels, and both aim much advertising at the general public, both to generate a favorable image of teachers and to get the public used to seeing education issues in a certain framework, favorable to the profession—for example, to equate more money for the public school establishment with "an investment in better education." Everything from television commercials to bumper stickers promote their cause, unopposed by any comparably organized counter-propaganda. Moreover, huge political campaign contributions assure teachers' unions favorable access to the seats of power in Washington and in the state capitals.

Given the political realities, it can hardly be surprising that public school teachers are among the most difficult of all employees to fire—regardless of the level of their competence or incompetence. Rates of pay likewise bear virtually no relationship to competence or incompetence, but are largely determined by longevity and college credits.[3] A teacher who ruins the education of generation after generation of students will be rewarded by continually rising pay levels.

Just how incompetent a teacher can be and still keep the job was illustrated by an extreme case in South Carolina, where a school tried to get rid of a teacher who had been warned repeatedly about her poor teaching and poor English. At a hearing where she was given a ten-word vocabulary test, she could neither pronounce nor define the word "agrarian." She could pronounce the word "suffrage" but defined it as "people suffering from some reason or other." The word "ratify" she defined as "to get rid of something." In her own defense, she said: "I'm not saying I was the best, but I don't think I did more harm than anyone else." A judge ordered her reinstated.[4]

To complete the tightly controlled monopoly, both the supply of customers and the supply of labor are almost totally under the control of the education establishment. Compulsory attendance laws guarantee a captive audience, except for about 13 percent of American youngsters who attend private schools,[5] and official requirements of education courses for permanent tenure keep out the unwanted competition of potential teachers from outside the existing establishment. These multiple monopolies serve the interests of two narrow constituencies: (1) public school teachers and administrators, and (2) those college professors who teach education courses—courses notoriously unattractive in themselves, but representing the toll gates through which aspirants must pass in order to acquire tenure in public school teaching. "Emergency" or "provisional" credentials can be obtained to enter the classroom, but education courses are officially required to stay there permanently as a teacher.

INTELLECTUAL LEVELS

The extremes to which job security for the individual and job barriers for the profession are carried suggest a desperate need to avoid competition. This fear of competition is by no means paranoid. It is very solidly based on the low levels of substantive intellectual ability among public school teachers and administrators, and among the professors of education who taught them.

Consistently, for decades, those college students who have majored in education have been among the least qualified of all college students, and the professors who taught them have been among the least respected by their colleagues elsewhere in the college or university. The word "contempt" appears repeatedly in discussions of the way most academic students and professors view their counterparts in the field of education.[6] At Columbia Teachers College, 120th Street is said to be "the widest street in the world" because it separates that institution from the rest of Columbia University.

Nor is Columbia at all unique in this respect. "In many universities," according to a study by Martin Mayer, "there is little if any contact between the members of the department of education and the members of other departments in the school."[7] When the president of Harvard University retired in 1933, he told the institution's overseers that Harvard's Graduate School of Education was a "kitten that ought to be drowned."[8] More recently, a knowledgeable academic declared, "the educationists have set the lowest possible standards and require the least amount of hard work."[9] Education schools and education departments have been called "the intellectual slums" of the university.

Despite some attempts to depict such attitudes as mere snobbery, hard data on education student qualifications have consistently shown their mental test scores to be at or near the bottom among all categories of students. This was as true of studies done in the 1920s and 1930s as of studies in the 1980s.[10] Whether measured by Scholastic Aptitude Tests, ACT tests, vocabulary tests, reading comprehension tests, or Graduate Record Examinations, students majoring in education have consistently scored below the national average.[11] When the U.S. Army had college students tested in 1951 for draft deferments during the Korean War, more than half the students passed in the humanities, social sciences, biological sciences, physical sciences and mathematics, but only 27 percent of those majoring in education passed.[12]

In 1980–81, students majoring in education scored lower on both verbal and quantitative SATs than students majoring in art, music, theatre, the behavioral sciences, physical sciences, or biological sciences, business or commerce, engineering, mathematics, the humanities, or health occupations. Undergraduate business and commercial majors have long been regarded as being of low quality, but they still edged out education majors on both parts of the SAT. Engineering students tend to be lopsidedly better mathematically than verbally, but nevertheless their verbal scores exceeded those of education majors, just as art and theatre majors had higher mathematics scores than education majors. Not only have education students' test scores been low, they have also been declining over time. As of academic year 1972–73, the average verbal SAT score for high school students choosing education as their intended college major was 418—and by academic year 1979–80, this had declined to 389.[13]

At the graduate level, it is very much the same story, with students in numerous other fields outscoring education students on the Graduate Record Examination—by from 91 points composite to 259 points, depending on the field.[14] The pool of graduate students in education supplies not only teachers, counselors, and administrators, but also professors of education and other "leaders" and spokesmen for the education establishment. In short, educators are drawing disproportionately from the dregs of the college-educated population. As William H. Whyte said back in the 1950s, "the facts are too critical for euphemism."[15]

Professors of education rank as low among college and university faculty members as education students do among other students. After listing a number of professors "of great personal and intellectual distinction" teaching in the field of education, Martin Mayer nevertheless concluded:

> On the average, however, it is true to say that the academic professors, with many exceptions in the applied sciences and some in the social sciences, are educated men, and the professors of education are not.[16]

Given low-quality students and low-quality professors, it can hardly be surprising to discover, as Mayer did, that "most education courses are *not* intellectually respectable, because their teachers and the textbooks are not intellectually respectable."[17] In short, some of the least qualified students, taught by the least qualified professors in the lowest quality courses supply most American public school teachers. There are severe limits to how intellectual their teaching could be, even if they wanted it to be. Their susceptibility to fads, and especially to non-intellectual and anti-intellectual fads, is understandable—but very damaging to American education. What is less understandable is why parents and the public allow themselves to be intimidated by such educators' pretensions of "expertise."

The futility of attempting to upgrade the teaching profession by paying higher salaries is obvious, so long as legal barriers keep out all those who refuse to take education courses. These courses are negative barriers, in the sense that they *keep out the competent*. It is Darwinism stood on its head, with the *unfittest* being most likely to survive as public school teachers.

The weeding out process begins early and continues long, eliminating more and more of the best qualified people. Among high school seniors, only 7 percent of those with SAT scores in the top 20 percent, and 13 percent of those in the next quintile, expressed a desire to go into teaching, while nearly half of those in the bottom 40 percent chose teaching. Moreover, with the passage of time, completion of a college education, and actual work in a teaching career, attrition is far higher in the top ability groups—85 percent of those in the top 20 percent leave teaching after relatively brief careers—while low-ability people tend to remain teachers.[18] This too is a long-standing pattern. A 1959 study of World War II veterans who had entered the teaching profession concluded that "those who are academically more capable and talented tended to drop out of teaching and those who remained as classroom teachers in the elementary and secondary schools were the less intellectually able members of the original group."[19] The results in this male sample were very similar to the results in a female sample in 1964 which found that the "attrition rate from teaching as an occupation was highest among the high ability group."[20] Other studies have had very similar results.[21] Sometimes the more able people simply leave for greener pastures, but the greater seniority of the least able can also force schools to lay off the newer and better teachers whenever jobs are reduced.

The dry statistics of these studies translate into a painful human reality captured by a parent's letter:

> Over the years, as a parent, I have repeatedly felt frustrated, angry and helpless when each spring teachers—who were the ones the students hoped anxiously to get, who had students visiting their classrooms after school, who had lively looking classrooms—would receive their lay-off notices. Meanwhile, left behind to teach our children, would be the mediocre teachers who appeared to have precious little creative inspiration for teaching and very little interest in children.[22]

With teachers as with their students, merely throwing more money at the educational establishment means having more expensive incompetents. Ordinarily, more money attracts better people, but the protective barriers of the teaching profession keep out better-qualified people, who are the least likely to have wasted their time in college on education courses, and the least likely to undergo a long ordeal of such Mickey Mouse courses later on. Nor is it realistic to expect reforms by existing education schools or to expect teachers' unions to remedy the situation. As a well-known Brookings Institution study put it, "existing institutions cannot solve the problem, because they *are* the problem."[23]

Teachers' unions do not represent teachers in the abstract. They represent such teachers as actually exist in today's public schools. These teachers have every reason to fear the competition of other college graduates for jobs, to fear any weakening of iron-clad tenure rules, and to fear any form of competition between schools that would allow parents to choose where to send their children to school. Competition means winners and losers—based on performance, rather than seniority or credentials. Professors of education are even more vulnerable, because they are supplying a product widely held in disrepute, even by many of those who enroll in their courses, and a product whose demand is due almost solely to laws and policies which compel individuals to enroll, in order to gain tenure and receive pay raises.

As for the value of education courses and degrees in the actual teaching of school children, there is no persuasive evidence that such studies have any pay-off whatever in the classroom. Postgraduate degree holders became much more common among teachers during the period of declining student test scores. Back in the early 1960s, when student SAT scores peaked, fewer than one-fourth of all public school teachers had postgraduate degrees and almost 15 percent lacked even a Bachelor's degree. But by 1981, when the test score decline hit bottom, just over half of all teachers had Master's degrees and less than one percent lacked a Bachelor's.[24]

Despite the questionable value of education courses and degrees as a means of improving teaching, and their role as barriers keeping out competition, defenders of the education schools have referred to proposals to reduce or eliminate such requirements as "dilutions" of teacher quality.[25] Conversely, to require additional years of education courses is equated with a move "to improve standards for teachers."[26] Such Orwellian Newspeak turns reality upside down, defying all evidence.

It should not be surprising that education degrees produce no demonstrable benefit to teaching. The shallow and stultifying courses behind such degrees are one obvious reason. However, even when the education school curriculum is "beefed up" with more intellectually challenging courses at some elite institutions, those challenging courses are likely to be in subjects imported from other disciplines—statistics or economics, for example—rather than courses on how to teach children. Moreover, such substantive courses are more likely to be useful for research purposes than for actual classroom teaching. When Stanford University's school of education added an honors program, it was specifically stated that this was *not* a program designed for people who intended to become classroom teachers.[27]

The whole history of schools and departments of education has been one of desperate, but largely futile, attempts to gain the respect of other academics—usually by becoming theoretical and research-oriented, rather than by improving the classroom skills of teachers.[28] But both theoretical and practical work in education are inherently limited by the low intellectual level of the students and professors attracted to this field.

Where education degrees are not mandated by law as a requirement for teaching in private schools, those schools themselves often operate without any such requirement of their own. The net result is that they can draw upon a much wider pool of better-educated people for their teachers. The fact that these private schools often pay salaries not as high as those paid to public school teachers further reveals the true role of education degrees as protective tariffs, which allow teachers' unions to charge higher pay for their members, who are insulated from competition.

Schools and departments of education thus serve the narrow financial interests of public school teachers and professors of education—and disserve the educational interests of more than 40 million American school children.

INSTITUTIONAL PROBLEMS

While the low—and declining—intellectual calibre of public school teachers limits the quality of American education, there are also institutional reasons why even these modest limits are often not reached. There are, after all, better and worse teachers, so that greater selectivity in hiring and a weeding out of the incompetent could, in theory at least, get the best performance out of the existing pool of people. However, the policies, practices, and legal constraints placed on educational institutions often prevent such rational maximization of teaching performance.

Even the bleak picture of the ability level among people who major in education leaves out institutional possibilities of better teaching, for it leaves out those people whose college majors were *not* in education but in other, more solid subjects, and who simply took education courses as well (either contemporaneously or later), in order to become teachers. Such people with *non*-education majors are in fact a majority among high school teachers.[29] Nevertheless, the attrition of the able and the institutional protection of the incompetent make American educational quality lower than it has to be, even with the existing pool of potential teachers.

Many of the constraints within which schools, school districts, and boards of education operate originate within the education establishment—with teachers unions, and schools of education, for example—but other constraints are imposed from outside. Legislators, for example, may mandate that new, non-academic subjects like driver education be taught in the public schools and judges may interpret laws and contracts in such a way as to make it an ordeal to get rid of either incompetent teachers or disruptive and violent students.

Incompetent Teachers

While mediocrity and incompetence among teachers limit the quality of work possible in public schools, institutional rules and practices often protect teachers whose performances fall far short of those limits. An academic scholar studying the problem of incompetent teachers during the 1980s discovered that several of the administrators he interviewed set aside $50,000 to cover procedural costs for every teacher they found to be a likely candidate for dismissal. Nor was this sum always adequate. One successful dismissal in California cost more than $166,000 in internal and external procedural costs, including more than $71,000 in legal fees to fight the teacher's court challenge. Had the school district lost in court, they would have had to pay the teacher's legal fees as well.[30] Moreover, only truly egregious cases are likely to lead to attempts at dismissal. More common responses include (1) ignoring the problem, (2) transferring the teacher, if parental pressures become irresistible, and (3) buying out an older teacher near retirement age.

At the heart of this pattern of evasion of responsibility for firing an incompetent teacher is the iron-clad tenure system and its accompanying elaborate (and costly) "due process" procedures for dismissal. Although tenured teachers are 80 percent of all California teachers, they were less than 6 percent of those involved in dismissals. Meanwhile, temporary teachers, who were only 7 percent of all California teachers, were involved in nearly 70 percent of all dismissals.[31] These statistics are especially striking because the research scholar discovered what data on test scores already suggest—that "incompetent teachers are much more likely to appear among the most senior segment of the teaching force than among the least senior."[32] In other words, where the problem is the worst, less can be done about it. The most senior teachers simply have too much job protection for an administrator to attempt dismissal, except in the most desperate cases. The teacher must not only be incompetent (or worse), but must also be recognized as such by many complaining parents, and these parents in turn must be people who know how to push a complaint through the system and exert influence.

Low-income and minority parents are less likely to complain and less likely to know how to make their complaints effective. Administrators are well aware of this and respond (or do not respond) accordingly.[33] In any kind of neighborhood, however, the mere fact that the teacher is incompetent and known by the authorities to be incompetent is unlikely, by itself, to lead to any action without parental complaints. As one school district administrator put it:

Principals are apprehensive about moving against a teacher. They need a reason to act other than the teacher is incompetent because it can be very difficult to prove.[34]

Another administrator:

Without parent complaints, we leave the teacher alone.[35]

Still another administrator:

You need a lot of external complaints to move on a teacher. The administrator is not willing to make tough decisions until he has to; that time comes when there are complaints.[36]

Even when a chorus of parental complaints forces an administrator into action, that action is unlikely to be dismissal. Transferring the teacher to a different school is far more common. This buys time, if nothing else. If and when the parents at the new school begin to complain about the same teacher, then another transfer may be arranged, and yet another. These multiple transfers are so common that they even have nicknames, such as "the turkey trot" or "the dance of the lemons."[37] From the administrator's point of view, the problem is not that the teacher is incompetent but that the parents are complaining. If the teacher can be put in a low-income neighborhood school, where many students are transient or the parents unable to make effective complaints, then the problem has been solved, as far as the system is concerned, without the expensive and time-consuming process of attempting dismissal.

Non-Academic Orientations

The academic deficiencies of American teachers and administrators, and the institutional insulation of incompetence, are only part of the story. Such factors might go far toward explaining the academic shortcomings of American schools, but there is an equally pervasive phenomenon in American education—an ever-growing intrusion of *non-academic* materials, courses, and programs into schools across the country. These non-academic intrusions include everything from political ideologies to psychological-conditioning programs, and their sponsors range from ordinary commercial interests (such as automobile manufacturers pushing driver education) to zealots for a vast array of "causes."

That outside interests should see 40 million school children as a captive audience to be exploited is not so difficult to comprehend as the fact that educators themselves are not merely acquiescent, but are often enthusiastic apostles of these innumerable non-academic courses and programs. Throughout most of the twentieth century, public school educators have pressed—usually successfully—for the inclusion of ever more non-academic materials in the curriculum, while the counter-pressure for more academic rigor, "back to basics," and the like, has come primarily from laymen.[38] As laymen have urged more emphasis on teaching mathematics, science, languages, and other traditional academic subjects, educators have promoted such personal concerns as nutrition, hygiene, and "life adjustment" in an earlier period, or sex education and death education more recently, along with such social crusades as environmentalism and the anti-nuclear movement, or such exotic topics as the occult. While the particular subjects that are fashionable change over time, what has been enduring is the non-academic thrust of the professional educators. As far back as 1928, John Dewey lamented the anti-intellectual tendencies of so-called "progressive education,"[39] though many educators had used his theories as a justification for abandoning or de-emphasizing traditional disciplines.

Strange as it may seem that people hired to teach academic subjects should be straining to do something else instead—for decades and even generations—this is far less strange in light of the academic backgrounds of the people who constitute the teaching and administrative staffs of the American educational system. It is not simply that they are academically deficient. They are not *academically oriented.* Nor is it reasonable to expect them to have a dedication to academic work, which brought them so little success when they were students in high school or college.

In addition to particular outside interest groups pushing to get their own interests and views represented in the school curriculum, there have been general theorists providing rationales for abandoning traditional academic education in favor of a wide variety of psycho-therapeutic activities known collectively as "affective education," designed to re-mold the emotions and values of students. Whether called by general names like "values clarification" or by more specific titles like "death education," "sex education," or "drug prevention," these psycho-therapeutic activities have flourished in the public schools—without any evidence of their effectiveness for their avowed purposes, and even despite accumulating evidence of their counterproductive effects (as will be seen in subsequent chapters). The theorists or gurus behind these ideas and movements have been very influential with educators highly susceptible to non-academic fashions and dogmas. The net result has been a deflection of public schools' efforts, interests, time, and resources from academic objectives toward what can only be called classroom brainwashing.

CHAPTER 3

Classroom Brainwashing

Many parents wonder why they lose their children to a
whole new value system.
— DONNA MULDREW, *parent and educator*[1]

A VARIETY of courses and programs, under an even wider variety
of names, have been set up in schools across the country to
change the values, behavior, and beliefs of American youngsters
from what they have been taught by their families, their
churches, or the social groups in which they have grown up.
These ambitious attempts to re-shape the attitudes and consciousness of a generation are as pervasive as they are little
known, partly because they have kept a low profile, but more
often because they are called by other, high-sounding names—
"values clarification," "decision-making," "affective education," "Quest," "drug prevention," "sex education," "gifted
and talented" programs, and many other imaginative titles.
The particular door through which such programs enter the
school curriculum is far less important than what they do after
they have gained entrance.

Drug prevention and sex education might seem to be very
different activities, and a program for gifted and talented students still more different from both of these. But that is true
only where these programs are legitimately confined to what
they claim to be. Far too often, however, these words are mere

flags of convenience under which schools set sail on an un-
charted sea of social experimentation in the re-shaping of young
people's emotions and attitudes. People who have looked beyond the labels to the concrete specifics have often discovered
that the ostensible subject of special curriculum programs—
drug education, sex education, etc.—occupies a minor part of
the textbooks or class time, while psychology and values are a
major preoccupation.

So-called "sex education" courses and textbooks, for example, seldom involve a mere conveying of biological or medical information. Far more often, the primary thrust is toward
a *re-shaping of attitudes*, not only toward sex but also toward
parents, toward society, and toward life. The same pattern is
found in many other programs claiming to be about drug prevention, smoking prevention, or many other worthy purposes.
Typical of this pattern was a so-called "drug prevention" program in New Hampshire, which a parent found to be about
one-fourth "informational" while "the other three-quarters
deal with values, attitudes, etc."[2] The same could be said of
the widely used sex education textbook, *Changing Bodies,
Changing Lives*. Similarly, in a widely distributed book used in
school anti-smoking campaigns, "smoking goes unmentioned"
except for inclusion in a list of "many new decisions" teenagers
will face.[3] A North Carolina teacher, testifying before the U.S.
Department of Education, pointed out that a federally funded
"drug education" curriculum "does not emphasize any information or facts about drugs, per se." Instead she found:

> This curriculum is 152 pages long, and yet only four pages
> make any mention of drugs, either directly or indirectly. The
> program is divided into three phases. The first phase is self-
> awareness followed by a series of exercises that permit stu-
> dents to gain "a wider understanding and appreciation of
> their values as autonomous individuals."[4]

If these programs are often not what they claim to be, then
what are they?

They are attempts to re-shape values, attitudes, and beliefs
to fit a very different vision of the world from what children
have received from their parents and the social environment
in which they are raised. Instead of educating the intellect,
these special curriculum programs condition the emotions.

This is sometimes called "affective education," as distinguished from intellectual education. It can also be called brainwashing.

BRAINWASHING METHODS

A variety of programs used in classrooms across the country not only share the general goals of brainwashing—that is, changing fundamental attitudes, values, and belief by psychological-conditioning methods—but also use classic brainwashing techniques developed in totalitarian countries:

1. *Emotional stress, shock, or de-sensitization*, to break down both intellectual and emotional resistance
2. *Isolation*, whether physical or emotional, from familiar sources of emotional support in resistance
3. *Cross-examining pre-existing values*, often by manipulating peer pressure
4. *Stripping the individual of normal defenses*, such as reserve, dignity, a sense of privacy, or the ability to decline to participate
5. *Rewarding* acceptance of the new attitudes, values, and beliefs—a reward which can be simply release from the pressures inflicted on those who resist, or may take other symbolic or tangible form

Stress and De-sensitization

There are all too many examples illustrating the use of these methods in psychological-conditioning programs in the public schools. For example, viewers of the ABC network television program "20/20" on September 21, 1990, may have been surprised—or upset—when they saw school children being taken to a morgue and being encouraged to touch the corpses, as part of "death education." Some viewers may have thought this exercise pointless as well as tasteless, and an imposition on the children. That may all be true, when looking at this as an *educational* activity, in the sense of something intended to convey information and develop the student's ability to analyze logically and weigh evidence. But this exercise was by no means pointless as part of a psychological-conditioning program. On the contrary, it was an example of the first step in brainwashing—stress and de-sensitization.

Some children undoubtedly found the experience stressful, some perhaps shocking, and more generally it served to desensitize normal inhibitions. An historical study of brainwashing techniques in various countries and in various periods of history found "emotional disruption" to be "essential" to the process.[5] The trip to the morgue was not a pointless exercise, from this perspective. Public schools do not have the degree of control maintained by totalitarian governments, but the targets of their brainwashing are younger and more vulnerable to milder versions of the same brainwashing techniques used under Stalin or Mao.

De-sensitizing experiences have been common in "death education" programs, as well as in many other kinds of psychological-conditioning programs. For example, assignments for students receiving "death education" have including writing their own epitaphs,[6] writing a suicide note,[7] discussing deaths which have occurred in their families[8] and—for first graders—making a model of a coffin for themselves out of a shoe box.[9]

Among the associated psycho-dramas in some schools are (1) having the children imagine that they are the children in the school bus that was buried underground in the infamous Chowchilla kidnapping case,[10] and (2) discussing lifeboat dilemmas in which there are more people than the boat can hold, so that a decision must be made as to who is to be left to drown.[11] Sometimes it is a fall-out shelter with limited capacity, so that some must be left outside to die of radiation poisoning after a nuclear attack.[12] Sometimes these dilemmas as to whose life is more important to be saved are extended to the point of asking the child to decide which members of his own family should be sacrificed in life-and-death situations.[13]

Because these are psychological experiences, stage-managing can be important. One handbook for teachers contained the instruction, "dim the lights," followed by: "Tell the students to pretend they are now dead." Later, the teacher is to arrange "a field trip to a local funeral home," "have each student briefly write what kind of funeral he wants for himself" and "write in ten words or less the epitaph he wishes to be remembered by."[14] Another book which prescribes a funeral home visit has more specific instructions for the students, including the following:

> Go through all the procedures to pre-arrange your own funeral.
>
> Select a casket as well as vault that meets your particular desires as well as financial needs.

Among the questions to be asked the students are:

> "How will you die?"
> "When will you die?"
> "Have you ever known anyone who died violently?"
> "When was the last time you mourned? Was it expressed in tears or silent pain? Did you mourn alone or with someone else?"
> "Do you believe in an after-life?"[15]

Another book outlines a series of "death education" class sessions, including funeral music, a filmstrip of funeral customs around the world, and many personal questions about the student's own emotional responses to death. Outside assignments include visits to a funeral home and a cemetery, with a list of data to be collected from tombstones.[16] This and other "death education" programs clearly envision many class sessions being devoted to the subject, for a period of weeks. This would be hard to explain or justify on purely educational grounds. But, if the purpose is to replace a whole set of attitudes with new attitudes preferred by those who design and administer such programs, then the time allotted is in keeping with the magnitude of what is being attempted.

Sex education of course is a very different subject—but the same pattern of de-sensitizing has been central. A parent who visited a fifth-grade classroom in Oregon testified at U.S. Department of Education hearings as to what she saw:

> I was present when a plastic model of female genitalia with a tampon insert was passed around to the boys so they might understand how tampons fit.[17]

From an educational standpoint, such information was obviously of limited practical use to eleven-year-old boys, but as a de-sensitizing experience it made sense—for purposes of brainwashing them into new attitudes. Similarly understandable for such purposes was a movie shown to a sixth-grade class in Kansas. A parent who was present testified:

> The first three minutes of the footage was the actual birth of a baby.
>
> It started out with a lady with her legs up and apart, and her feet in stirrups or something like that, with a doctor. It was very graphic and very detailed.
>
> The children in the 6th grade witnessed three actual births. I sensed a state of shock in the little boys and girls that it was all new to see a man doing what a doctor does to deliver a baby.[18]

In a North Carolina classroom, one of the children fainted when shown a childbirth movie.[19] In the Kansas classroom, when the parent questioned the nurse who showed the movie in a "health" class, the nurse's reply was: "Well, someday they need to learn about these things."[20] The more fundamental question was: What gave her the right to usurp the decision as to when that someday was, and to make it the same day for all the children, regardless of their individual emotional development? Clearly, she must have realized that it was a usurpation, for the movie was billed as a film on *vitamins*! Indeed, two-thirds of the movie was on vitamins, though the parent who watched it "did not see any correlation between the live births and the vitamins."[21]

Other de-sensitizing movies have shown a man's genitals,[22] a naked couple having sex "in living color" and "complete with sound effects,"[23] and masturbation.[24] Less graphic but more personal de-sensitizing techniques have included asking students questions about their own sexual attitudes and behavior.[25] A so-called "health" class in a junior high school in Washington state required all the boys to say "vagina" in class and all the girls to say "penis." When one embarrassed girl was barely able to say it, the teacher "made her get up in front of the class and very loudly say it ten times."[26]

Another common classroom technique is pairing boys and girls, so that each couple jointly studies and discusses sex education material, such as the sexual organs and their parts[27] and/or have conversations with each other using synonyms for penis, vagina, intercourse, and breast.[28] Again, the educational value of such pairing is much less apparent than its value as a de-sensitizing experience.

Death education and sex education are by no means the only special curriculum topics dealt with by brainwashing techniques. The difference between genuine education and psychological conditioning to change attitudes can also be illustrated by so-called "nuclear education," which deals with political-military issues involving nuclear weapons. Like any other controversial topic, nuclear weapons issues have generated numerous arguments on both sides in books, articles, speeches, and editorials. Moreover, there have long been two opposite schools of thought on the more general question as to whether peace is more likely to be preserved through military deterrence or through disarmament.[29] Leading intellectual and political figures of the past two centuries have argued on either side of this issue.[30]

In short, there is an ample literature on both sides for comparing opposing arguments, analyzing their logic, scrutinizing their evidence, and otherwise treating this as an *educational* topic. Instead, psychological conditioning has been widely used to lead children toward the pre-selected choice of disarmament. For example, tenth-grade children were introduced to the subject by the showing of a movie called "Hiroshima/ Nagasaki":

> In grisly detail these generally well-off upper middle-class kids were obliged to observe Japanese women and children being incinerated by the fire storm set in motion by the dropping of nuclear bombs. The youngsters sat riveted in their seats. Sobbing could be heard. By the conclusion the general mood of the class was well expressed by an emotional young lady who asked: "Why did we do it?" The teacher responded by saying, "We did it once; we can do it again. Whether these weapons of destruction are used depends on you." So began the unit on nuclear weapons.[31]

Note that the girl's question was never answered, but instead was side-stepped and used to lead toward anti-nuclear activism. As a study of various nuclear education programs concluded:

They encourage kids to "talk their hearts out." But they do not encourage an appreciation of the historical events leading to that tragic bombing in 1945.[32]

In short, this subject—like others—is treated as an emotional rather than an educational experience. The consequences of emotionalizing nuclear education, sex education, and many other subjects are not simply that an incorrect conclusion may be reached, or even that general intellectual development may be neglected. There are psycho-somatic effects as well.

A father in Oregon testified that his daughter required medical treatment as a result of tension created by such programs.[33] One young woman recalled, years later, the nightmares she had after viewing a movie shown in a high school course.[34] Many parents, doctors, and teachers have reported children bursting into tears in class during psychological-conditioning sessions[35] or after coming home.[36] Another parent reported that physicians had seen students with such symptoms as nightmares, stomach aches, vomiting, sleeplessness, and stuttering after they were subjected to a program with the high-sounding name "Exemplary Center for Reading Instruction."[37]

A research assistant who viewed numerous school movies, as part of the preparation for this book, likewise reported that she had trouble sleeping afterwards—even though she is a mature, well-educated woman who has lived in three countries and speaks two languages. What she had been seeing were movies routinely shown to students in American elementary and secondary schools.

Isolation and Cross-Examination

The success of brainwashing depends not only on the stress brought to bear on the targeted individuals but also on the extent to which their resistance can be undermined. Isolation—disconnecting them from the psychological support of those who share their values, or who are tied to them personally—is one way of undermining their resistance.

Totalitarian regimes often hold political prisoners in isolation, but even such regimes can find it excessively costly to do so when large numbers of people must be brainwashed simultaneously. An ingenious solution was found under Mao in China: The victim would be given a preliminary interrogation and then released with a "warning that it is a criminal offense to tell anybody—his friends, his relatives, or even his wife— that he is under examination by the police." Any individual who violated this warning was subject to a long prison sentence, even if he was never convicted of the offense for which he was being investigated.[38] This situation produced the desired psychological isolation and emotional tension, without the government's incurring costs for incarceration.

Even an accompanying physical threat, such as imprisonment, is not always essential. Richard Wright, leading black writer of the 1940s, left a haunting sketch of an internal Communist Party "trial" he witnessed in Chicago, where a fellow Party member confessed to false charges after a long and skillful presentation of the Party's worldwide struggle left him psychologically isolated.[39]

The emotional vulnerability of school children makes psychological isolation easier to achieve. A witness testifying at U.S. Department of Education hearings reported observing the treatment of a first-grade child who failed to have his values re-shaped to the teacher's liking:

> The teacher then asked how many of the students agreed with him. By the tone of her voice, they knew no one should raise a hand, so no one did. The little boy was so humiliated by the peer pressure and class manipulation by the teacher that he began to cry.[40]

A similar manipulation of peers against a recalcitrant was discovered by another parent in another school.

> Mr. Davis, the teacher, would bring up a controversial moral issue, such as premarital sex or homosexuality, and call on members of the class to defend their positions on the issue. He would call upon those with opposite moral beliefs from Jon, thus exerting peer pressure on Jon to change his moral views. Jon was consistently called on up to 23 times per class session to defend his values before his friends with opposing views. When Jon mentioned to Mr. Davis that he was calling

on him more than anyone else, Mr. Davis just said, "Oh", and continued calling on him.[41]

In yet another school, a parent testified, a junior high school girl "was required to defend her religion and values under extreme ridicule from the group leader and from her peers."[42]

Isolation from peers is only part of the process. In one way or another, students must also be emotionally isolated from the support of parents. Some psychological-conditioning programs have the children sit in a circle, called a "magic circle," where everything that is said there is confidential.[43] Some programs explicitly tell the children that they are not to tell their parents what is said or done.[44] Moreover, as will be seen later, the undermining and discrediting of parents is a recurring theme in the most disparate programs—whether called "sex education," "transactional analysis for tots," or called by many other labels. While it is parents who are undermined directly, it is the child who is thus isolated to face the brainwashing alone.

Stripping Away Defenses

In Maoist China, where the term "brainwashing" originated, an important part of the process was "the writing of autobiographies and diaries," which were then discussed by the group to which the individual belonged. This was not a matter of acquiring facts, but of discovering psychological vulnerabilities and putting the individual on the defensive. As one individual who had been through this process described it:

> A straight narrative of your past life was not enough. For every action you described, you had to give its motive in detail. Your awakened criticism had to be apparent in every sentence. You had to say why you smoked, why you drank, why you had social connections with certain people—why? why? why?[45]

Many irrelevant details, once they became "public property" in the discussion group, could then be used by the director of the group to probe for "sore spots" at which the individual was emotionally vulnerable—and that was very relevant to the brainwashing process.[46] George Orwell described a similar technique in his novel *1984*.[47] This same technique is widely used by psychological-conditioning programs in American public schools.

A seventh-grade "health" class in Corvallis, Oregon, for example, required "a private journal to be kept by the student on his feelings"—not events, but feelings. Nor was this to be a traditional journal for such traditional educational purposes as developing better use of the language. As the mother of one of these children testified: "No efforts were made to correct grammar, punctuation, sentence structure or continuity of thought."[48] Neither the keeping of diaries nor the disregard of their academic quality was peculiar to this school. Such diaries, focussing on feelings, including feelings about confidential family matters, are common around the country.[49] Utter disregard of the spelling, grammar, or punctuation in these diaries is likewise a pattern widely reported from around the country.[50] In short, this is not an educational activity but psychological conditioning.

In fourth-grade and sixth-grade classes in Tucson, diaries were assigned with the specific instructions that the student "could write about her personal problems and family relationships even if they were bad because the teacher is her friend and would not tell."[51] Similar assurances of confidentiality *from parents* were made in New Hampshire, though the sharing of these diaries in the group meant that family confidences were betrayed to strangers.[52] There is no special program to which such practices are confined. While these diaries were assigned in "health" classes in Oregon and New Hampshire, in various other places they have also been assigned in history, English, and social studies classes.[53]

In the Orwellian Newspeak widely found among advocates of psychological-conditioning programs, assignments creating pressure or compulsion to reveal personal and family matters are referred to as an *opportunity*—for example, "an opportunity to generate meaningful information about themselves which can be shared with others."[54] Obviously, people always have an opportunity to reveal anything they choose, to anyone they choose, at any time they choose. Psychological conditioning programs do not provide opportunity but pressure or compulsion. A leading book on the so-called "values clarification" approach to attitude-changing likewise refers to giving the student "the opportunity to publicly affirm and explain his stand on various values issues." During this "opportunity," the teacher "may ask the student any question about any aspect of his life and values."[55] All this is called "helping students get acquainted with each other on a more personal basis."[56]

When the class is further broken down into small groups, this "provides students with an opportunity to share on a more intimate basis" than when addressing the whole class.[57] Something called "privacy circles" is called strategy number 21, which "gives students the opportunity to find out whom they are willing to tell what."[58] While students are not directly forced to talk in this particular approach, they are encouraged to talk—and to talk at length. The authors' instruction to the teacher is:

Quantity is encouraged. Quantity eventually breeds quality.[59]

Among the questions which school children were given an "opportunity" to answer were the following:

What disturbs you most about your parents?
Would you bring up your children differently
    from the way you are being brought up?
    What would you change?
As a child, did you ever run away from home?
    Did you ever want to?
Who is the "boss" in your family?
Do you believe in God?
How do you feel about homosexuality?
Do you have any brothers and sisters? How
    do you get along?
What is the saddest thing you can remember?
Is there something you once did that you are
    ashamed of?[60]

In addition to questions, students have an "opportunity" to tell things, such as:

Describe a time of your greatest despair.[61]
Tell where you stand on the topic of
    masturbation.[62]
Reveal who in your family brings you the
    greatest sadness, and why. Then share
    who brings you the greatest joy.[63]

Tell some ways in which you will be a
  better parent than your own parents
  are now.[64]
Tell something about a frightening sexual
  experience.[65]

This book is not unique in asking such questions. Another "values clarification" book has blanks to fill in, such as:

Someone in my family who really gets me angry
  is ———.
I feel ashamed when ———.[66]

The U.S. Department of Health, Education, and Welfare in 1979 produced a questionnaire for "health education" which included these questions:

How often do you normally masturbate (play
  with yourself sexually)?
How often to you normally engage in light
  petting (playing with a girl's breast)?
How often to you normally engage in heavy
  petting (playing with a girl's vagina
  and the area around it)?[67]

Critics have often been so outraged by such questions that they have not sought to discover why these kinds of questions are being asked in the first place—from the standpoint of those who are asking. Such questions strip away all defenses and leave the student vulnerable to the brainwashing process. As Richard Wright said of his Communist Party comrade who had confessed voluntarily to false charges:

His personality, his sense of himself, had been obliterated.[68]

On a practical level, not only the child but the parents are left vulnerable as well. Family secrets revealed by children in school can be used to claim that objections to these programs are attributable to the parents' own psychological problems.

Another technique for stripping away defenses is to make the targeted individual a forced participant in emotionally in-delible experiences—that is, to make the individual *play a role* chosen by others. An example of this role-playing technique in China's brainwashing program was given by an inmate who later described "a trip by the whole school to a nearby village to watch and participate in the beating to death of an old woman 'landlord' who was hung up by her wrists before a mob of over a thousand people."[69]

While the powers of a totalitarian government vastly exceed those of a public school in the United States, very similar techniques have been used against more vulnerable subjects in the milder form of classroom role-playing. For example, a program on "Holocaust Studies" assigned to students the roles of concentration camp guards, Jewish inmates, and the like. A scholar who had studied the Holocaust found very little substantive information about the Holocaust contained in many school programs on the subject, some of which paid more attention to leading the students toward anti-nuclear activism.[70] With "Holocaust Studies," as with "sex education," "drug prevention," or other psychological programs, the ostensible purpose often has little to do with what actually takes place. Role-playing is an integral part of many psychological-conditioning programs, whether in "sex education" classes where boys and girls are paired to have a conversation with each other about sex,[71] or in "death education" classes where students are sent to funeral homes to arrange their own funerals,[72] or in "values clarification" classes where they are assigned to play the role of political demonstrators.[73]

BRAINWASHING AGENDAS

Attitude-changing programs involve so many thousands of schools, so many teachers, administrators, and "facilitators," and so many commercial, ideological, and other interests, that it is impossible to ascribe a single purpose to all involved. Yet such a pronounced pattern is found in these programs— whether their ostensible purpose is death education, sex education, drug prevention, or other concerns—that a broad consensus in approach and agenda can be discerned.

The most general—indeed pervasive—principle of these various programs is that decisions are *not* to be made by relying on traditional values passed on by parents or the surrounding society. Instead, those values are themselves to be questioned and compared with the values and behavior of other individuals or other societies. This is to be done in a neutral or "non-judgmental" manner, which does not seek to determine a "right" or "wrong" way, but rather to find out what feels best to the particular individuals. This general approach has been called "values clarification." Its focus is on the feelings of the individual, rather than on the requirements of a functioning society or the requirements of intellectual analysis.

Psychologists have been prominent among the proponents and creators of these programs, including the late psychotherapist Carl Rogers and a whole school of disciples gathered around him. Critics have called this approach "cultural relativism," for a recurring theme in attitude-changing programs is that what "our society" believes is just one of many beliefs with equal validity—so that individuals have the option to choose for themselves what to believe and value.

Central to this questioning of authority is a questioning of the role of the central authority in the child's life—the parents. Alternative ways of constructing individual values, independently of parental values, are recurring themes of curriculum materials on the most disparate subjects, from sex to death. The risks involved in the process of jettisoning what has been passed on from the experience of generations who went before are depicted as risks worth taking, as an adventure, or as a matter of subjective feelings of "trust" in oneself, in one's peers, and in the values clarification approach.

Attitude-changing programs and their promoters will be examined in more detail after first seeing how their general agenda is carried out in their treatment of parents, peers, and risk.

Parents as Pariahs

The sex-education textbook *Changing Bodies, Changing Lives* illustrates patterns which reach far beyond sex education courses. "There isn't any rule book to let you know when, where, or how to make the moves," it says in its opening pages.[74] "There's no 'right' way or 'right' age to have life experiences," it says on the next page. In short, standards are dispensed with early on, even though *Changing Bodies, Changing Lives* is primarily a book about social behavior, with only a fraction of it being biological or medical. Although it takes a dismissive attitude toward "many people in our parents' generation" who had "negative attitudes toward bodies and sex"[75] and also dismisses "old-fashioned stereotypes,"[76] "society's moralistic attitudes" and "religious traditions,"[77] it implicitly sets up another reference group for purposes of guidance: "We spent three years meeting and talking with several hundred teenagers all across the United States."[78] What those teenagers said is used again and again throughout the book to illustrate what is possible—and permissible.

The contrast could not be greater between the largely uncritical acceptance of selected statements from these teenagers and the repeatedly negative references to parents, who get "hung up"[79] or who "have a hard time letting go,"[80] parents who "go overboard"[81] or "have serious problems."[82]

In short, in *Changing Bodies, Changing Lives* as in other textbooks, parents are not presented as guides to follow, or as sources of valuable experience, but as problems to contend with, or perhaps even as examples of what to avoid. These repeatedly negative pictures of parents were epitomized in a free-verse poem about a girl who was trying to get her father's attention after dinner, when he had his face buried in a newspaper. The poem ends:

> Dad I gotta talk with you.
> Silence.
> Ya see dad I've got this problem.
> Silence.
> Dad I'm PREGNANT!!
> Did you say something honey?
> No dad go back to sleep.[83]

Again it must be emphasized that this anti-parent pattern is not peculiar to this particular textbook or to sex education. In a "values clarification" curriculum in Oregon, for example, third-graders were asked: "How many of you ever wanted to beat up your parents?"[84] In a so-called "talented and gifted" program, fourth graders were shown a movie in which children were in fact fighting with their parents.[85] In a so-called "health" class in Tucson, a high school class was asked: "how many of you hate your parents?"[86] Among the questions asked in a "values clarification" class in Colorado, was: "What is the one thing your mom and dad do to you that is unfair?"[87]

These were not isolated episodes. They were part of curriculum materials and approaches being used nationwide. As a parent in Tucson said, after surveying many such materials used in the local school, they "eroded the parent-child relationship by inserting a wedge of doubt, distrust and disrespect."[88] In some schools, students in various psychological conditioning kinds of courses are explicitly told *not* to tell their parents about what is said in class. This pattern too is very widespread—and not just in *avant-garde* places like California or New York. Hearings before the U.S. Department of Education turned up examples from Georgia, Maryland, Pennsylvania, Arizona, and Oregon.[89]

The undermining of parents' moral authority can begin quite early. An author in the "transactional analysis" school of psychology—often known as "T.A."—has produced a book designed for children from pre-school to third grade, entitled *T.A. for Tots*. One of the pictures has a caption: "Hey, this little girl is crying" and a butterfly on the side of the picture says: "Oh! oh! Looks like she got a spanking." The picture on the next page shows the same girl spanking her doll and saying "No No!" The caption reads: "Ah ha! Now she is being bossy and spanking her doll. Who taught her to do that?" The butterfly in the corner says: "Could it have been Daddy and Mommy?"[90]

The recurring theme of the book is that little boys and girls are born as little princes and princesses. At first, in infancy, they are treated that way and feel that way. But parents end up turning these princes and princesses into frogs, in their own minds, by constantly criticizing and punishing them. One of the morals of the story is:

> Sometimes things happen you don't like.
> You have the right to be angry without being afraid of being punished.
> You have a right to tell Mommy or Daddy what you don't like about what they are doing.[91]

This book sold nearly a quarter of a million copies within four years, so apparently many pre-schoolers and early elementary school children have received this message about their parents.

That the undermining or discrediting of parents should be a common feature of a wide variety of programs with such ostensibly different aims is by no means inexplicable. Parents are the greatest obstacle to any brainwashing of children, and it is precisely the parents' values which are to be displaced. If parents cannot be gotten out of the picture, or at least moved to the periphery, the whole brainwashing operation is jeopardized. Not only will individual parents counter what the brainwashers say; parents as a group can bring pressure to bear against the various psychological conditioning programs, and in some places get them forced out of the schools.

Advocates of such programs have written about ways for teachers or administrators to deflect or counter objections by parents. For example, one "sex education" curriculum which uses explicit color slides of both homosexual and heterosexual acts, warns that students "should not be given extra copies of the form to show to their parents and friends."[92] It is one of a number of programs which warn against letting parents know the specifics of the material being used.[93] Where parents nevertheless learn of what is happening and object, there are standard procedures used by boards of education to dismiss their complaints:

> Board members quickly learn to tell parents they are too inexperienced to speak on the subject of education, that all the experts oppose their point of view, that scientific evidence proves them wrong, that they are trying to impose their morals on others, and that they are the only people in the community who have raised such complaints.[94]

Any or all of these assertions may be completely false, but most parents do not have the time or the resources to prove it—which makes such claims politically effective. However, the very fact that supporters of such programs have written tactical suggestions for dealing with parents and other critics hardly fits the claim that few people have objected.

In some cases, laws may require parental consent or notice for the use of these psychologically-oriented programs on their children, but this requirement can be rendered virtually meaningless in practice by concealing the specifics. An Oregon program labelled Talented and Gifted (TAG) was a typical anti-parent, anti-values program, but it was very difficult to discover this beforehand. One persistent parent, who endured insults and misdirection to find out what was happening, testified before the Department of Education:

> Parents are notified before students participate in these programs, but it is not an informed permission. Most parents whose children are recommended for the TAG program think that they are going to be given advanced academic education. They don't know that, in these workshops, attempts will be made to alienate their children from them and from moral values, or that their children will be taught to substitute the judgment and will of the group for that of individual judgment and responsibility.[95]

Such programs and such deception are not confined to the public schools. A private secondary school in Los Angeles, obtained parental permission for something called "senior seminar" by describing what was to be done in only the most vague and lofty words, while the actual specifics remained unknown until it was too late. (Yanking a student out of class in mid-semester of the senior year is especially difficult in a school whose students are usually going on to college.) Any suggestion of indoctrination or emotional manipulation was wholly absent from the materials supplied to parents before this program began. Much of what was said in this material would in fact suggest the very opposite, that it was some kind of advanced academic training. The "objectives" listed when the "senior seminar" was instituted began:

1) develop the ability to analyze and synthesize ideas and information among disciplines
2) recognize and practice effective listening and speaking skills as well as critical thinking and effective writing techniques
3) make better decisions and contribute to their own personal growth

The list went on and on, accompanied by pages of other material containing an inundation of words on the mechanics and aspirations of the course—and nothing on the specific content. The list of objectives concluded:

10) improve research and library skills
11) write a Senior Thesis

Who could possibly object to such things? Yet, despite the intellectual emphasis of these statements, psychological manipulation began immediately. The first specific assignment involved betraying family confidences to strangers in an "autobiography" that included the student's relationship with a family member. The student was to describe "what gives you satisfaction and dissatisfaction in your family." Among later "units" in the course were "aging, death, and dying," featuring movies about the terminally ill, visits to local hospices serving terminally ill patients, arranged visits to funeral homes and to cemeteries, and a speaker on euthanasia. This went on for weeks, culminating in oral presentations in class. None of this was revealed until *after* permission had been obtained through glowing generalities.

Peers as Guides

While parents are finessed aside in one way or another, and the values they have instilled are made to seem arbitrary or outmoded, students are repeatedly told that it is they *individually* who must determine the values on which to make decisions—and the guidance repeatedly held out to them is the example of their peers.

"It's up to you alone"[96] is the message repeated again and again. What you do "will have to be your decision."[97] It is not merely that the child or adolescent must choose—but must also choose the underlying set of values on which the particular decision is made. Right and wrong are banished from the scene early on. "Remember, there are no 'right' or 'wrong' answers— just *your* answers," according to the textbook, *Learning About Sex*, which also says:

> I cannot judge the "rightness" or "wrongness" of any of these behaviors. Instead, I hope that you can find the sexual life-style which is best for your own life . . . "[98]

Concepts of "normal" or "healthy" sex are dismissed because "each of us has his or her own legitimate set of sexual attitudes and feelings."[99] Homosexuality is a matter of "preferences"[100] "Sado-masochism may be very acceptable and safe" for some people.[101] Although it is illegal and "exploitation" for adults to "take advantage" of children sexually, "there may be no permanent emotional harm."[102]

In the same book, a chapter entitled "Different Strokes for Different Folks" begins:

> You have noticed how the kinds of food you like and dislike are different from some of those other people like and dislike. . . . It is much the same with the sexual appetites of human beings.[103]

Even parents' views may be all right—in their place. "If you are interested in their ideas," you may talk with your parents, but if "disagreement" occurs or "the discussion turns into an argument," then parent and child alike should see the other's point of view "as *different*, not wrong."[104] In short, all views are equal, though it turns out that some are more equal than others, for the examples offered in the psychological-conditioning literature and classroom programs emphasize the feelings, attitudes, and behavior of peers. For example, the textbook *Changing Bodies, Changing Lives* begins many sentences:

> "Most of the teenagers we interviewed. . . ."[105]
> "Lots of people. . . ."[106]
> "Some people. . . ."[107]
> "Many people. . . ."[108]
> "Most teens. . . ."[109]
> "Almost everyone. . . ."[110]

Again and again, issues are posed in terms of what "many teenagers,"[111] "teenagers we've interviewed,"[112] "many people,"[113] or "many teens"[114] feel, believe, or do. By adopting the "non-judgmental" attitude which pervades such books, courses, and programs, the values and behavior of peers are left as the only guides. Nor is there any way for the reader to know whether the particular teenagers quoted are typical, or merely typical of what the brainwashers wish to promote.

Risk as Adventure

A recurring pattern in the attitude-changing, psychological-conditioning literature is the depiction of risk-taking in a wholly positive light. Numerous examples of the benefits of risk-taking are to be found in this literature—and virtually no examples of its disadvantages. Nothing bad ever seems to have happened to anyone as a result of taking risks, and certainly nothing catastrophic. The "objective" specified in one part of a so-called "gifted and talented" curriculum is: "To be a *risk taker* by having the courage to expose oneself to failure or criticisms, to take a guess, to function under conditions devoid of structure or to defend one's own ideas."[115] The epigraph to this handbook is:

> Better is one's own path though imperfect
> than the path of another well made.

This motto is offered, not to seasoned and mature adults, but to children in grades 4 through 6.

Carl Rogers, one of the gurus of the attitude-changing movement, rhapsodized about teachers who were "risking themselves, *being* themselves, *trusting* their students, adventuring into the existential unknown, taking the subjective leap"[116] by abandoning traditional methods for his kind of program. The often-cited book *Values Clarification*, by Sidney Simon and others, gives as the purpose of its strategy number 20, "learning to build trust so that we can risk being open."[117] Much of what is done in trust-building exercises—having classmates lead a blindfolded student, for example—may seem to be innocuous, and perhaps pointless, when viewed in isolation. It is, however, one of a number of aptly named "strategies" designed to induce a certain state of mind, including a relaxation of inhibitions against the unknown and reliance on peers. In short, youngsters are encouraged to extrapolate from these exercises in a highly controlled environment to the unpredictable dangers of real life.

Sometimes the step-by-step increase of riskiness can at some point reach serious levels of danger, even within the context of the trust-building exercises themselves. For example, in the *Values Clarification* handbook's strategy number 45, children go riding in a police car, or go into a ghetto, among other risk-taking activities. This handbook's "note to the teacher" proclaims the philosophy behind such activities:

> All new experiences are risk-taking experiences, because we never know how they might turn out. Generally, the more the student has to do, the newer the experience for him, the greater the risk he has to take, the deeper will be the sensitivity which results from it.[118]

In short, there is a coherent—though unproven—structure of beliefs behind these psychological exercises. Individual teachers are not usually the source of these beliefs, which typically originate with psychologists or psychological gurus who package programs for use in schools. Educators simply carry out such "innovations" and experiments on a captive audience of school children, while promoting the whole philosophy of life which attitude-changing programs represent. Particular trust-building exercises are just part of a larger pattern of inducing attitude changes by psychological means.

In attitude-changing programs, trust and risk are repeatedly depicted in a positive light, as if there were no dangers—psychological, physical, or financial—in ill-advised trust. Like so much in this approach, it simply *assumes* what is crucial, namely trustworthiness in this case. Carl Rogers was sanguine enough to make this assumption explicit, when he referred to "a profound trust in the human organism"[119] as a prerequisite for the kind of education he advocated. More generally, such sweeping trust and corresponding willingness to risk are prerequisites for abandoning the values and inhibitions which have been distilled from the experience of previous generations. Unfortunately, the greatest risks are not taken by teachers or promoters of attitude-changing programs, but by vulnerable children and the parents who will be left to deal with the consequences.

SPONSORS AND PROMOTERS

Who is pushing psychological-conditioning or attitude-changing programs into the public schools? And why?

Some are doing so out of simple self-interest. When pharmaceutical companies provide material promoting birth-control products for sex education courses, the financial self-interest is obvious. Similarly when an automobile manufacturer provides material for driver education. Moreover, the selling of curriculum materials of a more general nature is a substantial business in itself. A captive audience of more than 40 million school children is attractive to all sorts of people for all sorts of reasons. The susceptibility of educators to such fasionable "innovations" is what opens the floodgates to permit the intrusion of such programs into the public schools. This susceptibility is only partly spontaneous. Organizations pushing curriculum programs engage in massive and sustained promotional activities all across the country, sponsoring conferences, retreats, and traveling exhibits, to reach an audience of education officials with the power to choose curriculum materials for vast numbers of children.

Some idea of the amount of promotional activity that goes on, on behalf of attitude-changing programs, may be suggested by a schedule covering just six weeks of promotional meetings in 1990 by just one organization, Quest International:

DATE	CITY	DATE	CITY
November 5:	Columbus	November 15:	Chicago
			Nashville
			Rochester (Minn.)
			San Francisco
November 7:	Omaha		
November 8:	Grand Island (Nebr.)	November 16:	Gary
			Madison (Wisc.)
			Sacramento
November 12:	Green Bay (Wisc.)	November 26:	Bloomington
	St. Cloud (Minn.)		Denver
			Hartford
November 13:	Anaheim	November 27:	Indianapolis
	Atlanta		New York City
	Duluth		Tulsa
	Milwaukee		
November 14:	Columbia (S.C.)	November 28:	Albany
	Elgin (Ill.)		Oklahoma City
	Minneapolis		Springfield (Ill.)
	Oxnard (Calif.)		

DATE	CITY	DATE	CITY
November 29:	Davenport (Iowa)	December 6:	Richmond (Va.)
	Portland (Oreg.)		St. Louis
	Syracuse	December 7:	Boston
			Kansas City (Mo.)
November 30:	Buffalo	December 11:	Albuquerque
	Des Moines		Charlotte
	Seattle		Houston
			Toledo
December 3:	Cincinnati	December 12:	Cleveland
	Fort Lauderdale		Dallas
	(Fla.)		Greensboro (N.C.)
	Pittsburgh		Phoenix
December 4:	Louisville	December 13:	Akron
	Orlando (Fla.)		Corpus Christi
	Washington, D.C.		Las Vegas
			Raleigh (N.C.)
December 5:	Allentown	December 14:	Austin
	Evansville (Ind.)		
	Roanoke		

Note that this was only the schedule of *promotional* meetings during these two months. There was another busy schedule of three-day training sessions by the same organization in cities from coast to coast for teachers who were going to be using the "Quest" programs. "Minimum implementation fees" were $975 in 1990 for a program in a given institution, including the training of one person, with additional training fees of $375 each for additional participants.[120] Quest International also offered for sale audio and video materials to be used with the program, as well as T-shirts and coffee mugs. Moreover, it offered information on how the money to pay for its programs could be raised from foundations and civic organizations.[121]

According to the promotional material for Quest, its program for adolescents "has been adopted by over 12,000 schools in North America and 22 countries"[122] reaching "more than 1.5 million young people each year throughout the world."[123] Quest International is clearly a multimillion-dollar enterprise. While it characterizes itself as "a non-profit organization," whether the money coming in is called profit or something else does not affect its financial ability to expand the organization, or to reward those who operate it, or who are affiliated with it.

Ideology is another potent force behind the promotion of attitude-changing programs and shapes much of the content, the psychological-conditioning methods, and the circumvention and undermining of parents. Advocates of secular humanism, for example, have been quite clear and explicit as to the crucial importance of promoting their philosophy in the schools, to counter or undermine religious values among the next generation. As an article in *Humanist* magazine put it:

> I am convinced that the battle for humankind's future must be waged and won in the public school classrooms by teachers who correctly perceive their role as the proselytizers of a new faith: a religion of humanity that recognizes and respects the spark of what theologians call divinity in every human being.
>
> These teachers must embody the same selfless dedication as the most rabid fundamentalist preachers, for they will be ministers of another sort, utilizing a classroom instead of a pulpit to convey humanist values in whatever subject they teach, regardless of the educational level—preschool day care or large state universities.[124]

While the organized secular humanist movement might seem to be a small fringe group, its impact on education is out of all proportion to its size. For example, Carl Rogers—the psychotherapist who was one of the leading figures in introducing psychotherapeutic techniques into schools—was proud of having been named Humanist of the Year by the American Humanist Society,[125] Rogers' dismissive attitude toward religion, and his contempt for American culture in general,[126] are reflected in a vast literature, reaching well beyond his own considerable corps of disciples, and found in other schools of psychotherapeutic approaches to education.

Promoters of internationalism have likewise seen a need to undermine patriotism or other national cultural traditions through "global education." Gay rights advocates have also been active in promoting the use of school materials, including movies, promoting the homosexual lifestyle, and boosting the social image of homosexuals.[127] One of the largest organizations, with one of the oldest and most thoroughly elaborated ideologies and most sophisticated promotional operations, is

Planned Parenthood. The very name is deceiving, for the last thing they are planning is parenthood. Planned Parenthood is an organization with a population-repression ideology.

While the ideologies of these different groups have different emphases, they overlap to a considerable degree and reinforce one another. Moreover, they are all pushing ideas which cannot be openly and plainly labeled, so they all have an interest in maintaining lofty euphemisms and labels which obscure or misdirect. Their simultaneous emergence on a large scale in the public schools during the past two decades was neither a coincidence nor a conspiracy, but grew out of new opportunities provided by large infusions of federal money into public school systems long controlled and financed at the local level. Professor Jacqueline Kasun, who has studied the sex education aspect of this phenomenon extensively, concluded:

> . . . Congress created the conditions for massive growth in the sex education and birth control movement. From a crank obsession subsidized by drug companies, it became a growth industry with big money prizes for those who qualify for the multimillion-dollar federal grants. It could now not only operate more programs, but it could undertake massive "research," publishing, and promotion; it could employ high-powered "experts," operating out of its own proliferating offices located in the very heart of the public bureaucracy. Parents who questioned the new programs for the schools soon found that they were up against an entrenched power structure with a virtually limitless financial base.[128]

Although organizations such as Planned Parenthood present themselves as rationalistic and scientific, the hysteria they promote about alleged "over-population" in the world is contradicted by considerable empirical evidence to the contrary.[129] The population control ideology is simply one branch of the general ideology of an elite controlling the lives of the masses, for their own good—a view once openly expressed.[130] Although Planned Parenthood and others who have promoted sex education in the schools have used the argument that it would reduce teenage pregnancy, their bottom line has been population control, so that these programs have been a success from their perspective when abortions prevent population growth, even though more teenagers get pregnant.

The role of federal money is crucial, for it means that both commercial and ideological interests have a large market for their products. The fact that the money comes from Washington, rather than from locally controlled sources, means that local control or parental influence are less effective barriers to the intrusion of this material into the classroom.

Whatever influence parents might have is further diluted by education administrators' reluctance to let the public know about the introduction of any potentially controversial material. For example, an academic study of a controversial curriculum called *Man: A Course of Study* (*MACOS*) found that "school administrators were reluctant to acquaint parents and the general citizenry with their district's use of *MACOS*, either prior to or following its installation." Among the comments often heard from these administrators were: "Keep the lid on" and "do not want controversy," and expressions of fear of "flack from the community."[131] Nor did those who introduced this program believe that students would be any more receptive. Among teachers trained to present the *MACOS* curriculum, only 4 percent gave as their reason for adopting it that they thought students would like it.[132]

The sense of mission, of excitement, of being part of a vanguard promoting advances beyond the ken of ordinary people, should not be discounted as a factor behind the spread of attitude-changing programs. The notion that they are doing something "scientific," as opposed to merely "traditional," is part of this mystique. A doctoral dissertation on the *MACOS* program even referred to "scientific values," with no definition of what that might mean (inasmuch as values are not science and science is not values). Nevertheless, the dissertation depicted the controversy which erupted over *MACOS* as a clash between those with "scientific values" and those with "traditional values":

> Proponents of *MACOS* and scientific values believe . . . that it is not only appropriate but important for value issues to be discussed within the context of classroom lessons. They assert that because the world is constantly changing, students must have an opportunity to deal as first-hand as possible with problems and realities of that world. Issues of the present and future, then, to a large degree are paramount (though not to

the total exclusion of issues of the past) to those in favor of scientific values, whereas those in favor of traditional values tend to focus on the past.[133]

Just as Orwellian use of the word "opportunity" to describe compulsion is not uncommon among defenders of brainwashing programs,[134] so is use of the word "scientific" in a wholly unscientific sense, as verbal garnish for a set of idological fashions. Invocations of "science" as a characterization of educational fashions and dogmas go back for decades.[135] Moreover, the same note of self-congratulation was apparent in Abraham Maslow, a disciple of Carl Rogers and himself one of the early gurus of psychological conditioning in schools, when he said, "traditional value systems have all failed, at least for thoughtful people," so that "we are now casting about in a new direction, namely the scientific one."[136] Apparently school children are to be drafted for this "casting about" experiment.

The vague, lofty, and self-congratulatory note was also apparent in the titles, as well as the content, of books by Carl Rogers: *The Right to be Human* and *Freedom to Learn*—the latter another Orwellian phrase for public school children being compelled to be guinea pigs. Another writer on values clarification said: "I conceptualize man as a total, unified person."[137] This kind of pretentious mush has provided the ideological rationale for displacing intellectual studies from the schools in favor of psychological conditioning.

ASSESSMENT

Attitude-changing curriculum programs can be assessed in a number of ways, including (1) how effective they are in the specific area in which they claim to be effective (drug prevention, for example), (2) the academic and emotional costs they entail, and (3) their wider social consequences.

Remarkably little attention has been paid to the actual consequences of programs which have claimed to reduce drug usage, teenage pregnancy, fear of death, and so on. Glowing words and confident claims have often been considered a sufficient basis for subjecting millions of American youngsters to psychological conditioning. Often the promoters of such programs have been content to quote statements by those children who liked the programs, or by teachers who liked running the programs. But selected testimonials about how some people feel are hardly evidence as to whether these activities accomplish their declared aims. Moreover, some children and some teachers also like the traditional academic subjects, which psychological programs displace.

The most openly promoted and most widely introduced non-academic program has been so-called "sex education." The public has been told that these programs are ways of reducing teenage pregnancy and venereal diseases, including in recent years AIDS. The 1970s have been called "the heyday of the growth of sex education."[138] What was the situation before massive, federally-funded "sex education" programs began and how has it changed since?

Teenage pregnancy was *declining,* over a period of more than a dozen years, before so-called "sex education" programs spread rapidly through American schools in the 1970s. Teenage pregnancies then *rose* sharply, along with federal expenditures on "sex education" programs and "family-planning" clinics, many located in schools. The pregnancy rate among 15 to 19 year old females was approximately 68 per thousand in 1970 and 96 per thousand in 1980.[139]

Sex education advocates cite different statistics—on fertility or live births—to claim success. There was, as they claim, some decline in adolescent birth rates during the 1970s, when abortions among pregnant teenagers more than doubled, so that the dramatic increase in pregnancies was statistically offset by abortions and miscarriages.[140] However, even the modest decline in live births could not be attributed to sex education or to so-called family-planning clinics. Fertility rates among teenage girls had been declining since 1957,[141] long before the massive, federally funded programs of the 1970s and before *Roe v. Wade* made abortion legal in 1973.

Although sex education advocates have seized upon fertility declines to claim success, what they themselves predicted beforehand was a decline in both pregnancies and abortions—both of which increased.[142] Moreover, the sex education "experts" were wrong in other fundamental ways: (1) in their insistence that abstinence was not a viable option among today's teenagers because "everybody" was having sex and (2) their depiction of the role of parents and traditional values as ineffective or counterproductive.

There was no evidence that a majority of teenagers were engaging in sex before the sex education programs spread. As late as 1976, a majority of high school students were still virgins, and as late as 1987 only half of all 18-year-olds had had pre-marital sexual relations. Even among the so-called "sexually active," 14 percent had been "active" only once in their lives, and half had not engaged in sex in the month preceding their interview.[143] In short, "everybody" was not doing it, and only a minority were promiscuous. Although abstinence is often dismissed as impossible, it remains a way of life for many teenagers—however inconvenient that fact may be for those peddling an ideology or seeking money to support their programs.

Empirical evidence also shows that parents with traditional values have had much more positive impact than the "experts" have assumed. More than 80 percent of adolescent girls whose parents did not permit dating in their early teens were virgins, compared to only about half among those who began dating at age thirteen.[144] When Utah passed a law requiring parental consent for minors to be given contraceptives, not only did teenagers' use of family-planning clinics and teenage abortions decline; so did pregnancy and birth rates.[145] In short, parental influence proved to be a more effective force against teenage pregnancy than so-called "sex education" or even contraceptive clinics. But, over the past generation, traditions that worked have been replaced by "innovations" that sounded good.

Much more research has been done on sex education than on other attitude-changing programs, but the results in other areas have been similar. A study of death education in two secondary schools found that fear of death *increased* among those students taking this program, well beyond the level among those students not taking death education, even though the students in the death education program initially had less fear of death.[146] Parents whose children have talked about suicide, or committed suicide, after taking death education courses have been understandably bitter, though cause and effect are obviously difficult to establish in such cases. Still, one mother of a boy who committed suicide accused the school of "playing Russian roulette" by offering such courses to a mixture of students, some of whom may not be able to handle it.[147]

There has likewise been controversy over the effects of so-called "drug prevention" programs—for example, over whether the program "Quest" is responsible for an increase in drug usage among students in its program.[148] Causation and correlation are not the same, but it is worth noting that controversies seem to be over how to apportion blame for bad results, rather than discussions of the good results so confidently promised or assumed when these programs were inaugurated.

With psychological conditioning programs, as with ideological indoctrination, the problem is not so much that the program will succeed in accomplishing what it sets out to do, but that it will do great damage in the attempt. With psychological conditioning programs, the damage can go much deeper than educational deficiencies.

"Values clarification" programs, for example, could more accurately be called values *confusion*, for its whole non-judgmental approach is at odds with any set of values that includes right and wrong—and without any concept of right and wrong, it is hard to see what "values" mean. One parent testified before the U.S. Department of Education that her son "came home one day very confused as to the rightness or wrongness of stealing" after going through "values clarification" and other psychological-conditioning programs.[149] Other parents report similar confusion among children after their parents taught them right and wrong and the schools said that there was no such thing. Things taught in the classroom "cause children to re-think values taught at home"[150] and caused children "to wonder whom to believe."[151]

The very phrase "values clarification" is fundamentally dishonest. When parents tell their children not to steal or not to have sex, there is no ambiguity as to what they mean. *Clarification is neither required nor attempted.* Instead, values are downgraded to subjective preferences of individuals or blind traditions of "our society," and contrasted with alternative values of other individuals and other societies—including, in some cases, the societies of various species of animals.[152] The "non-judgmental" approach which pervades such exercises provides no principle of logic or morality by which to choose among the many alternatives presented—except, implicitly, what peers or "experts" or "modern thinking" might prefer. "Clarification" is merely a word used to camouflage this process of undermining the child's existing values.

Programs which attempt to re-mold the values, beliefs, and attitudes of school children have often been criticized in terms of the particulars of the new values, beliefs, and attitudes. Thus there has been much discussion of the relative merits of secular humanism versus religious morality, or radical ideologies versus traditional values. While these are legitimate issues, the more fundamental question is: *Who is to decide*—and by what right—the values with which children are to be raised? More specifically, who authorized outsiders to intrude into family relationships, undermine parental authority, and use brainwashing techniques on children? The problems created by these programs are not confined to the particular subject matter of the programs or to those children who become convinced by the brainwashers.

The promoters of psychological-conditioning programs themselves inadvertently admit the illegitimacy of what they are doing by (1) the stealth with which such programs are introduced into schools, behind the parents' backs; (2) the many uninformative or misleading labels and descriptions of these programs, and the frequency with which these labels change, as more parents begin to understand what such terms as "values clarification" or "transactional analysis" really mean; (3) injunctions to secrecy upon students, teachers, administrators, and "facilitators" involved in these programs; and (4) the numerous tactics of delay, denial, adverse labeling, and plain hassles inflicted upon parents who question or challenge. Are these the tactics of people who are doing what they have every right to do—or of people who have to cover their tracks? Lofty assertions of "expertise" beyond the parents' understanding, and of unnamed "studies" which have supposedly "proved" the effectiveness of the various brainwashing programs, are likewise ways of *not* discussing the issues raised.

These programs are fundamentally irresponsible, not simply in an arbitrarily normative sense, but in the plain factual sense that those who promote and carry out such programs *pay no costs* if their notions turn out to be wrong, damaging, or even disastrous to some or all of those subjected to them. The smug and glib apostles of these programs do not support one baby born to a teenage girl, or one youngster who contracts AIDS from the risk-taking spirit of adventure promoted by such programs. It is the much disdained parents who are left to pick up the pieces—or to grieve and mourn when a child commits suicide, after getting in too deep to handle the problems.

It is precisely the pervasive pattern of undermining parents which makes brainwashing programs dangerous beyond their particular subject matter, whether that be sex, death, smoking, or drugs. Even youngsters who develop no problems in these particular areas may nevertheless have their ties with their parents weakened, confused, or otherwise made insecure—especially during the crucial and dangerous adolescent years. The constant conditioning to act independently of parents, and to use similarly inexperienced peers as guides, is an invitation to disaster in many ways, going far beyond those covered in a particular brainwashing program.

Parents are not simply a source of experience from their own lives; they are a conduit for the distilled experience of others in earlier generations, experience conveyed in traditions and moral codes responding to the many dangers that beset human life. Psychological-conditioning programs which enshrine current "feelings" fail to understand that it is precisely feelings of the moment which lead to many dangers, and that inhibitions toward some feelings have evolved for that very reason.

It is pseudo-rationalism to say that a child or adolescent should follow only such values as he or she can defend intellectually against the cross-examination of an adult trained specifically for such cross-examination—and for emotional manipulation. The values which have endured the test of time were not created by children, but evolved out of experiences distilled into a way of life by adults. Such values are often used precisely for the purpose of guiding people too young to have enough personal experience to grasp fully the implications of the rules they follow—or the dangers in not following them. In other words, many values would not be needed if youngsters fully understood why they existed.

A trained cross-examiner could no doubt also bring out a student's incomplete grasp of the underlying premises of mathematics and science, but no one would regard this as either a refutation of mathematics and science or as a reason why students should make up their own rules of arithmetic, or their own personal physics.

The superficial rationalism of telling school children that their parents are just "ordinary people with faults and weaknesses and insecurities and problems just like everyone else"[153] misses the deeper and more relevant point that the relationship of a child to a parent is no ordinary relationship. It is the most extraordinary relationship anyone is likely to have with anyone else. Moreover, at the particular period of life when this statement is addressed to school children, the parents have vastly more experience than the child or the child's peers—and a far deeper and more enduring stake in the child's well being than any teacher, administrator, or "facilitator."

Another common piece of superficial rationalism is to offer examples of alternative values in differing cultures as a reason to make values in general seem like arbitrary choices. This too ignores a deeper and weightier reality: All societies which have survived have had some particular set of values, some canons of right and wrong. To banish right and wrong is to attempt something which no society has achieved—survival without shared values. Different societies also have different ideas of what kinds of food to eat, but that does not mean that food is something arbitrary that we can do without.

Despite the affectations of a detached, objective, or "scientific" attitude in many programs, reckless experiments are not science. Chemists do not take chemicals at random and pour them into a test tube to see what happens. Few chemists would survive if they did.

Far from being in any way scientific, psychological-conditioning programs are often fundamentally anti-intellectual. They enshrine "feelings," not analysis; the opinions of inexerpienced peers, not facts; they induce psychological acceptance of fashionable attitudes rather than teach logical procedures for analyzing assertions, or canons of evidence for scrutinizing claims. In addition to displacing intellectual courses from the curriculum, brainwashing programs actively promote anti-intellectual ways of dealing with the realities of life. Unfortunately, non-intellectual and anti-intellectual approaches are all too congenial to too many people in the educational establishment.

It may seem strange, or at least ironic, that people of such marginal intellectual competence as many public school teachers and administrators should take on the God-like role of reshaping the psyches and values of children. Yet this is perfectly consistent with the centuries-old observation that fools rush in where angels fear to tread.

CHAPTER 4

Assorted Dogmas

AMONG THE MANY dogmas prevailing in American education, most can be divided into two broad categories—dogmas about society and dogmas about education. The most widespread of the social dogmas revolve around "multicultural diversity" and the educational dogmas include "relevance," educating "the whole person," and a general de-emphasis of authority. Not all these dogmas are exclusively American. Some have gotten a foothold in the educational systems of some other countries, usually with the same disastrous consequences as in the United States.

"MULTICULTURAL DIVERSITY"

Few catch-phrases have been so uncritically accepted, or so variously defined, as "multicultural diversity." Sometimes it refers to the simple fact that peoples from many racial, ethnic, and cultural backgrounds make up the American population. At other times, it refers to an agenda of separatism in language and culture, a revisionist view of history as a collection of grievances to be kept alive, and a program of both historical and contemporary condemnation of American society and Western civilization.

Despite frequent, chameleon-like changes in the meanings of multiculturalism, its basic components are three: (1) a set of ideological beliefs about society and the world, (2) a political agenda to make these beliefs the basis for the curriculum of the whole educational system, and (3) a set of beliefs about the most effective way to conduct an educational system.

Many critics of multiculturalism, such as former Secretary of Education William J. Bennett, have done battle over the ideological beliefs of the multiculturalists.[1] What is most salient *educationally*, however, is the attempt of multiculturalists to make these beliefs a new orthodoxy, to be imposed institutionally by the political authorities. What is also salient are the multiculturalists' educational methods, geared toward leading students to a set of pre-selected beliefs, rather than toward developing their own ability to analyze for themselves, or to provide them with adequate factual knowledge to make their own independent assessments.

The ideological component of multiculturalism can be summarized as a cultural relativism which finds the prominence of Western civilization in the world or in the schools intolerable. Behind this attitude is often a seething hostility to the West, barely concealed even in public statements designed to attract wider political support for the multicultural agenda. That such attitudes or opinions exist, and are expressed by some people, is to be expected in a free society. It is not these beliefs, as such, which are the real problem. The real *educational* problem is the attempt to impose such views as a new orthodoxy throughout the educational system, not only by classroom brainwashing but also by institutional power—expressed in such things as compulsory indoctrination programs for teachers, making adherence to multiculturalism a condition of employment, and buying only those textbooks which reflect multiculturalism in some way, even if these are textbooks in mathematics or science.

Some or all of these patterns can be found in public schools across the United States, in leading American colleges, and in educational institutions as far away as Britain and Australia. In all these settings, what the general public sees are not the ideological foundations or the institutional mechanisms of multiculturalism, but only their educational arguments. These arguments fall into a few standard categories:

1. Multiculturalism is necessary to enable our students to participate in the emerging global economy.
2. Multiculturalism is necessary because an increasingly diverse population within the United States requires and demands education in a variety of cultures.
3. Intergroup relations are better when people are introduced to each other's cultures in school.
4. Education itself is better when presented from various perspectives, derived from culturally different social groups.

Whatever the plausibility of any of these beliefs, supporting evidence has seldom been asked or given. On the contrary, evidence contradicting each of these claims has been ignored.

When a 1991 commission report, prepared for the New York state Commissioner of Education, referred to "the need for preparing young people to participate in the world community,"[2] it was echoing a familiar theme in the multicultural literature. Yet neither argument nor evidence was offered to show how the particular things being done as part of the multicultural agenda would accomplish that purpose, which was itself left vague. It would be hard to think of a more monocultural, insular and self-complacent nation than Japan—and yet the Japanese are among the leading participants in the international economy, in international scientific and technological developments, as well as in international travel and tourism. This is not a defense of insularity or of the Japanese. It is simply a piece of empirical evidence to highlight the *non sequitur* of the claim that international participation requires the multicultural ideology or agenda.

Another equally reckless claim is that the ethnic diversity of the American population requires multicultural education. The United States has been ethnically diverse for more than a century. Yet successive massive waves of immigrants have arrived on these shores and become Americans without any such programs as have been proposed by the multiculturalists. Nor is there the slightest evidence, whether from the United States or from other countries where similar programs have been tried, that the transition has gone better as a result of multi-culturalism.

Perhaps the most tendentious aspect of the claim that ethnic diversity requires multicultural education programs is the assertion that this demand comes from the various ethnic groups themselves—as distinguished from vocal activitists. Non-English-speaking parents, for example, generally seek to get their children to be taught in English, rather than in the foreign-language programs promoted by activists under the label of "bilingualism."[3] Asian Americans, as well as Hispanics, have been found in polls to prefer to have their children educated in English,[4] and bilingual activists have had to resort to pressure and deception to maintain enrolments in bilingual programs.[5]

The claim that groups will get along better when they are given multicultural education is a straightforward claim which might be straightforwardly tested against the facts—but it almost never is. Wherever group separatism appears or group animosity erupts in the wake of multicultural education, these are automatically attributed to the influence of the larger society. The educational benefits of multiculturalism are likewise often proclaimed but seldom documented. There is no *a priori* reason to believe such claims, especially in the face of multiple evidences of declining educational quality during the period when multiculturalism and other non-academic preoccupations have taken up more and more of the curriculum.

Multiculturalists themselves are quite clear that they do not see their philosophy as just one of many philosophies that different people may entertain, or as something to be optional in some parts of the school curriculum. "Multicultural perspectives should *infuse the entire curriculum, prekindergarten through grade 12*" (emphasis in the original), according to the official report to the New York state Commissioner of Education.[6] Because this report considered *"commitment to multicultural social studies education"* to be crucial, it called for *"extensive staff development"* which would "address attitudes"—i.e., indoctrination—and which would extend even to the schools' clerical staffs and bus drivers.[7] In short, the call for cultural "diversity" is a call for ideological conformity.

This pattern is not peculiar to New York state or even to the United States. A study of a multiculturally oriented school in Manchester, England, found the very same buzz-words—"sensitive," "child centred,"[8]—as well as a determination not to "bend to parents' prejudices,"[9] a similar disregard of teachers who criticized what was being done in the name of "multiculturalism," and a hiring and promotion of new teachers more in tune with the multicultural dogma.[10] In Australia as well, there is the same dogmatic sense of exclusive rectitude in a multicultural educator's dismissal of "assimilationist and melting pot thinking from some reactionaries."[11]

There are many variations on the theme of multiculturalism, but their basic ideological premises, political modes of implementation, and educational practices show a recurrent pattern, whether at the school level or the college level, and whether in the United States or abroad. In all these settings, a major ingredient in the political success of promoters of multiculturalism has been a concealment of both their ideological agendas and their educational results. One of the most politically successful of these "multicultural diversity" programs in the United States, so-called "bilingual education," has owed much of its political success to concealment of its educational reality.

"Bilingual Education"

The theory behind bilingual education is that youngsters who do not understand English can best be taught school subjects in their native language, taking English classes as a separate subject, rather than be subjected to an all-English education from the first day. The children of immigrants from Spanish-speaking countries have been the principal focus of bilingualism, but once the idea caught on in the political arena and in the courtrooms, it expanded to include school children of Asian, Middle Eastern, and other backgrounds, and ultimately drew into its orbit even native-born American children whose only language was English. While most of the bilingual programs have featured the Spanish language, some have been in Chinese, Armenian, Navajo, and more than a hundred other languages.[12]

A landmark on the road to bilingualism was the 1974 U.S. Supreme Court decision in *Lau v. Nichols* that it was an unconstitutional denial of equal protection to provide only an English-language education to non-English-speaking school children. While the Supreme Court did not specify what alternative education must be provided, organized ethnic activists now had leverage to push for bilingualism, using the threat of lawsuits and political charges of discrimination and racism against school systems which resisted the activists' agenda.

Both legally and educationally, there were many possible ways of dealing with the language difficulties of foreign school children, and both school officials and parents might have been given discretion to choose among various options. For example, the foreign students might have been given a course on English as a second language, while taking their other school subjects in English as well, either immediately or after a transition period. At the other end of the range of possibilities, the children might be taught in a foreign language for years, perhaps with only token gestures toward making them English speakers. The relentless political pressures of ethnic activists have been directed toward the latter system—that is, establishing whole programs taught in a foreign language.

The political clout of these ethnic activists was reflected in Congress' restrictions on what percentage of federal spending in this area could be on programs teaching English as a second language, rather than on programs taught in foreign languages and given the label "bilingual." During the Carter administration, only 4 percent of the money could be spent on programs featuring English as a second language. Even under the Reagan administration (which was more critical of bilingualism) this rose only to 25 percent. In short, parents and school officials alike have been restricted in their ability to choose how to deal with foreign students' language problems, if their choice did not coincide with that of ethnic activists.

These ethnic activists—the Mexican American Legal Defense and Educational Fund, the National Council of La Raza, and others—have developed a whole agenda, going well beyond the language problems of school children. They argue that the "societal power structure" of white, Anglo-Saxon, English-speaking Americans handicaps non-English-speaking children, not only by presenting education in a language with which these children will have difficulty, but also by making these children ashamed of their own language and culture, and by making the abandonment of their ancestral culture the price of acceptance in the educational system and in American society. Consistent with this general vision, the educational deficiencies and high drop-out rates of Hispanic students, for example, are blamed on such assaults on their culture and self-esteem.

Given this vision, the agenda of the ethnic activists is not one of transitional programs to acquire English-language skills, but rather a promotion of the foreign language as a medium of instruction throughout the curriculum, promotion of the study and praise of other aspects of the foreign culture in the schools, and (whether openly avowed or not) promotion of a sense of historic grievances against American society, both on their own behalf and on behalf of other presumed victims of American and Western civilization, at home and around the world. In short, the activist agenda goes well beyond language education, or even education in general, to encompass political and ideological issues to be addressed in the public schools at taxpayer expense—and at the expense of time available for academic subjects. This activist agenda has provoked counter-responses by various individuals and groups, including school teachers, parents, and such civic organizations as "U.S. English" and "LEAD" (Learning English Advocates Drive). The resulting clashes have ranged from shouting matches in school meetings to legal battles in the federal courts. Bilingual education has been characterized by the *Washington Post* as "the single most controversial area in public education."[13]

Studies of the educational effectiveness of bilingualism and of alternative approaches have been as much shrouded in controversy as every other aspect of this issue. Yet the preponderant weight of the political system and the educational system has been solidly behind bilingualism, just as if it were a proven success, and its advocates have kept bilingual programs well-supplied with school children, through methods which often circumvent the parents of both foreign and native-born children.

In San Francisco, for example, thousands of English-speaking children with educational deficiencies were assigned to bilingual classes, blacks being twice as likely to be so assigned as whites. Hundreds of other youngsters, who in fact had a foreign language as their mother tongue, were assigned to bilingual classes in a *different* foreign language.[14] Thus a Chinese immigrant child could be assigned to a bilingual program because of speaking a foreign language—but then be put into a Spanish language class. Similarly, a Spanish-speaking child might be put into a Chinese language class—all this being based on where space happened to be available, rather than on the actual educational needs of the particular child. "Bilingual-education classes," according to the leader of a Chinese American organization, have also been "used as a 'dumping ground' for educationally disadvantaged students or students with behavior problems."[15]

In short, maintaining or expanding enrollment in bilingual programs has clearly taken priority over educating children. Moreover, the deception common in other programs promoted by zealots has also been common in bilingual programs. District administrators interviewed by the *San Francisco Examiner* "downplayed the number of black students assigned to bilingual classes, first estimating the number at three"—an estimate subsequently raised to about a hundred, though the real figure turned out to be more than 750. A civil rights attorney representing minority children characterized the whole approach as a "mindless" practice of "assigning kids to wherever there is space." It is not wholly mindless, however. Children whose parents are poorer, less educated, and less sophisticated are more likely to be assigned, or to remain, in bilingual programs. "More vocal white parents manage to maneuver their kids out of bilingual classes," as the civil rights attorney noted.[16]

The San Francisco situation is by no means unique. A national study of bilingual programs found large numbers of English-speaking minority students in programs taught in foreign languages and ostensibly designed for youngsters unable to speak Enlish. Only 16 percent of all the students in such programs were students who spoke only Spanish—the kind of student envisioned when bilingual programs were instituted. A study in Texas found that most school districts automatically categorized as "limited English proficiency" students—eligible for bilingual programs—even those Hispanic children who spoke *only* English and whose parents only occasionally spoke Spanish at home. The study concluded that English was "the dominant language" of most of the students participating in the bilingual programs surveyed.[17] Again, the whole thrust of the policy was toward maximizing enrolments.

Hispanic youngsters are not spared in the ruthless sacrifices of school children to the interests of the bilingual lobby. American-born, English-speaking students with Spanish surnames have often been targeted for inclusion in bilingual programs. Forced to speak Spanish during so-called bilingual classes, such youngsters have been observed speaking English among themselves during recess.[18] A bilingual education teacher in Massachusetts reported speaking to Puerto Rican children in Spanish and having them reply in English.[19] Research in several California school districts showed that children classified as "limited English proficient" ranged from being predominantly better in Spanish than English in districts closer to the Mexican border to being predominantly better in English than in Spanish in districts farther north, with about two-thirds being equally proficient (or deficient) in the two languages in the intermediate city of Santa Barbara.[20] A large-scale national study of bilingual programs found that two-thirds of the Hispanic children enrolled in such programs were already fluent in English, and more than four-fifths of the directors of such programs admitted that they retained students in their programs after the students had mastered English.[21]

While the rationale for so-called bilingual programs has been presented to the public in terms of the educational needs of children whose native language is not English, what actually happens in such programs bears little relationship to that rationale. It bears much more relationship to the careers and ideologies of bilingual activists. A study of Hispanic middle-school students in Boston, for example, found that 45 percent had been kept in bilingual programs for six years or more.[22] The criteria for being taken out of such programs are often based on achieving a given proficiency in English, so that students are retained in bilingual programs even when their English is better than their Spanish. A bilingual education teacher in Springfield, Massachusetts, reported her frustration in trying for years to get such students transferred into regular classrooms:

> Each year we had the same disagreement. I argued that the students, according to test scores and classroom performance,

had made enough progress in English to be able to work in a regular classroom, with some further attention to their reading and writing skills. The department head argued that they must remain in the bilingual program as long as they were not yet reading at grade level. It did not matter when I countered that many American students who speak only English do not read at grade level, or that after six or seven years of heavy instruction in Spanish without achieving good results it was probably time to try a different approach.[23]

Students retained in bilingual programs for years, without mastering either English or Spanish, have sometimes been characterized as "semi-lingual," rather than bilingual. The bilingual label is often grossly misleading also in terms of the token amount of time spent on English—perhaps a couple of hours a week—in programs which are predominantly foreign language programs, where students may spend years before taking a single subject taught in English.[24] The great majority of Hispanic parents—more than three-fourths of Mexican American parents and more than four-fifths of Cuban American parents—are opposed to the teaching of Spanish in the schools at the expense of English.[25] Many Asian refugee parents in Lowell, Massachusetts, likewise declared their opposition to bilingual education for their children.[26] In Springfield, Massachusetts, the Spanish-speaking bilingual teachers themselves put their own children in private schools, so that they would not be subjected to bilingual education.[27] Parents in Los Angeles who did not want their children enrolled in bilingual programs have been pressured, deceived, or tricked into agreement or seeming agreement. By and large, ethnic activists oppose giving parents an option.[28]

That the wishes of both majority and minority parents have been over-ridden or circumvented suggests something of the power and the ruthlessness of the bilingual lobby. Much of this power comes from the U.S. Department of Education, where ethnic activists have been prominent among those writing federal guidelines, which go much further than the courts or the Congress in forcing bilingual programs into schools and forcing out alternative ways of dealing with the language problems of non-English-speaking children.[29] However, bilingual activists have also been active in state and local agencies, and have been ruthless in smearing or harassing those who do not go along with their agenda.[30]

More than ideological zealotry is involved in the relentless drive to maintain and expand enrollment in bilingual programs, at all costs. Federal and local subsidies add up to hundreds of dollars per child for students enrolled in bilingual programs, and teachers proficient in Spanish receive bonuses amounting to thousands of dollars each annually. Bilingualism has been aptly described as "a jobs program for Spanish-speaking teachers."[31]

Teachers from foreign countries who speak one of the languages used in bilingual programs can be hired in California without passing the test of basic skills required of other teachers, even if they lack a college degree and are not fluent in English.[32] At the University of Massachusetts, candidates for their bilingual teacher program were, for a number of years, not even tested in English—all testing being done in Spanish. Moreover, a non-Hispanic woman who was fluent in Spanish, and who had taught for years in Mexico, was rejected on grounds that she was not sufficiently familiar with Puerto Rico. Among the questions she was asked was the name of three small rivers in the interior of the island[33]—a tactic reminiscent of the questions once asked by Southern voter registrars to keep blacks from being eligible to vote.

The costs of bilingualism add up. In Dade County, Florida, it cost 50 percent more to educate an immigrant child than the cost of educating a non-immigrant child. Oakland, California, found that it was spending $7 million annually to provide native-language instruction.[34] Nationally, expenditures on bilingual education have tripled in a decade.[35] The largest costs, however, are paid by the students who go through programs which claim to teach them two languages but often fail to teach them mastery of one. Among adults, Hispanics fluent in English earn incomes comparable to other Americans of the same age and education level.[36] To deny them that fluency is to create a life-long economic handicap.

The virtually unanimous support of bilingualism among Hispanic activists, "leaders" and "spokesmen"—in contrast to Hispanic parents—is understandable only in terms of the self-interest of those activists, "leaders" and "spokesmen," who benefit from the preservation of a separate ethnic enclave, preferably alienated from the larger society. This is not peculiar to Hispanics. Similar patterns can be found around the world. Activists, "leaders" and "spokesmen" for Australian aborigines promote the teaching of aboriginal languages to aborigines who already speak English, just as Maori activists in New Zealand push the teaching of the Maori language to Maoris who have grown up speaking English. In these and other countries, separate language maintenance has been part of a larger program of separatism and alienation in general. In all these disparate settings, the education of school children has been sacrificed to the financial and ideological interests of activists.

Promoters of so-called bilingual education, like the promoters of other forms of separatism, often claim that they are promoting intergroup harmony and mutual respect. "Language diversity within a society reduces ethnocentrism," one such promoter claims,[37] but it would be hard to find concrete examples of this anywhere on this planet, while there are all too many counter-examples of nations torn apart by ethnic polarization in Malaysia, murderous riots in India, and outright civil war in Sri Lanka, to name just a few. Sri Lanka is an especially poignant example, for it was at one time justly held up to the world as a model of intergroup harmony—*before* language politics became a major issue.[38]

One of the most widely used, and most tendentious, arguments in favor of the foreign-language and foreign-culture programs operating under the bilingual label is that a changing racial and cutural mix in the United States requires such programs, in order for American society to accommodate the newcomers. "People of color will make up one-third of the net additions to the U.S. labor force between 1985 and 2000," according to one bilingual advocate, who has urged "second-language competencies by all students," because otherwise a merely transitional bilingual program for minorities will lead to "the erosion, rather than the maintenance of, the minority languages."[39]

First of all, when people say that racial, ethnic, or linguistic minorities will make up some projected percentage of "net additions to the U.S. Labor force," there is much less there than meets the eye. The American population and labor force are growing slowly, so that any given fraction of that small *increment* is not a major factor in the over-all composition of the country's population or labor force. Even if it were, it is a *non sequitur* to say that special language programs must be established for newcomers, in a country where millions of newcomers have flooded in for generations on end, without any such programs being established.

Inflating the size of the population affected by language policy by speaking of "people of color" ignores the fact that most of those people of color are black, native-born, English-speaking people. Finally, even for those people who come to the United States speaking a different language, they not only can learn English but are in fact learning English, just as other immigrants did before them. Virtually all second-generation Hispanics speak English and more than half of all third-generation Hispanics speak *only* English.[40] All the sound and fury of the bilingual advocates is directed toward countering this natural evolution, which will otherwise deprive them of the separate and alienated ethnic enclaves so useful to "leaders"—and so detrimental to minorities as a whole and to the society as a whole.

The political success of bilingual activists—despite the opposition of parents and teachers, and despite both scholarly studies and journalistic exposés revealing the fraudulence of their claims—has wider implications for the vulnerability of the political process to strident special interests who are organized and ruthless. Education at all levels is especially vulnerable to promoters of their own ideological or financial interests in the name of some group for whom they claim to speak. In Los Angeles, which has one of the largest bilingual programs in the country, more than three-quarters of the school teachers oppose such programs—but to no avail. Bilingual activists have been so successful in branding critics as "racists" opposed to Hispanic people that an organization critical of bilingualism keeps their membership secret.[41] Intimidation and character assassination tactics have proved effective all the way up to the college and university levels, and for other groups besides Hispanics. Sometimes it is sufficient to accuse people merely of "insensitivity" to accomplish the same political result.

"Sensitivity"

One of the most tendentious words in the vocabulary of multiculturalism is "sensitivity." When it is proclaimed that one must become more "sensitive" to various ethnic, linguistic, sexual, or lifestyle groups, neither a reason nor a definition usually accompanies this opaque imperative. Moreover, what is called "sensitivity" often involves being *less* sensitive, in order to be more ideologically in fashion. For example, it is considered "insensitive" to use the word "Orientals" instead of "Asians" (even though the Orient or east is ultimately just a direction—and no one considers it insensitive to refer to the West or to Westerners). But, where there is a substantive difference between "Orientals" and "Asians," the former is the more specific term, referring to persons of Chinese, Japanese, and related racial ancestry, while the latter geographical term encompasses as well the racially different peoples of India, Malaysia, Indonesia, and the Philippines.

In other countries as well, to be "sensitive" in the ideological sense is to be *insensitive* to finer distinctions. In Britain, for example, to be ideologically sensitive is to call all non-white Britons "black," whether they are in fact Chinese, Pakistani, or West Indian. In Canada, the phrase that lumps all non-whites together is "visible minorities." In the United States, the corresponding phrase is "people of color."

In plain English, to make finer distinctions is to be more sensitive, but in educational Newspeak "sensitivity" means going along with current ideological fashions. When racially and culturally heterogeneous groups are lumped together—whether as "Asians" in the United States, "blacks" in Britain or "visible minorities" in Canada—the ideological point is to depict them all as victims of whites, and their economic, educational, or other problems as being due to that victimization. What a finer breakdown would reveal is that some of these groups differ as much from one another as they do from whites, whether in race, income, education, or cultural patterns. In some cases, particular ethnic groups within the broad category depicted as victims actually exceed the income or occupational status of whites. The taboo against finer distinctions among such groups serves to conceal such ideologically inconvenient facts.

"Sensitivity" goes in only one direction. It is seldom considered insensitive to refer to individuals or groups as "Anglos" or "WASPs" (white, Anglo-Saxon Protestants), even when they are in fact Celtic, Semitic, or Slavic in ancestry or Catholic, Judaic, or agnostic in religion. Nor are the most sweeping stereotypes about "Anglos" or "WASPs" likely to be questioned, either as to taste or accuracy.

The charge of "insensitivity" applies far more widely than to names, though usually with the same one-sidedness. To be sensitive, as ideologically defined, requires that one not merely accept but "affirm" other people's way of life or even "celebrate" diversity in general. Like other demands for "sensitivity," this demand offers no reason—unless fear of being disapproved, denounced, or harassed is a reason. If the thought is that anyone who really understood, or tried to understand, others' cultures would necessarily approve, then this is simply an unsubstantiated dogma posing as a moral imperative. Moreover, automatic approval has no meaning, except as a symptom of successful intimidation.

If you have no right to disapprove, then your approval means nothing. It may indeed be distressing to someone to have you express your opinion that his lifestyle is disgusting and his art, music or writing is crude, shallow, or repugnant, but unless you are free to reach such conclusions, any praise you bestow is hollow and suspect. To say that A has a right to B's approval is to say that B has no right to his own opinion. What is even more absurd, the "sensitivity" argument is not even consistent, because everything changes drastically according to who is A and who is B. Those in the chosen groups may repudiate any aspect of the prevailing culture, without being considered insensitive, but no one from the prevailing culture may repudiate any aspect of other cultures.

The Flow of Racism

One of the claims for multicultural programs in schools and colleges is that they reduce intergroup conflict by making all groups aware of, and sensitive to, racial, ethnic, and cultural differences—and more accepting of these differences. Whatever the plausibility of these claims, they are seldom, if ever, backed up with any evidence that schools or colleges with such programs have less intergroup conflict than institutions without them. The real dogmatism of such claims comes out most clearly, however, where mounting evidence of *increasing* animosities among students from different backgrounds, in the wake of multicultural programs, is met by further claims that this only shows the racism of the larger society overflowing into the schools and colleges.

An editor of *The American School Board Journal* was all too typical in asserting—without a speck of evidence—that "the effects of society's racism are spilling over into the schools," and adding (also without evidence), "public schools are society's best hope of battling racism."[42] He urged adding multicultural programs to the school curriculum and quoted an education professor who said: "Few other instructional techniques promise to make such improvements."[43] That statement is no doubt true enough in itself. The real question is whether multiculturalism delivers on that promise—or whether it in fact makes racism worse. That empirical question is not even asked, much less answered, either by this editor or by numerous other advocates of "multicultural diversity."

This dogmatism by multicultural zealots is found from the elementary schools to the colleges and universities. It stretches across the country and internationally as well.

The chairman of a committee of inquiry into a race-related murder on a school playground in Manchester, England, reported: "At several stages of our inquiry, we were told that racism in school derives from racism in the wider community."[44] Yet, after reviewing the zealous "multicultural" and "anti-racist" policies of the schools—policies which the committee chairman generally favored[45]—he was forced to conclude that, in this instance at least, the actual implementation of these policies was "one of the greatest recipes for the spread of racism from the school out into the community."[46] The *very possibility* that racism is flowing in the opposite direction to that assumed is never considered in most of the vast international literature on multiculturalism.

The Manchester multicultural program was instituted despite a warning that such programs in the London area had proved to be "a fiasco," and "divisive," and had created "suspicion" and "squabbles."[47] Ordinary people in the neighborhood near the Manchester school, where a Pakistani boy was killed by a white boy, also had no difficulty considering the possibility that multiculturalism could be counterproductive.

"I feel that this enforced focus on multi-culturalism produces prejudices," one said.

"I feel that the best way to bring about avoidance of racial hostility would be to ignore people's ethnic origins and characteristics," another said.

Double standards in treating students were cited among the counterproductive fruits of multiculturalism: "The teachers are scared, they are frightened to take the white side in case they are accused of racism."[48] Such complaints of double standards, favoring non-white students, also came from white students in the school—and were confirmed by the predominantly *non-white* committee of inquiry, dominated by Labor Party members.[49] This panel's findings could not be dismissed in the usual way by labeling them white male conservatives.

Some of the criticisms of multiculturalism as a counterproductive factor in race relations may be only statements of plausibility—but so are the opposite statements of the multicultural zealots. Yet these zealots operate as intolerantly as if they had the certainty of a proven fact. Belief in multiculturalism became a litmus test for applicants for teaching positions in the Manchester school, for example, and initiatives from the principal and other multicultural zealots "were presented in a way that assumed everybody was racist."[50] None of this was peculiar to Manchester or to England. Such things as enforcement of ideological conformity, *a priori* accusations of racism, and double standards for judging students' behavior are common features of multicultural programs in the schools and colleges of the United States. So too is trying to force people to take part in foreign cultural experiences—in religion, food, and a useless smattering of foreign words, for example[51]—whether they want to or not, and regardless of the academic or other costs.

"Why do we have to eat their food?" a student in Manchester asked.[52] Their parents' questions included: Why are English children being taught to count in Punjabi, when they are having trouble counting in English?[53] Why are they being forced to take part in Moslem religious rites?[54] Similar questions can be raised wherever multicultural zealots gain dominance—and such questions are likely to be ignored elsewhere, as they were in Manchester.

In the United States, multiculturalism not only covers the kinds of practices and attitudes found in England. In the U.S., the very pictures in textbooks must reflect the multicultural ideology. As one education writer noted:

> ... the textbooks teachers rely on are required to reflect the growing insistence on inclusion of "underrepresented populations"—mainly racial and ethnic minorities, women, and the handicapped.[55]

In the two biggest textbook markets in the country, Texas and California, committees of the state legislature have "set up exacting goals for depicting these groups in a book's stories and illustrations." One free-lance artist stopped illustrating children's readers after receiving a set of "multicultural" instructions running to ten pages, single-spaced. As she described the pictures resulting from these instructions:

> The hero was a Hispanic boy. There were black twins, one boy, one girl; an overweight Oriental boy, and an American Indian girl. That leaves the Caucasian. Since we mustn't forget the physically handicapped, she was born with congenital malformation and had only three fingers on one hand. . . .[56]

The Hispanic boy's parents could not have jobs that would seem stereotypical, so they had to be white collar workers and eat non-Hispanic food—"spaghetti and meatballs and a salad." The editor even specified to the artist what kind of lettuce should be in the salad: "Make sure it's not iceberg: it should be something nice like endive." There also had to be a picture of a "senior citizen"—jogging.[57] Such nit-picking is neither unusual nor the idiosyncracy of a particular editor or publisher. A specialist in textbook production pointed out that virtually every textbook "has to submit to ethnic/gender counts as to authors, characters in stories, references in history books, etc. Even humanized animal characters—if there's two boy bears, there have to be two girl bears."[58]

Part of the double standards of multiculturalism often involves a paternalistic sheltering of disadvantaged minority children from things remote from their immediate experience. As one former teacher on a Wyoming Indian reservation put it, in asking for "textbook relevance" for his Indian students:

> The concept of an ocean would be foreign to them. The children of Wind River know Ocean Lake, so named because of its considerable size, and the occasional wind-driven waves. They couldn't fathom the idea of a real ocean.[59]

No such claim was made for the white children in Wyoming, or in any of the other land-locked states of the United States. More fundamentally, it did not address the question whether education is meant to open a window on a larger world or to paint the student into his own little corner.

With so many people bending over backward to be "sensitive," with so much attention to mixing people from different groups, not only in real life (through "busing" and the like), but even in textbook pictures, what has been the net result? A San Francisco high school presented a lunchtime scene all too typical of many American schools and colleges where "multicultural diversity" is only statistical:

> In the brick-lined courtyard, a group of black students gathers on benches. Outside a second-floor classroom, several Chinese girls eat chow mein and fried rice from takeout cartons. Inside the dreary cafeteria, a clique of Vietnamese students sprawls across two tables—where they have spent every lunch since September. Against the back wall, two lone Russian boys pass lunch in conversation.
>
> San Francisco schools have spent two decades and more than $100 million on integration programs. Yet outside the classroom—at the lunch counters, on the playgrounds and in the hallways—many ethnic groups still mix as well as oil and water.[60]

It should be noted again that California is one of the states where the very textbook pictures must conform to the multicultural ideology. Moreover, it is not at all clear that there was this much ethnic separatism in multi-ethnic schools in times past. This is not simply a California problem, however. Researchers around the country report internal self-segregation among students in schools racially "integrated" statistically. A two-year study by a professor at the University of Pittsburgh found that, on a typical day at a school being studied, only 15 out of 250 students ate lunch sitting next to someone of a different race, even though the school had equal numbers of black and white students.[61]

The more fundamental question—whether racism is increased or decreased in the schools by multiculturalism, and therefore whether the flow of racism is primarily from the schools to the larger society, or vice-versa—can be better addressed after discussions of multiculturalism in American colleges and universities in Part II. It is sufficient here to point out that that question is seldom even considered in the massive outpourings of words on "multicultural diversity."

MISCELLANEOUS PSYCHO-BABBLE

"Relevance"

Everyone wants education to be relevant. It is hard even to conceive why anyone would wish it to be irrelevant. Those who proclaim the need for "relevance" in education are fighting a straw man—and evading the crucial need to define what *they* mean by "relevance," and why that particular definition should prevail.

Beginning in the 1960s, insistence on "relevance" became widespread and the particular kind of "relevance" being sought was typically a relevance judged *in advance* by students who had not yet learned the particular things being judged, much less applied them in practice in the real world. Relevance thus became a label for the general belief that the usefulness or meaningfulness of information or training could be determined *a priori*.

"No one should ever be trying to learn something for which one sees no relevance," according to Carl Rogers.[62] The student should be asked:

> "What do you want to learn? What things puzzle you? What are you curious about? What issues concern you? What problems do you wish you could solve?"[63]

It is easy to see how this particular concept of relevance is consonant with trends toward more student choice, whether individually in choosing among elective courses in schools and colleges, or collectively in designing or helping to design the curriculum. Because the student has neither foreknowledge of the material to be learned nor experience in its application in the real world beyond the walls of the school, his emotional response to the material must be his guide. As Carl Rogers envisioned the process:

> I am talking about LEARNING—the insatiable curiosity that drives the adolescent boy to absorb everything he can see or hear or read about gasoline engines in order to improve the efficiency and speed of his "cruiser." I am talking about the student who says, "I am discovering, drawing in from the outside, and making that which is drawn in a real part of *me*." I am talking about any learning in which the experience of the learner progresses along this line: "No, no, that's not what I want"; "Wait! This is closer to what I'm interested in, what I need"; "Ah, here it is! Now I'm grasping and comprehending what I *need* and what I want to know!"[64]

At the heart of the "relevance" notion is the belief that current emotional responses are a reliable guide to the future usefulness or meaningfulness of education. Although this assumption is essential to the logic of the argument for "relevance," Carl Rogers was one of the few who made that assumption explicit when he said that the man who would "do what 'felt right' in this immediate moment" would "find this in general to be a trustworthy guide to his behavior."[65] If emotions are indeed so prescient and virtually omniscient, then of course there is little reason to rely on experience—which must mean the experience of others, in the case of inexperienced students.

It is hard to imagine how a small child, first learning the alphabet, can appreciate the full implications of learning these particular 26 abstract symbols in an arbitrarily fixed order. Yet this lifelong access to the intellectual treasures of centuries depend on his mastery of these symbols. His ability to organize and retrieve innumerable kinds of information, from sources ranging from encyclopedias to computers, depends on his memorizing that purely arbitrary order. There is not the slightest reason in the world why a small child should be expected to grasp the significance of all this. Instead, he learns these symbols and this order because his parents and teachers want him to learn it—not because he sees its "relevance."

Experience would be virtually worthless if it were possible to know *a priori* what will and will not be needed in the future. If an economist who has done 20 years of research and analysis has no better idea how much statistical analysis a beginner should master than that beginner himself has, then one can only marvel that 20 years of experience have been such a complete waste. If a new recruit beginning basic training in the army knows just as much as a battle-scarred veteran as to what one should do to prepare for battle, then there is no justification for putting experienced officers in charge of troops and no excuse for differences in rank. In no other field of endeavor besides education would such reasoning even be taken seriously, much less be made the basis of institutional policy.

The "relevance" argument becomes especially dangerous when it is used to justify teaching different things to students from different racial or ethnic groups, on the basis of those students' immediate emotional responses, or their uninformed sense of plausibility as to what might, for example, be "relevant to the black experience"—at a time of life when they do not have enough experience of any color to make such a determination. How can someone who sets out to study things "relevant to the black experience" know whether such statistical concepts as multicollinearity or such economic concepts as dynamic equilibrium will turn out to be among those things which provide a whole new perspective on racial issues? To say that such questions can be answered *a priori* is to assume at the outset the very competence which education is supposed to produce as an end result.

Although many who use the "relevance" argument may not see clearly how it depends crucially on the reliability of current emotions as a guide to the future value of education, the inner logic of the argument nevertheless shows through in the frequency with which people of this persuasion use the word "exciting" as a recommendation for some educational policy. Other investments—that is, current costs incurred for future benefits—are seldom assessed in terms of how "exciting" they are. Farmers do not say that planting a given crop is exciting. Their justification for choosing a particular crop, or for planting it in a certain soil at a particular time of year, is much more apt to be in terms of the likelihood of producing a good havest. Similarly, a financial investor seldom characterizes his choice of portflio as "exciting." Instead, his justification for choosing the particular investments in his portflio is likely to run in terms of his assessment of future rewards.

Education is one of the largest investments in the society, running into hundreds of billions of dollars annually. Yet this investment is often, and increasingly, assessed in terms of its current emotional appeal to students or teachers. In short, it is not treated as an investment but as current consumption. The Bible said: "By their fruits ye shall know them." Educators too often seem to be saying: "By their excitement ye shall know them." For those less blatant, the word "relevance" is a round-about way of saying the same thing.

The idea that inexperienced young people can judge in advance what will later turn out to be relevant over the next half-century or more of their life is part of a more general and romantic social vision. This vision underlies such things as denigration of authority derived from experience or specialized training. This vision has been not only part of many radical experiments in American education, beginning during the 1960s, but was also the foundation of even more radical educational experiments in schools and colleges in China during the "great cultural revolution." The results were very similar in these very different settings.

In China, as in the United States, ideologically defined "relevance" superseded traditionally defined skills, as academic criteria in general were subordinated to such social goals as group "representation," while elitism in general was decried. College entrance examinations were abolished, grades were no longer unilaterally assigned by teachers but were discussed or negotiated, and off-campus activities substituted for academic work.[66] Educators' authority was so undermined that teachers were "afraid to take firm charge of their students."[67] The educational results in China were also similar to those in the United States. Nearly half the middle-school students failed the tests of basic knowledge in science and technology, and more than two-thirds failed the mathematics examination. By 1979, a group of American educators found that China's college entrance examinations were no longer as sophisticated as they had been 20 years earlier.[68]

The biggest difference between China's educational experiments and those in the United States has been that the Chinese learned from their mistakes, and abandoned such policies, while American education continues on the same course. Chinese political leaders recognized that China was falling further behind world standards in science and technology as a result of its educational debacles, and proceeded to re-introduce the teaching of traditional subjects and college entrance examinations.[69] Ideologically defined "relevance" was no longer a sacred cow in China, though it remains so in the United States.

The "Whole Person"

The idea that one should teach "the whole child" goes back at least as far as John Dewey. Some today call it "child-centered education" at the elementary school level and teaching "the whole person" in high school or college. The idea of tailor-made education, varying with the social background and psychology of each student, is related to the notion of "relevance." It is also reminiscent of an idea once popular among some ambitious economists, that they could "fine tune" the economy—until embarrassing experience taught them that they were lucky to get the right channel.

Ambitious educational goals seldom seem to evoke the question as to whether we have the capability of achieving them. Nor are these ambitions noticeably moderated by the educational system's abysmal failure at teaching the most basic skills. That educators who have repeatedly failed to do what they are hired to do, and trained to do, should take on sweeping roles as amateur psychologists, sociologists, and social philosophers seems almost inexplicable—except that they are doing it with other people's money and experimenting on other people's children.

There is only one way to deal with "the whole person"—and that is superficially. Anyone who is serious about understanding just one small aspect of the whole person—the endocrine glands, for example—knows that it is the labor of a lifetime for highly trained people, working with unrelenting dedication. Merely to develop the whole person's photographic talents can take many years, as anyone can see by looking at the nondescript early photographs taken by the great photographer Ansel Adams. The reason for teaching mathematics, instead of teaching "the whole person," is that one may have had some serious training in mathematics, and so at least have the possibility of being competent at it.

Educational theory too often focusses on the *desirability* of doing something, to the complete exclusion of the question of our *capability* of doing it. No doubt it would be far more desirable to travel through the air like Superman, instead of inching along in a traffic jam. But that is no reason to leap off skyscrapers. Our educational system is full of the results of leaping off skyscrapers.

Other countries whose educational systems achieve more than ours often do so in part by attempting less. While school children in Japan are learning science, mathematics, and a foreign language, American school children are sitting around in circles, unburdening their psyches and "expressing themselves" on scientific, economic and military issues for which they lack even the rudiments of competence. Worse than what they are *not* learning is what they *are* learning—presumptuous superficiality, taught by practitioners of it.

The "whole person" philosophy is not simply a theory of education. It has become an open floodgate through which all sorts of non-educational activities have poured into the schools, relieving many teachers of the drudgery of teaching, and substituting more "exciting" world-saving crusades in place of the development of academic skills.

Whether the crusade concerns the environment, AIDS, foreign policy, or a thousand other things, it is far more often pursued as a crusade than as an issue with arguments on both sides. Moreover, it is not sufficient that the students be propagandized in the classroom; they are taught to *act* on the one-sided superficiality they have been given. At one time, the President of the United States received more letters from school children fulfilling classroom assignments on nuclear war than letters from any other group on any other subject.[70]

In the San Francisco public schools in 1991, teachers organized a letter-writing campaign in which thousands of students sent letters to elected state officials, protesting cuts in the school budget. One letter from an elementary school student said: "I hate you. I would like to kill you." Another letter asked about the official's wife and children and said, "I'm going to set your house on fire and get my homies to beat you up!"[71] In response to public outcry and to angry officials, California's State Superintendent of Public Instruction, Bill Honig, sent out a memorandum to county and district superintendents, warning that "it would be legally safer to avoid such activities."[72] As for the ethics and propriety of using the children in this way, a spokesman for Honig's office was quoted in the *San Francisco Examiner* as justifying such school assignments:

> "It's appropriate to have kids responding to a current issue directly involving their lives," she said. "So having kids use class time to address public officials on current events is appropriate."[73]

Those who emphasize the teaching of "issues" rather than academic skills fail to understand that "issues" are infinitely more complex and difficult to master than fundamental principles of analysis. The very reason why there is an issue in the first place is usually because no single principle can possibly resolve the differences to the mutual satisfaction of those concerned. Innumerable principles are often interacting in a changing environment, creating vast amounts of complex facts to be mastered and assessed—*if* one is serious about resolving issues responsibly, as distinguished from generating excitement. To teach issues instead of intellectual principles to school children is like teaching calculus to people who have not yet learned arithmetic, or surgery to people lacking the rudiments of anatomy or hygiene. Worse, it is teaching them to go ahead and perform surgery, without worrying about boring details.

"Role Models"

One of the most widely accepted—or at least unchallenged—dogmas in American education today is that students need "role models" from the same social background as themselves. From the kindergarten to the colleges and universities, the dogma holds sway that students are taught more effectively by people of the same race, ethnicity, culture, and sex as themselves. Empirical evidence is almost never asked for, much less given.

Many of those who espouse this doctrine have the most obvious self-interest in doing so. Teachers and directors of bilingual education programs, Afro-centric programs in schools and various ethnic studies programs in college, all preserve jobs and careers for themselves—free of competition from members of the majority population—by using the "role model" dogma. So do feminists, homosexuals, and others. Administrators who have caved in to demands for various enclaves and preserves for particular groups likewise have a vested interest in this dogma, as a defense against critics. Around this solid core of supporters of the "role model" idea, there is a wider penumbra of those who wish to be *au courant* with the latest buzzwords, or to be on the side of the angels, as currently defined.

Historically, there have been good, bad, and indifferent schools where students and teachers have all been of the same background, where students and teachers were of wholly different backgrounds, and all sorts of combinations in between. There is no empirical evidence that any of those similarities or differences are correlated with educational results, and considerable indications that they are not.

One of the most academically successful of the all-black schools was Dunbar High School in Washington, D.C., during the period from its founding in 1870 until its rapid deterioration in the late 1950s, in the wake of new rules for selecting students. In addition to producing good academic results in general during this period, Dunbar also produced an impressive list of "the first black" to enter a number of fields and institutions, ranging from West Point and Annapolis to the federal judiciary and the Presidential Cabinet.[74] Its curriculum, however, was hardly Afro-centric and was in fact so traditional as to include Latin, long after most American schools had abandoned that ancient language. While Dunbar's teachers were black, another equally high-quality black high school, St. Augustine's in New Orleans, was founded and manned by whites of the Josephite order.[75]

Among the European immigrant groups, the first Irish Catholic children were taught by Protestant Anglo-Saxon teachers, at a time when such differences were very important socially and economically. Later, when the Jewish immigrant children began flooding into the public schools, they were far more likely to be taught by Irish Catholic teachers than by Jewish teachers. Still later, among the Chinese and Japanese children of immigrants, it was virtually unknown for them to be taught by teachers of their own race, religion, or culture. Yet, from all this vast experience, no one has yet produced evidence that "role models" from the student's own background are either necessary or sufficient, or in fact make any discernible academic difference at all.

The "role model" dogma is pork barrel politics, masquerading as educational philosophy. That this wholly unsubstantiated claim has been taken seriously in the media and by public officials is one more sign of the vulnerability of our minds and our institutions to vehement assertions—and to strident attacks on all who question them.

"Self-Esteem"

The notion that self-esteem is a precondition for effective learning is one of the more prominent dogmas to have spread rapidly thorugh the American educational system in recent years. However, its roots go back some decades, to the whole "child-centered" approach of so-called Progressive education. Like so much that comes out of that philosophy, it confuses cause and effect. No doubt valedictorians feel better about themselves than do students who have failed numerous courses, just as people who have won the Nobel Prize probably have more self-esteem than people who have been convicted of a felony.

Outside the world of education, few would be confident, or even comfortable, claiming that it is a lack of self-esteem which leads to felonies or its presence which leads to Nobel Prizes. Yet American schools are permeated with the idea that self-esteem precedes performance, rather than vice-versa. The very idea that self-esteem is something *earned*, rather than being a pre-packaged handout from the school system, seems not to occur to many educators. Too often, American educators are like the Wizard of Oz, handing out substitutes for brains, bravery, or heart.

The practical consequences of the self-esteem dogma are

many. Failing grades are to be avoided, to keep from damaging fragile egos, according to this doctrine. Thus the Los Angeles school system simply abolished failing grades in the early years of elementary school[76] and many leading colleges and universities simply do not record failing grades on a student's transcript. Other ways of forestalling a loss of self-esteem is to water down the courses to the point where failing grades are highly unlikely. A more positive approach to self-esteem is simply to give higher grades. The widespread grade inflation of recent decades owes much to this philosophy.

While the "role model" dogma is more obviously self-serving than the "self-esteem" dogma, the latter is not wholly free of self-interest. It is much easier to water down academic courses, replace them with non-academic activities, or give automatic high grades for either, than to take on the serious and difficult task of developing intellectual competence among masses of school children. Whatever the intentions of John Dewey or other pioneers of the Progressive education philosophy, its practical consequences have been a steady retreat from the daunting task of making mass education a serious attempt to raise American school children to a standard, rather than bringing the standard down to them.

The history of American education, from the time when high schools ceased to be a place reserved for an academic or social elite, has been a history of a steady displacement, or swamping, of academic subjects by non-academic subjects or academic subjects increasingly watered down. A blue-ribbon committee formed in the 1890s identified 40 subjects being taught in American high schools but, within two decades, the number of subjects expanded to 274. As of the period from 1906 to 1910, approximately two-thirds of all subjects taught in American high schools were academic subjects, but by 1930 only one-third were academic subjects.[77]

Even when the educational reform movements of the 1980s were successful politically in getting academic-subject requirements written into law and public policy, the response of many school systems across the country was simply to increase the number of academic subjects taught at a lower level—including courses taught remedially or even meretriciously, as former non-academic courses were re-named to look academic on paper. Sometimes the proliferation of pseudo-academic courses led to an absolute decline in the number of students taking challenging academic subjects.[78]

The "self-esteem" doctrine is just one in a long line of educational dogmas used to justify or camouflage a historic retreat from academic education. Its success depends on the willingness of the public, elected officials, and the media to take such dogmas seriously, without the slightest evidence. American school children and American society are the ultimate victims of this gullibility.

PART TWO

COLLEGES AND UNIVERSITIES

CHAPTER 5

Damaging Admissions

SEEKING ADMISSION to college has become such a stressful process for so many high school seniors that it is hard to realize how recent a social phenomenon the "selective" college is in American history. In 1920, for example, a survey of 40 of the most prestigious colleges and universities in the country found that only 13 turned away any applicants.[1] Swarthmore College was one of the rare exceptions in having several times as many applicants as places for them.[2] Even for Harvard, the first year in which there were more qualified applicants than there was space in the class was 1936—three centuries after the college was founded.[3]

As late as the period immediately after World War II, the Harvard admissions staff consisted of one administrator with a part-time assistant.[4] By academic year 1982–83, however, the cost of the admissions office staff at Harvard was more than $400,000 annually.[5] Today, even a small college like Middlebury has a dean of admissions with 17 people on his staff.[6] Large prestige institutions have not only large admissions staffs, but also outside consultants, a network of contacts among high school counselors across the country, mailing material aptly described as "professionally produced brochures that Madison Avenue's finest could be proud of,"[7] a "public relations machine that would make P. T. Barnum blush," as one Cornell administrator put it,[8] and recruiting operations that extend across the ocean. Even though Harvard now admits less than one-fifth of those who apply, it has a recruiting program which writes to approximately 25,000 high school students who have made outstanding scores on various tests and who have outstanding high school grades.[9]

Colleges have become especially competitive as a result of the decline in the size of the college-age population. According to *The Chronicle of Higher Education*:

> As competition for new students grows tougher, college presidents are treating admissions directors like football coaches, firing those who can't put the numbers on the board.[10]

While this new pressure cost dozens of admissions directors their jobs in a single year,[11] it also increased the demand for those with a record of success. Although the median salary of admissions directors in 1989–90 was approximately $42,000,[12] successful ones were being lured away at salaries as high as $100,000—"a figure unheard of just a year ago,"[13] according to *The Chronicle of Higher Education*. The economic stakes are high. When fewer students than expected enrolled at Bowdoin College in the fall of 1990, the college faced a loss of $500,000 in tuition.[14] Colleges also lose room charges when enrollment fails to fill the dormitories, whose costs of upkeep are not much reduced when there are empty rooms.

Given this picture—"the admissions director, faced with the prospect of empty beds and qualms about his job"[15]—it is possible to understand the pious but reckless huckstering that has become part of the college admissions process. For example, an article on preparing college brochures, appearing in the *Journal of College Admissions*, gave as its first axiom:

> Perception is the ultimate reality.[16]

In other words, the image of the college is what really matters, not what actually happens on campus. After quoting Marshall McLuhan's dictum, "the medium is the message," and recommending as a model "the folks with the golden arches," this marketing research consultant advised using less prose and more photographs, captions, and lists to capture the student's attention. As he put it: "Keep body copy light"[17] and "pare your ideas down to their most simple form."[18] Likewise, the head of a consulting firm specializing in college "marketing" said of college admissions brochures: "You want them to be mostly pictures. To be successful, a viewbook shouldn't have too much content."[19] Outside consultants not only advise on such things as preparing college brochures but also produce the brochures themselves and, in some cases, cause the college curriculum itself to be changed in ways designed to make it more marketable.[20] In this huckstering atmosphere, accuracy counts for little. As one college guidebook notes: "At least fifty colleges proudly state that they are in the top twenty-five."[21]

Even the test scores so widely published, and so uncritically accepted, are often fudged. Most colleges' reports of their SAT averages are not based on the scores of the students actually enrolled there, but on the scores of the students they accepted.[22] Thus, if a young man with math and verbal scores of 700 each applies to six colleges, and is admitted to all, then 5 colleges he is *not* attending will also include his SATs in their averages. Since higher-scoring students are more likely to be making multiple applications to more selective colleges, this inflates the SAT data, not only at those colleges but also at whatever "safety valve" schools were included among their applications.

Other gimmicks to boost SAT averages include omitting the scores of athletes, minorities, or others admitted under special provisions. An admissions director at a leading liberal arts college estimates that about one-fourth of the students in such institutions are likely to be special cases who are omitted in compiling SAT averages.[23] The difference that this can make may be illustrated by the fact that the University of Rochester's class of 1993 had a mean composite SAT score of 1149 with everyone counted, but 1218 with the various special students omitted.[24]

Lofty deception is as common in higher education as in elementary and secondary schools. Yet educators have somehow managed to convince others that academia should be teaching ethics to people in other professions and institutions.

But, as the late Nobel Prize-winning economist George Stigler put it, "the typical university catalog would never stop Diogenes in his search for an honest man."[25]

THE HUMAN AND FINANCIAL COSTS
OF COLLEGE

One consequence of the hype surrounding college admissions—much of it originating in the colleges themselves and amplified by the media—is a whole body of myths and misinformation about the academic world in general, and about its prestige institutions in particular. It is difficult to exaggerate the frantic anxiety of students and their parents, as they focus their attention on a relative handful of big-name institutions. The Stanford University admissions office, for example, receives approximately 45,000 mail and telephone inquiries annually—including an "annual flood of telephone calls and unwelcome visits from irate students who were not accepted and their parents."[26] This desperate desire for admission to prestige institutions in no way reflects any greater likelihood of receiving a better undergraduate education there than at many high-quality, less-known institutions.

College Quality

Perhaps the biggest and most damaging myth confronting students and parents who are choosing a college is that a "big-name" institution is a prerequisite or an assurance of a top quality education and/or a successful career afterwards. It is no doubt true that graduates of Harvard, Stanford, or M.I.T. earn higher incomes than the average graduate of unknown state colleges, but that is very misleading. Youngsters who have taken a voyage on the *Queen Elizabeth II*, or who have flown on the *Concorde*, probably also will have higher future incomes than those who have never travelled on anything more exotic than a bus. But that is hardly a reason to go deep into debt to book passage on the *QE 2* or to strain the family budget buying a ticket for the *Concorde*.

Top colleges turn out extraordinary graduates because they

take in extraordinary freshmen. That tells very little about what happened in the intervening four years, except that it did not ruin these individuals completely. It tells even less about what would have happened if these same extraordinary people had been educated elsewhere. Whether a given individual will do better, either educationally or financially, by going to a big-name college is very doubtful.

Hard statistics on the percentage of a college's alumni who eventually become sufficiently prominent to be listed in *Who's Who in America*, or who successfully complete a Ph.D., show many relatively obscure colleges whose alumni achieve either worldly success or academic success more frequently than the alumni of much better known institutions. The percentage of Davidson College alumni who end up in *Who's Who* is nearly as high as the percentage of Stanford University alumni listed there—and is higher than the percentage at three Ivy League institutions (Brown, Penn, and Cornell), as well as higher than the percentage of such alumni of Johns Hopkins, Northwestern, or Duke. Little-known Cornell College in Iowa has a higher percentage of its alumni end up in *Who's Who* than the alumni of Cornell University.[27]

It is very much the same story when it comes to the percentage of alumni who go on to receive Ph.D.s. Number one in the country in that regard is little Harvey Mudd College in southern California, an institution almost unheard of, east of the Mississippi. Over a period of years, more than 40 percent of all Harvey Mudd graduates went on to earn Ph.Ds—compared to 16 percent at Harvard.[28] It is not that these two measures of alumni success are the be-all and end-all. But almost any other measure will also turn up big surprises for those who believe in big names. For example, the average medical school applicant from Franklin & Marshall College scored higher on the medical school test than the average applicant from Berkeley, Duke, Dartmouth, Penn, or Northwestern.[29]

All this is not to suggest that there are no differences in academic quality between institutions. There are in fact vast differences—but big names are not a reliable guide to those differences. Those big names are often a result of faculty research activity, whose effects on undergraduate teaching are at best questionable.

Even those who concede that educational quality bears little correlation with institutional prestige often believe, nevertheless, that a big-name degree is a great help in gaining admission to top postgraduate institutions in medicine, law, or other fields. While it is undoubtedly true that officials at the nation's leading postgraduate institutions have learned from experience which colleges send them the best-prepared students, and that this may well influence admissions decisions, it is also true that deans of the leading law schools ranked Davidson College graduates over the graduates of most Ivy League colleges, and deans of the leading graduate schools of engineering ranked the graduates of Rose-Hulman Institute and Harvey Mudd College among their best students—higher ranked than engineering students from such prestigious institutions as Duke, U.C.L.A., Penn, or the Universities of Texas or Wisconsin.

There are reasons for these anomalies. Academic prestige is usually research prestige, and it is often purchased by the neglect of undergraduate education. From this perspective, it is hardly surprising that students from teaching institutions like Davidson or Franklin & Marshall are able to hold their own in competition with students from more prestigious institutions, or even in some cases to excel over students who entered college with better credentials. It may well be, as one academic writer put it, "a small school is often better equipped to deal with the tenuous beginnings of intellectual life."[30] However, precociously brilliant students may thrive elsewhere. Some of the most prestigious institutions, such as Harvard or M.I.T., may receive such an extraordinary student body that such students can learn a great deal on their own, despite the shortcomings of classroom teaching.

Conversely, at the other extreme, some small colleges may have such cozy student-faculty relationships that the student can remain immature, dependent, or even irresponsible, missing an opportunity to develop fully, either intellectually or as a responsible adult who can meet deadlines, respect rules, and maintain standards. None of these characteristics, which affect the quality of education, is something that can be quantified in a formula or calibrated in a simple ranking.

Because the national media are concentrated in the northeast, colleges in this region get far more attention than comparable (or better) institutions elsewhere. West coast institutions like Pomona and Harvey Mudd are quite comparable academically to the best institutions on the east coast, and yet they remain relatively obscure nationally. Whitman College, in the Pacific northwest, may be superior academically to Bennington by virtually all the usual indices, and yet Bennington remains far better known. One director of a college placement bureau offers as a geographical "law" of academic visibility: "Any distance west from Washington is twice the same distance north or south."[31]

With colleges and universities, even the prices charged are not nearly as indicative of quality as the prices charged for most other goods and services. According to a Carnegie Foundation study, "substantial differences in cost do not necessarily connote significant differences in outcomes."[32] Partly this is because tuition is only part of a college's income, with varying other amounts coming from endowment income, federal or state money, and alumni donations. Some very mediocre institutions charge high tuitions and some top-rated institutions charge much less.

Various other economic factors prevent price and quality from being as closely related as they are outside the academic world. Obviously state financing is one. Another is the widespread availability of financial aid, especially at the most expensive colleges and universities. This means that the net prices actually paid vary much more than the "list prices" shown in college catalogues. That is, the tuition actually paid varies widely from student to student in the same college, as well as among institutions.

In addition to myths, there is also misinformation. Perhaps the most dangerous misinformation are the many rankings of colleges and universities by "quality," "selectivity," or other such labels. The most elaborate—and most misleading—of these rankings are published annually by *U.S. News & World Report* magazine and then republished in book form in *America's Best Colleges*. The fundamental flaw in all these rankings is that no college can possibly be "best" for everyone. Even brothers or sisters may thrive in very different kinds of institutions. It is hard even to imagine what kind of person would be equally at home at Bennington College or at West Point, Reed College or Brigham Young University, Georgia Tech or the Juilliard School of Music.

The atmosphere and personality of colleges vary enormously, quite aside from variations in academic standards and methods. The real problem is to *match* individuals with institutions, not to *rank* institutions. It may be meaningful to say that M.I.T. outranks the Florida Institute of Technology as an engineering school, but many an individual may be able to learn engineering at F.I.T. and unable to learn the same subjects at M.I.T., where these subjects may be taught at a faster pace or in a more abstract and theoretical manner, requiring far greater mastery of advanced mathematics to follow what is being said.

For any given individual, one of these institutions may be far preferable to the other, but the reverse may be equally true for the next individual. If a higher ranking means simply that the most highly qualified student can find a greater challenge or a better opportunity to develop his talents to the fullest at a given place, then such rankings may be meaningful. But, even in this limited sense, many rankings are meaningless—and therefore dangerously misleading.

Some kinds of rankings make sense because they are based on personal knowledge and experience with respect to the students, the faculty, or the facilities of various institutions. Graduate deans ranking the quality of students their institutions have received over the years from particular colleges have this kind of knowledge and experience to draw on. But college presidents trying to guess what quality of education goes on at competing institutions have no such access to the facts. As the president of Middlebury College wrote, in response to a questionnaire from *U.S. News & World Report*:

> The underlying premise of your survey is that college and university presidents have special knowledge about the strengths and weaknesses of most other institutions. I seriously doubt that any of us had anything more than a superficial knowledge of most other campuses. We simply cannot answer your questions with any degree of authority.[33]

At the graduate school level, the story is different. Professors at leading institutions become familiar with each other's publications in scholarly journals and books, and hire each other's graduate students as new faculty members, so that they are well aware where the best work is being done in their respective fields and which institutions' new Ph.D.s are the best trained. Here too, rankings based on professional knowledge often differ from generalized "prestige." Among graduate departments of philosophy, for example, the University of Pittsburgh was ranked third in the nation. In mathematics, New York University outranked most of the Ivy League, and in chemical engineering the University of Delaware outranked Princeton.[34] In ranking educational institutions, as elsewhere, there is a vast difference between expertise and gossip—even quantified gossip.

The more "scientific" or formula-ridden the college rankings are, the more remote they are from conveying meaningful information on the education of undergraduates. *America's Best Colleges*, which admits that its choices are "ranked according to a formula,"[35] is the worst offender. When it ranks the University of California at Berkeley 13th among the nation's universities, that is surely an unlucky choice. Does this seriously mean that there are only a dozen universities in the United States where a student can get a better undergraduate education than at Berkeley? Even the worst pessimist does not believe that, for Berkeley is notorious for its mass, impersonal education, its many classes taught by hundreds of teaching assistants, often unable to speak fluent English, and for bureaucratic and other obstacles to getting a decent education.

Although Berkeley is one of the leading Ph.D.-granting institutions in the country, both quantitatively and qualitatively, a smaller proportion of its own undergraduates go on to receive Ph.D.s than do the alumni of dozens of other institutions, including many small colleges like Wabash, Eckerd, Kalamazoo, and Occidental. Among universities as well, Berkeley is nowhere near the top when it comes to sending its own undergraduates on to receive Ph.D.s. In fact, Berkeley falls behind four other institutions in the University of California system (U.C. San Diego, Irvine, Riverside, and Santa Cruz) in that regard.[36] Berkeley is the flagship of the University of California system, in terms of world-class research prestige, but virtually no one believes its undergraduate education is top-notch.

It is not that alumni Ph.D.s are the only or always best indicator of the quality of undergraduate education. But *America's Best Colleges* has no real measure of the quality of undergraduate education. Its formula gauges faculty quality by such things as average faculty salary—almost certainly more a reflection of research than teaching at Berkeley—and by student-faculty ratios,[37] even though many of the faculty counted in these ratios never go near an undergraduate. Like so many formula-ridden approaches which affect a "scientific" air, *America's Best Colleges* inadvertently betrays the ignorance behind its pretensions—in this case, by misusing repeatedly the simple statistical concept of "percentile."[38] This is typical of the pseudo-precision and pseudo-objectivity of these rankings.

A more insidious problem is that the subjective rankings of institutions by college administrators reward institutions which have done something to bring themselves to the attention of administrators elsewhere. High-quality education is far less likely to do that than some "innovative" gimmick that gets media mention—"interdisciplinary" freshman courses (virtually a contradiction in terms) at Amherst[39] or a community service requirement for graduation at Wittenberg,[40] for example. The 1988 edition of *America's Best Colleges* itself characterizes "innovation" as the "answer to obscurity"[41]—which is not to say that it is the measure of quality. If you cannot measure quality, the next best thing is to avoid pretending that you can. *America's Best Colleges* is only the worst offender in this respect, but by no means the only offender.

One of the common practices in a number of college guides is to rank colleges by their "selectivity"—defined as the percentage of applicants accepted for admissions. But if college *A* attracts a large number of mediocre applicants and college *B* attracts a smaller number of well-qualified applicants, then college *A* may end up accepting a smaller percentage of its applicants—thereby looking statistically more "selective." Such a statistic would be completely misleading, both as to institutional quality and as to any given individual's probabilities of being accepted at the two schools. Moreover, where college *A* is more widely known, and college *B* has a better reputation among fewer people, to make statistical "selectivity" a factor in ranking them is to perpetuate a public misperception. Some colleges may even deliberately encourage applications from students who have no realistic prospect of being admitted, in order to be able to have a high percentage of rejections and thus be rated more "selective" by college guides.[42]

None of this means that college guides in general are worthless. On the contrary, many guides are very valuable—and especially so when they do *not* attempt pseudo-scientific rankings, but instead sketch something of the character and thrust of particular institutions, so that a given individual can determine which places would represent a match or a mismatch with that individual's own aspirations, ability, and personality. Books like *The Fiske Guide to College, The Insider's Guide to the Colleges,* or *The National Review College Guide* serve this important purpose.

Larger guides containing compilations of numerous institutional statistics—percentage of students who receive financial aid, or who go on to postgraduate education, percentage of faculty with Ph.D.s, percentage of students graduating in which fields—can also be useful, depending on the relevance of the particular statistics presented. The *Comparative Guide to American Colleges* or *The College Handbook* are among the more useful of these kinds of guides. Finally, there are those which do not focus on individual institutions but instead give an overview of the academic world, as an introduction to the whole process of college selection and the considerations to take into account. *Choosing a College* and *Looking Beyond the Ivy League* are these kinds of foundation books.

It is no more necessary, or possible, to rank these different kinds of books than to rank different kinds of colleges. The various kinds of guides are complementary and, even for a given kind of guide, both multiple opinions and even multiple statistics need to be checked against one another. All can be useful in getting beyond the myths and misinformation which abound on academic institutions.

Tuition and "Costs"

The average tuition at American colleges and universities rose every year throughout the decade of the 1980s, at a rate much higher than the general rate of inflation in the economy.[43] Private colleges have led the way, charging not only the highest tuitions but also taking a growing percentage of family income. In academic year 1976–77, the average tuition at private four-year colleges was less than 17 percent of median family income but, by academic year 1987–88, their tuition was more than 22 percent of median family income.[44] By academic year 1990–91, there were 255 private colleges where tuition alone was $10,000 per year or more.[45] By no means were these all distinguished institutions.

Mitigating the full impact of these charges were (1) the widespread availability of financial aid, (2) the fact that most private colleges charged less than $8,000,[46] and (3) the fact that most students attended public institutions.[47] Nevertheless, the sums which had to be paid represented serious sacrifices for many families, especially since travel costs, clothing, increasingly expensive textbooks, and other incidental expenses had to be paid for, in addition to charges for tuition, room, and board. The financial drain of all this requires some families to save up for college beforehand or to incur large debts to be repaid long after their son or daughter has graduated. Dartmouth, for example, is not unique in listing in its admissions and financial aid bulletin the availability of home equity loans which permit parents "to tap up to 80% of the equity in their homes as an educational resource."[48]

College and university officials have often responded to complaints about rapidly rising tuition with claims that rising costs have made these increases necessary. Like so much that is said by educational institutions, this claim sounds plausible at first, especially when backed up by statistics, but ultimately it cannot stand up under scrutiny. Even if not a single price except tuition had changed anywhere in the entire economy, "costs" would still have risen, as "costs" are defined in academic discussions.

Whatever colleges and universities choose to spend their money on is called a "cost." If they hire more administrators, or build more buildings to house them, or send the college president on more junkets, these are all additional costs. If they hire more research assistants for the faculty or more secretaries for the administrators, these are all costs. Doing more research, raising salaries, inviting more high-priced speakers to campus and many other things also increase costs. What colleges and universities seek to insinuate—misleadingly—by saying that costs have gone up is that the cost of doing what they have always done is rising, necessitating an increase in tuition. But colleges and universities have been greatly expanding what

they do—and, as long as they spend the rising tuition on something, that something will be called a cost. It is a completely
circular argument.

Expanding bureaucracies have been one reason for rising
costs—or, to put it more directly, it is one of the things on
which colleges spend their increased revenues. From 1975 to
1985, for example, while student enrollment nationally rose by
less than 10 percent, college professional support staffs increased by more than 60 percent. (By professional support staff
is meant people whose jobs require degrees but who do not
teach students.)[49] At Stanford University, for example, the president, vice presidents, and their staffs all added up to 47 people
in 1977, but this increased to 83 people by 1988.[50] Colleges and
universities have also created new campuses and student centers overseas. Stanford opened overseas student centers in Italy
and France in 1960, in Spain in 1968, Germany in 1975, England in 1984, Poland in 1986, Japan in 1989, and Chile in
1990.[51] Nor are overseas campuses or student centers limited
to a handful of elite institutions. Innumerable colleges have
them, either singly or collectively in consortium arrangements.[52] The University of Evansville, for example, has its own
55-acre campus in England and the University of Dallas has
its own campus in Rome.

At the University of South Carolina, the president has spent
as much as $879 a night for his hotel rooms while travelling
and $7,000 in one year for chauffeur services. The university
has also paid $350,000 in travel and salary to the widow of
Egyptian President Anwar Sadat, for teaching one class a week
for three semesters.[53] All of these are "costs." A federal investigation of "costs" which Stanford University charged against
government research grants turned up $3,000 for a cedar-lined
chest and $2,000 a month for flower arrangements, both at the
home of Stanford President Donald Kennedy, as well as more
than $180,000 charged as depreciation on a yacht privately
donated to the university's athletic department.[54] The taxpayers were also charged for part of the cost of a $17,500 wedding
reception when Mr. Kennedy remarried in 1987.[55]

While these odd examples are not intended to be typical,
they do demonstrate the enormous elasticity of the concept of
"cost," as used in the academic world—and hence its mean-
inglessness as a justification for tuition increases. A much more

common cost item are professors' salaries, which rose faster than the rate of inflation, every year during the decade of the 1980s.[56] Added to this is the normal tendency toward expansionism in organizations not checked by the competition of the marketplace and the grim realities of a bottom line. At Vassar College, for example, the vice president for finance said: "Vassar's departments are consulted for projected costs for the following year. Usually included are proposals for new materials and projects." The college administration then "tries to allow as much departmental expansion as possible"—and this in turn drives up tuition.[57]

As a comprehensive economic study of American colleges and universities concluded, "the cost of any institution is largely determined by the amount of revenue it can raise."[58] This was said, not by a critic, but by a man described as "the supreme defender of higher education."[59] In other words, it is the amount of money that colleges and universities can get— from tuition, endowment income, donations, etc.—which determines how much their spending or costs will go up, *not* the other way around, as they represent it to the public. To say that costs are going up is no more than to say that the additional intake is being spent, rather than hoarded.

When a college expands its range of expensive activities first, and then calls it "increased costs" later, when seeking more money from various sources, this tends not only to confuse the issue but also to erode the very concept of living within one's means. The financial problems of well-endowed Bowdoin College illustrate the process and the attitudes. Its own professors and administrators have blamed its ballooning deficits on a decade of expanding programs, jobs, and buildings. As the dean of the college put it: "People would come forward with plans that were good ideas—and because it was a period in which we could afford to grow, we just said Yes without being very deliberate about it." According to *The Chronicle of Higher Education*:

> Many faculty members did not even know of Bowdoin's financial problems until last year, when they read about them in a newspaper, *The Maine Times*. Several administrators say they also were unaware of the magnitude of the problem until last year.[60]

This situation was not unique to Bowdoin, or even to rich private colleges in general. A consultant looking into the finances of Oregon State University reached very similar conclusions: "It's amazing how much in a university, processes are added on and added on, and no one takes a critical look at it."[61]

In short, when parents are being asked to borrow against the equity in their homes to pay rising tuition, it is not simply to cover the increased cost of educating their children, but also to help underwrite the many new boondoggles thought up by faculty and administrators, operating with little sense of financial constraints. As an official of the U.S. Department of Education put it, many colleges "choose to increase tuition because they can get away with it." While colleges claim that the increased spending is to improve education, this official saw it as going into "the swelling of the ranks of vice presidents and deans" and to other costly endeavors which make little or no contribution to quality education, which is "not a function of money."[62] The availability of federal grants and loans to help students meet rising tuition costs virtually ensures that those costs will rise. A college which kept tuition affordable could forfeit millions of dollars annually in federal money available to cover costs *over and above* what students can afford, according to a financial aid formula.

Arguments have often been made that students are getting a good deal from college, because tuition does not cover the full costs of their education. Such statements are much more difficult to check than they might seem to be. First of all, education is not the only activity going on at research universities, and even at liberal arts colleges, research is increasingly expected of the professors. This research is paid for not only by faculty grants but also by reduced teaching loads—which is to say, by hiring far more professors than were required before to teach the same number of courses. These additional costs may be carried on the books as instructional costs, but they are in fact research costs. Almost anything can be treated as a cost of educating students—on paper. At the University of Texas, for example, more than $11 million of student fee payments were applied to paying for construction of a microelectronics research facility, located more than 6 miles away from the campus.[63]

The research imperative has spread across all kinds of institutions and down the academic pecking order. Virtually everywhere, the education of undergraduates is a joint product, along with research and other activities. As any economist knows, there is no such thing as the average cost of producing a joint product—that is, there is no such thing as the average cost of producing pig skin, because it is produced jointly with bacon, ham, and pork chops. There is an average cost of producing a pig, but not its components, which cannot be produced separately.

Even if it were possible to separate out the cost of undergraduate education, there is no reason why tuition should cover it, since alumni and other donors contribute money for the express purpose of subsidizing education. Endowment funds often were contributed for the same purpose. When college and university administrators expand their empires by raising tuition, this is not necessarily due to the rising cost of education. Nor are the "extras" necessarily an enhancement of education, nor something reflecting student demand through the marketplace. In the public institutions, where most students go, it is largely a matter of administrators' convincing legislators to contribute the taxpayers' money.

It may seem odd that college admissions directors are under heavy pressure to enroll more students, if the colleges are losing money on each student enrolled, as academic administrators so often claim. When Dartmouth vice-president Robert Field announced that the college was accepting more transfer students, in order to bring in more revenue, the *Dartmouth Review* asked editorially: "How can Field make money on new students when every time he raises tuition, he claims tuition pays for only half the cost of each student?"[64] This probing question goes to the heart of the economic issue, and its answer depends upon *incremental* costs. Once a college is built and its dormitories and classroom buildings are in place, the additional or incremental costs of adding more students is relatively low, so long as their numbers do not exceed the existing capacity. Within those limits, adding more students may well bring in far more additional revenue than any additional costs they represent.

The claim by college administrators that tuition does not cover the average cost of a college education is both meaningless and misleading. It is meaningless because there is no such thing as the average cost of a joint product, and it is misleading because there is no more reason why tuitions should cover all the costs of a college than there is for magazine subscriptions to cover all the costs of producing a magazine. Advertisers often pay most of the costs of producing a magazine or newspaper, each of which comprises joint products—journalistic writings and advertisements, just as academic institutions produce both teaching and research. No one believes that magazines are doing a favor to their subscribers by offering subscriptions at prices which do not cover the average cost of producing the magazine. Nor do magazines make any such sanctimonious claims.

It is commonplace in the ordinary business transactions of the marketplace for joint products to be sold simultaneously to different groups, no one of whom pays enough to cover the total costs of the business. A professional baseball team not only sells tickets to those who enter its stadium; it also sells television and radio rights to broadcasters who cover the game, and rents out the stadium to others who use it for rock concerts, boxing matches, and other events while the team is on the road or during the off-season. If ticket prices for baseball games rose to exorbitant levels, it would be no answer to the fans to say that they were still not being charged enough to cover the total costs of the baseball club. Yet colleges and universities use this as an argument against students and their parents who complain about exorbitant tuition.

In the ordinary transactions of the marketplace, competition from rival producers limits how much a given business can charge its customers. In the academic world, however, *organized collusion* among some of the most expensive colleges has stripped the students and their parents of this consumer protection. Each spring, for 35 years, the Ivy League colleges, M.I.T., Amherst, Northwestern, and a dozen other colleges and universities have met to decide how much money they would charge, as a net price, to *each individual student*, out of more than 10,000 students who have applied to more than one institution in this cartel. The lists of students have been compiled before the annual meetings and officials from the various colleges have decided how much money could be extracted from each individual, given parental income, bank account balance, home equity, and other financial factors. Where their estimates differed, these differences were reconciled in the meetings and the student then received so-called "financial aid" offers so coordinated that the net cost of going to one college in the cartel would be the same as the net cost of going to another.[65]

The U.S. Department of Justice began investigating these and other colleges in 1989. With a legal threat of anti-trust prosecution by the government, and a class action suit on behalf of students, hanging over this group of colleges, pending the outcome of the investigation, Yale and Barnard dropped out of the meetings in 1990, and in 1991 the meetings were canceled.[66]

A cartel or a monopoly maximizes its profits by charging not only a high price but also, if possible, a *different* price to different groups of customers, according to what the market will bear in each separate case. Seldom can most business cartels or monopolies carry this to the ultimate extreme of charging each individual customer what the traffic will bear, as the academic cartel did. But academic institutions are armed with more detailed financial information from financial aid forms than most credit agencies require, and for decades have been comparing notes when setting their prices, in a way that would long ago have caused a business to be prosecuted for violation of the anti-trust laws. In other respects, however, the colleges and universities use the same methods as business cartels or monopolies. Like monopolistic price discriminators in the commercial world, private colleges and universities set an unrealistically high list price and then offer varying discounts. In academia, this list price is called tuition and the discount is called "financial aid."

The widespread availability of financial aid—often received by more than half the students at the more expensive colleges—changes the whole nature of tuition. Back when scholarships were awarded to a needy fraction of the students, this was clearly a matter of philanthropy and reward for academic ability. Today, varying amounts of financial aid are awarded up and down the income scale, and very little of it has anything to do with the quality of the student's academic record or with philanthropy to the poor. Approximately two-thirds of the undergraduates at Harvard and four-fifths of those at Rice receive financial aid.[67] The average family income of financial aid recipients at Harvard in academic year 1990–91 was $45,000. These financial aid recipients included more than 400 whose family incomes were above $70,000, of whom 64 came from families with incomes exceeding $100,000.[68]

Harvard is not unique in this respect. At Marquette University, for example, out of 119 students in the class of 1989–90 who came from families with incomes of $60,000 to $70,000 and who applied for financial aid, 71 were declared eligible for it, as were 74 out of 192 students from families with incomes above $70,000.[69] Similar figures are common at other private colleges and universities. The President of M.I.T. noted that financial aid applicants at that institution "are distributed almost uniformly across the spectrum of family incomes."[70] The percentage of applicants who receive aid typically varies by income level and so does the amount of the aid received, so that the net price actually charged is adjusted to the most that can be extracted from each applicant's family.

Ordinarily, price discrimination does not work in a competitive marketplace, because those charged extortionate prices will be bid away by competitors, until the price is competed down to a level commensurate with the cost of producing whatever commodity or service is being sold. But this does not happen among high-priced colleges which engage in organized collusion. The picture is complicated somewhat by the fact that the term "financial aid" encompasses both paper discounts from tuitions listed in college catalogues and actual transfers of money—the great bulk of this money being government-provided or government-subsidized. Philanthropic aid also continues, enabling a needy fraction of students to cover their cost of living, as well as tuition. Fundamentally, however, college-provided "financial aid" is a method of producing a sliding scale of tuition charges, like ordinary price discrimination elsewhere—and like successful price discrimination elsewhere, it is a by-product of collusion. For example, when one student found that his financial aid package offered by Brown University and by Yale were inadequate to enable him to attend either institution, his efforts to get an increase were complicated by the fact that "each could alter a package only after consulting with the other."[71]

This collusion process has been made easier by the remarkable similarity of tuitions among those in the cartel—

despite differences in urban or rural location, endowment income per student, local cost of living variations, the size of the student body over which the institutional overhead was spread, and other such economic considerations which normally lead to price differences. A Carnegie Foundation study found "widely different costs per student" among institutions.[72] Yet in 1989–90, for example, the variation in tuition among the eight Ivy League colleges was less than 5 percent from the most expensive (Brown) to the least expensive (Cornell),[73] even though Ivy League colleges are scattered from Manhattan to rural New Hampshire.

Officials of some colleges and universities admit not only to sharing information on financial aid offers to specific students but also to sharing information on pending tuition increases and faculty salaries.[74] This has all the appearance of a multidimensional "price-fixing system that OPEC might envy," as the *Wall Street Journal* characterized it[75]—and a clear violation of American anti-trust laws when businessmen do such things.

THE ADMISSIONS PROCESS

As college and university admissions have become a major operation, especially in large and selective institutions, they have often become the province of administrators more so than faculty members. Moreover, even at elite colleges, the personnel attracted to college admissions are seldom themselves part of the intellectual elite. Yet their job is to select students unlike themselves, to be taught by professors unlike themselves, for careers unlike theirs. It can hardly be surprising that admissions personnel are drawn toward non-intellectual criteria and toward ideas not unlike the notion of judging "the whole person," as found among educators at the pre-college level. Over the years, all sorts of criteria from popular psychology and sociological speculation have assumed increasing weight vis-a-vis such standard intellectual criteria as academic records and test scores.

The net result has been that the highest test scores and even a perfect 4.0 grade point average in high school are no guarantee of admission to colleges where other students are accepted with uninspiring high school grades and SAT scores hundreds of points below the school average. At Amherst College, for example, among those applicants from the class of 1991 who scored between 750 and 800 on the verbal SAT, less than half were admitted—while 26 other students who scored below 400 on the same test were admitted.[76] A very similar pattern is found at Stanford University, which rejected a majority of those applicants who scored between 700 and 800 on the verbal SAT, while admitting more than a hundred other students who scored below 500 on the same test.[77] Duke University likewise rejected 35 applicants who scored 750 and above on the verbal SAT while accepting 293 students who scored more than 200 points lower.[78] Among the non-academic criteria which help explain such anomalies are personal qualities (real or imagined by the admissions committee), geographical distribution, alumni preferences, and ethnic "diversity" or racial quotas, however one chooses to phrase it.

The general mindset behind the weight given to non-academic criteria was expressed by the dean of admissions at Harvard:

> ... the question we ask is: how well has this person used the opportunities available to him or her? A young man from the Canadian prairies will have different opportunities and challenges from those faced by the young woman from a selective suburban high school. The committee's task is to understand—in the context of the candidate's interests and talents—how well he or she has risen to challenges and taken advantage of opportunities.[79]

In other words, the admissions committee takes on not only the task of judging "the whole person," but also of judging the whole person's whole context—a task which some would have left to God on Judgement Day. Nothing daunted, the admissions director declared, "we are trying to assess character and other personal qualities such as energy, self-discipline, and generosity." To this end, they require the student to write "a comprehensive self-portrait" and to have "a personal interview with one of our alumni/ae and/or a member of our staff."[80] Columbia University's distinguished dean Jacques Barzun long ago saw through this kind of "passion for fuzzy psychologizing" and declared: "No human being at any age should be asked to display worthy motives on command." In such a competition "the advantage goes to the precocious worldling who has found out 'the ropes,' or the instinctive hypocrite."[81] If this judgment seems harsh, consider the recent case of a criminal fugitive who gained admission to Princeton under an assumed name by claiming to be "a self-educated ranch hand whose mother was dying of leukemia in Switzerland." He, in fact, graduated from Palo Alto High School, across the street from Stanford University.[82] He knew the ropes.

Putting aside the very large question whether any admissions committee could possibly accomplish the task of assessing how well individuals have utilized their varying opportunities, the question remains: What purpose would that serve anyway? It might well be more of a personal achievement for a boy from an utterly blighted family, growing up in desperate social conditions, to have taught himself the rudiments of reading and writing than for a privileged lad from an expensive boarding school to have mastered Einstein's theory of relativity. But is college admissions a reward for past moral merit or an assessment of future intellectual accomplishment? It is by no means clear that most admissions committees have chosen the latter—or have even distinguished the two in their own minds.

Emphasis on non-academic criteria has in some colleges and universities led to friction between the faculty and the admissions offices that determine which of the applicants become their students. At the Massachusetts Institute of Technology, for example, faculty complaints that the students they were receiving were not as sharp as in earlier years were confirmed by data which showed that the admissions office was admitting a smaller percentage of the top-scoring students than they once did. Back in 1968, nearly two-thirds of all applicants who scored between 750 and 800 on the quantitative SAT were offered admission to M.I.T. By 1987, less than two-fifths of such students were being offered admission.

It was not that there was a decline in the number of applicants to M.I.T. with such high performances. On the contrary, there were even more students scoring in these lofty ranges who applied to M.I.T. than before. The admissions office just did not admit as many of them.[83] Although the M.I.T. admissions director raised questions about the validity of SAT

scores, the faculty complaints originated from their own observations of "a progressive decline in the quality of the performance of students, as compared with classes of earlier
years."[84] In other words, the test scores and the faculty observations both told the same story, even if the admissions director
did not want to believe it.

At Harvard, the faculty has likewise been at odds with the
admissions committee.[85] Despite the committee's enthusiasm
for non-intellectual criteria, based on psychological and sociological speculation, there has been no empirical evidence
asked or given to substantiate the predictive validity of those
beliefs.[86] One study of the admissions committee itself characterized its members as people who had *not* been "brilliant
students" themselves, nor "truly original and independent and
imaginative minds,"[87] but they shared a belief that they could
"identify the nuances in individual character and ability,"
while seeking students with "academic competence rather than
academic superiority."[88] As Harvard's dean of admissions put
it:

> We want to serve the best students from all backgrounds and
> we're trying to choose people who will be leaders later
> on. . . . If we're driven exclusively by academic qualities, we
> would have a much less rich and interesting student body
> than we currently have.[89]

What will look "rich and interesting" to superficial people
can of course differ greatly from what scholars who are masters
of their respective intellectual disciplines will find to be students able to plumb the depths of what they have to offer. Dull-
looking nerds can revolutionize the intellectual landscape and
produce marvels of science, even if their life stories would never
make a good movie or television mini-series.

Nothing in the literature generated by admissions committees at other colleges and universities suggests that they are
fundamentally different from Harvard's admissions committee. This literature abounds in statements about seeking students with "leadership" potential, "commitment," or other
elusive non-academic qualities, which will supposedly make
them valuable assets to the larger society in later years. Typically, not a speck of evidence accompanies such sweeping assertions. It is a field with "an abundance of hunches and

impassioned beliefs," as one study concluded.[90] Empirically, however, none of the assertions tested had any predictive power when it came to measuring the later-life impact of individuals.[91] As David Riesman has noted, in a study of American higher education for the Carnegie Foundation, deans and admissions officials "are rarely familiar with institutional research" and rely instead on selected anecdotes about the success of some "high-risk" student, while ignoring "the students who quietly drop out or who stick it out in bitterness and humiliation."[92]

Historically, elusive concepts like "leadership," "character," and the like were among the ways used to reduce the proportions of Jewish students admitted to Harvard and other selective institutions. Today, similar concepts are used to increase or decrease the enrollment of whatever groups the admissions committee wants increased or decreased, whether for the committee's own reasons or in response to various outside pressures. An outgoing dean of admissions at Stanford quipped, "If we only admitted students based on SAT scores, I wouldn't have a job."[93] There was more truth than humor in this remark. Sweeping presumptions about what admissions committees are capable of judging not only justify a costly administrative empire, with far-flung operations extending across the country and overseas, but also feed the egos of those who imagine themselves to be performing a difficult and vital task.

Self-delusions may be no more peculiar to academic bureaucrats than to business executives. However, the delusions of the latter receive swift and brutal correction from the marketplace, whether in the form of red ink or takeover bids. It is the insulation of academia from such forces which allows individual or collective delusions to persist, and fashions to flourish virtually unchecked.

Admissions Tests

Although the frantic pressure of students trying to gain admittance to a relative handful of prestigious colleges and universities is a phenomenon less than half a century old, there were standards of admission, even back in the days when virtually all applicants met those standards and virtually all were admitted. Dartmouth has been credited with setting forth the first explicitly articulated set of admissions standards in the early 1920s,[94] but even before then some colleges had their own entrance examinations or required certain grades in high schools, and in some other colleges the registrar simply decided unilaterally whom to let in. Harvard and Yale, for example, gave their own tests back in the nineteenth century.[95] Nationally, the picture was one of chaotically varying standards and some leading institutions were clearly insular and inbred. Harvard's students once came predominantly from elite preparatory schools and, up to the end of World War II, one-fourth of entering freshmen were the sons of Harvard parents.[96]

One of the major factors in breaking the near-monopoly of private preparatory schools in supplying students to the elite colleges was the development of a nationwide, standardized, college entrance test. The Scholastic Aptitude Test (SAT) is the best known and most widely used of these tests. It is taken by more than two and a half million high school students annually. The American College Testing program examination (ACT) is taken by several hundred thousand students annually. These standardized tests made it possible to compare students from coast to coast, from the most diverse schools, with radically different standards. They enabled elite colleges, especially, to select more socially diverse students, who were at the same time an elite of ability. As college attendance expanded substantially between the 1950s and the 1960s,[97] use of the Scholastic Aptitude Test increased approximately ten-fold—from more than 80,000 test-takers in 1951 to more than 800,000 in 1961.[98]

Since the 1960s, much controversy has developed around standardized admissions tests, with the SAT being the prime target, as befits the leading test. Various critics have claimed that such tests are not good predictors of academic success or life success, in general or especially not for disadvantaged minorities; that they have cultural bias, or that they test quick, superficial thinking rather than penetrating analytical reasoning. Although there has been a vast outpouring of writings on both sides of these controversies, there is no reason why some of these issues must be settled by debate. It should be axiomatic that the SAT, like everything human, is imperfect, so that the relevant practical question is how it compares to alternative tests (ACT, IQ, etc.) and to other criteria, such as high school grades and teacher recommendations.

These are empirical questions and there is no reason why there must be one answer for all institutions and all kinds of students. A substantial number of colleges and universities prefer the ACT to the SAT, some in the past have used I.Q. scores, and a few places like Bates College require no test scores at all. In addition, each admissions office gives these scores whatever weight it chooses, based on its own experience and judgment. There is no reason why "experts" must settle this question, once and for all, though they are of course free to produce a better test, if they can, and to enter it into the competition.

This does not mean that facts are irrelevant. Some of the most strident criticisms of standardized tests are demonstrably false. For example, it has been claimed—and repeated like a drumbeat—that standardized tests under-estimate the "real" ability of racial and ethnic minorities, and therefore predict a lower future performance in college than these groups will in fact have. Whatever the initial plausibility of this claim, there is no reason why there should have been more than 20 years of controversy over it (still continuing), because that means that more than 20 years of factual results have accumulated, and can be used to test the competing theories.

These facts have demonstrated repeatedly that the SAT (and numerous other tests) did *not* predict a lower academic performance (or other performance) for blacks, for example, than in fact later occurred.[99] SAT scores have in fact proved empirically to be *better* predictors than high school grades for blacks, though the reverse has been true for whites and Asians.[100] Insofar as there is any difference, on average, between the level of blacks' academic performance predicted by the SAT scores and their actually observed performance, the latter has been slightly lower. In short, every aspect of the argument that "cultural bias" makes test scores invalid as predictors of minority student performance turns out to be false empirically.

It would be impossible to understand the persistence and vehemence of these arguments against test scores without understanding the political purpose they serve. Arguments that test scores under-estimate the subsequent academic performance of minority students (1) serve to justify preferential admissions of minority students and (2) permit denial that these are in fact preferential policies, by enabling the claim to be made that different admissions standards merely adjust for the "unfairness" of the tests. In reality, the tests are not unfair. Life is unfair and the tests measure the results. Ignoring those results merely sets the stage for more and bigger problems, as will be seen in Chapter 6.

Many people are uncomfortable with any conclusion that tests, on average, reveal differences in the current academic capabilities of different racial or ethnic groups, because this conclusion seems too close to the theory that some groups are innately and genetically inferior to others. But these are, in reality, very different arguments—and the truth of one is perfectly consistent with the falseness of the other.[101] Even on so-called "intelligence" tests (as distinguished from "aptitude" or skills tests such as the SAT), whole nations have, over a period of decades, significantly increased the number of questions they can answer correctly, though this worldwide phenomenon has been inadvertently concealed by re-norming of I.Q. tests to produce the definitional average I.Q. of 100. In other words, the same number of correct answers which would have given an individual an I.Q. of 110 fifty years ago might give that individual's son or daughter an I.Q. of 90 today, because the average person today answers more questions correctly—and whatever the average number of correct answers might be at a given time is, by definition, equal to an I.Q. of 100.

When whole nations do significantly better on I.Q. tests over time, this undermines the claim that such tests (or any tests) measure "real" or genetically innate ability. So too does a change in the relative standing of different groups, such as the Jews, who scored below average on intelligence tests given to American soldiers in the First World War,[102] but who have since scored above the national average.[103]

Test results within some other nations likewise suggest that test scores may provide valid predictions without necessarily measuring so-called "real" ability or innate potential. In the Philippines, for example, people growing up in Manila tend to score higher on standardized tests than do people in the hinterlands. This may well be because of differences in social circumstances rather than differences in innate or "real" ability.

Yet low-scoring individuals from the hinterlands performed no better at the university than did equally low-scoring individuals from Manila.[104] Similarly, in Indonesia, people on the island of Java have averaged higher test scores than people from the outer islands. Yet outer islanders with a given score did not perform any better at the university than did people with the same score from Java.[105]

Whether in the United States or in other countries, *developed capabilities* differ significantly among people, depending upon the circumstances in which they have grown up and the cultural values which have influenced their own efforts to acquire education—or to direct their energies in other directions. The relationship between their innate potential and their developed academic skills may be quite loose—and yet differences in levels of academic skill cannot be sweepingly dismissed as "irrelevant" or as showing arbitrary "cultural bias" in tests. There is no point chasing the will o' the wisp of a "culture-free" test or any other culture-free criteria. Whatever anyone accomplishes anywhere in this world will always be accomplished within a given culture. No race, no country, and no period of human history has ever been culture-free.

Preferential Admissions

Colleges' preferential admission of different categories of people is not a new phenomenon. Athletes for the schools' sports teams have long had preferential admission, not only in powerhouse Big Ten schools but also in the Ivy League. Private institutions, attempting to develop loyalty among alumni families who will donate money, have likewise long given preferential admission to the sons and daughters of people who graduated from the particular college. Not all alumni children get admitted, but it is not uncommon for them to be put in a special category by admissions committees at many private colleges, including Harvard. The more difficult the school is to get into, the more valuable is this privilege—and presumably, the more generous the alumni are expected to be when donations are sought. State universities, as a matter of course, give preferences to students applying from within the state as compared to out-of-state applicants, not only in admissions but also in the tuition charged.

Since the 1960s, another category of preferentially admitted students has been added—racial and ethnic minorities. In the controversies which have arisen around the issue of preferential admissions by race or ethnicity, those on both sides of the issue have often argued as if the circumstances—and especially the academic failures—of minority students were unique social phenomena with unique causes. In reality, there is nothing uncommon about a high failure rate among people preferentially admitted to college. This pattern has long been common among college athletes, whether they were white or black. Even a highly privileged group like alumni sons at Harvard, during the era when more than half of those sons who applied were admitted, were disproportionately represented among students who flunked out.[106] Similarly, when students at the University of the Philippines could be admitted at the discretion of the university president, by-passing the usual academic competition, those preferentially admitted tended to be from the more privileged classes—and tended also to perform less well at the university.[107]

In short, preferential admissions tend to lead to substandard academic performance, whether those admitted are privileged or underprivileged. What has been unique about students preferentially admitted by race has been the large numbers involved, the magnitude of the preferences, the magnitude of the hypocrisy, and the magnitude of the academic and social disasters which have followed.

CHAPTER 6

"New Racism" and Old Dogmatism

INCREASING HOSTILITY toward blacks and other racial minorities on college campuses has become so widespread that the term "the new racism" has been coined to describe it. For example, a dean at Middlebury College in Vermont reported that—for the first time in 19 years—she was now being asked by white students not to assign them black room mates.[1] There have been reports of similar trends in attitudes elsewhere. A professor at the University of California at Berkeley observed: "I've been teaching at U.C. Berkeley now for 18 years and it's only within the last three or four years that I've seen racist graffiti for the first time."[2] Another Berkeley professor, recalling support for the civil rights movement on the campuses of the 1960s and 1970s, commented: "Twenty years later, what have we got? Hate mail and racist talk."[3]

Much uglier incidents, including outright violence, have erupted on many campuses where such behavior was unheard of, just a decade or two earlier. At the University of Massachusetts, for example, white students beat up a black student in 1986 and a large mob of whites chased about 20 blacks.[4]. A well-known college guide quotes a Tufts University student as

132

saying, "many of my friends wouldn't care if they never saw a black person again in their lives."[5]

Racism, as such, is not new. What is new are the frequency, the places, and the class of people involved in an unprecedented escalation of overt racial hostility among middle-class young people, on predominantly liberal or radical campuses. Painful and ugly as these episodes are, they should not be surprising. A number of people predicted such things many years ago, when colleges' current racial policies began to take shape. They also predicted some of the other bad consequences of those policies. These predictions and warnings were ignored, dismissed, or ridiculed by those who believed the prevailing dogmas on which academic racial policies were based. Now that these predictions are coming true, the dogmatists insist that the only solution is a more intensive application of their dogmas.

PREDICTIONS VERSUS DOGMAS

When the idea of special, preferential admissions for racial and ethnic minorities became an issue during the 1960s, two fundamentally different ways of evaluating such proposals emerged. One approach was to discuss the *goals* of preferential admissions, such as the benefits assumed to be received by minority students, by the groups from which they came, by the institutions they would attend, and by American society as a whole. This became the prevailing approach, which dominated both intellectual discourse and academic policy-making.

Another approach was to ask: What *incentives* and *circumstances* were being created—for the minority students, for their fellow students, for college administrators, and for others— and what were the likely consequences of such incentives and circumstances? When the issue was approached in this way, many negative potentials of preferential policies became apparent. However, relatively few people risked moral condemnation by asking such questions in public, so that there was little need for those with a goals-oriented approach to answer them. Now history has answered those questions, and these answers have provided both abundant and painful confirmation of the original misgivings, based on examining the incentives and constraints of academic racial policies.

The issue is not one of a simple, direct reaction to preferential admissions policy, though that by itself generates considerable resentment. The many academic and emotional ramifications of such policies set in motion complex reactions which pit minority and non-minority students against each other, and generate stresses and reactions among the faculty, administrators, and outside interests. Though many colleges and universities have been caught by surprise and have been unable to cope with the unexpected problems—or have responded in ways which have created new and worse problems—much of what has happened has followed a scenario set forth by critics more than two decades ago, and much of the intervening time has seen a steady building of tensions toward the ugly episodes of recent years, which have now been christened, "the new racism."

What was at issue, then and now, is not whether there should be larger or smaller numbers of minority students attending college, but whether preferential admissions policies should be the *mechanism* for making a college education available to more minority students. There are other ways of increasing the number of minority students—not only in theory, but as a matter of historical fact. Between 1940 and 1947, for example, there was a 64 percent increase in the number of non-white students attending post-secondary institutions[6]—due to financial aid under the G.I. Bill for veterans returning from World War II. This made a college education available to the black masses for the first time.[7] During a corresponding period of the 1960s—from 1960 to 1967—there was a 49 percent increase in the number of black students attending college, but this later increase was often accompanied by preferential admissions policies, while the earlier and larger percentage increase had been accomplished simply through more financial support.

The point here is that a substantial increase in minority student enrollment in higher education can be achieved with or without preferential admissions policies. Money is the crucial factor, given the lower incomes of blacks and some other minority groups. The case for preferential admissions policies must therefore stand or fall on its own merits, though the proponents of such policies often argue as if preferential admissions were the only possible way to increase substantially the numbers of minority students in college.[8] Unfortunately, proponents of preferential admissions policies have not only ignored history; they have ignored much of what has happened in the wake of these policies.

Although the taint of "insensitivity" or the outright charge of "racism" has often been applied to critics of preferential policies, many of these critics were in fact advocates of equal rights for blacks, long before that became a popular position in the 1960s. John H. Bunzel, for example, advocated equal rights for blacks back in the 1940s and Morris Abram, an attorney, took on the dangerous task of defending blacks in Georgia during the same era.[9] The late Bayard Rustin, organizer of the famous "march on Washington" in 1963, was a militant black civil rights activist and pacifist who went to jail for his views during World War II. They and others like them later became critics of preferential policies, when these policies emerged during the 1960s.

Shifting Students

One of the earliest attempts to analyze preferential admissions policies in terms of their effects, rather than their goals, was undertaken by Professor Clyde Summers of the Yale Law School who, like some other early critics, was someone with a track record of concern for minorities, going back years before that was popular. Back in 1946, Summers wrote a landmark article on racial discrimination in labor unions.[10] In a 1969 conference on preferential admissions to law school, he saw the key problem in such policies as being a pervasive *mismatching* of students and institutions, due to a systematic shifting of minority students from institutions where they could succeed to institutions where they were likely to fail. In short, the issue he raised involved the institutional *distribution* of minority students, not their aggregate numbers. Summers in fact characterized the shortage of minority lawyers as "disgraceful" and urged policies designed to "increase the number of minority group law students"[11]—but not through preferential policies, which he characterized as "an unreal solution to a real problem."[12]

While troubled by the fact that "what one writes may be seized upon and used by those who seek excuses for doing nothing and thus preserving the present pattern of deprivation,"[13] Summers nevertheless went to the heart of the problem of the preferential admissions approach—the systematic mismatching of minority students with institutions, thereby artificially fostering failure among students with the qualifications to succeed. Given that law schools, like the rest of the academic world, have a whole hierarchy of work standards, and a corresponding hierarchy of admissions standards, the issue was not whether a minority student was "qualified" to study law and become a lawyer, but whether his particular qualifications were likely to match or mismatch the institutional pace, level, and intensity of study under preferential admissions policies. While this issue was raised as regards law schools, the principle applies to the whole academic world.

Although institutions at the top of the hierarchy could dramatically increase their own minority student enrollments through preferential admissions policies, Summers warned them not to deceive themselves that they were creating any corresponding increase in the total number of minority students in law schools:

> If Harvard or Yale, for example, admit minority students with test scores 100 to 150 points below that normally required for a non-minority student to get admitted, the total number of minority students able to obtain a legal education is not increased thereby. The minority student given such preference would meet the normal admissions standards at Illinois, Rutgers, or Texas.[14]

Correspondingly, when institutions in the second tier of the academic hierarchy lower their standards for minority students, they attract applicants who would otherwise go to institutions in the third or fourth tier. Summers continued:

> Thus, each law school, by its preferential admission, simply takes minority students away from other schools whose admission standards are further down the scale. Any net gain in the total number of minority students admitted must come, if it

comes at all, because those schools whose admission standards are at the bottom of the scale take students whom they would not otherwise take. . . . In sum, the policy of preferential admission has a pervasive shifting effect, causing large numbers of minority students to attend law schools whose normal admission standards they do not meet, instead of attending other law schools whose normal standards they do meet.[15]

Academic and Social Problems

Summers' crucial objection was to the needless academic and social problems created by this "pervasive shifting effect." The "special social and psychological problems" of a preferentially admitted student "are multiplied if the student is not prepared to compete on even terms" with his classmates who enter with higher qualifications. An "intense anxiety and threat to the student's self-esteem" are among the costs incurred "whenever a student is admitted to a school whose normal standards he does not meet, even though he does meet the normal standards of other schools."[16]

This student does not get a better education because he is at a more prestigious school. On the contrary, he may well get a much worse education at such fast-paced institutions, in the sense of failing to learn things which he is perfectly capable of learning, in a learning environment that proceeds at a normal pace. Such a minority student may end up "confused, floundering and unable to keep up."[17] As Summers explained:

> He is thrust into first year class with students with much greater verbal facility and much more developed skills in manipulating ideas. He is denied the time necessary for him to perfect the process of case analysis or to learn to work through legal problems, for the educational process is not geared to his needs but the needs of students who make up the large portion of the class and who are prepared for the faster pace. . . . The situation almost insures a sense of lostness and defeat.[18]

What are the further consequences of such a situation? According to Summers, offers of remedial help or reduced course loads are further blows to the student's self-esteem and expressions of the institution's lack of confidence in him—and may be rejected for these reasons. The student's escape routes include absenteeism and an attitude of dismissal toward the standard curriculum as "unnecessary and irrelevant" and a redirection of energies toward "community activities."[19]

The consequences in terms of the reactions of white classmates are likewise negative, for racial mismatching can cause whites to carry with them from law school into the legal profession what Summers called the "monstrous" notion that minority lawyers are substandard.[20] Summers' recommendation was that more *money* be made available to enable more minority students to go to law schools—but without the preferential admissions which mismatch them institutionally.[21]

While Clyde Summers presented one of the fullest elaborations of the case against preferential admissions policies for minorities, others saw similar dangers. At about the same time as the 1969 conference at which Summers made his remarks, Judge Macklin Fleming was writing to Dean Louis H. Pollak of the Yale Law School to express his apprehensions over the fact that only 5 out of 43 black students admitted to that institution met the normal admissions requirements.[22] Judge Fleming too was concerned about the bad effects he anticipated for both black and white students. Among whites, he said, double standards in admissions "will serve to perpetuate the very ideas and prejudices it is designed to combat."[23] That was because it leads to blatantly different performance levels, which cannot be talked away:

> If in a given class the great majority of the black students are at the bottom of the class, this factor is bound to instill, unconsciously at least, some sense of intellectual superiority among the white students and some sense of intellectual inferiority among the black students. Such a pairing in the same school of the brightest white students in the country with black students of mediocre academic qualifications is social experiment with loaded dice and a stacked deck.[24]

In these circumstances, the faculty "can talk around the clock" about the disadvantages of blacks, Fleming said, and it will not erase the personal experience created by this mismatching of students.[25]

Meanwhile, black students cannot be "expected to accept

an inferior status willingly." To salvage their self-respect, they "inevitably will seek other means to achieve recognition and self-expression."[26] Those means include "agitation to change the environment from one in which they are unable to compete to one in which they can." He spelled this out:

> Demands will be made for elimination of competition, reduction in standards of performance, adoption of courses of study which do not require intensive legal analysis, and recognition for academic credit for sociological activities which have only an indirect relationship to legal training. Second, it seems probable that this group will seek personal satisfaction and public recognition by aggressive conduct, which, although ostensibly directed at external injustices and problems, will in fact be primarily motivated by the psychological needs of the members of the group to overcome feelings of inferiority caused by lack of success in their studies.[27]

Unfortunately, Judge Fleming's prediction of more than 20 years ago turned out to be true not only for law schools, but also for the academic world in general. It is equally enlightening, however, to note the response to his argument by Dean Pollak, for this response was typical of a mindset which pervaded the academic world and which still does, well beyond the boundaries of law schools. Dean Pollak's response was not in terms of incentives, constraints, or cirumstances created by preferential admissions policies, but rather was in terms of goals based on assumptions.

The law school admissions committee, according to Dean Pollak, has eschewed "uncritical application of the normal indices of past academic performance" in selecting minority students with "high promise not reflected in formal academic terms." What this "high promise" was based on was not specified, nor were any criteria suggested by which this belief might be tested empirically. Instead, Dean Pollak claimed that the blacks selected were being trained for future "leadership." As alumni, such students have "speedily demonstrated professional accomplishments of a high order"[28]—though demonstrated to whom and by what criteria were likewise matters left unspecified and undefined. Moreover, the "present admissions policies" will be "under continuing review by the faculty,"[29] so that presumably such policies could be changed if any negative evidence materialized. He ignored the very possibility that preferential admissions policies might become politically irreversible—indeed, that students preferentially admitted could become a militant pressure group demanding ever-expanding quotas.

As for Judge Fleming's central arguments, they were never confronted.

Empirical Evidence

Some factual evidence may be in order when evaluating these different views. As of the time of this discussion, admission to the leading law schools usually required a B+ average in college and a Law School Aptitude Test (LSAT) score of 650 or more.[30] As late as 1976, the total number of black students with LSAT scores of 600 or more and a B+ average in college was 39—in the entire country.[31]

Despite Dean Pollak's disparagement of the predictive value of LSAT scores and assertions of "high promise" detectable in other ways,[32] the law school grades of the black student in the top ten law schools ranked at the 8th percentile—that is, 92 percent of the other law school students outperformed them.[33] When disproportionately large numbers of black law school graduates failed their bar examinations, that simply set off more cries of "cultural bias" in the tests.[34] In short, the prevailing dogmatism remained unmovable and impervious to any evidence.

As for the psychological pressures, a black law student captured that graphically:

> Traditionally, first-year law students are supposed to be afraid, or at least awed; but our fear was compounded by the uncommunicated realization that perhaps we were not authentic law students and the uneasy suspicion that our classmates knew that we were not. . . . The silence, the heavy sense of expectation, fell on all of the blacks in the classroom whenever one of us was called on for an answer. We waited, with the rest of the class, for the chosen man to justify the right of all of us to be there. . . . And when the answer came, however poor it was, there would be relief visible in the faces of the

white students and the instructor, and audible in the renewed breathing of the rest of the black students.[35]

Not all black students reacted like this young man—and not all white students reacted like those in his class. Many black students organized to make demands on campus authorities, some sought—and received—special favors from professors,[36] and many whites increasingly resented the double standards in academic performance and personal behavior.

Just as these patterns were not confined to law schools, so those who warned against the policies behind such patterns were not all white. Among the early warnings was one in an article appearing in the *New York Times Magazine* of December 13, 1970, by a black professor named Thomas Sowell:

> When the failures of many programs become too great to disguise, or to hide under euphemisms and apologetics, the conclusion that will be drawn in many quarters will not be that these were half-baked schemes, but that black people just don't have it.[37]

Such conclusions are now part of the "new racism" spreading across college campuses from coast to coast.

PATTERNS VERSUS DOGMAS

One of the remarkable characteristics of many discussions of the statistical "representation" of various minority group students or professors on elite college campuses is an *utter disregard* of the size of the pool of minority individuals who meet the normal standards of such institutions.

Typically, students attending elite colleges average 1200 or above on their composite SAT scores, or 600 each on the verbal and quantitative portions of the test. As of 1985, fewer than 4,000 black, American Indian, Mexican American, and Puerto Rican students in the entire country scored 600 or above on the quantitative SAT and fewer than 2,000 scored 600 or above on the verbal SAT. The specific racial and ethnic breakdown of minority students scoring 600 or above on the verbal or quantitative SAT was as follows:[38]

Group	600+ Verbal SAT	600+ Quantitative SAT
American Indians	163	320
Blacks	1,032	1,907
Mexican Americans	515	1,230
Puerto Ricans	<u>218</u>	<u>472</u>
	1,928	3,929

If all these 3,929 minority students with quantitative SATs of 600 and above went exclusively to the 58 colleges, universities, engineering schools, and military service academies with composite SATs of 1200 and above, that would still average out to fewer than 70 minority students per institution. Based on verbal SAT scores, the average would be fewer than 35 minority students per institution. Yet, among schools in this bracket, Harvard has not admitted less than a hundred black students alone in any given year since 1970.[39] Stanford has had more than a thousand black, Mexican American and American Indian students combined on campus at a given time[40]—or about 250 per class—this at an institution where 88 percent of the students admitted in 1990 had composite SAT scores above 1200 and nearly half had composite SATs of 1400 or above.[41] Many other elite institutions have likewise had several times as many minority students as the average number with the same median test scores as their other students. Clearly, these elite institutions are going well beyond the pool of minority students who match the qualifications of their other students.

Asian Americans represent a radically different situation. More Asian American students scored above 600, on either verbal or quantative SATs, than these other four racial or ethnic groups combined. As of 1985, 3,572 Asian Americans scored 600 or above on the verbal SAT and 11,903 scored above 600 on the quantitative SAT.[42] Although Asian Americans are a minority—as are Jews, Armenians, and many other groups—they are seldom, if ever, given preferential admission. The term "minority," as it is used in academic admissions policy, is neither statistical nor social. It usually refers to such groups as must be preferentially admitted if they are to approach the same share of the student body as they are in the general population.

Sometimes qualifications are simply not mentioned. At other times, they are dismissed as arbitrary, irrelevant, or biased barriers. But, as the case of the preferentially admitted law students indicates, qualifications make a difference in the end results. When the same pattern was found among the preferentially admitted sons of Harvard alumni, then the effect of lower admissions standards are clear, even if those admitted are predominantly affluent and white.

In those very rare cases where an institution releases its students' test scores by race, the double standards are blatant. At the University of Texas Law School, for example, the admissions office uses an index incorporating test scores and college grades. The median index among black students admitted was lower than the lowest index with which any white student was admitted. There were 81 whites turned down in 1990 with a higher index than all but one of the black students admitted. Only two white students were admitted with an index as low as the median index among Mexican Americans admitted.[43] At Georgetown University Law School, similar data were revealed by a student who had worked in the admissions office. In a sample of more than a hundred white students accepted, none had an LSAT score (new scale) less than 39, while the median LSAT scores for blacks admitted was 36.[44] The student who revealed this was, predictably, denounced as "racist" and his expulsion was demanded. Equally predictably, the dean of the law school said that "median LSAT scores for a group tell nothing about what individuals can and will achieve"[45]—this despite empirical studies to the contrary.

Having admitted minority students mismatched with the other students and with the institution's own academic standards, many colleges and universities have been surprised by results which were not only predictable but almost inevitable. While there have been variations from campus to campus, the general pattern of these results has included minority student academic problems, social problems, and militant political activism centering on demands for special admissions, special programs, and special hiring of minority faculty. Most of the more prominent colleges and universities have not only acceded to most of these demands but have also promoted double standards—both academic and social—for minority students.

Academic Double Standards

The mismatching problem was dramatically demonstrated at the Massachusetts Institute of Technology, where the average black student scored in the top 10 percent, nationwide, on the mathematical portion of the Scholastic Aptitude Test—and in the bottom 10 percent at M.I.T. Nearly one-fourth of these students failed to graduate at M.I.T., and those who did had significantly lower grades than their classmates.[46] Such wholly needless failures among highly qualified students was the price of M.I.T.'s having a racial "representation" that would enhance its image and keep hundreds of millions of federal dollars coming in, without being jeopardized by charges of discrimination based on "under-representation" statistics. As for the other students at M.I.T., the *Wall Street Journal* reported "a widespread if rarely stated perception that black students somehow lack what it takes to make the grade." Nor is this perception lost on the black students at M.I.T. "It's not blatant," one of them said, "It's like you're the last person picked as a lab partner, or someone will lean over you and ask the person sitting next to you what the professor said—like you wouldn't have understood it."[47]

M.I.T. is not unique. At Berkeley, where black students' average composite SAT scores of 952 were above the national composite average of 900, though well below the Berkeley average of 1181, more than 70 percent of the black students failed to graduate.[48] Again, these were *artificial* failures, on an even larger scale than at M.I.T., in the sense that these black students' academic qualifications would have been more than adequate for the average American college or university, though not adequate for competing with Berkeley's white students who scored 1232 or Berkeley's Asian students who scored 1254.[49]

Despite a rising number of blacks admitted to Berkeley over the years—the great majority under "affirmative action" standards—fewer blacks graduated in 1987 than graduated eleven years earlier.[50] What was accomplished by admitting more black students and graduating fewer? The benefits are far more obvious for Berkeley than for the students. The racial body count enabled the university to proclaim that its student body is "wonderfully diverse" and that "we are excited that the class closely reflects the actual ethnic distribution of California high school graduates."[51] It also enabled Berkeley to continue receiving vast sums of state and federal money without being distracted by the inevitable legal and political complications which an "under-representation" of blacks or Hispanics would have entailed.

The U.S. Air Force Academy likewise sought racial "diversity" through double standards. A 1982 memorandum on Air Force Academy stationery, with the notation "for your eyes only," listed different cut-off scores to use when identifying possible candidates for the Academy from different racial ethnic groups. *Composite* SAT scores as low as 520 were acceptable for blacks, though Hispanics and American Indians had to do somewhat better, and Asian Americans had to meet the general standards. For athletes "lower cut-offs" were permissible.[52] Given that composite SAT scores *begin* at 400 (out of a possible 1600) a requirement of 520 is really a requirement to earn only 120 points out of a possible 1200 points earned. Given that the general composite SAT average for students admitted to the Air Force Academy is 1240,[53] a special cut-off score of 520 composite for black students is an invitation to mismatching.

At the University of Texas, where the SAT scores of black undergraduates averaged more than 100 points below the SAT scores of white undergraduates, the grade point average of black freshmen was 1.97, compared to 2.45 for white freshmen.[54] Their graduation rates have been about half that of whites.[55] Many other colleges and universities keep such information under lock and key. At Stanford University, for example, voluminous statistics are published on all sorts of other things, including numerous body-count statistics on minority students and faculty,[56] but *not* information on the academic qualifications and performances of minority students. Even statistics on the percentage of minority applicants who are admitted have been characterized by an official Stanford publication as "so confidential that we cannot even discuss trends."[57] But wherever hard data have been available from other colleges and universities, these data have shown time and again, at otherwise disparate institutions, that test scores cannot be dismissed as "irrelevant" without disastrous results for minority students.

The issue is not whether minority students are "qualified" to be in college, law schools, etc., but whether they are systematically *mismatched* with the particular institutions they are attending. In the Georgetown University Law School case which attracted national media attention, the median test scores of the black students was at the 75th percentile[58]—higher than the median test scores of all students at many respectable law schools, though lower than the score with which any white student in the sample was admitted to Georgetown. Although the student who revealed the LSAT scores was denounced by *The New York Times* for "an obsession with numbers"[59] and was falsely accused by *Chicago Tribune* columnist Clarence Page of claiming that black students were "unqualified,"[60] his real complaint was about double standards. The larger issue is the impact of such double standards—both academically and socially.

Dogmatists have attributed the high attrition rates of minority students to racism on white campuses,[61] rather than to the mismatching indicated by test scores. However, if one goes beyond dogmas to evidence, the role of supposedly "irrelevant" academic criteria becomes clear: While only 22 percent of the Hispanic students preferentially admitted to Berkeley had graduated five years later, more than half the Hispanic students admitted under normal academic standards had graduated. Figures for black students were similar.[62] If the all-purpose explanation is racism, then why did this racism have such radically different effects on people of the same race with different test scores?

As Professor Clyde Summers predicted long ago, this mismatching problem has not been confined to the top echelon schools. As each tier finds its normal pool of minority students pre-empted by a higher tier, it must in turn pre-empt the minority students who would normally qualify for the colleges in a lower tier. Thus San Jose State University ended up, like Berkeley, with more than 70 percent of its black students failing to graduate.[63] The problems of mismatching and artificial failure proceed on down the academic pecking order. Nationwide, 74 percent of black students have failed to graduate, five years after entering college.[64]

The problem starts at the most selective institutions, because that level is where there is the most extreme shortage of minority students matching the prevailing academic standards. That is also the level at which there is the greatest pressure to have a visible minority presence, both for maintaining "appearance" and academic "leadership," which are part of the mystique of prestige institutions, and for the very practical purpose of maintaining the continued in-flow of large amounts of government money, uninterrupted by any charges of "discrimination" based on minority "under-representation."

As for the minority students themselves, many—and probably most—of their academic failures throughout the various levels of colleges and universities can be traced to the systematic mismatching resulting from preferential admissions policies. Certainly that seems clear from the statistical data from those colleges and universities which release data by race and ethnicity—and the secretiveness of other institutions suggests that they have a similar story to hide. Certainly the graduation rate of black students is generally below that of their white classmates at numerous institutions where this information is available.[65] Nationwide, black students' graduation rate is about half that of whites.[66] Yet these explicit failures, large as they often are, do not measure the full damage, either to the students or to the institutions.

Part of the damage is concealed by double standards in grading. Many minority students are helped along academically by what David Reisman of Harvard has called "affirmative grading,"[67] either because of the unwillingness of individual professors to flunk minority students, or because of the intervention of minority affairs officials on campus, who ask that failing grades be "reconsidered," or by the creation of courses or programs—various ethnic "studies," for example—where minority students can expect to receive passing grades (or better) without undue effort. At Stanford, a black student who referred to "extreme exceptions" that some faculty members will make for black students used herself as an example: "I did really poorly on this one physics midterm," she said. "I went to see the professor about it. He was really easy with me and said, 'No problem. Don't worry about it.' He said he would drop it off of my quarter grade and that it wouldn't even count, which was against his own rules. Right after I went in, this white student went in to ask him if he would drop his midterm grade because he did really bad too. The professor said, 'No way.' "[68] Even at the Harvard Medical School, there have been instances where pressure has been put on professors to find ways to pass black students who have failed examinations repeatedly[69]—though one of the medical school's own professors called it "cruel" to "allow the trusting patients to pay for our irresponsibility."[70]

Some institutions have organized sessions to make faculty members become more "sensitive" to the problems of minority students, and an untenured faculty member, especially, can hardly fail to understand the possible consequences for his career of becoming known as "insensitive" for being hard-nosed about applying the same academic standards to minority students as to everyone else. Neither black nor white students or faculty are unaware of these double standards, nor are any of them likely to be unaffected by that awareness. This is another ingredient in the backlash known as "the new racism."

Highly qualified minority students can also lose. They are often offended and resentful when their white classmates and white professors betray surprise at discovering that they are quite competent. Nor does it end there. Employers may be skeptical about taking at face value the grades which a minority student has fully earned by four years of hard work, because employers cannot be sure which grades are real and which have resulted from pressures for double standards. All this is part of the price of preferential admissions policies and the consequences to which they lead.

Minority Faculty and Programs

As preferentially admitted minority students began to turn from academics to activism, including disruption and violence, among their recurring demands were more minority faculty and more "relevant" courses and programs. Both demands were widely met at colleges and universities across the country, as minority faculty, various racial and ethnic "studies," and special minority cultural and social centers all became familiar parts of the academic landscape.

In their haste to meet politically defined demands for minority faculty, colleges and universities again proceeded with an utter disregard of the size of the pool of qualified people. As of the early 1970s, when these patterns were established on many campuses, various surveys and estimates showed that there were fewer than 4,000 black Ph.D.s in the entire country.[71] That was less than two for each college, even if every black Ph.D. went into the academic world, with not one going into industry, government, think tanks, or other endeavors. Moreover, the number of black doctorates awarded annually still had not reached 1,300 by the mid 1980s.[72] Hispanics and American Indians, put together, did not earn as many doctorates as blacks, so that all these conventionally defined "minorities," put together, did not receive 2,000 Ph.D.s annually[73]—which is to say, there were not enough of them for each college in the country to add one minority Ph.D. to its faculty annually. As of 1989, these three groups, combined, received fewer than 1,500 doctorates[74]—not enough for *half* the colleges in the country to hire one new minority Ph.D.

Nevertheless, various colleges and universities have set up numerical goals for hiring minority faculty—sometimes without regard to whether these faculty members' professional fields matched the institutions' vacancies. Bucknell and the University of Iowa, for example, have done this. At other institutions—including San Francisco State, Ohio Wesleyan, and Wayne State—administrators have specified that existing vacancies were to be filled solely by minority candidates.[75] More circumspect institutions have gone through the motions of considering non-minority, and non-female candidates, while in fact setting the position aside for minority or female faculty members.

The size of the qualified pool may be resolutely ignored, but its consequences remain inescapable. Black faculty have lacked a Ph.D. more often than white faculty, received Ph.D.s (when they did) later in life, and published much less than white faculty.[76] Those teaching in white colleges and universities have often complained that they were not taken very seriously by their colleagues, and were not often asked to co-author scholarly studies.[77] Clearly, intellectual interaction with colleagues is part of the individual's own development, so that being perceived as substandard becomes itself a barrier to the full realization of one's potential. By the same token, others cannot afford to waste time with someone hired for racial body count purposes, if they wish to develop their own potential to the fullest.

Given the widespread political demand for minority faculty

and the very small supply of individuals academically qualified to meet those demands, it can hardly be surprising that both the people hired and the programs they set up have often been a painful embarrassment, even at highly prestigious institutions. A report on an Afro-American Studies course at Princeton, for example, noted that some students found it "simply a three-hour 'rap session,'" where the assigned readings "were certainly not necessary," for there was only "nominal discussion of their content during seminar discussions."[78]

Another Afro-American Studies course at Princeton was described as being "a lot of fun" and to have a workload that was "very light." In yet another course in the same department, students reported that the topics for class discussion "were seldom related to the topics on the outline" and the required reading was both "light" and "easy." Harvard's Afro-American Studies department was likewise described by the students' *Confidential Guide* as a department in need of repair—one with "fading student interest and faculty discontent"[79] and a department which was "a touchy subject" because of "its political history."[80] More explicitly, David Riesman said, "the program was widely recognized as of poor quality by black Harvard undergraduates as well as by black and white faculty members at other leading universities."[81]

Here again, what happened had been predicted many years earlier. Black civil rights activist Bayard Rustin warned back in 1969 that "black studies must not be used for the purpose of image-buiding or to enable young black students to escape the challenges of the university by setting up a program of 'soul courses' that they can just play with and pass."[82] The same year, NAACP Executive Director Roy Wilkins condemned the creation of "sealed-off black studies centers" for "racial breast-beating." While sympathetic to "the frustrations and anger of today's black students," he nevertheless said:

> In their hurt pride in themselves and in their outrage, they have called retreat from the tough and trying battle of a minority for dignity and equality. They don't call it a retreat, of course. They have all sorts of fancy rationalizations for their course.[83]

Today, those rationalizations are now an established part of the racial dogmatism in academia.

Across the country, black studies programs arose in the wake of black student demands and fell as many of those same students declined to major in the subject, or even to enroll in sufficient numbers to keep many of the programs alive. It is hard to explain this apparently inconsistent behavior, except on the ground that the demands were symbolic, expressing an emotional need rather than a serious interest. In any event, there were about a thousand black studies programs in the country in the early 1970s but these had declined to no more than 500 by 1988.[84]

Looking at this from the standpoint of the incentives and constraints facing minority faculty members in black (or Hispanic or Native American) studies, their careers were precarious and their futures uncertain if they were either wholly in these racial or ethnic studies, or if they held joint appointments split between some traditional department and such programs. A Carnegie Foundation study by David Riesman found "nonscholarly black faculty members who seek to maintain their precarious hold on academic life by building up a cadre of militant followers, threatening to charge the institution with racism if it releases them."[85] Clearly, the jobs of these minority professors are more secure the more minority students are on campus, the more politicized those students are, and the more of a credible threat of disruption or violence they represent, should anyone seek to scale back the racial and ethnic studies programs.

Finally, as increasing evidences of white backlash became apparent, racial and ethnic studies courses were promoted as a *requirement* to be imposed on all students, as the "solution" to intergroup hostility. Ironically, such programs were now being promoted as a way to help "de-ghettoize the university as a whole,"[86] when in fact they were part of the process which produced campus ghettoes in the first place. Moreover, to believe that imposing substandard courses taught by substandard faculty will improve race relations strains credulity.

Whatever the rhetoric, the brutal reality of ethnic studies programs is a struggle to preserve turf and jobs. This was perhaps epitomized by a controversy which erupted at San Francisco State University in 1990, when the political science department offered a course on black politics. Although the course was taught by a black professor, the School of Ethnic

Studies staged a disruptive protest demonstration. One faculty member described it as a "life and death" issue and saw the overlapping course as an attempt by the administration "to destroy the School of Ethnic Studies."[87]

More than job security is involved, however. Minority faculty hired preferentially face exactly the same problem of self-respect as the students admitted under double standards. It is fundamentally the same mismatching stituation: A professor who would be a respected member of a department at an average college or university may be completely overshadowed in a department where colleagues are publishing regularly in the leading scholarly journals of the world, writing landmark books in their field, and receiving national and international recognition, honors, and prizes.

In these circumstances, for mismatched minority faculty to accept the intellectual standards around them and the scholarly thrust of their colleagues means losing their own self-respect. But to denounce the standards they do not meet, and decry as "irrelevant" the scholarship they cannot match, at least enables them to hold their heads up and to achieve some recognition as a force on campus. However, to maintain even this tenuous respectability requires that they have behind them the support and implied threat of minority students—which in turn requires that they promote among those students not only a sense of separatism but also of paranoia, a sense that white professors are out to "get" minority students, that low grades are symptoms of repressive racism, etc. Bizarre as some of these notions might seem to an observer, they appear to be far more plausible to minority students who have sailed through substandard high schools with A's and B's, and who now find themselves struggling to get C's—and often losing that struggle.

Incentives to push paranoia are inherent in the situation, not only for minority faculty, but also for the growing number of minority affairs administrators and for student activist "leaders," whose effectiveness depends not only on the number of minority students on campus but also on their attitudes and cohesiveness. How many of these key individuals are cold-bloodedly promoting paranoia in pursuit of their own self-interest, and how many are following the all too human pattern of rationalization, are questions to which no answer is possible.

What is clear is what the built-in incentives promote, however much other considerations may lead particular minority individuals to "play it straight."

Some campus minority leaders, however, have been quite clear that what they needed were not simply more minority students, but more *disgruntled* minority students. Don't be "happy campers," warned the head of the black students' organization at Carleton College, who also quoted Louis Farrakhan to back up his call for alienation.[88] Similar promotions of paranoia have been common elsewhere. One tactic used by minority mini-establishments on a number of campuses has been to gain influence on the recruitment and admission of minority students—and to use that influence to *block* the admission of highly qualified black students[89] who are likely to fit in, both academically and socially—and therefore *not* be part of the kind of political constituency desired. At a time when the Harvard Medical School was bending the rules to allow some black medical students to become doctors, the school's black recruiters were passing over highly qualified blacks who did not fit the social or ideological profile they were seeking.[90]

Like mismatched minority students, mismatched minority faculty have sought refuge in non-intellectual pursuits, such as community activities and campus political activism, in denunciations of standards they do not meet, and in complaints about the moral shortcomings of colleagues, or of American society in general. Given the stark alternatives of (1) losing one's self-respect by accepting the prevailing academic standards and values, and (2) protecting one's self-respect by repudiating those standards and values, it can hardly be surprising that many have chosen the latter.

Clearly, not all minority faculty have followed this pattern However, those who have "played it straight" have been overshadowed by activists—regardless of the numerical proportions between the two kinds of minority faculty—and have been largely treated as expendable by administrators preoccupied with placating those with a potential to cause trouble. It has thus been the activist minority faculty who have played a key role in the racial and ethnic patterns which have emerged on campus. A few examples of these minority activists may make the pattern more concrete.

Perhaps the best known of the minority faculty activists is Professor Derrick Bell of the Harvard Law School. He has urged black students at elite colleges in general toward activism.[91] He vocally supported a student sit-in at the Harvard Law School dean's office, trying to force the hiring of tenured black female faculty. On other issues, he has argued that "direct action" is more effective than law, that "reform requires confrontation" which "can't be intellectualized."[92] While admitting that "few minority scholars have national reputations or are frequently published in the major law reviews," Bell attributed this to whites' "exclusion" of them.[93] Blacks with a different outlook are dismissed by Bell as people who merely "look black" but "think white."[94]

An episode at the Stanford Law School when Bell was a visiting professor captures the atmosphere of the times. According to the dean of the law school:

> Students in Prof. Bell's class criticized his teaching and complained that they were unable to learn the subject from him. Many began auditing other instructors' constitutional law classes. These events ultimately led to the idea of a series of public lectures in basic constitutional law to be given by various faculty members. Although these lectures would be open to the student body as a whole, their unstated purpose was to offer Prof. Bell's students a supplement to his course. The series was called off after members of the Black Law Students Association protested the first lecture on the ground that both the students' dissatisfaction and the unprecedented lecture series were tainted by racism.[95]

Bell likewise attributed the students' complaints to their having "viewed me as a token, visiting presence of questionable competence." There was "an insult inherent in the lecture series," it was "a denial of my status as a faculty member and my worth as a person."[96]

Hispanic Professor Richard Delgado has argued that the predominance of white males among the writers most often cited by law journals and in court decisions shows an "exclusion" of minority writers.[97] However, in promoting this thesis, Professor Delgado did not even attempt to establish specifically which less-cited, minority-written publications were superior to which often-cited, white-written publications. Instead, he used rhetoric about "imperial scholars"[98] with "indifference to minority writings."[99] Finally, he used the "may" tactic as a substitute for argument: Whites "may be ineffective advocates" for minority rights or "may lack information" or "may lack passion" or they "may pull their punches."[100]

"May" arguments require not a speck of evidence, so that there is no way to answer them, except by constructing an alternative list of "may" possibilities. Since almost anything is possible, there is no way to resolve conflicts based on "may" statements. However, with Delgado as with others who use the "may" tactic, this tactic serves as an emotional prelude (as distinguished from a logical foundation) to other unsupported assertions—in this case, the assertion that white writers should stop writing about civil rights, so that minority writers can get published and cited more.[101]

Although Asian students and faculty tend not to be as politicized as those from some other groups, there is a fringe of politically activist Asian academics as well, and their arguments follow along lines very similar to those among black or Hispanic activists. Professor Mari Matsuda, for example, has urged that "the process of eradicating apartheid in legal knowledge" be promoted by buying, reading, citing and teaching "outsiders' scholarship"—defined as writings "written by white women, women of color and men of color." Like Professor Delgado and others, she simply *assumed* that minority writers had better insight than other writers who were better known, without even attempting to argue this from specific examples.

Double Standards of Behavior

The passing years have seen an ever-widening double standard of behavior, by race, on many campuses. At the University of California at Berkeley, for example, when some partying fraternity members pinned a confederate flag outside the frat house, the administration imposed "sensitivity" training on the whole fraternity and asked them to seek more minority members, but it took a very different view when the feelings of Jewish students were involved:[102]

Two female members of the Jewish Student Union were recruiting for the organization when members of the Black Mus-
lim Union spotted them, and began loudly harassing them
with anti-Semitic remarks. A small crowd gathered and egged
the Muslims on. The women, in tears, fled and reported the
incident to the Student Conduct Office, wanting the fighting
words code invoked. They were told that they ought to develop
"thicker skins" and nothing was done.

On many other college campuses as well, the standards for
"racism" themselves vary by race. For example, when a white
woman at the University of Pennsylvania expressed her "deep
regard for the individual and my desire to protect the freedoms
of *all* members of society," she was chided by an administrator
who said that the word "individual" is "considered by many
to be RACIST."[103] The reason is that emphasis on the individual
could be construed as "opposition to group entitlements." At
Stanford, an even more strained use of the word "racist" grew
out of a conflict that had nothing to do with race. When a
fraternity student was punished for insulting a homosexual
resident advisor, a few of his fraternity brothers staged a silent,
candlelight vigil as a protest, wearing hockey masks to shield
their identity and avoid having this protest be seen as a frater-
nity-sponsored action. Some observer decided that this silent,
candlelight vigil was reminiscent of the Ku Klux Klan and
contacted the Black Students Union, 30 of whose members then
appeared on the scene.

Although the fraternity protesters expressed surprise at the
racial interpretation put on their vigil, an altercation was only
narrowly averted. The fraternity men were condemned as "insensitive" by Stanford President Donald Kennedy for not re-
alizing the racial implications of their actions,[104] even though
those actions were not directed at any racial or ethnic minorities and involved entirely different issues. But the Stanford
administration had no such condemnation when the head of
the Black Students Union publicly declared, "I do not like white
people." He said:

> Unfortunately, for blacks, we only get our pictures in the
> paper when we protest or fail and not when we succeed.
>
> My response, and you may quote me, is "kiss my black
> behind!"[105]

No one in the Stanford administration called him "insensitive"—or said anything at all publicly. Had a white student made similar remarks concerning blacks, he would be lucky to escape expulsion—not only at Stanford, but at many other colleges and universities across the country. Formal prohibitions on statements that can be construed as racist (or sexist or homophobic) have become common, along with stringent penalties for violations of their broad and vague provisions. What has also become common are double standards in applying these codes. The lattitude permitted members of minority groups (or homosexuals, feminists, and others) has been extremely broad. Moreover, the students themselves know that such double standards exist.

At Vassar College, a black student had a public outburst that included such epithets as "dirty Jew" and "f--king Jew."[106] He was neither suspended nor expelled, as the Vassar administration focused its efforts on keeping the story from being published by the *Vassar Spectator*, a student-run publication, which became a target of intense criticism—and retribution—when it published the story anyway.[107]

A number of black student organizations on various college campuses have invited as a speaker Louis Farrakhan, noted for his fiery denunciations of Jews. However, Minister Farrakhan is by no means unique in this respect. Other speakers invited to address black student groups on various campuses have made such comments as "the Jew hopes to one day reign forever," that Jews are a "violent people,"[108] that the "best Zionist is a dead Zionist,"[109] or have referred to "Columbia Jewniversity in Jew York City."[110] Official condemnations of "racism," which are freely proclaimed in other situations, are seldom if ever forthcoming when minority students, faculty, or invited speakers attack other racial or ethnic groups.

Double standards extend not only to words but also to actions. When dozens of minority students have invaded classrooms to shout down the professor, intimidate the students, and prevent the lecture from being given, they have done so with impunity at San Francisco State University, at Berkeley, and at the City College in New York.[111] On the campus of the State University of New York at Binghamton, a public lecture by a 70-year-old retired professor was invaded and disrupted by dozens of students—mostly minority—carrying sticks. One of the black students blew his nose on a tissue, which he then deposited in a cup of coffee from which the professor had been drinking—to the cheers of the mob, while an administrator sat silently in the audience, grinning.[112]

Despite a readiness of university officials to interpret all sorts of words and deeds by whites as racist, even outright physical assaults by blacks against whites are unlikely to be labeled that way. When two white students at Brown University were victims of unprovoked street attacks by blacks, according to the student newspaper the head of campus security "was quick to point out that 'There is nothing at all that would tend to indicate that this is a racially motivated incident'."[113] After a similar unprovoked street attack on two white students by five blacks at the University of Wisconsin (Madison), the student newspaper there similarly reported that campus police "do not believe the attack was racially motivated, although 'racial slurs' were used." Indeed, when the students asked why they were being attacked, the answer was: "Because we're black and you're white."[114] But, officially, it was still not considered a racial attack. At Wesleyan University, where thinly-veiled hints of violence from black student activists both preceded and followed a fire-bombing of the university president's office,[115] the president of Wesleyan likened the arson to an "automobile accident" and called for "healing."[116]

A series in the *Christian Science Monitor* on campus racial problems included this episode:

> When a dozen black youths crashed a Theta Delta Chi fraternity party at Berkeley last fall, pulling knives, hurling epithets, and putting two whites in the hospital, the student paper didn't cover the story. "There were 11 cops and two ambulances—and *we* were the ones worried about a lawsuit!" says fraternity member Jon Orbik. "Can you imagine the media if it had been the other way around?"[117]

Double standards and hypocrisy are recurring complaints about the way racial issues are handled on campuses across the country. The specifics range from double standards of admission to charges of racism by minority students or faculty who make racist statements themelves, to self-segregation by students who claim to be "excluded."

As regards preferential admissions, Dartmouth professor Jeffrey Hart wrote:

> The white student who gains admissions to a good college has undoubtedly worked hard for four years in secondary school and experienced the heavy anxiety of filing application for admission and waiting for acceptance or rejection. Such a student is very likely to be a competitive personality. That a black skin or a Hispanic surname is worth several hundred Scholastic Aptitude Test points sticks in the craw.[118]

Even those who are themselves admitted often feel resentment on behalf of relatives or friends who were not admitted, despite better records than minority students admitted preferentially.[119] As a Rutgers University undergraduate said on the McNeil-Lehrer news program: "The reason why we have racial tensions at Rutgers is they have a very strong minority recruitment program, and this means that many of my friends from my hometown were not accepted, even though they are more qualified."[120] This was not peculiar to Rutgers. When two Californians from the same preparatory school applied to the University of California at Berkeley, this was the result:

> Student A was ranked in the top third of his class, student B in the bottom third. Student A had SAT scores totaling 1290; student B's scores totaled 890. Student A had a record of good citizenship while student B was expelled the previous winter for breaking a series of major rules. Student A was white; student B was black. Berkeley rejected student A and accepted student B.[121]

Similar stories abound. At Dartmouth, a student with uninspiring SAT scores and poor high school grades was admitted, even though students with far better academic records have been turned away. This young man had some trace of American Indian ancestry, though he was blond and blue-eyed.[122]

Whatever resentments grow out of this issue are compounded when college authorities stifle any complaints about it. At U.C.L.A., for example, a comic strip in the student newspaper contained an episode in which a student sees a rooster on campus and asks how he got admitted. "Affirmative action" was the rooster's reply. The editor was removed from his job— and when the student newspaper at Cal State Northridge criticized this action editorially, illustrating the editorial with the comic strip in question, that editor was also removed.[123]

At the University of Wisconsin (Eau Claire) a cartoon in the student newspaper showed two white students with faces darkened from a bucket of paint labeled "Minority in a Minute" and "E-Z 2-ITION." One student says: "Who needs to work so hard to get a perfect G.P.A. or money for tuition, when ya have this stuff?" The other sings "Free tuition here we come."[124] A Michigan State University student who displayed this cartoon on his dormitory door was suspended.[125]

Self-segregation by minorities is another common complaint. Sometimes this extends from eating together—the "black table" is a common phenomenon at many colleges—to socializing exlusively within one's own racial or ethnic group, to having separate dormitories. Nor is all this spontaneous. Often there are social pressures, sometimes abetted by college administrators in various ways.

The process begins even before the minority student sets foot on campus. Racial identity information on the admissions application form triggers racially separate listings of students, with these lists then being shared with the local Black Students Union or other minority organizations on campus. Students may be invited to campus as individuals, only to discover after arrival that the gathering is all-black, all-Hispanic, etc. In short, they do not join minority organizations the way Jewish students may join Hillel or Catholics may join Newman clubs; they are *delivered* to campus minority organizations.[126]

Pressures to self-segregate and adopt groupthink attitudes begin early. As an observer at Washington University in St. Louis said:

The minute they get on campus, the Legion of Black Collegians tells them that they are going to be discriminated against. So they stick together and ostracize any that might get involved on campus.[127]

Mark Mathabane, black South African author of *Kaffir Boy*, traveled to America to go to college and escape apartheid—only to discover its philosophy flourishing here:

When I was in college, I and a few other black students were labeled Uncle Toms for sitting with whites in the cafeteria, sharing with them black culture, working with them on projects and socializing with them.[128]

Similar attitudes can be found among other minority groups, including Asians on some campuses. An Asian American student at Carleton College reported:

> Students of color are looked down upon and sometimes openly criticized by their peers for having too many white friends, not doing enough for their respective multicultural groups, or just being too "Americanized" or trying too hard to blend in. Using the Asian American experience as an example, terms like "banana" (yellow on the outside, white on the inside) are sometime used and questions like "How come you don't have an Asian first name?" come up in everyday conversation.[129]

The term "banana" for Asians who reject separatism parallels the use of the term "Oreo" (black on the outside, white on the inside) for blacks and "coconut" (brown on the outside, etc.) for Mexican Americans who reject separatism. In short, campus political activists in various groups attempt to stigmatize those students of their own race who do not join their political constituency and share its groupthink. Such activism is, however, less common and less extreme among Asian Americans, though the general pattern is similar in those cases where Asian campus activists are at work.

The cumulative effects of self-segregation pressures eventually take their toll on many minority youngsters. An observer described the process among black students at Dartmouth:

> Most have a healthy attitude when they come here. They want to meet all kinds of people, and expand their intellectual and cultural horizons. Yet, if they happen to make more white friends than black ones, they quickly learn the ugly reality of Dartmouth's reverse racism. Normally-adjusted blacks are called "incogs" and "oreos," meaning that they are "black on the outside and white on the inside." Most frequently, it is blacks themselves who call other blacks by these hateful names.
>
> Many black freshmen can't withstand the pressure.... They begin to eat together, live together, and join all-black fraternities and sororities.... At first, they resisted the pres-

sure to abandon their well-integrated circle of friends, yet were unable to keep up the resistance.[130]

As on other campuses, the Dartmouth administration abetted this process, not only by arranging a special orientation weekend for blacks (at first not so labeled) and then by providing *de facto* segregated housing:

> Dartmouth participates in the segregation process by providing Cutter Hall for black housing and the Afro-American Society. Although housing in Cutter is ostensibly available for anyone who wants it, the last time a white student lived there was the winter of 1986. Cutter's militant, ingrown atmosphere ensures that few whites will ever cross the threshold, let alone consider living there.[131]

At Berkeley, self-segregation is achieved by matching room mates by race. "I came here expecting to have friends, even room-mates, of other races," a white student at Berkeley said. Of the minority students she said, "They go around calling everybody 'racist,' but they're the ones insisting on being separate." She added: "If white students got together on the basis of race, they'd be considered Nazis."[132]

Sometimes self-segregation endures right on through to graduation itself. The Stanford *Campus Report* for June 13, 1990, listed a "Black Baccalaureate," a "Native American Graduation Dinner" and an "Asian American Graduation Reception" at separate locations.[133]

Minority students who insist on going their own way as individuals, not only socially but ideologically, face special pressures and even physical threats—often to the complete disinterest of college administrations. In Allan Bloom's *Closing of the American Mind*, he reports going to Cornell University's provost on behalf of "a black student whose life had been threatened by a black faculty member when he refused to participate in a demonstration." The provost expressed sympathy but did nothing, because (1) the administration was preoccupied with current racial tensions on campus and (2) campus politics in general were such that "no university in the country could expel radical black students or dismiss the faculty members who incited them."[134]

At about the same time, black educator Kenneth B. Clark

resigned from Antioch College's board of directors in protest against the administration's silence as militant black students "intimidate, threaten, and in some cases physically assault" other black students who disagreed with them.[135] Similar patterns can still be found on elite college campuses today. Threats of violence against a black student who was also editor of the conservative *Dartmouth Review* evoked a similar lack of interest on the part of the Dartmouth administration,[136] even though the student named names and had faculty witnesses. At Stanford, Hispanic students who complained of intimidation by more militant, organized Hispanic students found a similar indifference on the part of the administration. Moreover, a copy of their letter of complaint, complete with signatures of the complaining students, was turned over to the militant Hispanic organization.[137]

Often, college administrators deal with the most vocal minority organization as if it represents "the" blacks, "the" Hispanics, etc.—regardless of whether it does in fact. Hispanic students at Stanford, for example, claimed that "only 15.2 percent of Chicano/Latino students have ever participated in any way whatsoever" in any of the activities of the organization which speaks in their name.[138] Nevertheless, such organizations tend to monopolize administrators' attention, whether because of ideological affinity, administrative convenience, or because they represent a credible threat to campus tranquility.

Because college officials respond to the organized and vocal elements within each minority group, the whole racial atmosphere on campus tends to reflect the issues raised by these vocal elements and by administrators' policy responses to their charges and demands. What *most* minority students think may carry far less weight. Sad as it is to have tensions between two racial groups when they disagree, it is tragic insanity to have racial tension when these groups as a whole are in fundamental agreement For example, a survey of 5,000 students at 40 colleges showed that, at predominantly white colleges, 76 percent of black students and 93 percent of white students agreed that all undergraduates should be admitted by meeting the same standards At predominantly black colleges, more than 95 percent of the students of both races agreed.[139] This divisive issue inflames campuses across the country because college officials respond to the vocal activists.

Another factor not to be overlooked in explaining college policies is the sheer, blind imitativeness of the academic world. Even colleges and universities which have lagged behind in the developments which have brought turmoil to other campuses, often decide later to imitate their less fortunate compatriots. For example, Whitman College, a somewhat traditional institution which escaped much of the turmoil and fashions of the 1960s, nevertheless chose later to establish a Director of Minority Affairs, and he in turn chose to invite to campus a speaker on racism, described—by the speaker's own promotional literature—as someone who "draws out anger," who is "loud, verbally brutal, demeaning, cold and oppressive."[140]

Why invite such a man to Whitman College? According to an official of Whitman's Multi-Ethnic Student Organization: "Just because we don't have any real problem (at Whitman) doesn't mean there is no problem. . . . Racial sensitivity is what we're after."[141] In other words, they could not resist stirring up problems, instead of leaving well enough alone. This is all too typical of the mindset which has led to escalating racial polarization on many campuses—a polarization which, however, enhances the visibility and importance of people associated with "multicultural" and minority affairs.

Bringing on campus people who are specialists in emotional confrontations on race relations is not a practice unique to Whitman College. There is in fact a whole industry of "diversity consultants" or race relations specialists who give talks or conduct seminars on campus, advise administrators on racial matters, participate in freshman orientation programs, hold off-campus retreats for faculty members and administrators, prepare films, videotapes or other materials, hold conferences around the country, and publish newsletters and magazines devoted solely to "diversity."[142] While individual styles vary, a common theme is that *everyone* white is racist, with the only distinction being between those who are overt and those who do not realize their own racism, those who admit it and those who engage in psychological "denial." To minority individuals, the message is: Racism is pervasive around you, whether you realize it or not. Ambiguous situations should always be interpreted as racial affronts. "Never think that you imagined it," one speaker at a Harvard workshop said, "because chances are that you didn't." This speaker was an official of the university.[143]

Colleges and universities across the country utilize race relations consultants. Tulane University, for example, has subjected its administrators to two-day seminars off campus, operated by an Atlanta organization which uses methods described as "confrontational" and based on the usual *a priori* presumption of racism that has to be rooted out by these consultants. This Atlanta organization has also received money from the Ford Foundation to bring together high officials of universities throughout the region for similar sessions.[144] Yale University paid several thousand dollars to a New York-based firm to conduct workshops on its campus, with one of the consultants suggesting that students who had chosen to go to class rather than attend the workshops were racist.[145] At a week-long series of workshops at Harvard, the presumed breakdown of racism was quantified as 85 percent subtle racism and 15 percent overt racism. Yet, despite this air of scientific precision, an observer found that the atmosphere surrounding the keynote address "resembled a religious revival meeting."[146] This too is not uncommon. Psychological techniques used by old-time itinerant revival-meeting preachers have proved effective in evoking feelings of guilt and repentance in academia. At the University of Wisconsin, for example, an itinerant race relations specialist evoked "the repentant sobs of white students" at one of his workshops, while pushing his message that virtually all white people are racists and all black people are angry.[147] Sometimes the old-fashioned revival meeting techniques are combined with modern psychological devices like role-playing.[148]

The very possibility that self-interest might be involved in consultants' commercial promotion of polarization on campus never seems to be mentioned, even though these secular Elmer Gantry's have made a career for themselves by practicing an art requiring little academic qualification and facing no empirical check regarding either assertions or consequences.

As with so many other non-academic intrusions into education at all levels, the problem is not that these activities will necessarily succeed at their avowed purpose, but that they can do enormous damage in the process. Perhaps the most ironic venue for racial polarization has been Oberlin College, whose long tradition of liberalism (in the original sense) on racial issues goes far back into the nineteenth century, when Oberlin was a stop on the "underground railroad" that helped blacks escape from slavery. Today, while workshops are being held on the Oberlin Campus with such themes as "fighting oppression" and "celebrating diversity," blacks and whites go their separate ways, letters to the student newspaper are filled with angry recriminations among the various fractionalized groups, and there is a search for "ever more rarefied units of racism," according to the college's own president.[149]

The prevalence of the idea that frequent and sweeping charges of racism are going to improve intergroup relations cannot be explained either by its plausibility or its track record. On the contrary, it feeds the polarization which benefits only those minority activists and apparatchiks who promote this approach. Increasingly, white students are becoming not only hardened against such denunciation but openly resentful of it. As a student at the University of Texas (Austin) wrote:

> Racism has become an epithet against which there is no defense. The charge of racism needs little support, is nearly impossible to refute, and is more damaging to a person than any other label. It has become the insult-of-choice to many liberals.[150]

A University of Michigan student said, "the word *racism* is thrown around so often that it is in danger of losing its meaning."[151] Certainly the term had lost its sting for the *University Review of Texas*, which responded to accusations of racism by calling them "boring and uncreative."[152] A recently graduated Stanford law student referred to "panhandlers for minority representation" on campus and to "minority advocates who greet any opposition to their agenda of quotas and preferences with charges of racism."[153] At colleges around the country, there have been bitter complaints about the double standards used in determining what is and is not racism. A student at the University of Virginia, for example, noted:

> Apparently there is a double standard for racism at the University. When a sign was found on Route 29 containing a racial slur, the entire University was up in arms. However, when a

black fraternity distributed a flyer with a picture of a black man holding a sword in one hand and the decapitated head of a white man, entrailes and all, aloft in the other, no one seemed concerned. The same was true when a representative from the Nation of Islam speaking at the University claimed to have words only for black students saying, "to hell with the rest of them."[154]

A Stanford undergraduate likewise declared that the racism on his campus was a racism "against whites." He added:

There is a quiet, powerful resentment growing among whites here who feel that they are paying an increasingly burdensome toll for the crimes of their, or someone else's, ancestors. The fact that this resentment is not expressed in campus literature or open conversation does not mean it is not there; on the contrary, its lack of expression will ensure that it festers and grows.[155]

An observer at an "anti-racism" seminar at Oberlin reported:

Throughout the three-and-a-half hour session, no participant raised an objection, yet I subsequently heard that many were dismayed. Why had they not spoken out? "It's not worth it," one senior told me. "You just get attacked."[156]

A professor at Kenyon College said:

Black students . . . are regularly permitted the most outrageous expressions of anti-white racism and, increasingly, anti-semitism, while white students must be extraordinarily careful in their choice of words and in their actions lest they be accused of racism and punished accordingly.[157]

The student newspaper at Bryn Mawr and Haverford reported a "backlash" at these colleges against the *a priori* charges levelled against white students:

From the moment they arrived on campus, they have been called racist, sexist or classist.[158]

Not all the students take it. A white student at Haverford, responding to a complaining and accusatory article by a black classmate, said:

You come off in your article as a most embittered person—
"pity me" you write: "pity me more because I am Black."
Though you make good points about disadvantages Blacks
have, I found your letter offensive to me as a person who
happens to be white. I did not chose to be this color any more
than you chose to be Black; and I respect that which is distinct
in the Black culture, but I refuse to be ashamed because I am
white.[159]

Some white students at Berkeley complain that it is a problem just to avoid setting off criticism by not being up to date
on ever-changing names for different groups:

It's Chicano now, or Chicana, or Mexican, Latina, Hispanic,
I mean . . . every year it changes. . . . If you say the wrong
thing you're either racist or they yell at you. . . . But we're
always the white honky . . . we don't get to change our name
every year.[160]

Another Berkeley student complained of "whites hearing
all year they are racists." He said:

I grew up with white, yellow, black. I mean half my buddies
on the football team were black, and I come here and read
every other day in the paper I'm a racist. It irritates me.[161]

Neither whining nor breast-beating are sounds that anyone
wants to hear incessantly. Nevertheless, the search for grievances over racism remains unabated. In some cases, charges
are fabricated. The Tawana Brawley hoax in New York has had
a number of campus counterparts. A black instructor at Ohio
Dominican College resigned after claiming to have received
racial hate mail from one of her students—and after detectives
found evidence suggesting that she had forged the letters herself.[162] Other reports of racial incidents at Tufts University, at
Smith College, at Emory University, and at the University of
Texas have also turned out to be false, and an incident at Columbia University was described by more than 20 eyewitnesses
very differently from the way it was first reported in the media.
The attorney for the black students in the Columbia University
case was C. Vernon Mason, who was also an attorney for Tawana Brawley.[163]

Both false and true racial incidents reveal something of the atmosphere on college campuses, an atmosphere whose complex cross-currents derive ultimately from the needless pressures generated by double standards and double talk, both of which poison the atmosphere required for people to get along. As race relations have worsened in the wake of policies designed to make them better, there has been no re-thinking of the original assumptions on which these policies were based. On the contrary, there has been a renewed insistence on more of the same dogmas. In addition, the escalating racial and ethnic strife has generated some new dogmas as well, based on the same general vision as the old.

NEW DOGMAS FOR "NEW RACISM"

Three responses to the growing backlash of insulting, harassing, and violent incidents against blacks and other minorities across the country have been common among academics:

1. Blaming it on the racism of the past, continuing into the present
2. Blaming it on the racism of the larger society, spilling over onto college campuses
3. Blaming it on the conservative mood of the times, exemplified by the election and re-election of President Ronald Reagan

What these three explanations have in common is that they wholly ignore *the very possibility* that the policies and practices of the colleges themselves may have been responsible for the hostile racial climate on campus. They also completely ignore facts which go counter to each of these three explanations. In addition, the "remedies" suggested or taken extend or accentuate the racial double standards which have been so much resented. Moreover, the "experts" consulted in such matters have often been ethnic studies professors and minority affairs administrators, who have the most blatantly obvious vested interest in continuing and expanding these double standards.

Typical of the closed mind on such issues in academia was a long feature article in *The Chronicle of Higher Education* of January 27, 1988, focusing exclusively on the views of those with the three explanations already noted. Of the thousands of words in its story, not one was from anyone with a different perspective, challenging the prevailing social vision or the policies based on it. According to *The Chronicle of Higher Education*, "black students are finding that white campuses are often hostile environments in which vestiges of the 'old' racism persist."[164] But the "vestige" argument is contradicted by the fact that the racial outbreaks on many campuses are both more numerous and more severe than anything witnessed in past decades on these same campuses, even though minority students have been attending such colleges for generations. By definition, a vestige is not larger or worse than what it is a vestige of. Nuclear bombs are not a vestige of bows and arrows. Moreover, the geographical distribution of racial incidents also belies the "vestige" argument.

In the 1960s, there were many violent resistances to the racial integration of colleges and universities in the South, while today such violence is far more prevalent in the North. Tabulations of outbreaks of racial or ethnic violence by the National Institute Against Prejudice and Violence in 1988 and 1989 both found more such incidents in the state of Massachusetts alone than in the entire region of the South. Yet the "vestige" doctrine is by no means confined to *The Chronicle of Higher Education*. It is part of a far more general dogmatism in academia, which refuses even to consider the possibility that its own policies have contributed to the disasters it is experiencing.

Professor Troy Duster of Berkeley echoed a widespread view among academics when he blamed racial strife on "the society that generated the students who come here."[165] This ignores the observations of others who have said that the racial strife on campus is more severe than that normally encountered in the larger society,[166] as well as more severe than in the past.[167] A professor at San Jose State University noted among his painful experiences hearing a black woman who "said she'd never been called a nigger till she got to this campus."[168] An Hispanic student at Cornell likewise said that she "had never experienced racism in my face before I came to Ithaca."[169] When 70 percent of the graduating seniors at Stanford say that racial tensions have *increased* during their time on campus,[170] that does not suggest a "vestige," if only because a growing "vestige" is a contradiction in terms.

On most campuses, however, the very possibility that institutional policies are themselves adding to racism is not even mentioned. Instead, it is dogmatically assumed that the racism on campus must have originated off campus. When Dr. Ira M. Heyman, then chancellor at Berkeley, blamed racial hostilities on that campus on "the larger framework of the general mood in the U.S.,"[171] he ignored Berkeley's own racial quota policies under his administration—policies which turned away more than 2,000 white and Asian students with straight A averages in one year,[172] in order to admit black students who overwhelmingly failed to graduate.

Professor Duster, while likewise blaming campus racial problems on "the mood in the country" more explicitly blamed a "conservative era," in which "Reagan has made racism a more legitimate thing."[173] Similar views have been echoed by many others, including Professor Philip G. Altbach of the State University of New York at Buffalo, who said that "the racial crisis on campus is very much a part of the legacy of Reaganism."[174] But Massachusetts has never been Reagan country and the problems plaguing liberal or radical institutions like Berkeley or the University of Massachusetts have seldom erupted on more conservative campuses.

Very conservative Pepperdine University, for example, has a higher percentage of non-white students than the more liberal or radical University of Massachusetts[175]—and yet it is U. Mass which has had headline-making racial violence. The conservative University of Oklahoma, with a predominantly white undergraduate student body, elected a black woman president of the student body by a majority vote—which is to say, a larger vote than that received by the three other candidates combined.[176] At a time when black students at many liberal Northern campuses express alienation and dissatisfaction, and engage in self-segregation, a college admissions counselor visiting conservative Rhodes College in Memphis found the black students on that Southern campus expressing feelings of being part of the campus community.[177] While this evidence is suggestive rather than decisive, the larger point is that the very concept of evidence is not applied by those who repeat the academic dogma that racial polarization is caused by conservatism, wholly ignoring the possibility that this polarization may be a backlash against double standards promoted by liberals and radicals.

The argument is often made that what really angers white students is the loss of coveted places in elite colleges to black and other minorities, and their consequent loss of numerical predominance or "cultural hegemony"[178] on various campuses, as the numbers of minority students has increased. But, although this theory is often asserted, it is almost never tested empirically. For example, on many elite campuses, Asian students often substantially outnumber black students and are a significant percentage of the total student body, without provoking nearly as much hostility or violence as that directed against blacks, Hispanics, and others who are admitted under double standards—and who are permitted double standards of behavior.

Asian students outnumber blacks at seven of the eight Ivy League colleges and on all nine campuses of the University of California, as well as at Stanford, Case Western Reserve, Union College, Haverford, Davidson College, Franklin & Marshall, the Illinois Insitute of Technology, Lehigh University, and Whitman College, among other places. They outnumber black, Hispanic, and American Indian students—put together—at Cal Tech, the University of Chicago, Harvey Mudd College, Renssealaer Polytechnic, Cooper Union, the Rose-Hulman Institute, and Worcester Polytechnic. Asians are more than 20 percent of the student body at more than a dozen institutions.[179]

Why does this large-scale taking of places from whites not provoke the same reactions against Asians as against other nonwhites? As an old song said: "It ain't what you do, it's the way that you do it." Asians have done it by outperforming whites. A white student at San Jose State University expressed the different reactions to the two kinds of minority admissions:

> Just because 150 years ago some people were treated poorly doesn't mean I have to repay their descendents. Simply because I'm white, should somebody who's not white get my slot?
>
> I think it stinks. The Asian with a better grade point average—that person should have that slot.[180]

Neither Asians nor Jews have been wholly immune to all forms of student resentment and Asians have been adversely affected to some extent, like the Jews, in the racial backlash and polarization which has struck many campuses. It has been a common pattern in a number of countries, and in various periods of history, that heightened group hostility between groups *A* and *B* also adversely affects attitudes toward groups *C*, *D*, and *E*—who have nothing to do with the strife between *A* and *B*. Increased group chauvinism is a threat to everyone. Nevertheless, Asians have seldom been targets of outright violence, even on campuses where they are a large presence. If whites' real resentments were over a loss of slots or a loss of "cultural hegemony," the Asians would be their prime targets on elite campuses across the country.

On any of these issues revolving around the "new racism," people might differ and argue—but they almost never do in academia. Views contrary to the prevailing ideology are simply not mentioned, much less debated. That is the essence of the dogmatism which makes any solution, or even improvement, in the campus racial scene unlikely for many years to come.

The obviously self-serving nature of the usual administrative responses to racial incidents—free speech restrictions, making ethnic studies courses mandatory, larger quotas for minority students and faculty—provide an impetus to new and ever-escalating rounds of double standards and racial backlash. Where will this self-reinforcing spiral end? In other countries, group preferences and quotas in higher education have led to widespread bloodshed (as in India) or to outright civil war (as in Sri Lanka). The growing evidences of racial hostililty and sporadic outbreaks of violence which we in the United States call "the new racism" may be an early warning that we are heading in the same direction as other countries which have promoted preferences and quotas longer and more strongly. But the prevailing dogmatism among academics suggests that the real meaning of these early warnings may not be understood until long after it is too late.

CHAPTER 7

Ideological Double Standards

RACIAL DOUBLE STANDARDS are not the only double standards pervading the elite colleges and much of the academic world. So many decisions have been dominated by ideology rather than principle that the term "politically correct" has arisen to describe these double standards. It has become such a familiar term among academics that it is often abbreviated as "P.C." A comic strip character named "politically correct person" appears in Brown University's student newspaper, dressed like Superman but with "P.C." rather than "S" on his costume.

Students, for example, may go unpunished for major violations of campus rules, including disruptions and violence, if these actions were undertaken to forward some ideological agenda currently in favor among academics. But mere infringements, or even inadvertent actions construed as infringements, may be very severely punished, up to and including suspension or expulsion, when those accused are ideologically out of step. Sometimes it is not the purpose but the group from which the offender comes which is crucial in defining what is "politically correct." Homosexuals, ethnic minorities, radical feminists, Marxists, and environmentalists are among those likely to be

174

forgiven their transgressions, or even praised for the "idealism" behind them, but no such leniency can be expected for those whose ideals are conservativism, especially if they fall in the suspect category "white males."

Many invited speakers have been prevented from speaking at Harvard by disruption and violence, and the university has either done nothing at all or has given only the most nominal punishment—when the disrupters were "politically correct" and the speaker was not. Such conservative figures as Caspar Weinberger, the Reverend Jerry Falwell, Contra leaders, and others have been disrupted and assaulted with impunity at Harvard by radical students.[1] In one episode, the speaker—Contra leader Aldolfo Calero—was ready to resume his talk after having been physically assaulted, but was prevented from doing so by Harvard University authorities. One rationalization for this surrender to the opponents of Calero was that there was now "a solidly conservative audience" remaining in the lecture hall, which would create the impression that the sponsors "were trying to exclude liberals."[2] The impression that free speech was being excluded was apparently less troubling to those who wanted to be "politically correct," or to practice the administrative tactic of pre-emptive surrender to those who were.

In the wake of demands that Harvard protect speakers and /or punish disruptors, Dean of the Faculty of Arts & Sciences A. Michael Spence said: "We rely on basic human decency as the ultimate corrective mechanism to insure freedom of speech."[3] Dean Spence has in fact suggested limiting the number of controversial speakers, in order to reduce security costs.[4] Since the only speakers who are "controversial" at Harvard, in the sense of being likely to be disrupted or assaulted, are those who arouse the wrath of the political left, this too was "politically correct." Such concern for frugality was not apparent, however, when one of the leftist causes—divestment in South Africa—was involved. As the *Harvard Salient* reported:

> When divestiture protesters illegally erected shanties in Harvard Yard last spring and refused to dismantle them when the University asked them to do so, the administration spent thousands of dollars every week to give them a twenty-four

hour police guard; the college even ran an electrical line out to the shanties to enable the protesters to use their televisions and lamps while they lived in symbolic poverty.[5]

Double standards are the essence of political correctness. Harvard has not been unique, but in fact all too typical of elite institutions, in permitting the politically correct to use storm trooper tactics against the politically incorrect. Ambassador Jeane Kirkpatrick has been driven off the stage at Berkeley by disrupters shouting and throwing objects—and has been similarly disrupted at the University of Wisconsin, the University of Washington, and other institutions. Former Black Panther leader Eldridge Cleaver, once welcome on campuses across the country during his radical days, has now turned against the left after living in countries with left-wing dictatorships—and has been prevented from speaking by disrupters at Berkeley, Wisconsin, and Minnesota. Other speakers opposed to the prevailing leftism on campus have likewise been shouted down or otherwise disrupted when trying to give talks at Columbia, Northwestern, U.C.L.A., Wisconsin, University of Colorado, and Wellesley, among other places.[6]

These are not merely the personal vicissitudes of particular speakers. These are systematic patterns of stifling free speech and preventing academic audiences from hearing anything which challenges the prevailing vision of the left currently monopolizing many elite colleges and universities. The problem is not that most professors are politically on the left, but that alternative visions are kept off campus—by force if necessary—and that colleges and universities themselves are selectively permissive toward disrupters, though capable of dealing harshly with those who challenge (or even appear to challenge) the "politically correct" views.

Among professors, those holding "politically correct" views may turn their classrooms into indoctrination centers and staging areas for political activism, but those with different views may be accused of "insensitivity," "racism," or "sexism" on the basis of nothing more than a failure to use politically correct language—"Native American" rather than "American Indian"; "he or she," rather than the generic "he"—or a failure to include "issues of race, class, and gender" in their courses. No such squeamishness applies in the other ideological direction. As two retired faculty members report:

> Professors have felt free to call conservative students "Neanderthals." Feminist professors have felt free to call non-feminist females "Barbie dolls."[7]

At a more serious level, professors whose courses have deviated from "political correctness" have not only been made targets of campus smear campaigns based on innuendos, like Stephan Thernstrom at Harvard, or Reynolds Farley at Michigan,[8] but have sometimes even had their classrooms invaded by masses of outside students who prevented the enrolled students from hearing the professor, as has happened at Berkeley.[9] In all these cases, no punishment was meted out to the students—and the rights of the professors and their enrolled students were not even verbally defended by college officials, who either maintained a discreet silence or else treated the professors as being under suspicion.

While the brainwashing in colleges and universities tends to be ideological rather than psychological, echoes of the psychological and social agendas from high school days may still be heard, including an anti-parent orientation and a "sex education" approach that focuses on attitude-changing more so than biological information. In short, what is "politically correct" encompasses the social, the ideological, the educational and the administrative.

SOCIAL AGENDAS

Social agendas on campuses across the country show double standards in a number of ways. For example, they attempt to reduce parental influence over the student in the name of individual autonomy, while violating that autonomy themselves with sustained attempts at indoctrination, buttressed by punishment for those who step out of line from the officially approved attitudes. One of the areas in which colleges and universities have the most consistently one-sided set of policies is in sexual attitudes and practices, all the while affecting a "non-judgmental" posture. As with racial double standards,

those awarded preferential status based on their presumed vic-
timhood as homosexuals respond in ways which create new
polarization and hostility.

Parents

The attempt to downgrade the role of the parents of college
students begins even before those students set foot on campus.
High school counselors, college admissions directors, and others often try to reduce or eliminate the role of parents in influencing the decision as to which college the student chooses to
apply to or to attend. Once the freshman enters college, parents
are likely to hear once more how they should stay out of the
student's decisions, whether on choice of subject to major in
or matters of personal lifestyle. One of the guides for parents
whose children are going to college is called *Letting Go*. Cornell
University President Frank Rhodes says that parents should
"stand back; don't push."[10] The admissions director at the College of William & Mary advises parents to "overcome the protective urge."[11] "Stop meddling" is the more blunt advice of
the director of admissions of New College of the University of
South Florida.[12]

Much of this kind of advice is ostensibly based on the college
student's need for autonomy and respect. Obviously, these are
legitimate concerns and there is no single answer as to how far
parents should go in these matters. Unfortunately, all sorts of
activists with their own ideological agendas, including administrators and professors, show little or no regard for students'
autonomy or need for respect. Parents who heed the constant
drumbeat of advice to get out of the picture are only making
it easier for others to get into the picture, with their own special
agendas.

Sex

Nothing perhaps illustrated the calibre of people promoting
avant-garde social agendas on campus as an episode at Stanford
University in 1986, when Dr. Ruth Westheimer gave a talk
there. "Dr. Ruth," famous as a free-wheeling sex counselor in

the media, is regarded as daring by many but she was not nearly radical enough for Stanford. When asked if it was all right for a girl to get undressed and engage in sexual preliminaries with a boy—and then decide to say "no," Dr. Ruth replied:

> If there is foreplay and there is passion—for somebody who does not want to engage in sexual activity, then to play like this with fire is just not fair and right.[13]

This statement immediately set off a storm of controversy which began with a counter-attack by Alice Supton, Stanford's Assistant Dean of Student Affairs, and which continued for a week afterwards in the pages of the college newspaper, *The Stanford Daily*. Ms. Supton criticized Dr. Ruth, both at the lecture and later in print, on grounds that women have the right to refuse "at any point along the path of sexual intimacy."[14]

Dr. Ruth was accused by a campus radical group of teaching the "acceptability of date rape."[15] The coordinator of Stanford's Date Rape Education Project found Dr. Ruth's statement "infuriating"[16] and said that "Dr. Ruth is essentially denying a person the right to say no."[17] Dr. Ruth's view was depicted as a "blame-the-victim" mentality which "perpetuates the myth that everyone who engages in foreplay really wants to have sex," so that "Dr. Ruth is guilty of unfairly portraying women who say 'no' as teases."[18] One man who identified himself as a "proud advocate of feminist values" declared himself "outraged at Dr. Ruth's Victorian attitude and chauvinistic advice," which "undermines all the important gains of the feminist movement."[19]

Not everyone at Stanford shared those views. There was applause from the audience when Dr. Ruth made her statement of plain common sense—a rare commodity at Stanford. Yet the letters printed in the *Stanford Daily* were overwhelmingly those supporting the radical feminist viewpoint. One of the few letters it published on the other side, by a young woman, said: "The best way to avoid date rape is not to pray that your date is someone noble, who manages to challenge all life's basic assumptions."[20] Another young woman pointed out the many programs of sexual incitement promoted by the university itself and the "150 to 300 unwanted pregnancies at Stanford each year."[21]

Assistant Dean Alice Supton has been prominent in promoting the idea of "getting in touch with your sexuality." However, she is not alone, either at Stanford or in the academic world in general. Expressing one's sexuality takes many forms. At Northwestern University's Women's Center, a picture prominently displayed in the living room is "an artistic rendering of the female genitalia."[22] At San Francisco State University, movies in one class showed humans having sex with animals.[23] More organized expressions of an *avant-garde* view of sex appear in so-called "sex education" material, routinely passed out to students as part of their normal registration for courses.

In college as in the public schools, so-called "sex education" is not so much a matter of conveying biological or medical information as it is a matter of *changing attitudes* toward sex—in an avant-garde direction. Stanford's sex education kit, for example, contains a booklet entitled "SAFE SEX EXPLORER'S ACTION PACKED STARTER KIT HANDBOOK," which says: "MUTUAL MASTURBATION IS GREAT—but watch out for cuts on hands or raw genitals."[24] Among its other advice:

USE CONDOMS FOR FUCKING: with several partners, ALWAYS CLEAN UP AND CHANGE RUBBERS BEFORE GOING FROM ONE PERSON TO ANOTHER![25]

These so-called "sex education" kits are passed out routinely to young students, away from home for the first time. It conveys not merely biological or medical information but a whole set of attitudes, fundamentally in conflict with the values with which many, if not most, of these students have been raised. Further challenges to these values are made through such things as Stanford's annual condom-testing contests, where students are urged to use various brands of condoms—supplied free—and then vote on which brands and types they found most enjoyable. An accompanying booklet says: "Try out the condoms by yourself, with a partner, or partners. Be creative! Have fun! Enjoy!"[26] Included is a ballot on which various brands and types of condoms are to be rated for various characteristics, including taste and smell. Condoms weeks are also common events on other campuses, such as Berkeley, San Jose State, Virginia Tech, and the universities of Iowa and North Carolina.[27]

Like Stanford's sex-education kit, condoms are routinely

distributed to students—in this case, by The Stanford AIDS Education Project. To the outside world, the name suggests an organization trying to fight a deadly disease. In reality it is an attitude-shaping effort, under a lofty title, and whether it is likely to increase or decrease the incidence of AIDS is very problematical. Nor is Stanford unique in using AIDS-prevention as a cover for attitude-changing material. At the University of Puget Sound, the Northwest AIDS Foundation took out a full page ad in the student newspaper, showing two cartoon individuals, with little hearts around them, and the message:

> WHEN IT CAME TO SAFE SEX, I THOUGHT HE'D BE LIKE ALL THE REST.....QUICK, BORING AND THEN LONG GONE. HOW COULD I HAVE KNOWN THAT HE HAD BEEN TO THE WORKSHOP? HOW COULD I HAVE KNOWN HE WAS ABOUT TO GIVE ME THE MOST SEARINGLY ROMANTIC NIGHT OF MY LIFE? AND HOW COULD I HAVE KNOWN HE WOULD WANT TO STAY? HE GAVE ME. . . . A DOZEN RED CONDOMS.[28]

Dartmouth's sex education kit has an accompanying form letter, saying that its booklet is "educational," that it "is not intended to moralize or be judgemental," but the actual contents of the booklet are in fact promotional, in the sense of favoring a particular set of attitudes, very much like those promoted in high school "sex education" courses. For example, sex is a matter of "how you feel" and it is a decision "too important and personal" to let "someone else" decide for you. It is all a matter of "your feelings and expectations" and sexual relationships "can be heterosexual or they can be homosexual." You might "clarify your feelings by talking to friends," but parents are not included in the list of people who have any clarification to contribute.[29] Only after a sexual relationship turns out to be "devastating," are parents included among those to whom one might turn for emotional support.[30]

Any "negative" attention to homosexuality can only be due to "prejudice and hostility," according to this Dartmouth pamphlet. Any "derogatory terms" are to be avoided and the "acceptable name" of "gay" used. Although homosexuality was once considered an illness, "the American Psychological Association no longer considers it a mental disorder."[31] This last statement is misleading because it neglects to mention that this change did not result from any new scientific evidence, but from a threat by homosexuals to disrupt the American

Psychological Association's meetings, when they were held in San Francisco.[32] But whatever the merits or demerits of the pamphlet's reasoning or conclusions, it is clearly a brief in favor of a particular attitude—despite its "non-judgemental" claims.

Being non-judgmental in one direction is part of the double standards surrounding the "politically correct" social agenda on many campuses. For example, homosexuals are free to publicly proclaim the merits of their lifestyle, as they see it, but anyone who publicly proclaims the demerits of that lifestyle, as he sees it, is subject to serious punishment. At Yale University, for example, "Gay and Lesbian Awareness Days" have been an annual event celebrating homosexuality. A sophomore with different views put up posters parodying the homosexuals' posters. For this alone, he was suspended for two years. The dean of Yale's own law school called the decision "outrageous."[33] In the face of this and other outcries, Yale reduced the punishment to probation—with a warning that anything like this again would mean expulsion.

At Harvard, a freshman named Samuel Burke inadvertently got into trouble in December 1985, merely trying to help some strangers find a table on which to eat lunch in a crowded dining room. Spotting an empty table, he removed a sign that read: "Reserved HRGLSA," and invited them to sit there. It turned out that those initials stood for the Harvard Radcliffe Gay and Lesbian Students Association—which made this an ideological offense against one of the "in" groups. Sam Burke was taken to the Freshman Dean's Office. According to the *Harvard Salient*, a student publication:

> Sam offered to apologize publicly to the GLSA for his thoughtless act. But according to friends, he was nonetheless pushed to the brink of tears by the official inquisitors who questioned his motives at every turn and threatened him with severe punishment.

Heavy pressure on this young man, at an institution where deliberate disruption and even violence have repeatedly gone unpunished, was all the more remarkable because the Freshman Dean's Office knew that Samuel Burke was already burdened with personal problems. A high school football star, he had just been told by a physician that he could not play football in college. Moreover, his father had recently been killed in an automobile accident. But no humane considerations tempered the zeal of those determined to do the politically correct thing. Sam Burke was hit with disciplinary probation just before the Christmas holidays.

He did not return from the holidays. He committed suicide.[34]

Being "politically correct" means deciding issues not on the basis of the evidence or the merits, but on the basis of what group those involved belong to or what ideology they profess. Many colleges and universities have become blind partisans with no sense of proportion, or principle, or of fairness. Objections to the special privileges which are created for some groups in the name of equal rights are treated as betraying malign attitudes toward those groups—"racism" or "homophobia," for example—which are to be rooted out by "re-education" campaigns and punished severely where brainwashing fails.

As regards homosexuals, almost never is the issue one of whether they should be left in peace to live as they wish. Much more often, the issue is whether others must be subjected to a steady drumbeat of strident propaganda by gay activists. As a group of students at the University of Massachusetts said in a jointly signed statement in the student newspaper:

> I am not homophobic and I do not endorse homosexuality but I accept it. I am just tired of having the issue continually in my classrooms, in my paper, in my building, on my campus.[35]

A Wesleyan University student reported a similar situation there:

> It is nearly impossible to enter the campus center without being inundated by propaganda about gay men, lesbian women, and bisexuals.[36]

"Re-education" is a common punishment for those judged guilty of such ideological crimes as "homophobia." At the University of Vermont, a fraternity which rescinded an invitation to a pledge when they learned that he was homosexual, had among its punishments attendance at workshops and lectures against "homophobia."[37] Homosexuals are only one of a number of special groups about whom students are no longer free to have their own opinions, nor are free to choose not to associate, even though such groups remain free to be as separatist and exclusive as they wish.

When one of the ordinary frictions of human life happens to involve a member of one of these special groups, such incidents are immediately inflated into a *cause célèbre*, even when there is no clear or present danger of any larger problem on campus. A homosexual student at Amherst College admitted to the student newspaper "that he had not experienced any other forms of hostility while at Amherst beyond 'a look that said stay away from me.' "[38] Yet he expressed fear of homophobic violence because one student had written anti-homosexual words on the door of two other gay students. Both the administration and the campus gay organization made a public issue about this one incident and the student newspaper made it a front page story.

This hypersensitivity to their own interests has not led homosexual activists to be at all sensitive as to the rights or feelings of others. On the contrary, intolerance by vocal activists has become as common among homosexuals as among other groups given special privileges on campus. Lesbians at Mount Holyoke College objected to a campus lecture by James Meredith, the first black man to attend the University of Mississippi, because he was promoting the traditional family.[39] As with other intolerant people, disagreement did not imply debate but suppression. For themselves, however, Mount Holyoke's organized lesbians claimed not only freedom but license, chalking up the sidewalks with slogans like "lesbians make great lovers" and "try it—you'll like it."[40] At Cornell likewise, homosexuals have chalked up the sidewalks with slogans like "Sodomy sucks but we can lick the problem" and have removed the American flag from a university building, replacing it with a flag containing a pink triangle, the symbol of homosexuality. Although campus security people were present, the chalkers were neither stopped nor punished.[41] At Harvard, pictures of individuals engaged in homosexual acts were posted all around campus by a homosexual organization.[42]

Disregard of the feelings of others extends far beyond words or pictures. Students who use the men's toilets on some campuses encounter sexual solicitations from homosexuals, or become unwilling witnesses to the homosexual activities of others. College toilets have become sites for homosexual activities to such an extent that a book of favorite places around the country for such gay encounters has been published and updated annually. It lists three buildings at Georgetown University, for example, as well as libraries at Howard University, the University of Maryland, and Catholic University, and the student center at George Washington University. Homosexuals from off-campus can often gain access to these places to meet young male students.[43]

At the University of Florida, middle-aged gay men from as far as 40 miles away are among those who gather in a college library toilet for "oral, anal or hand sex." So-called "glory holes" have been drilled in the panels between toilet stalls there, to facilitate anonymous homosexual acts. Maintenance workers have had to line these panels with stainless steel to prevent these holes from being drilled again after they have been closed up.[44] Dartmouth, Georgetown, and the University of California at San Diego have also had to seal up "glory holes" drilled in the panels separating toilet stalls.[45] Numerous complaints about homosexuals soliciting sex in the men's toilet at a library at San Jose State University led to the arrest of two men—one of whom was a professor at the university.[46]

While some academic institutions take some precautions against the worst excesses of homosexuals' publicly forcing their activities into the lives of other people, other institutions actually promote the introduction of homosexuality as a subject to be brought to the attention of students. At Stanford, the university has explicitly advertised for homosexuals for the job of resident advisers in the student dormitories. *The Stanford Daily* of March 7, 1990 carried an advertisement from the Office of Residential Education which said: "Because a residence staff which includes lesbian and gay RAs helps to raise discussions about sexuality and sexual orientation and works to combat homophobia at Stanford, gay and lesbian students are encouraged to consider applying for RA positions".[47] These "discussions," incidentally, can hardly be free exchanges of ideas, since those who oppose homosexuality are subject to punishment under restrictions against "harassment"—very loosely interpreted. In short, dormitories are to become "re-education" camps.

While mere words of criticism of homosexuality are enough to put students in jeopardy of punishment at Stanford—and at many other institutions—outright threats against the conservative *Stanford Review* by a homosexual university employee not only went unpunished but even un-investigated, even though the editors of that publication supplied the name and university phone number of the employee in question.[48] Homosexuality is clearly one of those issues on which double standards are "politically correct."

Colleges and universities have often proclaimed that they are no longer in the business of regulating sexual behavior, or of acting *in loco parentis* in general. This is a half-truth, at best. Many of the colleges which have abandoned any control over the sexual activities of their students nevertheless require their students to live in the dormitories, regardless of how individual students or their parents feel about the behavior or atmosphere in those dormitories, and regardless of whether an eighteen-year-old away from home for the first time wants to sleep in a room with a stranger who has sexual interests in people like themselves, or in a room where other people are having sex. Moreover, colleges are actively promoting a particular set of attitudes toward sex.

One of the dormitories at Stanford University has a coed shower, for example, and the *Stanford Daily* of October 18, 1990, featured a front page photograph of four people of differing sex having a shower together. The resident assistant in another dormitory promoted a swap of room mates, so that male and female students could become room mates for a week, in order to demonstrate that people of opposite sex could share a room in a platonic relationship.[49] Another front page photograph, on the *Stanford Daily* of December 5, 1990, showed a male student holding a plastic model of a penis while a female student was putting a condom on it. They were fulfilling a requirement in a psychology course.[50]

Whatever the merits or demerits of any of these activities, they represent behavior actively promoted by institutional policy and institutional personnel. In short, many colleges are not following the hands-off policy they claim to be following. They are being permissive in one direction, and even inciting in one direction, but they are not permitting students who do not want to be part of the avant-garde scene to live in a single-sex dormitory, to live off-campus, or to refuse to sleep in a room with someone who is sexually attracted to people like themselves. Penn State University, for example, has made explicit what is only implicit on some other campuses—that objections to being housed with homosexual room mates will not result in room changes.[51] Georgetown University has punished a student for not attending what was billed as an "AIDS awareness" session in the dormitory, but which also included promotion of avant-garde sexual attitudes.[52]

The claim is that colleges are treating students as adults, when in fact they are treating them as guinea pigs. Moreover, it is precisely because students are so young, so inexperienced, and so vulnerable that they attract the attentions of brainwashers.

The vision of a brave new world of ultra-rational attitudes toward sex, which is promoted by advocates of the sexual revolution, is in painful contrast with soaring pregnancy and abortion statistics on many campuses across the country. At Brown University, for example, the campus health service reports about 40 to 50 pregnancies per academic year—slightly more than one a week—and virtually all of these end in abortions.[53] This rate is characterized as similar to the rate at comparable institutions "like the Ivies and other coeducational, non-religious schools." Stanford University has had more than a hundred positive tests for pregnancy annually, Auburn University two hundred and Indiana University several hundred. Moreover, not all pregnant students are tested on campus, so the total numbers of pregnancies may be even higher. U.C.L.A. and the University of Maryland are among the institutions reporting that at least 90 percent of their pregnancies end in abortion. Altogether, nearly one-third of all abortions in the country are performed on women in schools.[54]

Because pregnancies and abortions are so widespread on so many college campuses does not mean that they have little impact on the individuals involved. A young woman at Indiana State University, who became pregnant soon after she arrived as a freshman, recalled:

> I knew I had to tell my boyfriend. When I told him, he just started crying. We both cried.

After she had an abortion, the two of them split up:

—— couldn't take it. I can't say that I blame him. He carried a lot of guilt, and my state of mind didn't help much. He needed to try to forgive himself and have me forgive him, but I couldn't even forgive myself. All I could do was cry about it.[55]

At this stage, those activists who promote the adventurous spirit of the sexual revolution are seldom involved anymore.

IDEOLOGICAL AGENDAS

The mere fact that professors, administrators, or students may have their own individual ideologies, or even that a particular ideology may be dominant in any or all of these groups, does not in itself mean that an institution has an ideological agenda or "politically correct" double standards. One of the early arguments for academic freedom was that what professors believed or did as private individuals should not be a basis for firing them, so long as they did their jobs competently, and did not use the classroom to indoctrinate students. Today, not only the classroom but also the dormitories, administrative committees, and the platform for invited speakers are all used to express the prevailing ideologies and to stifle opposing views. An editorial in the student newspaper at the University of Virginia complained of "being force-fed an endless stream of so-called 'awareness days' that emphasize differences rather than commonality."[56] Often the ideological agenda includes not only propaganda barrages but also double standards when dealing with those who agree and those who disagree.

Campus Discipline

Ideological double standards in punishing students or faculty for violations of campus rules are apparent not only in individual instances of injustice, or even in the pattern of such injustices, but also in the very nature of the rules themselves. Orwellian use of the word "harassment" to cover situations in which no one approached, addressed, or even noticed the supposed target of this "harassment" has enabled colleges and universities to punish behavior to which the only real objection is ideological. At Tufts University, for example, a young man who wore a T-shirt listing "15 Reasons Why Beer is Better than Women at Tufts" was punished for *harassing* women by the mere wearing of such a T-shirt.[57] But nothing that feminists (or racial or ethnic minorities) put on a T-shirt is likely to get them punished for harassment, either at Tufts or elsewhere. At Northwestern University, for example, a T-shirt being sold in a campus cafeteria showed a gun-wielding black militant and the caption: "By Any Means Necessary." The back of the T-shirt read: "It's a Black Thing. You wouldn't Understand."[58]

While examples of ideological double standards in punishing—or judging—misbehavior can be found from coast to coast, some of the most egregious examples have occurred at Dartmouth College. For example, in 1982 a black professor whose course was criticized in the *Dartmouth Review* (which has also panned numerous white professors' courses) went to the dormitory where the student-writer lived and—at 8:30 A.M.—shouted obscenities outside her door, returning at 10:30 to attempt to force the door open. It so happened that the student who wrote the criticisms was not there, but her roommate was—and was in tears. The professor received only an official reprimand from the Dean of Faculty, who said: "I don't know what it's like to be a black man. He's obviously under emotional stress."[59]

Three years earlier, Dartmouth reacted far more strongly to an episode which many would consider relatively innocuous. At the end of half-time in a hockey game, three white students, dressed in American Indian regalia, skated out onto the ice— to the cheers of the Dartmouth crowd, which rose to sing the Alma Mater. As soon as these students' identities became known, they were abruptly suspended from the college. Their crime was ideological. Their actions implicitly challenged the "politically correct" view that Dartmouth's long tradition of calling its athletic teams "Indians" was wrong and racist. Although the team name had been changed, the hockey crowd's emotional response to the old traditional symbol of the school provoked an angry reaction in the Dartmouth administration and among the politically activist elements on campus. All classes were cancelled, being replaced by campus speeches and declarations against "racism" and other related and unrelated topics of an ideological nature.

Although efforts by the campus police to discover the identity of the "Indian" skaters had failed, the students voluntarily came forward to identify themselves, and at least one apologized for any offense. Nevertheless they were suspended, with just one week left in the term—which meant that they received no credit for all their academic work that term and received no refund of their tuition.[60] Only after outcries from alumni, some of whom began raising money to finance a lawsuit against the college, did the administration relent. The new punishment, according to one of the students, was: "I have been ordered to conduct public seminars, whenever I can get students to listen, about the evil of the Indian symbol. In addition, I've been commanded to take an Indian to lunch once a week for a year."[61] (Incidentally, no one considers it racist that Notre Dame's athletic teams are called "the fighting Irish" or that Hope College's teams are called "Dutchmen.")

Many of Dartmouth's double-standard episodes have involved students on the staff of the *Dartmouth Review*, a conservative publication located off campus and often referred to by its critics as "racist" and "sexist," though it has been run in various years by a black editor, a female editor, and editors from India—and its editorial policy has been consistently pro-Israel and critical when anti-Semitic speakers have been invited on campus. "Politically correct" epithets are intended to perform the political task of discrediting, rather than the cognitive task of achieving accuracy. Yet even *Rolling Stone* magazine, hardly a conservative publication, reported on the cameraderie among the multi-racial, multi-national staff of the *Dartmouth Review*, "co-existing in the kind of casual harmony liberals yearn for."[62]

Before the first issue of the *Dartmouth Review* was published, its editors were threatened with a lawsuit by the college's attorney if they used the word "Dartmouth" in their title.[63] The administration tried in various ways to prevent alumni from donating money to the publication.[64] A black administrator who physically assaulted a Dartmouth student who was distributing the *Dartmouth Review* on campus received only a short suspension—with pay—and the faculty voted 113 to 5 to censure the student, rather than the administrator, even though it was the latter who was fined in a court of law.[65]

A *Dartmouth Review* editor who published information marked "cleared for release" by the College News Service was nevertheless disciplined because the release proved embarrassing to the medical school.[66] A *Dartmouth Review* reporter was suspended from the college on a charge of plagiarism in 1990, on the unsupported suspicions of a left-wing professor, with no citation of any writing from which his essay was supposed to have been plagiarized. The professor herself said: "I just have a general feeling that the writing was beyond his ability . . . I don't have sufficient evidence to prove or disprove my accusation."[67] While his essay was generally well written and well reasoned, it was nothing beyond the range of a bright undergraduate,[68] and was certainly not beyond the range of the particular student who wrote it—a young man who achieved a perfect score on his advanced placement English examination.[69] Yet, on the basis of unsupported speculation, he was not only suspended but given a record that will follow him for life, as a violator of the honor code—a cheat.

When word of this episode received national media attention, the waters became muddied, as the Dartmouth administration pulled back somewhat and offered a compromise to the suspended student, who was anxious to resume his education. Their proviso was that he agree not to sue. The original claim of plagiarism was changed to the more nebulous charge of failing to cite sources properly, and the two-term suspension was reduced to a one-term suspension in a negotiated settlement.[70] That a freshman at Dartmouth, in his first semester of college, may have failed to cite sources is hardly plagiarism. That he should have been punished more severely—and more indelibly—than others who committed disruptions and even violence is precisely what is meant by the ideological double standards known as political correctness.

An even more severe permanent punishment was inflicted on a Stanford graduate student named Steven Mosher, who was not even on campus when he committed his violation of political correctness. Like many graduate students who have completed their course work, Mosher was no longer in residence but was pursuing other activities elsewhere, pending the writing of his doctoral dissertation in anthropology. Elsewhere in this case was China, which had only recently agreed to allow some American scholars into the country.

After his stay in China, Mosher shocked much of the world by revealing that country's widespread compulsory birth control program, including compulsory abortions, imposed on Chinese women by the Communist government. His book, *Broken Earth*, became a best-seller and helped shatter the rosy picture of Maoist China being promoted by many Western intellectuals on the left, including academics on American college campuses. In addition to rubbing Stanford's left-wing anthropology department the wrong way ideologically, Mosher's book also jeopardized the newly available access of American research scholars to China. Chinese government officials wrote to Stanford, denouncing Mosher's activities in China.

Steven Mosher was terminated as a graduate student from Stanford, prevented from earning the Ph.D. which plays such a crucial role in an academic career. As with so many other punishments inflicted on those who have violated political correctness, the basis for Mosher's expulsion was left vague and inconsistent. Not one stated requirement for the doctorate in anthropology was even claimed to have been violated, nor the facts in his book challenged. Instead, criteria of personal behavior were created *ex post* as a reason why the department "could not certify you as an anthropologist," even if the remaining academic requirements of a doctoral dissertation were met.[71]

These new personal behavior criteria included "responsibility for the welfare of those he is studying" and a "professional imperative for sensitivity to others." Moreover, these nebulous personal behavior standards were repeatedly and insistently depicted by Stanford University's President Donald Kennedy as *professional* criteria in anthropology, rather than university rules about personal conduct[72]—for the latter have due process protections which Mosher was never accorded. Instead, Mosher was given one hour in which to make his case and denied the presence of his attorney, on grounds that "presence of counsel would make for an adversarial confrontation rather than informative colloquy"[73]—even though this "informative colloquy" could ruin his whole professional career.

To complete the Alice-in-Wonderland reasoning, Mosher was repeatedly denounced by Kennedy for "lack of candor"[74] because Mosher's letters to his professors did not reveal many aspects of his personal life in China, nor his misadventures with the Communist authorities there, as he sought out information that they did not want him to have. Yet there were neither university rules nor departmental Ph.D. requirements that he write to his professors at all, much less that he detail his relations with the opposite sex,[75] his legal difficulties with the Communist authorities,[76] the informal favors he did to gain access to the information he wanted,[77] or his payment to a local Chinese man to drive him into areas which both knew to be off-limits.[78] Yet failure to adequately disclose these things were among the key reasons given for expelling him from Stanford's Ph.D. program.

President Donald Kennedy waxed indignant that "Mosher was not candid about the very relevant fact that he and the 'translator' are now married,"[79] that he "failed to mention" his arrest in China "until directly asked,"[80] and cited Mosher's "possible dissimulation to the Chinese officials," as part of a picture of "manipulativeness and lack of candor."[81] Even if every charge and every interpretation in the thousands of words in Kennedy's official decision were 100 percent correct, there would still not be a single violation of the existing rules for receiving a Ph.D. in anthropology at Stanford.

Of all the many campus injustices across the country, what happened to Steven Mosher was the academic Dreyfus case of our time. But there was no Émile Zola to write "J'Accuse." A man who attacked both Communism and birth control was obviously not "politically correct" and so could expect few defenders.

While some individuals receive favorable treatment on college and university campuses because of their race or sex, it is not simply the biological category to which one belongs but the ideological category that is crucial. An Asian American woman at the University of Connecticut, for example, was severely punished for violating an ideological taboo. A sign on the door to her dormitory room listed "people who are shot on sight," including "preppies," "bimbos," and "homos." After gay rights activists complained, she was ordered to move out of the dormitory and off campus, and was forbidden to set foot in any dormitory or college cafeteria—in other words, she was sentenced to virtually total social isolation. Only under threat of a federal lawsuit did the university later allow her to move back on campus.[82]

Even matters involving the physical safety of students and faculty can be determined by ideological double standards. Dartmouth College has hired forensic experts to try to trace anonymous, abusive letters to feminists and blacks, but it took no action when one of its professors received death threats because he co-sponsored a speaker (on the sinking of the *Titanic*) with the *Dartmouth Review*. Nor was the Dartmouth administration interested when a black writer on that newspaper was threatened, even though he had faculty witnesses and named the other black students from the Afro-American Society who had threatened him. There was a similar disinterest when members of the same society threatened another black student, even though he is handicapped and in a wheelchair.[83]

It is hard to know how much of the ideological double standards found on college campuses reflects the ideologies of the administrators themselves and how much is a pragmatic caving in to vocal ideologues among the students and faculty, or a pre-emptive surrender to their presumed desires. The swiftness with which administrators have sometimes reversed themselves when counter-pressure was applied suggests that they still have that "versatility of convictions"[84] with which Thorstein Veblen credited them long ago.

During the Persian Gulf war of 1991, for example, officials of the University of Maryland made students take down displays of the American flag and other signs of support for the U.S. war effort in the Middle East. "We have a big population to be sensitive to," one administrator explained, while another said, "what may be innocent to one person may be insulting to another." Yet when the story made front page headlines in the student newspaper and also appeared in the *Washington Post*, the administration quickly reversed itself and declared that it "strongly supports" such displays "as expressions of freedom of speech."[85] A very similar episode occurred at Cornell University, where students were threatened with expulsion if they did not remove their American flags and yellow ribbons from their windows during the Gulf War. Again, the administration backed down only after the story reached the media.[86]

Student Fees as Political Subsidies

One of the most remarkable symptoms of the politicization and partisanship of academic institutions has been the widespread practice of automatically deducting part of students' fees to be turned over to off-campus organizations promoting the ideological views associated with Ralph Nader. Called Public Interest Research Groups (PIRGs), these organizations exist in states across the country, as CalPIRG in California, MassPIRG in Massachusetts, ConnPIRG in Connecticut, and with similar names in other states.

The sums of money deducted tend to be small individually—four dollars per semester for MassPIRG from each Wellesley student, six dollars for the Minnesota PIRG from each student at Carleton[87]—but even a small college like Wellesley has had more than $13,000 a year extracted involuntarily from its students for this ideological cause, while CalPIRG at one time collected automatically more than $52,000 annually from fees paid by students at the University of California at Santa Cruz, more than $57,000 from student fees at UCLA, more than $124,000 from Berkeley students, and more than $135,000 from fees paid by students at the University of California at Santa Barbara.[88]

With substantial sums of money being extracted from students on many campuses from coast to coast, whether at private institutions like Tufts or on the multiple campuses of the University of Minnesota and other state institutions, a very large amount of money is being funneled into a political movement through a privately levied tax, rather than through voluntary donations. PIRGs are unique in having this privilege.

Defenders of this extraordinary arrangement claim that the donations are "voluntary" because each student has a legal right to demand a refund of his own contribution and the campus has collectively voted to establish such a check-off system. Both claims are shaky, however. Students and parents who receive college bills totaling thousands of dollars may or may not check every item costing a few dollars. Moreover, getting a refund is not always quite as easy as PIRG advocates claim.

Defenders of MPIRG at Carleton College said that "each student has the opportunity to have their money refunded during the fiscal refund period of each year."[89] But this means that only those who act within a given span of time can retrieve their money. When CalPIRGs operated at the University of California at Santa Cruz, each student had to hand-deliver his request for a refund in writing to the organization or to the college registrar.[90] At Carleton College, according to a critic of the Minnesota PIRG, each student must either "contact the business office directly or request a refund from MPIRG at the very beginning of each year or term from MPIRG."[92] At Wellesley, the waiver is not sent out with every bill.[92]

Claims of being democratic are likewise suspect. One class' vote can bind subsequent classes to pay, through an automatic check-off, and small voter turnout allows the organized PIRG supporters to carry the day with much less than a majority of the student body. At Wellesley, for example, only 37 percent of the students voted on the issue in 1987 and only 19 percent favored such a system—but these 19 percent were a "majority," whose votes bound not only its own class but subsequent classes as well,[93] until a 1989 vote narrowly overturned this system.[94] MassPIRG's defeat at Wellesley was all the more remarkable because its supporters mounted a major campaign to maintain its privileged position and the ballot proposition was so worded as to suggest that the issue was whether the organization could continue to exist on campus. A separate question as to whether *any* student organization should "have the right to have a line item on the tuition bill/comprehensive fee bill" received a resounding rejection by a vote of nearly three to one.[95] Getting the automatic "contributions" to PIRGs stopped on other campuses has likewise been an arduous process. In California, it took an act of the university regents in September 1990 to end the practice on the various University of California campuses.[96] At Rutgers University, it took a lawsuit to stop the local PIRG from continuing to collect hundreds of thousands of dollars from the various campuses of that state university.[97] The automatic check-off still remains in place on many other campuses.

That such a system of commandeering students' money (for a cause which they might not support voluntarily) should have been instituted in the first place speaks volumes about the academic mindset and its ideological double standards. Other organizations are permitted no such direct levy on students and it is unthinkable that any such arrangement would even be considered for organizations with opposing views.

"Residential Education"

Traditional college dormitories have in recent years been subtly transformed into places where organized indoctrination efforts have become routine, under the title "residential education." These indoctrination efforts may be frequent or sporadic, subtle or heavy-handed, depending largely on the style and zeal of the resident adviser or resident assistant. At Stanford, where there is a "department of residential education," one of the resident assistants said: "I tried soft sells like putting up cartoons of episodes in African-American history in the bathroom stalls, but some people complained, 'I can't escape this multiculturalism stuff anywhere.' " The same RA admitted "often frosh told me, 'I'm so sick and tired of multiculturalism.' "[98]

Stanford's "residential education" program has expanded to the graduate level, creating a multicultural theme house for graduate students—whether they want it or not. Despite the efforts of the resident assistant there and ten theme coordinators who organize "events such as multicultural film series, minority guest speakers and parties celebrating different cultures," the RA expressed disappointment at the "apathy" of the students. Only about 15 of the 115 graduate students in this house were active in the theme house's activities. He attributed this to the fact that their academic work "tends to drain their energy."[99] Considering the workload of Ph.D. students at a top-tier university, it is amazing that anyone would have sought to intrude ideological programs into their lives in the first place, but this is done not only at the multicultural theme house, but to a lesser degree in all of the other graduate dormitories as well.[100]

At Harvard, the minority affairs dean handpicked and assigned "designated race relations tutors" to each house to "monitor the racial atmosphere," report "violations of community," and "raise consciousness" among the students. She also engaged an outside "facilitator company" to conduct "house workshops" on racism. Among the material used in this consciousness-raising operation was a pamphlet which presumed students guilty of racism *a priori*. The pamphlet urged students to "accept the onion theory, that they will continue to peel away layers of their own racism for the rest of their lives." Even a "Back to the Fifties" party by dining-hall employees was denounced as "racism" by the minority affairs dean, on grounds that the 1950s were a racist decade.[101]

Like other fashions which begin at the most prestigious colleges and universities, "residential education" has spread across the country and down the academic pecking order. A student at the University of California at Santa Cruz reports: "Many dorms have begun to require residents to attend sensitivity workshops where students are taught the 'proper' beliefs regarding race, gender, and sexual preference."[102] A member of the board of regents at the University of Michigan reported receiving "many complaints from parents and students" about "indoctrination sessions" in the dormitories.[103]

At trendy colleges and universities, "multicultural diversity" is much more than simply "an appreciation of different cultures and values,"[104] as a devotee innocently characterized it. It is a whole elaborate set of beliefs and attitudes, covering everything from homosexuality to Western civilization. Moreover, these beliefs and attitudes are not simply part of the marketplace of ideas. They are institutionally imposed. Few things are as one-sided as so-called "diversity," which has a "politically correct" response to every issue. As Oberlin College president S. Frederick Starr put it, the word "diversity" has come to mean in practice "subscribing to a set of political views."[105] The dogmatism behind the concept was inadvertently captured by a headline on the front page of *The Chronicle of Higher Education*:

Racial Tensions Continue to Erupt on Campuses Despite Efforts to Promote Cultural Diversity

The very possibility that these "cultural diversity" efforts themselves may have contributed to the tensions was not mentioned anywhere in the accompanying story.

While the Stanford resident assistant who prided himself on his "soft sell" approach admitted that some other RA's were "overzealous,"[106] he did not reach the deeper question:

Why were there such cultural *Gauleiters* in the first place, and why were students' campus homes becoming re-education camps? Such brainwashing operations make a mockery of attempts to get parents out of their children's lives, on grounds that the latter's autonomy and self-development must be respected.

FRAUDULENT DEFENSES

In the face of bitter criticisms from around the country that double standards are being applied on campus, according to the ideological or biological group to which individuals belong, defenders of the prevailing practices have repeatedly chosen to ignore this charge completely, and to reply instead with defenses of their own beliefs and social goals.

Thus, a dean at Rutgers defends those accused of political correctness as people whose goal is "bringing about change"— as if there has ever been a time in the history of the world when change was not going on. Generic "change" has never been an issue. Only specifics are an issue, and a flight into vague generalities is an evasion of issues. Professors interviewed by *The Chronicle of Higher Education* denounced the term "politically correct" as an "epithet to discredit new policies meant to make campuses more hospitable to women and minority groups."[107] In other words, it is all a question of different intentions. *The Stanford Daily* likewise posed the issue in terms of "the goals of the progressive movement."[108]

In addition to those who simply refuse to address the issue of double standards in the application of institutional rules and policies, there are others who deny that these transgressions are widespread. To Michael Kinsley of *The New Republic*, for example, "anti-PC diatribes" and "hysteria" are based on "suspect anecdotes."[109] Similar dismissals of charges as "vastly overblown" or as showing an "hysterical attitude" have appeared in *The Chronicle of Higher Education* and in *The New York Times*.[110] However, as to the sheer quantity of episodes, no book small enough to be hand-held could contain all the instances of institutional double standards in judging and punishing behavior, or even all the instances published in student newspapers across the country. Given the physical limitations on how much can be covered in one place, claims that "selective" examples have been used are misleading at best. More fundamentally, some episodes have implications that reach far beyond those directly involved, whether because of the grossness of these episodes, by the official sanctions they embody, or the clear, chilling message of intimidation that they convey.

When a college or university takes no official action against disruption and violence by some sets of students, while threatening, punishing, or expelling others for such non-violent behavior as flying an American flag during the Gulf War, skating out onto a hockey rink at half-time in costume, seating people at a reserved table, or turning in a paper without footnotes, then this sends an unmistakable message whose implications reach far beyond the particular individuals involved. Moreover, it is not just the particular episodes themselves, but the *institutionalized apparatus* which has been created to impose conformity on an on-going basis—the propaganda machines of "residential education," the "sensitivity" workshops for faculty and students, the whole industry of "diversity consultants," and the "speech codes" which claim to be protecting against gross insults,[111] but whose power to punish extends into the most nebulous areas. This use of imaginary horrors to acquire power to punish a wide range of behavior is not unlike the technique of bait-and-switch advertising.

This is not to say that there are no real horrors, but these are typically either violations of the law or are committed clandestinely, which is to say, beyond the reach of speech codes. What speech codes do is to create a vast penumbra of proscribed behavior, reaching far beyond the horror stories used to justify the codes. Often the horrors were amply covered by existing rules, as at Stanford University, where students could be expelled for failure to show "respect for order, morality, personal honor, and the rights of others"—*before* the new speech code prohibited any words or deeds which "stigmatize" anyone.[112] No one familiar with the double standards at Stanford seriously expects that anyone from any of the approved "victim" groups will ever be found to have "stigmatized" anyone else, while anyone who addresses or replies to what they say will have to walk on eggshells.

It is by no means clear that a negative editorial comment on such programs as "affirmative action" in the student newspaper would escape the ban on "stigmatizing" fellow students. At Vassar College, an editorial in a student newspaper brought charges of "political harassment." Since most of what is said in most editorials in most newspapers could be called "political harassment," this charge may seem to be merely silly. However, three students on the staff on *The Vassar Spectator* were forced to spend hours answering these charges in college hearings, held at a time when they needed to be preparing for their final examinations in their courses.[113] What will or will not lead to charges on a given campus with a vague speech code can only be determined *ex post*, and may well depend on what the accuser or the college administration thinks will fly politically. Nebulous speech codes are a hunting license for harassing those who are out of step ideologically. Nor is this merely a speculative possibility. Colleges and universities with a history of ideological double standards are precisely the ones most prone to have vague speech codes.

Being "politically correct" is *not* simply a matter of holding certain opinions on various social or educational issues. Political correctness is *imposing those opinions on others* by harassment or punishment for expressing different views. For example, the issue is not whether one prefers so-called "gender-neutral" language and chooses to use it—but whether students are to have their grades lowered by politically correct professors for saying "Congressman" rather than "Congressperson," or whether professors are to have their lectures repeatedly interrupted by politically correct students whenever the professor uses the generic "he" instead of saying "he or she." The issue is not whether there shall be "a curriculum that includes more works by women and members of minority groups,"[114] but whether readings shall be chosen by the physical characteristics of their authors rather than the intellectual qualities of the publications themselves—and whether those who don't have the right race and gender counts on their reading lists are going to be harassed. Group labeling of intellectual products is taken very seriously on many campuses today, though this represents something that has not been attempted in the Western world since Hitler distinguished "German physics" or "German mathematics" from their Jewish counterparts.

CHAPTER 8

Teaching and Preaching

> . . . the good professor is underpaid at any salary, while the
> poor professor is overpaid no matter what he receives.
> —Anonymous[1]

TEACHING AND LEARNING are at the heart of what most people think of as the function of a college or university, even if research or social engineering or other activities may preoccupy the faculty or the administration. There is almost always a favorable response when some president of a research university announces that there will now be a renewed emphasis on teaching,[2] however often such announcements have been made periodically in the past, without any visible changes following.

Complaints about teaching, especially the teaching of undergraduates, are legion. What is difficult is to sort out passing gripes from enduring and serious problems. What can be even more difficult is to know what to do about them, given that most of the usual panaceas are either unworkable or prohibitively costly. Some problems, however, are sufficiently gross that the only challenge they present is to the courage of administrators.

Teaching is both one of the hardest and one of the easiest jobs in the world, depending on how conscientiously it is done. It is also one of the noblest and one of the most corrupt occupations—again, depending on how it is done. Because of the greater freedom of professors, compared to school teachers, the sweep of the variations tends to be even more extreme in higher education. Few responsibilities weigh so heavily as the responsibility for the development of a young mind and few temptations are so corrupting as the temptation to take advantage of the trust, inexperience and vulnerability of students. Cheap popularity, ego trips, and ideological indoctrination are just some of the pitfalls of teaching. Where good teaching exists—and there is much of it in many kinds of institutions—this is not merely because the faculty are professionally competent but also because they have the character to resist the temptations inherent in a situation of large disparities in knowledge, experience, and power.

Some professors misuse their position (and their tenure) for everything from ideological indoctrination to obtaining sexual favors from students. One professor at Rutgers was accused of forcing two students to work in his garden and do household chores for him.[3] A Stanford professor committed suicide in the wake of accusations of sexually molesting the son of one of his graduate students—and he was posthumously honored by the university, which created an award in his name.[4] Most complaints about professors and other aspects of collegiate education are much more mundane, but the extremes give some sense of the lax environment within which professors operate.

COMMON COMPLAINTS

While various signs of student discontent with their education are widespread, both geographically and across varying kinds of institutions, the level of discontent does seem to differ significantly by type of institution. Fewer than half the students surveyed at state research universities reported that they were satisfied by their contacts with faculty members and administrators—compared to nearly two-thirds at private four-year colleges.[5] Access to faculty, or to particular courses, is only one of the common complaints. Others include irresponsibility and ideological bias.

Access

One of the commonest complaints about professors is simply the difficulty of gaining access to them. Sometimes this means the difficulty of enrolling in their courses and sometimes it means the difficulty of seeing them outside of class, even after being enrolled.

Many courses at many universities are simply not taught by professors but often by graduate students. The undergraduate college at the University of Chicago, which has resisted this tendency longer than some other institutions, has been nevertheless giving in to this trend in recent years. One of its professors referred to "the excruciating problem" of "steady pressure from graduate departments on the College to allow grad students to teach as is the case at Harvard or Stanford."[6] Another University of Chicago professor said, "a first-year student could take his Humanities core, Social Sciences core, a year of calculus, and a year of a foreign language without ever being taught by a professor."[7] At the University of North Carolina, about half the freshman courses are taught by teaching assistants and only about a third by full-time professors.[8] A senior majoring in economics at the University of Minnesota said: "I am graduating from one of the best economics departments in the country and I've never had a professor."[9] She had been taught by graduate students and part-time instructors.

A somewhat different access problem is getting enrolled in the courses desired. Where the student is denied admittance to a course required for graduation, that can have serious consequences. A carefully planned sequence of courses may have to be disrupted in ways that make no sense educationally, simply in order to take the required course in some future term when it may be available. In a worst case scenario, graduation itself may have to be postponed, at considerable cost to student and parent alike. Yet, despite the serious consequences of denying students admittance to courses required for graduation, it happens with considerable frequency at some institutions. At the University of Texas, for example, nearly a thousand students were turned away from a required English course.[10]

Being shut out of full courses has been a problem not only at huge institutions like the universities of Texas or Illinois[11] but also at some small colleges like Davidson, Carleton, and Wellesley.[12] At the University of Virginia, it has become a practice for a student to write notes to several professors simultaneously, each note saying why it is especially important to be allowed to enroll in that particular professor's course. However, the professor who grants the request may then find the student *not* enrolling. Such notes have become simply a tactic to use to ensure a choice of courses (including back-up courses) when over-crowding makes access a problem.[13] It is much like multiple applications to colleges.

Even when enrolled in a course, access to the professor may be quite limited. Huge classes with hundreds of students seldom permit any interaction during the lecture, and little immediately after class or in the professor's office. The magnitude of this problem varies with the institution. A small college may have no class with more than 50 students but Brown University's largest class has nearly 500 students[14] and the largest class at the University of Iowa has more than a thousand students.[15] The sheer numbers of students can limit how much interaction is possible, even when the professor is interested or cooperative. Moreover, a Carnegie Foundation study found that only 35 percent of the full-time faculty members at research universities considered teaching their chief interest, compared to 71 percent of faculty members at all institutions combined.[16] A science professor at the University of Michigan put the situation bluntly when he said: "Every minute I spend in an undergraduate classroom is costing me money and prestige."[17]

For untenured faculty members, spending large amounts of time with students or in preparing carefully crafted lectures can cost them the job itself. It has become commonplace for an untenured faculty member to win a teaching award and then be told that his contract will not be renewed. At M.I.T., for example, the teaching award "is frequently referred to as 'the kiss of death' because its recipients are often denied tenure."[18] In the up-or-out system of academic employment, being denied tenure is equivalent to being fired.

Neither this pattern nor this phrase is peculiar to M.I.T. Both have been recurrent at Ohio State University, for example.[19] At Stanford, a lecturer in biology received a number of teaching awards over the years and was then denied tenure.[20]

At the University of Pennsylvania in recent years, professors of English and of political science have been denied tenure after receiving teaching awards.[21] Some academics dispute the belief that a teaching award is the kiss of death, either in general or at a particular university.[22] However, the very fact that there can be a controversy over the issue suggests how widespread the phenomenon is.

The direct competition of research versus teaching for the professor's time is accentuated when a particular individual in a research-oriented department devotes himself to teaching. Although Columbia University, like other research universities, says that "high effectiveness as a teacher" is a necessary (though not a sufficient) requirement for tenure, a faculty member denied tenure there both disputed this claim and provided an insight into the dynamics of the teaching-versus-research process:

> ... if you are unlike many members of the senior faculty (that is, you are a good teacher who cares about undergraduate instruction), you attract lots of students. This gives you a disproportionate amount of work, making it less likely that you'll be able to publish enough to get tenure.[23]

A teaching-award winner at Harvard who was likewise denied tenure, despite being described by a senior colleague as "an extraordinarily gifted scholar," blamed his own allocation of time to teaching for his having to leave. According to the student newspaper, the *Harvard Crimson*, "he plans to reduce the portion of time he spends teaching in his new job."[24] Not only junior faculty members, but even graduate teaching assistants and advisers, learn that spending too much time on undergraduates imperils their own future. One Harvard teaching assistant refused to reveal his last name to his students until the last day of the term, in order to prevent their phoning him.[25]

Advising students on setting up their academic programs is another important function which often gets short shrift at research-oriented institutions. At Columbia University, the student newspaper complained that the advisers, who supposedly help undergraduates shape their education through their choice of courses were in fact elusive, uninterested, and uninformed:

Students often see their advisers only to get a signature on their program filing forms, and advisers in every department sometimes seem more ignorant of departmental requirements than their advisees are.

. . . Since being a good adviser offers few rewards, faculty do not hesitate to let their advising responsibilities slide. Thus students often find their advisers unnervingly indifferent to their academic program and surprisingly uninformed of school and departmental policy.[26]

Careless advising can mean not only that the student does not take the best selection of courses for his own intellectual development; it can also mean that his graduation will be postponed, if all the departmental or college requirements are not met by the program of courses approved by the adviser. None of these problems is peculiar to Columbia. At the University of Virginia, 40 percent of the students surveyed declared themselves dissatisfied with their freshman-year advisers, and the student newspaper referred to "the distaste with which some professors seem to view their advising duties."[27] At Stanford, 42 percent of graduating seniors rated as "poor" the advising they had received before choosing a major and another 27 percent rated it "fair," with only a minority giving it a rating of "good" or better.[28] David Riesman's study of higher education in general concluded that advising was "at most large universities, including my own, at best an embarrassment, at worst a disgrace."[29]

All these examples are from major research universities. They provide a clue as to why small liberal-arts colleges so often produce better results in undergraduate education, even when neither their students nor their professors have as impressive credentials as those in the more prestigious universities.

Classroom Performance

The most visible aspect of education, though not the most important, is the classroom performance of the teacher. This is what students see and respond to most strongly. When they speak of a "good" teacher, they typically mean a teacher who is good at this and when they speak of a "bad" teacher, they typically mean a teacher who is bad at this.

One kind of teaching is that described by *The Confidential Guide*, published annually by the student newspaper at Harvard:

> ...Coles' random, often guilt-inducing lectures can be fascinating, if not always relevant. Coles is a brilliant orator, and he prides himself on the fact that he doesn't use any notes. His delivery is frequently awe-inspiring, and he uses words like fuck and shit just to prove how down-to-earth he is.[30]

This course had an enrollment of 800, the largest enrollment of any course at Harvard.[31] The charismatic professor, or teacher as preacher, is only one of the kinds of ego trips or other self-indulgences by faculty members. Another Harvard professor described in the student-written guide was a variation on the same theme:

> You will be going to the most expensive theater show of your life—a couple of thousand bucks to watch a famous guy stroke his ego in front of 300 students.[32]

Conceding that the professor "does have reason to be proud of his research," *The Confidential Guide* says, "he does not have a reason in the world to be proud of his personal conduct during class, or for the course itself." Among other things, he has been known to "waste 50 minutes talking about the World Series" in a course on geology.[33] Such professors are not peculiar to Harvard.

At the University of Texas, a biology professor was noted for opening every class "by playing his favorite ditties (by Gershwin and Brubeck) to the students while waddling sleepily across the stage." According to the *Texas Review*:

> He is at his most enthusiastic during the sex education stages of his 303 classes; without warning he flicks up eye-popping slides of female genitalia onto the cinema-sized screen of AC21 and accompanies them with comments such as "this is not my wife" and "I did not take these pictures, ha, ha."[34]

At Arizona State University, a student in a course on "Human Sexuality" testified before the institution's board of regents that the slides shown included not only "genital penetration from a variety of positions and angles" but also oral sex, to the accompaniment of such professorial comments as "I sure hope she doesn't sneeze" and "Imagine if she got a cramp in her jaw now." Another student in the same course, a young woman who missed an examination, reported that she was told by the professor that she could make it up by writing a ten-page paper on her own sexual experiences.[35]

Sometimes there is method in a professor's madness: "Known for cutting class short to manage his tennis schedule," a sociology professor at Northwestern "often arrives with racket in hand," according to a student newspaper. The class itself is conducted in the same self-serving way: "Pitting black students against white," this professor "relies on their emotional arguments to fill class time."[36]

In addition to gross self-indulgences, professors have also been criticized for simple ineptitude, carelessness, and callousness. An anthropology professor at Berkeley was described as giving lectures so "unorganized" that "it's hard to figure out exactly what she is trying to say."[37] The lectures of an economics professor at Princeton were characterized as "sleep-inducing," those of a colleague "unorganized and incoherent," and those of another "quite confusing." Yet another Princeton economist was noted for his "general impatience in responding to questions" and still another tended to get "lost in his own equations." In electrical engineering, one professor was noted for "mumbling" and another "literally read the book aloud in his lecture." A Princeton math professor was noted for "proofs begun and never finished."[38]

In Duke University's Asian and African Languages department, a professor whose class discussions usually "went off on a tangent" was also someone who "embarrasses and insults students." The report on one of his colleagues in the same department was "many students find that his condescending and sarcastic attitude discourages them from asking questions, disagreeing, or expressing ideas."[39] In the computer science department at Duke, one professor's lectures were described as "disorganized," another's "boring and slow." Another colleague "wandered off the subject" and for yet another computer science professor, the most noted experience in his course was "falling asleep in class and knowing you hadn't missed a thing."[40]

Professors are not the only classroom performers. Teaching assistants, popularly known as TA's, teach many classes on their own, especially in mathematics and the sciences. Many of these TA's are foreign graduate students, and their hard-to-understand English is a chronic complaint from undergraduates. One TA teaching at Harvard was described as "functionally illiterate in the English language," someone whose "spelling errors, thick accent, and chaotic grammar render him incomprehensible."[41] A similar complaint about foreign teaching assistants who "cannot speak English clearly" was made at the University of North Carolina.[42] Such complaints are echoed at universities across the country. At Stanford, most of the teaching assistants in an introductory statistics course "spoke only fragmented English."[43] At the University of Chicago, "unfamiliarity with English" and "problems with her command of English" were among the complaints against those teaching elementary mathematics courses.[44] At the University of Maryland, a student enrolled in introductory calculus was glad that he had learned to speak Korean in the Air Force, for that made him one of the few students able to converse with the graduate student teaching the course.[45]

Complaints about the poor English of foreign teaching assistants have become so widespread that legislators in some states have introduced bills requiring that foreign teaching assistants receive instruction in speaking comprehensible English.[46] Whether any of these bills will become law is another question. At Johns Hopkins University, where complaints about the English spoken by teaching assistants also abound, a faculty member suggested a different solution: "Undergraduates should try to be more accepting and to understand the difficulties facing the TAs."[47]

Ideological Indoctrination

Complaints about political indoctrination in the classroom have been made on a number of grounds, including (1) their time-wasting irrelevance to the course in which the students enrolled, (2) their lack of balance, undermining the whole concept of education, and (3) the factual or logical deficiencies of the particular ideologies being promoted.

The strongest of these objections is the first, for students who are paying to take accounting or literature are not paying to hear their professor's opinions on foreign policy or endangered species. When the money comes from parents who are asked to borrow against the equity in their home to pay inflated tuition, it seems especially unconscionable that professors should blithely indulge their own emotions after contracting to supply their expertise. Yet this pattern is widespread in American higher education, and especially so at its leading institutions.

An English professor at Dartmouth, for example, "doesn't mind wasting your time by indulging in political diatribes," according to a student report, while a radical feminist colleague in the same department turns the study of literature into "a tedious hunt for crotch symbolism."[48] At Arizona State University, a political science course described in the catalogue as being about political ideologies like "Marxism, liberalism, conservatism," turned out instead to be dominated by the professor's own anti-nuclear opinions and "overpopulation" worries.[49] Quite aside from the merits or demerits of the professor's views on these subjects, they were not what the catalogue said the course was about, not what students signed up for, and not what the professor was paid to teach.

A required course in American history from 1492 to 1865, at the University of Texas (Austin), gave over whole lecture periods to things that happened long after 1865. Two class periods featured slides of poverty-stricken people from the Great Depression of the 1930s and another class period was spent denouncing the Reagan administration's foreign policy. Along the way during the course were all sorts of other editorial comments far removed from the ostensible subject of the class, including "I'm a fucked-up man" and "You can't disagree with the values of a bunch of people without pissing them off." This last remark the professor had the class repeat aloud.[50] At Harvard, a professor of divinity spent a class period praising the "nuclear freeze" movement and explaining why he was involved in it. According to a student present, the class began with "people handing out material on how to get involved with the nuclear freeze movement" and ended with "a girl with a guitar" singing "a folk-song about how we should all join hands against nuclear arms."[51]

Required courses, with their captive audiences, seem especially susceptible to being abused for ideological purposes. Freshman composition has thus become focussed on ideological indoctrination at the University of Massachusetts[52] and was scheduled to do so at the University of Texas (Austin), until a public outcry, led by a local chapter of the National Association of Scholars, forced a change of plans.[53] At Cornell University, the freshman seminar program has become "filled with courses of political orientation."[54] At the University of Michigan, introductory biology—used to satisfy students' natural science distribution requirement—became a setting for films and slides about Nicaraguan politics, denunciations of Ronald Reagan and George Bush, and other unrelated matters.[55]

In addition to introducing ideology into courses in which the ostensible subject matter has nothing to do with ideology, there are other courses more or less blatantly taught ideologically. For example, the professor in a University of Massachusetts (Amherst) course entitled "Contemporary American History" declared: "I am biased. I'm not going to give you both sides to every question." He also said: "This course will be consistently anti-American," that this was "not a course that is going to make you happy to be an American."[56] Like brainwashing in the public schools and in Maoist China, this course requires "personal experiences" to be dealt with, beginning with a question on the first assignment: "Where's your head and how did it get that way? What are your politics?"[57]

Where the fundamental purpose of a course is ideological, grades tend to vary ideologically, not only to reward those who espouse the ideology and punish those who oppose it, but more generally to attract a larger audience for the cause with easy grades. All this makes sense when education is regarded as simply a continuation of politics by other means. Thus a music course at Dartmouth, notorious for its obscenity-laden ideological ramblings, was also regarded as "a notorious gut."[58] A Harvard course on "Women and the Law," taught from a "feminist perspective," was characterized by the student guide as one in which it is "virtually impossible to do badly when exam time comes around" and one in which the term paper can be on "any topic you can think of that is even remotely related to the course's topic."⁵⁹ At the State University of New York at Buffalo, an English class regarded as "a snap course," was given over to political issues and a student who challenged the professor was given "one of the lowest grades in the class"— an A minus!⁶⁰ A professor at St. Cloud State University in Minnesota gave extra credit to students in his course who took part in a protest demonstration—5 points for marching and 20 points for carrying a sign.⁶¹

Marxist professors, who have on more than one occasion openly advocated the use of the classroom for ideological indoctrination,⁶² have likewise openly used their grading power to reward students who espouse the Marxist line and punish those who do not. The syllabus for a course on Marxian economics at the University of Texas (Austin), for example, says that this course "provides you with an opportunity to learn how to view the world from a new point of view and the tests are aimed at evaluating whether and to what degree you have learned to do this."⁶³ Aside from the familiar Orwellian use of the word "opportunity," this course is, by its own description, not oriented toward the educational goal of analyzing or evaluating Marxian economics, but is instead oriented toward the ideological goal of accepting Marxism as the basis for evaluating the world—with the professor's power of the grade hanging over the student's head.

Despite high grades and lax standards in ideological courses, students who oppose the brainwashing may be dealt with severely. A leftist professor at Dartmouth has been described as a "political grader" who "tolerates no intellectual diversity in her class."⁶⁴ In a Religious Studies class at Humboldt State College in California, when a student stated arguments against the professor's anti-nuclear views, he was cut off with "That's not what I am looking for" and it was suggested that he not come back to class.⁶⁵ When a student challenged the material on Central American politics introduced into a biology class at the University of Michigan by the professor, he was told—in front of the class—that the professor wished he would go to El Salvador and get blown up, the professor offering to sponsor this "independent study program" for him.⁶⁶

In a course at the State University of New York at Farmingdale, where one of the assigned texts was the professor's own parody of Ronald Reagan and the Bible, a student who questioned the accuracy of some of the professor's statements was ordered out of the class and then security guards were called to eject him.[67] Most propagandizing professors do not go to this extreme, nor are 100 percent of them on the political left. A conservative economics professor at the University of Texas (Austin) was criticized by the conservative *Texas Review* for teaching and evaluating his students like his counterparts on the other end of the political spectrum: "Like most *leftist* classes, this reeks of ideological indoctrination." Moreover, "like most *liberal* faculty members," this conservative professor expected students to follow his ideology on the tests.[68] Again, the fundamental problem is not ideological imbalance to the left, but classroom brainwashing itself. When students must be "well-practised parrots"[69] as the *Texas Review* says, in order to get good grades in ideologically oriented courses, the real problem is not with what they are parroting but with the fact that they are not learning to use and develop their own minds, in the process of reaching their own conclusions.

COMMON PRESCRIPTIONS

While the many examples of professorial misconduct already cited do not show what is typical, they do show what is wrong— how lax the system is. Before considering some of the cures being prescribed, it is necessary to look at the other side—the professors who are conscientious, effective, and even inspiring. They too can be found across a wide spectrum of institutions.

At even the most research-oriented institutions, there are still some dedicated professors. At Stanford, four out of five seniors graduating in 1990 rated their education at least "very good" and nearly a third rated it "excellent."[70] At the University of Chicago, there were calculus teachers who received unanimously excellent ratings by their students[71] and an economics professor was praised "almost unanimously" for "eloquent, clear and interesting lectures" and for responding to questions "cordially" and "thoroughly."[72] "All of the students thought very highly of the instructor" in another economics course[73] and yet another instructor was "universally praised as an excellent lecturer who was easy to understand, organized, and clear."[74] In a geography course at Chicago, "not one negative comment was received concerning the instructor or any aspect of this class,"[75] and a history professor received "rave reviews."[76] Another historian's lectures were called "fantastic and phenomenal" and his ability to direct class discussions "brilliant."[77]

At Duke University, an economics professor was described as "enthusiastic, knowledgeable, considerate and easily accessible outside of class." Another "received rave reviews from the great majority of his students." Yet another gave "dynamic and well-presented lectures" and was "always willing to meet with his students to help their analysis and to discuss any other problems." Still another economist at Duke received "unanimous praise for his sense of humor, excellent organization and amount of time he devotes to his students."[78] While the mathematics department at Duke did not fare as well, on the whole, still a number of math instructors received general student approval. One was rated "excellent," another "superb" and yet another "qualifies for sainthood in the eyes of his students."[79]

At the University of California at San Diego, the conservative *California Review* gave high ratings to some professors described as being politically on the left. One was described as a "well-respected and published teacher whose lectures can accurately be described as spell-binding." Of another professor, it said: "Leftist or not, Professor Schiller is a great teacher. He is tolerant of opposing viewpoints and respectful of his students." Another top-rated professor "never lets on to his political leanings in the class room."[80]

"Never less than fascinating to listen to," is the evaluation of an English professor at Northwestern University. Of a colleague in history it was said: "You can always find a long line outside her office as she is firmly committed to helping students learn."[81] Even at Berkeley, widely regarded as epitomizing the research university where undergraduates are ignored, a professor of computer science has been described as always "lucid and organized," and "a pleasure to study under." A professor of English there was described as "a terrific lecturer and very approachable in office hours," while a professor of rhetoric was likewise praised for having a "well-organized" class and for being "always willing to give students personal attention during office hours."[82]

At Harvard, a statistics professor was rated 5, on a scale

from 1 to 5, by 30 of her 36 students and 4 by the other 6. An English professor did almost as well, with a five rating from 20 of his 28 students, the other 8 being 4's. An economics professor had 22 fives out of 29 students, a professor teaching Japanese received 56 fives from 71 students, a professor teaching Latin lyric poetry received 15 fives from 17 students, and a professor teaching Greek received 21 fives from 26 students, while an anthropology professor received a perfect score of 5 from all of his six students.[83] Very similar high ratings are found, in varying proportions, among professors at Princeton, Dartmouth, the University of Texas, and many other colleges and universities, both well known and little known.

The point here is not to attempt to strike a balance or to estimate an average quality of teaching. Both these goals are unattainable. The point is to demonstrate the incredible range of classroom performances at the same institutions—and the almost total lack of institutional quality control which this implies, at least at research universities. There is probably nothing else purchased which has such a large impact on family finances, or on the future of the next generation, which has such lax quality control. Yet many prescriptions for establishing such quality control are likely to fail unless the factors involved, and the balance of power on campus, are understood.

Among the most popular prescriptions for better college teaching are more weight given to student evaluations of their professors, classroom observation of their teaching by peers or administrators, or a stricter control of the appointment and tenure process by administrators, giving more weight to teaching, rather than research. All these approaches have serious flaws.

Student Evaluations

Many colleges and universities already have student evaluations, some of which are published for the benefit of other students, and all of which are available to department chairmen, deans, and college presidents, to do with as they will. These evaluations often contain very useful information on those things which students are qualified to evaluate—the conscientiousness, clarity, and accessibility of professors, for example. The crucial problem, however, is that students are not qualified to evaluate what matters most, the quality of their education.

They can spot blatantly shoddy stuff, some of which can be found in even the most prestigious institutions. But to evaluate the real quality of a course which the student found challenging, interesting, and even inspiring, would require the student to know how that course compares to similar courses elsewhere, how much of what is vital to the subject was included or left out, and how much of a foundation the course provides for later and deeper work and thought in the same or related fields. These are the unknowns which are almost certain to remain unknown for years after the student's evaluation has been turned in.

No administrative reforms, no statistical techniques, no in-depth interviews, nor any other methods or gimmicks can substitute for the missing knowledge—which is inherently missing. If the student knew enough to evaluate the course by such criteria, there would be no point in his taking the course in the first place. By the time he is working on his Ph.D., he may be able to look back over the years at the introductory courses in his field and evaluate how well, or how poorly, they laid the intellectual foundations for later study or for later work in that field. But, by then, the student is long gone from college and his assessment of what he learned may be radically different from what it was at the end of the course. As Dean Henry Rosovsky of Harvard put it:

> All of us who have reached advanced years can recall teachers whom we vigorously detested in high school or college, only to discover in more mature years the excellence of their instruction. . . . Most of us will also remember some much beloved "old doc so-and-so"—unfortunately a fixture on so many American campuses—who in our more mature memories reveals his true self to us as a pathetic windbag.[84]

Because students cannot evaluate what is crucial, someone else with more training and experience must do that evaluating. Student evaluations, gossip among themselves, complaints to administrators, and choices of courses all play an important role in trying to keep professors honest. But someone else must assume responsibility for things that go beyond that. Whether that someone must be departmental colleagues, campus administrators, or the leading scholars in the profession who pass judgment on the individual professor's research—or some combination—is another and larger question.

Classroom Visits

A perennial panacea for substandard teaching is the classroom visit, whether by senior colleagues, the department chairman, deans, or others. These people can no doubt detect, and perhaps deter, gross misbehavior, but so can the students. The officials may be more sophisticated but the students are far more numerous and see a far larger sample of the professor's classroom performance, over a period of months. A canny administrator has his ear to the ground and knows enough of what is going on, on campus, that he can tell whether a given professor is rotten or decent in the classroom. Not much more than that is likely to be learned from a visit.

A dean, for example, cannot possibly be an authority on all the subjects taught in a college, nor even one-tenth of the subjects. A small liberal arts college is likely to have about 20 departments and, for a major university, there will be at least twice as many departments, each with more numerous specialties than a department in a liberal arts college. The most that a dean can observe are classroom management skills. When it comes to the intellectual substance—the heart of the educational process—the dean is probably as much of an amateur as the students, if not more so. A dean who is a former professor of English literature is unlikely to understand the substance of what is being said in an engineering class, and is certainly unlikely to understand it as well as a student with a couple of other engineering courses already under his belt.

Those who believe that a classroom visit is likely to be a great source of information about teaching repeat the fatal fallacy of education professors, that there is such a thing as teaching, separate from the substantive knowledge being taught. The conveying of that knowledge, and of the intellectual skills and discipline which give it meaning, is ultimately what teaching consists of. If these things are conveyed from one mind to another, then the teaching has been successful, no matter how chaotic or clumsy the classroom management may be. By the same token, if it fails to happen, then teaching has been a failure, no matter how smoothly or impressively the classroom has been managed, or how happy or inspired the students feel.

The futility of observing a classroom reflects the fact that *that is not where education takes place.* What has happened in the professor's mind before he sets foot in the classroom, and what happens in the students' minds after they have left it and pursued their assignment—that is what determines the quality of the education. Two professors may be pretty much the same in a classroom and yet, if one has greater mastery of the field and deeper insights into what issues need covering—and how and why—then what they bring into that classroom, and what the students derive from different assignments, reflecting these fundamental differences in depth of understanding, can be profoundly different, even though wholly invisible to a dean observing the scene.

This would be obvious in almost any other field. No one would expect to acquire any real grasp of military operations by sitting around a field headquarters (or even the Pentagon) watching a general handing out sealed orders to officers going out on their assignments. It is what happened *before* those orders were conceived and written up that constitutes military strategy and it is what those officers do later, in battle, that determines whether it will work. Observing the transfer point tells you nothing substantive, no matter how long you observe it.

If a dean or a college president cannot learn much of any real significance by being in a classroom, perhaps the department chairman could, given that he is trained in the same discipline as the instructor. Unfortunately, specialization is so far advanced in many fields that even this belief has a large element of wishful thinking in it. The department chairman may be an economist, for example, but if his specialty is international trade and the instructor is teaching industrial organization or labor economics, then the chairman is not much better off than the dean, when it comes to assessing the validity or relevance of what is being taught. The instructor may be wonderful at conveying the peripheral aspects of his field, while omitting or failing to bring out the significance of what is the central focus of his specialty. Someone else, more clumsy or chaotic in classroom management, may be a far better teacher in focussing the students' attention on what is crucial to an understanding of the subject.

Here, as in the case of student evaluations, there is no sub-stitute for knowledge—no way to fake it. Unfortunately, the natural desire of an administrator to have some report in his files which he can use to justify a decision on appointment, promotion, or tenure, is likely to give a spurious importance to any document, whether it was generated from student eval-uations or classroom visits. The more cynical administrators may not even believe in these documents themselves, except as cover if their decisions come under fire.

Administrative Responsibility

Many faculty misdeeds are too well known to require much investigation. The real question is whether administrators can do anything about them. This is not simply a matter of the administration's legal or institutional authority. A dean or a provost may have the full authority to terminate an untenured faculty member, for reasons which deserve termination, and yet may have many practical considerations to weigh before exercising that power. If the junior faculty member is the pro-tegé of an influential senior professor, and especially if the younger scholar is a vital member of a multi-million dollar research project at the university, then the exercise of the dean's power or the provost's power may require more reck-lessness than courage.

When the student editorial writers on the *Columbia Daily Spectator* said that faculty members who neglect their advising responsibilities "must be held accountable for their perfor-mance by the deans and by their department heads,"[85] they assumed a degree of leverage which these administrators may or may not have. After all, what real leverage does a dean or department head have with a senior faculty member whose research and ability to bring grants on campus make him much in demand by rival institutions? Even to hold back a raise for such a faculty member risks losing someone who is a financial asset to the university. Moreover, as others see a distinguished scholar being punished by a dean, they too may keep an eye out for greener pastures.

Some courses are an abuse in and of themselves, irrespective of the professor's classroom skills—courses on tea-leaf reading, television soap operas, and the like. Easy courses and high grades may be offered to attract students, thereby building enough enrollment to justify the professor's job or the departmental budget. As two retired faculty members have said, "junk courses fill classroom seats"—partly because "they are the only kind of course that unqualified students can endure."[86] Administrators may have formal authority to put a stop to both the junk courses and the admission of students who do not meet the academic qualifications. Whether college officials are willing to pay the price of exercising that authority is another question.

This does not mean that nothing can be done. It does mean that some *institutional* changes may be needed to rein in professors and allow a campus to have some coherent principles, rather than be simply a collection of baronial fiefdoms run by tenured faculty members.

INSTITUTIONAL ISSUES

Given the enormous variation in the quality of teaching, even on the same campus, the most expensive tuition paid cannot guarantee that the education received will be first-rate—or even adequate. Whether the heavy costs of a college education are borne by the taxpayers or by parents, there is very little institutional assurance as to the quality of what they are paying for.

With the disintegration of the curriculum at many colleges and universities, students may graduate from prestigious institutions wholly ignorant of entire fields of human knowledge, such as economics, mathematics, biology, history, government, chemistry, and sociology. Brooke Shields in fact graduated from Princeton without taking a single course in any of these subjects.[87] Loose curriculum requirements are damaging, as William F. Buckley put it, "not because you cannot get a good education at Harvard, but because you can graduate from Harvard without getting a good education."[88]

Because most people pass through college only once in a lifetime, and at a time when they have little experience with life in general, they cannot all be presumed to be knowledgeable consumers, especially since the central purpose of education is to make them knowledgeable. In short, institutions of higher education have weighty responsibilities, both to their students and to society, but lack the institutional means of carrying out these responsibilities effectively. It is not simply the difficulty of making tenured faculty members give serious attention to teaching, or otherwise obey institutional rules; the tenured faculty themselves make the rules—and they make them in their own interests. Thus, it is not uncommon for an English department to leave freshman composition courses in the hands of teaching assistants, junior faculty, or even part-time or "gypsy" faculty, hired just for doing the "menial" work of the department, while the senior tenured professors devote themselves to esoteric theories of literature. No amount of money will cause American students to receive much-needed, first-rate instruction on how to write decent English, so long as the institutional rules allow professors to structure the curriculum to suit their own convenience and leave them free to pursue "research" that will enhance their own individual prestige.

English departments are by no means unique in this respect. Most introductory calculus courses at Harvard are taught by teaching assistants.[89] This is a common pattern in mathematics departments at research universities across the country. So is a widespread use of foreign graduate students with incomprehensible English as teaching assistants.

Given the repeatedly demonstrated mathematics deficiencies of American students and given the key role of calculus as the foundation for the study of higher mathematics, as well as for use in other fields such as economics and physics, the decision to throw responsibility for this course on to inexperienced graduate students whose English is difficult to understand can only be explained by the self-interest of mathematics professors. These professors gain no recognition or prestige in their profession by teaching a first-rate introductory calculus course—and lose nothing by refusing to teach it at all.

Once again, the point here is not to condemn all professors, nor even to determine with any precision the prevalence of the neglect of teaching. The point is to consider the reasons why academic institutions are unable to control even the most gross neglect of undergraduate education. Among the principal reasons are academic research, tenure, and faculty governance.

Academic Research

Like many things, academic research is neither good nor bad absolutely. The issue is one of proportion, of costs, and of methods. Even as regards teaching, research has an important contribution to make, however much an excessive emphasis on research has undermined teaching at many institutions.

Limitations on evaluating teaching by observation—whether by students or administrators—are inherent in the fact that education is invisible, taking place in the minds of teachers and students. It is possible to test what students have learned in college on Graduate Record Examinations, Law School Aptitude Tests and the like—but that tells very little about which particular professors were more effective in teaching them. Neither can the student tell, for though he knows what he was taught, and how effectively he was taught, he has no way to know what he was *not* taught. Virtually every course has a far larger potential content than any content which can be squeezed into the time available. The selection of what is important, what is peripheral, and what is expendable, is one of the most important tasks of a teacher and reflects the depth of his grasp and mastery of the subject. It is usually a task completed before the first class meets.

Given a decently conscientious effort to teach, the quality of that teaching is essentially the quality of the mind of the teacher. At the very least, that is the limiting factor—and, for many, that is a very limiting factor. Those most competent to judge the quality of a professor's mind, his grasp and mastery of the subject, are typically not even on campus. They are, his peers in his specialty, scattered around the country or around the world. It is these whom the professor addresses when he publishes. For this audience, it is no longer a question whether he can impress the sophomores three mornings a week, but whether those who have made the specialty their life's work find his work solid or lacking.

"Publish or perish" is a misleading phrase. One can perish by publishing, if one's work is rejected time and again by all the leading scholarly journals, and can only emerge shame-facedly into print in some peripheral publication. Even those who make it into print in a respectable academic journal may find their article devastated by a cross fire of criticisms in later issues. In short, academic publication is a sorting process and this process is valuable to the profession, not only when it uncovers gems, but also when it exposes frauds. Indeed, it may be more valuable when it exposes frauds, however impressive those frauds may be to students who see only the charisma or feel only the personal warmth, which may be quite genuine. Publication to one's scholarly peers is the acid test of what education is all about—intellect.

To fulfill its role as a quality-control process, academic pub-lication need not require a massive or continuous outpouring of research. A scholarly article once every few years may be sufficient to maintain the intellectual credentials of a professor at a teaching institution and such a pace is in fact not uncom-mon among the faculty at leading liberal arts colleges. At major research universities, the pace is of course much faster, as books, articles, and monographs are expected to follow on one another's heels, if the prestige of the individual and the insti-tution are to be maintained. Vast amounts of federal research money have added yet another reason to engage in research, well beyond the point where it is a complement to good teach-ing and well into the region where its effects on teaching are largely negative. Many academic scholars themselves are in-creasingly critical of the pressures to publish in large volume. Much of what is being mass-produced under the label of schol-arship has been variously characterized as trivial, routine, or even meretricious.[90] A survey of more than 35,000 professors at nearly 400 colleges found that more than one-fourth regarded research pressures as interfering with their teaching. At public research universities, 44 percent said that research pressures were interfering with their teaching.[91] In very research-oriented institutions, the average faculty member spends more than twice as many hours per week on research as he spends on teaching preparation.[92]

Ironically, much of the massive federal spending on aca-demic research has been seen, politically at least, as support for higher education—even though teaching and research are obviously competing for the time of professors. No one would be surprised if massive federal subsidies to Sears had an adverse effect on Penney's or Montgomery Ward, but many seem not to notice that throwing billions of dollars annually at academic research has taken more and more professors away from the classroom. Moreover, faculty research stars who are able to attract millions of dollars in research grants become as uncontrollable as feudal barons, for the large institutional "overhead" payments which accompany these grants make the university more dependent on such professors for money than the professors are on the university for a job. When, if, and how they will teach are not matters on which department chairmen or deans are in any position to say very much.

The heavy dependence of many colleges and universities on federal research money has yet another major consequence. The need to avoid the political appearance of racial discrimination, in order to retain these grants, makes minority youngsters valuable as bodies and expendable as students. Their large numbers on campus and small numbers on graduation platforms reflect this fact of life. Science professors, with large research grants at stake, have especially strong incentives to vote for the admission of mismatched minority students, knowing that such youngsters are unlikely to become science students. Similar attitudes have been observed among mathematicians at Harvard.[93]

Tenure

Two concepts dominate discussions of tenure—"academic freedom" and "deadwood." Often neither term is defined very clearly.

The original impetus toward academic freedom in its current institutional form came from a series of firings of professors for their political or social views in the early twentieth century. The American Association of University Professors was formed in 1915, and from its first meeting came a declaration which called for tenure as a protection of academic freedom. The conception of academic freedom at the time was that of a protection of professors from reprisals for their activities or beliefs *outside the classroom*. Inside the classroom, the original AAUP report said, the professor must avoid "taking advantage of the student's immaturity by indoctrinating him with the teacher's own opinions before the student has an opportunity fairly to examine other opinions upon the matters in question."[94] Over the years, however, the doctrine of academic freedom was turned completely around to protect whatever professors did *inside the classroom*. By 1969, a survey of professors found more than four out of five agreeing that "faculty members should be free to present in class any idea that they consider relevant."[95]

Jacques Barzun, drawing upon his experience as dean at Columbia University, said: "I have personally known men who thought it fair to indoctrinate the captive freshman, and yet called it a violation of academic freedom when they were cautioned or restrained."[96] Academic freedom had thus been transformed into *carte blanche* or academic licence, and it has protected not only intellectual independence but also personal failings and misconduct. As a knowledgeable academic has noted, it protects tenured professors "in whom signs of deterioration, incompetence, gross neglect of duty and willful flouting of academic authority are only too evident."[97]

Although academic freedom has become, in practice, faculty unaccountability, many fear that the erosion or disappearance of tenure would mean the disappearance of intellectual freedom at colleges and universities. However, institutions with personnel very similar to those in academic institutions have operated very well without tenure. The closest institutions to academic institutions are the various "think tanks" such as the Brookings Institution, the Hoover Institution, the RAND Corporation, and many others scattered around the country. These think tanks typically employ scholars with Ph.D.s who write articles and books very similar to those of their academic counterparts—and in fact, many think tank scholars are former academics, academics on leave, or part-time academics. Though lacking tenure, these think tanks have produced at least their share of controversial individuals and controversial writings.

Tenure is neither a necessary nor a sufficient condition for intellectual boldness. Other occupations with iron-clad tenure, such as civil servants, have been more notable for people quietly keeping their noses clean while waiting for retirement on pension. It may even be that tenure attracts into an occupation more than its fair share of people too timid to take their chances in the marketplace. Even a defender of tenure has pointed out that "it is inconceivable to professors how matter-of-factly people outside academia look for new jobs."[98]

Tenure and its ramifications make looking for a new job a much more traumatic process for academics. Tenure does not increase over-all job security in colleges and universities. It distributes the insecurity in a peculiar pattern, concentrating it on the younger, less experienced, lower-income, and untenured faculty members—the most vulnerable people. Every guarantee of a job to a tenured professor is an exclusion of an untenured professor who may be equally, or more, qualified. In few other occupations does someone who is doing a good job (or even an outstanding job, as measured by teaching awards) have to fear being thrown out of work at a flourishing institution. Yet leading universities routinely fire the bulk of their untenured faculty members when their contracts run out after a few years. This system of hiring far more junior faculty than are likely to be retained exists because of the impossibility of knowing, in advance, which of the promising new Ph.D.'s emerging from graduate school will prove to be among the top research scholars who will meet the standards for being granted tenure. By hiring a dozen promising assistant professors, a top-level department may be able to find one or two who meet their criteria for promotion and permanence.

This whole Draconian process—the "up-or-out" system— is made necessary by tenure and by the AAUP rule that the tenure decision cannot be postponed indefinitely. Because tenure means a commitment to pay an associate professor's salary, or more, for decades to come, it is a commitment of more than a million dollars to one individual. To avoid being stuck with "deadwood," the institution must make a once-and-for-all decision on each individual faculty member within a few years. In turn, this means that the untenured faculty member is under great pressure to "produce"—that is, to produce published research—at the beginning of his career, while putting together courses for the first time, and perhaps while supporting a new family as well. The higher up in the academic institutional pecking order a new faculty member begins, the greater the likelihood of having to relocate, tearing up the family's local roots and starting over again hundreds of miles away, or even on the other side of the country, wherever the best new opening appears. Therefore job changes tend to be more disruptive for academics than for secretaries, accountants, or computer programmers. Changing jobs in academia typically involves geographic relocation, because comparable colleges and universities are seldom located in the same community.

Anyone who has been through this experience is likely to find it a horror not to be repeated. Those who must try two or three institutions before finally achieving tenure can spend the better part of a decade in limbo, without as much job security as a factory worker in a viable business. When tenure is finally attained, it is not only likely to be regarded as precious, but also as something whose abolition would mean a return to debilitating insecurity and chaotic disruptions of family life. Yet the gypsy life of an untenured faculty member is itself largely a function of the existence of tenure for others, and the incentives which expensive tenure commitments create for institutions to protect themselves against mistakes—against "deadwood"—at all costs.

The concept of "deadwood" is also worth examining. The classic example is the tenured professor who resolves the conflict between teaching and research by doing very little of either. The costs of "deadwood" are even higher than the salaries of those individuals who are not pulling their own weight. Where the tenured professor ceases to keep up with the ongoing development of his field, someone who is up to date may have to be hired, and parallel courses created, so that the department does not suffer the national (or international) embarrassment of turning out Ph.D.s who are found to be obsolete in some specialties.

Like other concepts, "deadwood" varies with the context. A professor who publishes a good scholarly article once every five or six years may be a very respectable member of a liberal arts college, especially if his teaching is first-rate. Yet he would be considered "deadwood" in a research university where his department is vying to become recognized as one of the top ten in the nation. The existence of tenure, however, inhibits the transfer of individuals from where they are "deadwood" to where they are not. It also protects those who are "deadwood" everywhere.

Given its high costs, what benefit does tenure confer in return? For the profession as a whole, it does not increase job security but merely concentrates the insecurity on vulnerable new faculty members. This leaves as its principal claim that it protects academic freedom, at least for the tenured faculty. In turn, the image of academic freedom is that it is a protection against ideological conformity, imposed from outside, and stifling the free exercise of the mind which is at the heart of teaching and learning. With the passing years, however, this conception has grown ever more remote from reality.

Since the 1960s, at least, the conformity of the academic world has been an *internally* imposed conformity of the left, culminating in the "political correct" fashions of the 1980s and 1990s. Tenure and academic freedom have not protected individual diversity of thought on campus but instead have protected those who choose to impose the prevailing ideology through classroom brainwashing of students and storm trooper tactics against outside speakers who might challenge this ideology. The related concept and practice of "faculty self-governance" has allowed this ideological intolerance to enter faculty hiring decisions as well, so that conservative "think tanks" like the Hoover Institution have flourished on the services of scholars who are ideologically *persona non grata* in universities to which their published research would otherwise give them ready access.[99]

As in other cases where results are the opposite of intentions, incentives are the key to understanding what has happened. Tenure not only insulates professors from outside pressures of a political nature, but also from accountability for carrying out their teaching responsibilities in a responsible manner, or for protecting the academic and behavioral standards of the university from internal subversion. Moreover, the tenure and self-governance powers of the faculty likewise restricts the ability of administrators to enforce these standards. When President Nathan Pusey of Harvard was repudiated by his faculty in 1969 for having had students ejected from a building they had forcibly occupied (and from which they were leaking confidential files to the media), this epitomized the institutional unaccountability of the faculty and the irresponsibility to which it leads.

Less dramatic but more pervasive examples include the structuring of everything from the course curriculum to the scheduling of class hours to suit the convenience of professors—regardless of how this affects students or the mission of the institution. For example, faculty insistence on having classes scheduled at times convenient for themselves means having courses meeting at times clustered together, making it impossible for students to take many courses they would like because so many classes meet at the same time. The ramifications go beyond students' inconvenience or a missing of particular courses; graduation can be delayed, at great and needless cost.

A recurring complaint in many fields and in many colleges and universities is that the faculty teach courses in esoteric sub-specialties, while foundation courses in the field go untaught. When a college's philosophy department offers no course in logic but does offer a course on "Philosophical Perspectives on Gender,"[100] or when a history department offers no history of Germany or France but has a course on "Images of Minorities in Cinema,"[101] then faculty sub-specialties are being indulged at the expense of students' education in fundamentals. Self-indulgence at the expense of taxpayers, donors, and tuition-paying parents is also common, not only in the numerous individual frills and extravagances in academia but also, and more fundamentally, in the whole approach to academic financing, in which money is spent or committed first and then funding sources are asked to help the institution meet "rising costs."

There are many kinds of costs besides money costs. Among these have been grade inflation and other deteriorations of academic standards, the mindless proliferation of costly "innovations," and a growing toleration (and even praise) of mob rule, which has future as well as current implications for academia—and for the country as a whole, as students emerge from college expecting to settle the issues of the day by riots. The fundamental institutional failing of colleges and universities is that many of its decision-makers need not give any serious weight to the many costs they create, because those costs are paid by others.

The institutional incentives created by faculty self-governance are for mutually indulgent log-rolling, especially when tenure ensures that many professors must regard each other as "facts of life" for years to come. This was understood more than two centuries ago, when Adam Smith wrote: "They are likely to make common cause, to be all very indulgent to one another, and every man to consent that his neighbour may neglect his duty, provided he himself is allowed to neglect his own."[102]

Outsiders also pay the non-monetary costs created by academic decision-makers. When rules are bent to pass minority medical students at Harvard, no professor loses anything, even though unsuspecting patients may pay for years, and some may even pay with their lives. Yet there is nothing whatever in the institutional processes to force a re-thinking or to prevent more such "feel good" decisions from being made, with other bad results, in other areas. As the distinguished Columbia University dean Jacques Barzun said, nearly half a century ago: "Most of the heartburnings in the academic world come from somebody's yielding to the temptation to be nice at the wrong time."[103]

If deans "love peace and hate trouble," as Barzun said,[104] they can also buy peace with someone else's money and reap the benefits of avoiding trouble. They can, for example, avoid being called racist, sexist, or homophobic by subsidizing new programs demanded by campus activists, and pass the costs along to the taxpayers at a state university or to parents in higher tuition at a private college in a tuition-setting cartel. Institutional non-accountability makes such self-indulgences possible.

CHAPTER 9

Athletic Support

WHERE CAN YOU take in more than nine and a half million dollars annually and still be classified as "amateur"? In Division I-A college athletics, where the average annual revenue is nearly $9.7 million per institution.[1] More than 20 colleges have received a million dollars or more on a single day—New Year's day—led by the two Rose Bowl colleges, eligible for $6 million each.[2] In basketball, television receipts alone for Division I conferences totaled nearly $70 million in academic year 1990–91.[3] College athletics are a big-money operation—except for the players, whose exploits, aches and pains, and risks to life and limb, make it all possible.

Coaches and athletic directors are by far the biggest individual financial beneficiaries of college athletics. While the average athletic director had an official salary of about $47,000 in academic year 1989–90—about the same as the average faculty member[4]—top coaches in Division I football and basketball had incomes more than ten times as high as that, and greater than the salary of any professor, college president, or President of the United States. Typically, this income comes under various labels from the college, so that "salary" is only

232

one form of institutional compensation, quite aside from outside sources of income from endorsements, media shows, and
numerous other lucrative activities, any one of which may
bring in five- or six-figure sums. At least 50 college football and
basketball coaches each earn a quarter of a million dollars or
more annually, and several make well over half a million[5]—
all this in "amateur" sports.

Ironically, in view of the pay, perks, and privileges of athletic coaches, even the top-rated sports teams seldom bring in
enough money to cover their costs. "Creative accounting" is
often necessary, just to make them appear on paper to be self-
supporting. Some states have laws forbidding the use of taxpayers' money to subsidize athletic programs, but these laws
are easily circumvented by having coaches and their staff ap-
pointed as instructors in physical education, and their salaries
charged as academic expenses.[6] Athletic scholarships are likewise often charged to the college's general scholarship fund,
rather than to the athletic department's budget.[7] Medical personnel serving the athletic team may be charged to general
student health services,[8] and legal problems may be handled
by the college's attorney rather than being charged to the athletic department's budget.[9] Stadiums and sports complexes can
be financed by student fees or tax-free bonds—again, without
appearing in the athletic department's budget.[10]

Even with all these diversions of costs, a survey by the
National Collegiate Athletic Association (NCAA) found that the
vast majority of athletic programs lose money.[11] Colleges in all
divisions of the NCAA had higher costs than revenues from
athletics, except for the big-time sports programs in Division
I-A, where revenues exceeded expenses—by less than one percent—in fiscal year 1989.[12] Independent estimates are that only
10 to 20 athletic programs make a consistent profit, however
small, and another 20 to 30 break even—out of more than 2,000
programs in the country.[13] Whatever money is brought in by
college sports, even when it is millions of dollars at some institutions, is almost invariably spent entirely on college sports.
The late A. Bartlett Giamatti, Commissioner of Baseball and
before that president of Yale University, summed up the situation succinctly: "I have yet to see the laboratory or library or
dormitory built with football or basketball revenues."[14]

Like so much else in academia, intercollegiate sports programs survive on myths and dogmas which facilitate the extraction of money from students and taxpayers, and the diversion of money from donors seeking to support academic programs, but in fact supporting lavish spending on coaches and an athletic empire. These myths and dogmas are related not only to the economics of intercollegiate sports but also to the effects of these sports on the young people who participate in them—the so-called "student-athletes," more accurately described as semi-pro players hoping for a rare shot at professional athletics after completing their "education."

THE ECONOMICS OF ATHLETICS

If the economics of athletics seem crazy—for example, paying enormous salaries to coaches running money-losing operations—that is partly because the usual competitive marketplace does not exist. However competitive intercollegiate sports may be on the playing field, their financial operations are those of a tightly controlled cartel, the National Collegiate Athletic Association, nominally composed of hundreds of academic institutions but in reality controlled by the athletic directors of those institutions. The NCAA makes the rules for athletic competition among its member colleges, including the rules for bowl games and basketball tournaments, negotiates multi-million dollar contracts with television networks, and prescribes rules for coaches and players.

It is the NCAA which forbids players from being openly paid salaries and which, in collusion with professional sports leagues, has kept them tied to NCAA programs for four years, even after their skills would otherwise make them eligible for the National Football League, the National Basketball Association, and the like. In exchange, the NFL, NBA, and other professional sports leagues benefit from a minor league farm system which is free to them, though costly to colleges, students, and the taxpayers. Above all, this cartel is financially beneficial to the coaches and athletic directors who run the NCAA.

Another major factor which prevents intercollegiate sports from operating like any other multi-million dollar business in a competitive marketplace is that athletic programs are heavily subsidized by institutions which themselves have no "bottom line" to control their own economic activities. State institutions simply go to the legislature with their red ink to plead their "needs" and private institutions appeal to alumni and other donors. Moreover, the elite private institutions have their own cartel, enabling them to extract all that the traffic will bear from parents' income and assets, including the equity in their homes.

Internal as well as external sources are raided when necessary to cover athletic department deficits. At the University of Nevada at Reno, $175,000 was taken out of the student union fund to help cover a deficit from athletics, with the university president explaining, "we had to find the money somewhere." The same explanation was used at the University of Houston, when the athletics department's share of students' fees rose from $400,000 in 1985 to $900,000 in 1987 and then to $1,720,000 in 1988.[15] At Utah State University, there was a half-million dollar reduction in medical insurance benefits for faculty and staff while the athletics department ran up an $800,000 deficit.[16] As a University of Massachusetts professor specializing in sports management has said, athletics directors "know that the universities are going to come in at the end of the year and make up their deficits by raising student fees by siphoning off profits from other places."[17]

In short, in athletics as in other areas, colleges and universities tend to run up bills for whatever they want and then scrounge the money from wherever they can, claiming that "costs" have risen. Between 1985 and 1989, for example, the cost of living rose 15 percent but the expenses of athletic programs at NCAA colleges and universities rose by at least double that rate in all divisions, and by more than three times that rate in two divisions.[18]

In an academic context, the phrase "costs have risen" often has exactly the same meaning as the phrase, "we chose to spend more money." Meanwhile, college administrators try to make it seem almost immoral for donors to earmark their donations, as this will "tie the hands" of the institution. Unfortunately, the real problem is that their hands are not tied securely enough, for money contributed for academic purposes is readily diverted to athletics, administrators' perks, and other purposes by verbal sleight of hand and "creative accounting."

Even with all due allowance for the difference between the inherent discipline of a competitive marketplace and the looser and more self-indulgent practices of academia, the question still remains: Why are coaches in such demand that their salaries are bid up to enormous levels, when they are usually in charge of money-losing operations? Indeed, why do athletic programs survive at all? Most of the usual explanations do not stand up under scrutiny.

The grand myth of all, that students are engaging in a recreational activity as amateurs, is believed only by the most naive. This myth serves as a formal justification for not paying college athletes, thereby leaving more money for coaches and athletic directors. Almost as unbelievable is the claim that college athletes are students who receive a free education in exchange for their services. Most big-time varsity athletes in football or basketball do not receive even a degree, much less an education. Exceptions do exist—athletes who not only graduate but who do so in a serious subject. The NCAA gives maximum publicity to such "student-athletes" but their scarcity is perhaps epitomized by the fact that Byron "Whizzer" White is still being cited as an example, decades after he became a Supreme Court Justice.

A more plausible-sounding claim is that athletic programs give visibility to a college or university, and that this visibility translates into academic prestige, alumni donations, and student applications. But the evidence not only fails to support this dogma; it suggests that the opposite is at least equally likely—that academic prestige may be overshadowed by an institution's image as a "football school."

The University of Notre Dame, for example, is far better known for its "fighting Irish" football teams and "win one for the Gipper" than it is for having a chemical engineering department ranked among the top ten in the nation for its faculty's research publications. The University of Southern California has likewise been better known as a football power than because it has graduate departments ranked among the top ten in the nation in computer sciences and electrical engineering.[19] Conversely, schools like Cal Tech and Columbia University have suffered no visible loss of prestige from having had monumental losing streaks in football, nor did the University of Chicago suffer any loss of prestige from having no football team at all for decades.

As for donations to colleges and universities, these seem to come from two sharply different groups for sharply different purposes. Athletic "boosters"—typically not alumni—contribute heavily to athletic programs and have often been involved in scandals about under-the-table payments to college athletes. These boosters seldom support academic programs, however, and because their support perpetuates a program which usually loses money over all, they are no net addition to a college or university's financial ability to engage in academic pursuits.

The actual alumni, on the other hand, tend to donate to academic programs or general funds, and various studies indicate that this support is little affected by whether the college's sports teams are winning or losing.[20] During UCLA's glory days as a basketball power, its alumni contributed less than the alumni of other institutions in the same conference. Conversely, after Tulane University discontinued basketball entirely, alumni donations rose by $5 million the following year. When Wichita State University suspended its football program, alumni donations doubled the next year.[21] Individual examples are not conclusive evidence, but the dogmas so widely believed seldom offer any evidence at all.

All this does not mean that it is wholly irrational for a college or university administration to maintain an athletic program which is losing money. Economists have long known that it is perfectly rational—as well as common—for a commercial business to continue in operation during periods of financial losses, not only where there is some prospect of red ink turning to black in the future, but even where there are only more losses to look forward to. Sometimes the only alternative to a given loss from continuing to operate is an even larger loss from shutting down—especially where there are large fixed costs which go on, regardless of whether the business produces anything or not.

An athletic stadium or a basketball arena represents a large, fixed cost: The debt incurred to build it must be repaid, even if not a living soul ever goes in there to see a game again. In purely financial terms, it may pay the college or university not only to keep playing games but also to spend heavily for a coach who can field the kind of team that will keep the turnstiles turning to minimize the losses. For example, when attendance at Stanford Stadium declined between 1989 and 1990, the university lost $568,000 in ticket sales.[22] A coach who could have eliminated that loss—or cut it in half, or prevented it from doubling—would have been worth paying a considerable salary.

In the long run, however, when the issue arises whether or not to replace the stadium or sports complex when it wears out, the financially rational and responsible decision would be to shut down the athletic program entirely if it is losing money. But few administrators take this long run view because their tenure may not extend into the long run—and indeed, their tenure may be shortened by publicly advocating any such policy, especially if they have been approving huge athletic department budgets for years and now claim that it is all a losing proposition. Financial losses from athletic programs are so widespread and so commonplace that there are innumerable rationales to justify them, and innumerable accounting practices to understate their real magnitude, so that the path of least resistance may well be to let the red ink continue to flow and let sleeping dogs lie.

In short, the decision to keep subsidizing athletic programs indefinitely is not an irrational decision for college and university administrators, even if it makes no sense financially from the standpoint of the institution, the students, or the taxpayers. If academic accounting practices were less creative and more bluntly honest, the huge losses created by many college sports programs might be carried on the books as career insurance for college administrators.

COLLEGE ATHLETES

Students who engage in sports as an avocation for exercise or recreation must be sharply distinguished from those college athletes for whom sports are the central, consuming purpose of their presence on campus, determining the courses they take, the time these courses are scheduled (so as not to interfere with practice), and determining also whether or not the money to pay their tuition and living expenses will continue to be forthcoming, or will be cut off for athletic deficiencies, as distinguished from academic deficiencies.

Players in campus intramural sports are not really college athletes in this sense, nor are most intercollegiate competitors in swimming, tennis, and other "non-revenue sports," nor perhaps varsity athletes in any sport at some of the smaller colleges where sports are taken casually. Whitman College, for example, was more than a hundred years old before it won a national championship in any sport—skiing, in this case.[23] At Haverford, the head coach of women's tennis and volleyball was able to run up an impressive won-and-lost record while working on her own doctorate in physical education.[24] But these are not big-time college athletics.

The classic college athlete in the sense used here is the big-time football or basketball player, competing in major conferences for the prospect of post-season play and a post-college professional career. Big-time athletics involve major investments of students' time and the college's money. Even at an academically highly-rated institution like Stanford University, where intercollegiate athletics are not an overwhelming interest, the athletic director dispenses more than 250 full scholarships, worth $5.7 million a year—some of this paid by earnings on a $38 million athletic endowment raised for this purpose.[25] This is more than is officially reported at some colleges and universities where intercollegiate sports play a larger role than at Stanford, for many of these other institutions channel money for athletes through the regular financial aid office, so as not to call it all athletic scholarships.[26]

Ivy League colleges award no athletic scholarships, but they are also seldom prominent among the nation's top-rated football or basketball teams. Big-time sports means big-time money—and big-time pressure on the college athletes. It is significant that Ivy League teams were once able to compete with top teams from around the country, half a century or more ago, but that was before television and other big-money forces made college football and basketball too demanding of students' time and institutional resources to be compatible with maintaining high academic standards for college athletes.

The Athletic Cartel

The basic relationship between the college—which is to say, the coach—and the college athlete is very asymmetrical. With minor exceptions, the athlete is committed to the institution for four years, whereas the institution is committed to the athlete for only one year at a time. If his athletic performance falls below expectations, financial aid can be terminated, but if his performance reaches a professional level before the four years are up, he is expected to remain in college.

Until relatively recently, the professional leagues abided by their collusive agreements with the NCAA and would not touch such athletes until their college eligibility was up, or until 5 years after their class had entered college. A lawsuit forced the National Basketball Association to violate this collusive agreement and individual legal challenges have forced the National Football League and the NCAA to make more exceptions.[27] However, it speaks volumes about the mismatch between coaches and college athletes that such one-sided arrangements could have been created and endured so long.

There are few, if any, transactions in any marketplace with as gross a mismatch between the transactors as those between a high school athlete negotiating with a college coach for a place on the team. Not only is the coach likely to be more experienced by decades, but he also controls vast sums of money, from both inside and outside the university, carries much weight with the college admissions committee (even in Ivy League schools),[28] and has contacts and influence with high school coaches, for whom he can do various favors,[29] and who in return can influence their athletes in an apparently disinterested way, "for their own good," to sign with college coach X rather than college coach Y. Most important of all, the coach belongs to a tight, nationwide cartel—the NCAA—which sets the basic terms within which individual coaches compete for players.

As if these were not enough mismatches, big-time coaches have dealt with generations of students but the student is facing his first encounter with the labyrinthine world of college athletics. Finally, a disproportionate number of top athletes in football and basketball are black youngsters from poor backgrounds, poorly educated themselves and with poorly educated parents, and are often the first members of their families to go to college, so that they are unlikely to have any informed guides to rely on. Having seen many black professional athletes with huge salaries, they may not realize that more than 90 percent of all college athletes in football, basketball, or baseball will never play professionally.[30] Black collegiate athletes who do not go on into professional sports are especially bad off. Only 27 percent of black athletes in Division I colleges have graduated five years after entering college, compared to 52 percent among white Division I athletes. The black athletes typically entered college with much weaker academic records and 43 percent leave in bad standing, compared to 20 percent among white athletes in the same Division.[31] These youngsters have simply wasted their time and risked their bodies to entertain and enrich other people.

In effect, the college athlete in big-time sports is buying a lottery ticket and paying for it with his body and with four years of his life. He may also pay for it through the corrosive cynicism generated by participating in the various shabby tricks designed to maintain his eligibility to play, by pretending to be a student while avoiding the demands of real education.

Athletics versus Education

Being a college athlete is a full-time job. A study commissioned by the NCAA showed that Division I athletes spent an average of 30 hours a week on their principal sport, during the season for that sport, and 18 hours a week even during the off-season. In both cases, this was more time than the average college athlete spent in classes and laboratories. During the sport season, the time spent on athletics exceeded both class and lab time, and the time spent preparing for class, all combined.[32]

While this was a study of Division I institutions, Division I is itself divided into three parts, with Division I-A representing the most intense competition—big-time sports. Professor Harry Edwards, a sociologist at Berkeley specializing in studies of athletics, has estimated that Division I-A basketball players spend 50 hours a week on their sport and football players up to 60 hours. Moreover, he points out, the gruelling nature of this activity often means that fatigue, aches, and pains render their remaining hours less effective for academic work. Others knowledgeable about college sports have made similar estimates of the time they consume in the top conferences.[33]

Athletics versus Academics

Given the demands of high-pressure sports and the sub-standard academic backgrounds of many college athletes, there is little prospect of serious academic work for many of those who compete in the top athletic conferences. Yet they must pass enough courses to remain eligible to play under NCAA rules. Therefore they "major in eligibility," as it is cynically phrased. That is, they find such courses and such instructors (including athletic coaches) as will enable them to get by without spending time that would cut into the athletic requirements of practice, learning plays, physical conditioning, and travel. At Miami University, a basketball player who never attended a class nor did any assignment was given an A by the instructor—who was his coach. At Hampton University, the academic records of football players were simply altered.[34] Even at Harvard, courses characterized by the student guide as "gut" courses were also noted for attracting athletes.[35]

Often the team has tutors or advisors who help players with their choice of courses, as well as helping them in those courses. One such academic counselor boasted that he could keep a cockroach eligible for two years.[36] Periodic scandals of illiterate athletes going through college suggest that the exaggeration was not as great as might be thought.[37] Some idea of how modest the requirements of eligibility can be may be indicated by the record of a University of Iowa football player who took courses on billiards, coaching football, soccer, and bowling as a freshman and ended up with a 1.62 grade-point average (D+) out of a possible 4.0. By making a D in a summer school course, he rescued his eligibility for his sophomore year.[38]

Even with such lenient standards, some athletes fail to maintain their eligibility—and some colleges let them play anyway. Florida State University, for example, allowed a star athlete to play in the Sugar Bowl after he flunked all his fall semester courses.[39] At North Carolina State University, basketball players' grades were changed under pressure from coaches.[40] For some athletes, ignoring the rules and having them bent or disregarded by academic authorities is a pattern that begins even before they reach college. A high school teacher in Waco, Texas, was fired after refusing to change a student's grade to maintain his eligibility.[41] A Detroit high school teacher discovered that many grades he had given athletes had been changed from failing to passing before being entered into the official record.[42] A former dean of Arizona State University put it this way:

> There are certain truths in life. You don't spit into the wind, you don't tug on Superman's cape, and you don't mess around with star football players.[43]

Despite such favoritism and scandal, most top-level (Division I-A) football and basketball players do not graduate—partly because this favoritism is focussed on keeping them eligible to play, not getting them a degree, much less an education. Once again, it is necessary to distinguish the big-time varsity athletes in large, revenue-producing sports like football and basketball from athletes at colleges which do not have high-pressure sports programs and from athletes in such other sports as tennis, swimming, volleyball, or track, whose demands do not usually have such devastating impacts on academic performance.

It is true, but misleading, to say that college athletes as a group graduate from college at a slightly higher rate than students in general[44] because this lumps together athletes in a wide spectrum of sports and institutions. In all the major Division I-A conferences—the Big Ten, the Atlantic Coast Conference, the Pac-10, etc.—football players graduate at a *lower* rate than other students and basketball players graduate at an even lower rate than football players.[45] In the Southeastern Conference, only 14 percent of the basketball players admitted in 1984 had graduated by August 1989.[46] It can also be misleading to point to colleges like Stanford with high academic standards and numerous athletic championships, when those athletic championships have been in sports like tennis, water polo, volleyball, and swimming.[47] Credit is due to some institutions like Georgetown University, where 90 percent of the basketball team graduated, but such institutions are more than

COLLEGES AND UNIVERSITIES

244   COLLEGES AND UNIVERSITIES

counterbalanced by places like Memphis State, where no basketball player graduated for an entire decade.[48]

The big-time college athlete is often as isolated from the
social life of a college as he is from its academic life. Many top
football teams have special separate dormitories for their players—usually with better accommodations and better food than
those for the regular students receive at the same colleges.[49]
Moreover, coaches and boosters have even been known to come
to the rescue of athletes when they get into trouble with the
law.[50] Then, when the student's eligibility eventually runs out,
he usually finds himself out on the street with no skills, no
degree, and perhaps no character.

PART THREE

ASSESSMENT

CHAPTER 10

The Empire Strikes Back

Today the NEA is far larger than the United Auto Workers, larger than the Electrical Workers, larger than the State, County, and Municipal Employees, and larger than the Steelworkers. My friends, we are now the largest union in all of America by a half million members.

—Mary Hatwood Futrell, President
National Education Association[1]

EDUCATION is a vast empire. Both the National Education Association and its chief rival, the American Federation of Teachers, are huge unions with large sums of money available to support political lobbying, and significant blocs of votes to throw onto the scales at election time. The headquarters of the National Education Association in Washington employs more than 500 people and spends well over $100 million dollars a year. The N.E.A. is also the dominant teacher's union in every state except New York, where the rival American Federation of Teachers holds sway.[2] At both the national and the state and local levels, the N.E.A. has vast sums of money available for political purposes and for propaganda campaigns to get the public to see the world as the N.E.A. sees it—for example, to equate bigger school budgets with better education.

Both the elementary and secondary schools, on the one hand, and higher education, on the other, encompass large numbers of people and huge sums of money. With more than $170 billion being spent annually on the education of more than 40 million elementary and secondary school students,[3] education is a major sector of the economy. Higher education is also a very significant part of the education empire, with more than 12 million students, of whom more than 7.2 million are full time and 6.5 million are full-time undergraduates.[4] Colleges and universities spend more than $105 billion annually.[5] Both in higher education and in the elementary and secondary schools, by far most of the money comes from government—whether state, federal, or local.

With millions of jobs, millions of students, and hundreds of billions of dollars at stake, the education establishment has not welcomed criticism or critics. As N.E.A. President Mary Hatwood Futrell put it:

> The Nation's students today are threatened only by the failure of policymakers to give education the money it deserves.[6]

In pursuit of that money, the N.E.A. has become a political power, as well as the largest labor union in the country. In Minnesota, for example, the state affiliates of the N.E.A. and the American Federation of Teachers together often contribute more money to politicians running for statewide office than *all other political organizations in the state*, put together.[7] In higher education as well, there is the same sense of entitlement to other people's money—and the same sense of not needing to justify their own performance. As tax-exempt entities, some colleges and universities have joined in campaigns to raise state taxes from which they benefit.[8] Nor is this sense of entitlement to other people's money limited to tax money. At a meeting of dozens of academic fund-raising organizations, the head of one such organization denounced corporate donations that were earmarked for particular purposes as "something we can't live with."

"How dare they do this?" he asked, and challenged those present: "What are we doing to hold these companies accountable?" *The Chronicle of Higher Education* reported that his speech "was met with wild applause."[9]

While it may be taken as axiomatic in some education establishment circles that they need as much money as possible, with as few restrictions as possible, there is also a sense of a political need to respond to critics. But this is only a political necessity, to be met in ways that are politic, without necessarily being substantive. Both the schools and the colleges and universities have developed many ways of responding to criticism, and ways of seeking to discredit critics, *without having to confront the specifics* of their criticisms. Tactics, rather than arguments, have become standard responses.

ARGUMENTS WITHOUT ARGUMENTS

Even though educators consider themselves to be "thinking people," there is a remarkable absence of substantive arguments in their responses to critics. These responses include evading the specifics of the criticisms and arbitrarily attributing Utopian beliefs to critics. Schools and colleges each have additional substitutes for arguments, specialized for their respective issues.

Evading the Specifics

Critics of particular policies or programs are often depicted as "bashing" the entire enterprise of education or the entire function of teaching. It is as if critics of corruption in the Teamsters' Union were answered by saying that they were "bashing" trucking and failing to understand its vital role in the American economy.

A word like "bashing" conveys absolutely no information, other than a dislike of the criticism, and contributes nothing to a logical or factual assessment of its validity. The issue is not one of critics' "blanket contempt" for the country's universities, as a former Stanford professor has claimed,[10] or that critics "condemn the whole of higher education," as retired Harvard president Derek Bok has charged.[11] Rather, the issue is one of very specific criticisms which such distortions evade, without having to produce any substantive arguments. When Johns Hopkins University president William Richardson said that America "could not and would not do without universities," he was demolishing one of the most flimsy and shabby of all straw men.[12]

Hiding the specifics which have been challenged inside some larger and more innocuous generality is a common tactic at all levels of education. For example, critics of psychological-conditioning or attitude-changing programs in the public schools are depicted as people who "do not want students to call on their personal experiences for any oral or written response to any question or assignment."[13] In other words, the broad generality of "personal experiences" is substituted for the specific kinds of interrogations and assignments imposed by teachers and "facilitators" in brainwashing courses.

Straw Man Utopias

Anyone who argues that particular educational policies and programs have made things worse, and who points to evidence that things were in fact better before such policies and programs were initiated, is almost certain to be depicted as someone who believes in a "golden age" of the past. This trivializing distortion has become common among educators, including the president of Williams College,[14] the president of Harvard University and the dean of its faculty, and a professor at the University of Pennsylvania who responded to criticism of so-called "Afro-centric history" by saying that its critics seem to believe that "if we went back to an earlier time there was a perfect history."[15] Critics are seeking "an intellectual Camelot that never existed," according to Dartmouth president James Freedman.[16] "Edenic" is the characterization of critics' "diatribes" by Duke University Professor Stanley Fish.[17]

The widespread use of such sweeping pronouncements in lieu of arguments raises a fundamental question: Is no policy to be judged by whether it makes matters better or worse, simply because its proponents arbitrarily choose to characterize its critics as believing in a golden age, Eden, perfection, or Camelot? This tactic is one of a number of ways of seeming to argue, without actually using any arguments. Misdirection has long been one of the skills of the professional magician. It is increasingly one of the skills of the professional educator.

THE SCHOOLS

The public schools' responses to criticism have been both verbal and institutional. The verbal responses have been largely tactical, rather than substantive—typically blaming the shortcomings of the school on the problems of others or the demands of others.

The Problems of Others

Blaming social problems outside the school for academic short-comings inside the school has become a common tactic of educators. Typical of this trend was the response of a California teacher who said, "the real culprit is the dramatically changing student population," including "pistol-packing gang members, Third World immigrants," and the like.[18]

There is no question that serious social problems exist outside the schools and beyond their control. But the real question is whether such facts can account for the downward trends of the past generation. Gang violence, for example, no doubt takes its academic toll in many inner-city schools, but is that where the decline in test scores has been concentrated? Mexican American youngsters have in fact had small *increases* in their S.A.T. scores in recent years and black students have had even greater increases—all while the national average has been drifting downward.[19] As for immigrant children from the Third World, so many Vietnamese youngsters have excelled academically, become valedictorians and won prizes, that this is scarcely considered news anymore.

As noted in Chapter 1, the problem is not that more low scores from disadvantaged children are being averaged in, thereby bringing down the national average. On the contrary, there has been a sharp decline *at the top* in the number of high-scoring youngsters.

While the arguments of the education establishment will not stand up under scrutiny, the more fundamental and intractable problem is that they are not subjected to scrutiny in the first place, either by educators themselves or by those in the media who uncritically repeat and amplify their excuses.

The Demands of Others

Just as comedian Flip Wilson says, "The devil made me do it," so education officials often say, in effect, "The public made me do it," when defending practices which are otherwise difficult to defend. Thus the intrusions of all sorts of non-academic material, activities, and programs into the public schools have been depicted as responsibilities loaded onto the school system by "society." But this claim too will not stand up under scrutiny. Throughout most of the twentieth century, there has been an on-going tug-of-war between educators and laymen, with the National Education Association and other establishment groups pushing for the introduction of innumerable non-academic courses and programs into the public schools, while the laymen have attempted to promote a concentration on academic subjects.[20] In recent times especially, the public is often kept uninformed, or is deliberately misled about such programs, precisely in order to avoid adverse public reactions to fashionable "innovations."

Even a sympathetic writer, describing the introduction of a program called *Man: A Course of Study* into the Oregon public schools, found that education officials kept it as quiet as possible to avoid parental opposition, and even among those teachers who were themselves enthusiastic about teaching this curriculum, only 4 percent favored it on grounds that the students would like it.[21] Yet promoters of this program have depicted it as a course that will "permit children to gather data" and "formulate hypotheses" through cross-cultural comparisons.[22] If one takes this seriously, a picture emerges of elementary school children demanding to "formulate hypotheses" in anthropology and to test these hypotheses against data graciously supplied by those willing to "permit" them to do so.

This picture of such spontaneous desires hardly fits the facts. Like other programs such as "Quest," *Man: A Course of Study* was heavily promoted nationwide. The National Science Foundation spent at least $200,000 annually "to hold promotion conferences for school decision-makers and officials, to lobby them to buy the program." This was in addition to millions of dollars in federal money spent to develop the program in the first place and "NSF grants to train teachers in the MACOS philosophy and pedagogy."[23] As with so many other claims by educators to be responding to public demand, this claim was a phoney, used to disguise the self-interest of promoters and brainwashers.

A "death education" curriculum has likewise been defended as a way to "help students learn about the function of funerals and the funeral director in our society."[24] Again, it is pictured as if students want to do this, and the teacher is just trying to help, like a good Samaritan. Moreover, the theme of meeting an unmet need is reinforced by the sentence introducing a chapter in a textbook for this psychological curriculum: "Death and dying are often considered to be taboo areas for discussion in our society."[25] Like so much else that is arbitrarily assumed in the field of education, the assumption that death was not commonly discussed before in schools turns out, upon investigation, to be utterly false.

In reality, death and dying were very common themes in the old *McGuffey's Readers* of an earlier era.[26] Death was dealt with not only often, but sensitively—but not in the manner of so-called "death education" today. The difference in tone and approach may be illustrated by a *McGuffey's Reader* story about a child whose mother, suffering from a long illness, asked her to go get her a glass of water. The daughter recalled, years later:

> I went and brought her the water, but I did not do it kindly.
> Instead of smiling, and kissing her as I had been wont to do,
> I set the glass down very quickly, and left the room.[27]

Feeling guilty later that night, she decided to ask forgiveness in the morning—but the next morning she found her mother dead. The daughter recalled:

> I bowed down by her side and sobbed in the bitterness of my
> heart. I then wished that I might die, and be buried with her;
> and, old as I now am, I would give worlds, were they mine
> to give, could my mother but have lived to tell me she forgave
> my childish ingratitude.[28]

This was not the gimmicky approach of today's "death education," with its "dim the lights" instructions to teachers,[29] or its self-congratulation at discussing a subject ignorantly assumed to have been "taboo" in the past. Nor was this the creation of pompous jargon like "thanatology" for death education or "Type II (HD-II)" to convey the simple fact that two types of "horrendous deaths" were being discussed.[30] Such pathetic attempts to seem "scientific" only betray the hollowness so characteristic of "affective education" in general.

No matter how false, the claim to be responding to an unmet need, expressed in public demands, is a recurring theme in a wide variety of attitude-changing programs. Many of those promoting new curriculum packages are quite sophisticated in their backstage efforts, which often means making the demand seem to be coming from "society" at large. Planned Parenthood, for example, has instructed its followers on how to create the appearance of a demand for its programs: "Pack the board room with your supporters," it said and "avoid a public encounter" with "the opposition."[31]

However much attitude-changing programs claim to be responding to public demands, the tactics used to get them inaugurated and continued suggest a clear awareness by their proponents of a need to *avoid* public scrutiny. One symptom of this awareness is the repeated changing of curriculum titles. As a writer who has studied this phenomenon said: "Titles proliferate because once the public catches on to the nature of a program in one place, the same curriculum re-emerges somewhere else under a new title."[32] The "Quest" program warns its teachers and "facilitators" to avoid using terms which "tend to raise 'red flags' among the critics." These terms include "values clarification," "role-playing" and "self-concept"[33]—terms whose concrete meanings have become too well known over the years to be useful any longer as smoke screens.

Institutional Defenses

Verbal tactics are not the only tactics used by the educational empire as it strikes back at critics. These critics include not only outsiders but also individual teachers. These latter are, however, the easiest for the educational establishment to deal with. Ultimately, the teacher who is critical or skeptical of fashionable "innovations" can be dealt with by threatening his or her career, but some can be brought into line by more subtle means. These include special rewards for teachers who first jump on the bandwagon of a new program,[34] hostile responses to teachers who are reluctant or questioning,[35] or a side-track-ing of teachers in favor of "facilitators" who come in from outside to conduct the psychological program sessions.[36] Similar tactics have been used in England.[37]

The testimony of an Arizona parent before the U.S. Department of Education in Washington suggests something of the untenable position of a teacher critic: "I had one teacher express to me that she would lose her job if she showed any support at all for the parents who were questioning the program."[38] Another parent, appalled at a movie showing "masturbation in detail" in a so-called "Human Development" curriculum received help from a teacher, but in a manner indicative of the pressures the teacher was under:

> A teacher called me anonymously and said she had a copy of the 13-year curriculum guide and she would leave it in her top desk drawer. I would come in when she was out, take it, and use it any way I wanted. I xeroxed 200 copies, spread it around the school, and both the program and the principal were removed from the school.[39]

That such cloak-and-dagger methods are necessary suggests something of the obstacles put in the way of the facts coming out.

Parents who seek through official channels to see specific materials used in a curriculum can be stalled, told to come back another day, given only part of the material, told that a committee will be convened to look into it—and these tactics can go on for months, or even years. A Department of Education hearing officer who has followed attempts of parents to see various program materials, and the educators' tactical responses, concluded, "the primary aim was to wear them down."[40] If parents sense the futility of their individual efforts and organize, then these organized groups will be depicted as "censors" trying to stifle "freedom" in the schools. However, people who argue this way never say that *McGuffey's Readers* were "censored" when they were replaced by other textbooks. Only after the kinds of books they want are in place is any criticism of these choices called "censorship." However, this has often proved to be a politically very effective tactic, substituting for an argument.

School Choice

Few things arouse such all-out opposition from the educational establishment and their media allies as proposals to allow parents a choice as to the schools their children attend. Here the empire strikes back with a long litany of objections, of which these are the most common:

1. Parents would make bad choices.
2. Parents who make good choices would take their children out of substandard schools, leaving behind in hopelessness the children of parents with less knowledge, concern, or initiative.
3. Parental choice would destroy the American tradition of the common school for all, replacing it with schools segregated by race, income, religion, and other social divisions.
4. It would lead to an unconstitutional government subsidy of religious schools.
5. It would be prohibitively expensive.

The first objection goes to the heart of the issue, for this objection stands or falls on the assumption that parents lack the knowledge, interest, and initiative to make as good choices as those made by the educational establishment. After more than a quarter of a century of declining school performances, the claim that educators have some mysterious "expertise" which parents cannot grasp is a claim that is hard to take seriously. Most members of the educational establishment do not in fact phrase this claim in the form of an explicit comparison, but instead deplore the possibility of "schools that pander shamelessly to parents,"[41] suggest that parents are unlikely to choose on the basis of "rigorous standards."[42] or claim that "poor families" are too beset with problems to be able to "cope with the added responsibility" of "evaluating different schools."[43]

Although such arguments dwell on, or exaggerate, the deficiencies of parents, the alternative receives no such critical scrutiny, whether that alternative is allowing children's schools to be chosen by the very educators who have produced disaster after disaster, or allowing the child's school to be chosen by the accident of arbitrary school boundary lines.

Despite paternalistic concerns expressed that disadvantaged minority children might be left behind in various parental choice schemes, due to the apathy of their parents, polls have repeatedly shown that support for parental choice has been higher among blacks than among whites.[44] In Chicago alone, there are dozens of private, non-Catholic schools that are predominantly or wholly black[45]—in addition to the Catholic schools located in black neighborhoods. In Berkeley, one third of all the children in Catholic schools are black, and in Oakland 62 percent of the children in Catholic schools are black.[46] Clearly, there are black parents in black neighborhoods who are not only concerned about their children's education, but who are also prepared to make financial sacrifices out of below-average income, in order to get their children a decent education. Often, most of the black children in a Catholic school are not Catholic, but are being sent there for educational reasons.

Not all parents are conscientious, of course, whether among blacks, whites, or any other group. But any policy must be compared with an alternative, not with an ideal. One of the most remarkable objections to parental choice is that not all children would benefit. This Utopia-or-nothing approach has been expressed, among other places, in a *New York Times* editorial which asks, "what's to be done about the children left behind, whose parents are indifferent, afraid or absent?" The *Times* is especially opposed to enabling "the cream of the crop of poor children to attend non-public schools."[47] In other words poor children who are ready *right now* to go elsewhere, to get a decent education denied them in their substandard schools, are to be held hostage in those schools until such indefinite time as either (1) all the other children around them are also ready for quality education, or (2) one of the innumerable educational "reforms" that come and go finally works. It is hard to imagine a more unconscionable sacrifice of flesh-and-blood children to ideological visions. Moreover, if this is such a wonderful principle—either morally or educationally—then why do we permit the children of the affluent (such as editorial writers) to escape being used as hostages for the greater glory of social justice?

Seldom does any social advance take place simultaneously among all members of any large social group. Typically, the most far-sighted or most venturesome members of the group try the new way, or migrate to a new place, and others follow in their wake as their success becomes apparent. To demand that low-income people alone must all be ready at once is to demand what is seldom, if ever, found among any other people in real life. As to those youngsters initially left behind in substandard schools, it is hard even to conceive how they could be worse off educationally then they are today. The only difference from today would be that now they would have before them the living examples of neighbors, friends, and relatives who are getting the benefits of better schools. Some of those initially left behind would undoubtedly follow their classmates. Moreover, the exodus from substandard schools would itself create incentives for those schools to improve, to prevent more losses of students and the inevitable losses of budget and jobs which follow.

An equally baffling argument is often used that it would be "unfair" to the public schools to leave with them the worst students, especially with the public schools operating not only under the handicap of having to accept everyone, but also under the additional handicaps of innumerable mandated rules, policies, and commitments whose rigidity and red tape interfere with the educational process. However, the very concept of "fairness" applies to relationships between *human beings*—not institutions. Institutions are merely a means to an end, that end being to serve human beings. There are no moral obligations to institutions which do not serve human purposes as well as other institutions. The most important fairness is fairness to children.

This does not mean that public schools are to be banished categorically. The whole point of allowing parental choice is to permit a widespread monitoring of school performance to replace arbitrary policies based on *a priori* beliefs. Those public schools which prove to be able to do a good enough job will undoubtedly survive the competition, just as many public schools survive and flourish in many affluent communities today, where private schools are both available and affordable to the high-income people in those communities. In other cases, where the public schools are too snarled in red tape to compete effectively, then competition provides an incentive for the educational establishment itself—the teachers' unions, the state education departments, etc.—to work to get rid of the red tape, in the interest of institutional survival. If the red tape nevertheless proves to be impossible to get rid of, that is all the more reason to let institutions die off when they are incapable of doing their job.

The argument that parental choice would be socially divisive is painfully ironic, in view of the deep social divisions in the public schools as they exist today. A nationwide study, headed by the widely respected scholar James S. Coleman of the University of Chicago, found that "blacks and whites are less segregated within the Catholic schools than are blacks and whites in public schools."[48] Moreover, the gap in academic performance between black and white students was less in the Catholic schools than in the public schools.[49] The education establishment's claims of social divisiveness have been carried to the extremes of claiming that parental choice could lead to schools representing ideological fringe fanatics of the left or right, religious cults, or purveyors of bizarre philosophies. Yet existing private schools, especially those sought out by parents from disadvantaged groups, have tended to be more traditional than the public schools. Indeed, it is precisely in the public schools that brainwashing with *avant-garde* ideas, and even the occult, have been increasingly introduced into the curriculum.

The constitutionality of parental choice plans that would allow public money to be used to pay for children to attend private, religiously affiliated schools is a legal question for the courts. The courts already allow some federal money to be spent in religiously affiliated educational institutions. However, even under a worst-case scenario, the worst that could happen would be that expanded options would not be as wide as they could be—but they would nevertheless be wider than they are today.

Finally, the most unfounded claim of all is that parental choice plans would be costlier than the present public school education. In reality, the average cost of educating students in private schools is less than the cost of educating them in the public schools. The Catholic schools tend to be especially low-cost. In Oakland, for example, the Catholic schools spent only about one-third as much per pupil as the public schools in the same city.[50] It has been commonplace for private schools to produce better education for less money.

The opposition of the educational establishment to school choice proposals has not been limited to presenting arguments. They have also used their political muscle to get choice plans scaled back, under-financed, or encumbered with red tape, where they have been unable to stop such plans completely. For example, almost never do such plans for parental choice allow the student who transfers out of the system to take along as much money as the system spends per pupil. Having done as much as possible to cripple the choice actually offered to parents, the educational establishment then points triumphantly to the fact that parents have not been as enthusiastic for the shriveled options presented to them as choice advocates had suggested when advocating a full-bodied set of options. Moreover, the National Education Association engages in tricky manipulations of statistics, in order to understate how much use is made of parental choice. Although the whole point of allowing parental choice is to permit a selection among *schools*, the N.E.A. measures the usage of such choice by how many transfers take place out of the school *district*.[51] Obviously, few parents are going to send their children great distances from home, but the N.E.A.'s tricky statistics conceal how many transfer among schools within the district.

COLLEGES AND UNIVERSITIES

Critics of American colleges and universities have made four principal criticisms—that (1) the quality of American college education has declined and is unacceptably low, that (2) ideology has supplanted academic skills in too many social science and humanities courses, that (3) campus racial policies have had disastrous consequences, and that (4) free speech has been sacrificed to the ideological conformity of "politically correct" thinking.

By and large, academic leaders have not confronted any of these arguments, but have instead sidestepped them and then struck back in various ways. These ways include claims that "the public made me do it," radical redefinitions of words to create a protective academic Newspeak, and a general burying of specific issues in larger and more innocuous generalities. Among the things the academic establishment defends in this way are ideological double standards on campus, the declining quality of college education, the price-fixing cartel which set tuition for decades, and the tenure system at the heart of so much academic irresponsibility. That academic spokesmen should seek to defend colleges and universities from critics is understandable. That they so often resort to tactical responses rather than substantive arguments makes those defenses suspect.

The Demands of "Society"

The public school administrators' claim that "the public made me do it" is echoed in higher education as well. Former Harvard University President Derek Bok has called most of the charges by critics of academia "flawed" because "they ignore basic conflicts and contradictions in the demands society makes on universities."[52] Yet almost all the academic policies attacked by critics—propaganda courses, racial double standards, the erosion of curriculum requirements, skyrocketing tuition, and ideological intolerance—are responses to *internal pressures* generated by various constituencies within the academic world itself.

Preferential admissions policies, for example, are not demanded by the public. Indeed, they have even been repudiated by a majority of black students[53]—a majority ignored by academic administrators, who respond instead to organized, vocal, and threatening minority "spokesmen." The public has not demanded that people who attempt to speak on campus be shouted down or be assaulted by those who disagree with them, that students in their dormitories be targets of officially sanctioned thought-police, or that campus disciplinary procedures become kangaroo courts when ideological issues are involved. The public has certainly not demanded higher tuition or the reduced teaching loads and expanded boondoggles which make them necessary, nor the academic cartel arrangements which made possible charging all that the traffic will bear.

These developments in American higher education exist precisely because academic decision-making under faculty self-governance is so insulated from the public's knowledge or influence. The panic in academia when alternative, uncontrolled channels of information about campus events open up to the public—a small newspaper published periodically by Accuracy in Academia, or weekly or monthly independent student newspapers—suggests that academics know all too well that what they are doing is not at all in line with what the public wants, and will come under increasing pressure if the public finds out about it. Saying "the public made me do it" would not be a valid excuse, even if the public did in fact favor the things being done. Its falsity only highlights the absence of an argument.

Sometimes it is not the general public but a student constituency to whom the academic establishment claims to be responding. Harvard's Dean Henry Rosovsky, as well as its former president Derek Bok, has made the argument that believers in a free market are inconsistent in criticizing colleges and universities, which are responding to what students want and are willing to pay for.[54] This was said by officials of an institution at the center of a cartel that has been meeting annually, for decades, precisely in order to *prevent* this from being a free market.

Organized coordination of tuition-setting and of financial aid is further abetted by the magnitude and mechanisms of government financial aid programs. Part of what is called "financial aid" in academia is simply a fancy name for a discount on paper, as it would be called more plainly and more honestly in ordinary commercial transactions, even transactions with used-car dealers. Where there is real money changing hands on behalf of students, that financial aid is largely provided by, or guaranteed by, the federal government. In academic year 1988–89, for example, the federal government either directly or indirectly provided nearly $20 billion out of a total of nearly $27 billion in student financial aid nationwide, including the paper discounts of the colleges and universities themselves.[55] The "free market" of which Messieurs Bok and Rosovsky speak is this government-subsidized academic cartel.

The specific terms under which the government provides student financial aid virtually guarantees tuition escalation to unaffordable levels in private colleges and universities. (State colleges and universities are under political pressures to keep tuition low.) The federal formula for determining how much aid a student gets first determines the "expected family contribution," based upon family income, assets, number of children, and other measures of ability to pay. Federal aid begins where tuition and other charges exceed this "expected family contribution."[56] A private college or university which kept its tuition affordable—that is, no greater than the "expected family contribution"—could forfeit millions of dollars annually in federal money. For example, if College X can provide a good education at a tuition of $8,000 a year, while its average student's family can afford $9,000, then it loses opportunities to receive federal money. By raising its tuition to $12,000, it not only gets an additional $1,000 per student from their families but also an additional $3,000 per student from the government. In short, there is no incentive to keep tuition affordable and every incentive to make it unaffordable.

Dean Rosovsky, an economist, surely knows that government subsidies to agriculture make food more expensive than it would be in a free market, and government subsidies to the maritime industry make shipping more expensive than it would be in a free market, so it can hardly be surprising that government subsidies of college tuition make these tuitions higher than they would be in a free market. Moreover, in any sector of the economy where price competition is reduced or eliminated, there is also a common economic phenomenon called "non-price competition," in the form of frills added to the basic product or service being sold, in order to woo customers. Professor Chester E. Finn, Jr., of Vanderbilt University, a noted authority on education, has described this phenomenon in the academic world:

> Instead of vying to offer the best, trimmest product at the lowest possible price, colleges compete to erect elaborate facilities, to offer trendy new programs, and to dangle before prospective students the gaudiest array of special services, off-campus options, extra-curricular activities, snazzy dorms, and yuppified dining-hall menus. . . . A Mount Holyoke dean terms this the "Chivas Regal strategy."[57]

Such frills are not a response to a free market but are common symptoms of non-price competition in a market that is *not* free. Before commercial airlines were deregulated, their passengers were much more likely to receive various kinds of frills. But the advent of price competition after deregulation meant that passengers received what they wanted more than they wanted frills—that is, to get where they were going at a lower cost. If the academic world ever becomes the "free market" of which Rosovsky and Bok speak, many academic frills can be expected to fall by the wayside as well, as institutions compete to keep tuition within students' ability to pay—instead of having incentives under present conditions to make sure that tuition exceeds what most people can afford.

Another prominent member of the education establishment, Harold Howe II, former U.S. Commissioner of Education and Ford Foundation executive, has likewise argued that the long list of ancillary services provided by colleges help justify "obviously necessary tuition increases." This was said in response to what he called "grousing" by former Secretary of Education William J. Bennett concerning tuition increases. According to Howe, college education today is "a bargain." Nothing, however, is a bargain unless it supplies what the consumers most want at a price representing its cost of production. But because tuition payments are supplemented by endowment income, government subsidies, and other sources of money, the price of education is able to rise far beyond the costs necessary to produce it.

In the absence of stockholders, who could receive the excess as dividends, this excess is absorbed by the kinds of ancillary activities which Harold Howe lists, as well as by many other expansions of administrative bureaucracy and faculty perquisites. Nor is the government financial aid, which is so much a part of this process, primarily a matter of helping "needy students," as Howe claims.[58] That is the image of the past but the reality of today is large-scale price discrimination and a government subsidy system which rewards colleges for making tuition unaffordable.

So-called "need-based" financial aid can be as oblivious to academic ability as it is to ability to pay. Some colleges in deep financial trouble have staved off bankruptcy by admitting semi-literate derelicts and other unlikely "students" whose tuitions, paid through government financial aid programs, would enable the college to survive. At least one free-lance recruiter has made a lucrative career out of performing this service for several colleges and numerous "students." Many of these "students" have simply taken the expense money from their government-guaranteed loans and disappeared into the streets from which they came.[59] While these are extreme cases, they illustrate a principle at work in less extreme cases: Scholarships are no longer a reward for being a scholar. They are part of a larger scheme of price discrimination and subsidization of colleges. Scholarships earmarked for minority students are a further extension of the principle of funnelling money into colleges without safeguards, for the students in question need not be either poor or deserving.

A remarkable example of the education empire striking back occurred when a U.S. Department of Education ruling in 1990 called into question the legality of race-based financial aid. A chorus of outcries from academics and politicians prompted a quick reversal, on the self-contradictory ground that poor minority students would be denied an education. Obviously minority students who were poor would be eligible for *need-based* aid, rather than race-based aid. Indeed, most minority students on financial aid were in fact receiving that aid on income grounds rather than racial grounds.[60] Yet the knee-jerk response of the media, academia, and politicians enabled money to continue flowing to individuals without any demonstrated financial need, nor any other entitlement besides their ancestry.

Academic Newspeak

Among the many academic substitutes for argument is the special use of words, redefined like Orwellian Newspeak, to mean something wholly different from what virtually everyone else understands these words to mean. As already noted, the word "opportunity" is widely used to describe compulsory assignments in psychological-conditioning programs in the public schools. At leading colleges across the country, the word "harassment" is used in a similarly dishonest way to include the expression of any adverse opinion about any behavior, group or organization that the college views favorably, whether or not that expression occurs within sight or earshot of those criticized, and even when it involves no personal contact whatever.

When a conservative student newspaper at the University of Pennsylvania included a campus homosexual organization on its list of the biggest wastes of money by the university,[61] it was deemed guilty of "harassment," lost its official recognition, and the university bookstore stopped advertising in it.[62] M.I.T.'s report urging an anti-harassment policy defined harassment to include, among other things, anything which creates an "offensive environment." This includes things said or done, "on or off campus" and penalties range "up to and including termination of employment or student status."[63] At the University of Connecticut "harassment" includes "misdirected laughter" or even "conspicuous exclusion from conversation."[64] When not talking to someone becomes "harassment," Newspeak clearly reigns.

A special class of tendentious rhetoric has been created by the simple use of words which refer to conditions *before the fact*—"access," "prejudice," "privilege," "exclusion," "opportunity," etc.—to refer instead to results *after the fact*. Outside of academia, no one would say that Babe Ruth had more "opportunity" to hit home runs than his team mates had. If anything, he had less opportunity, because pitchers became very cautious about how they pitched to him and often walked him, rather than take a chance in a critical situation. What was different about Babe Ruth was his performance—that is, the results *ex post*. Yet, in academia, performance and behavior are shunted aside by rhetoric which implicitly assumes that whatever result is observed *ex post* is a measure of circumstances *ex ante*.

For example, writings which have become classics because many generations of educated people have appreciated them, are referred to in many academic circles as "privileged" writings, taught to the "exclusion" of other works. Typically, no argument or evidence has been considered necessary to support such characterizations. This *utter disregard of behavior and performance* runs through all sorts of academic Newspeak, confusing *ex post* results with prior conditions. For example, any adverse judgment of the behavior or performance of any of a number of groups currently in favor is automatically dismissed as racism, sexism, or homophobia—that is, as prejudices before the fact rather than assessments after the fact.

Again, these are arguments without arguments, because it is not even considered necessary to advance a speck of evidence to support such characterizations. It is, presumably, impossible for various individuals or groups to have done anything to merit any adverse conclusion on any aspect of their behavior or performance. Conversely, any groups or segments of the population with higher achievements are called "privileged." Although this kind of rhetoric is especially prevalent among ideological zealots, it has spread well beyond their circles to become part of mainstream academic thinking. Thus Derek Bok has argued that to apply the same admissions standards to minority applicants as to everyone else would be to "exclude them from the university."[65]

Academic Quality

The quality of American college education has been under attack in recent years from a number of critics, of whom former Secretary of Education William Bennett and best-selling author Allan Bloom have been the most prominent. But, while critics tend to focus on the problems of undergraduate education, defenders tend either to shift the focus to the graduate level or to lump the two together, as President James Duderstadt of the University of Michigan did when he said, "we've developed the strongest system of higher education in the world."[66] Harvard's Derek Bok also shifted the focus as he struck back against critics:

> In international opinion surveys, our universities invariably dominate. We are the country of choice for students around the world seeking to pursue their education abroad. Business leaders and government officials from overseas extol the quality of our academic research and admire its stimulative effect on the economy.[67]

Statistical studies of the contribution of education to American economic development seem to confirm the conclusion that education has been a major positive force.[68] However, both the statistical and the impressionistic evidence suffer from the same fundamental flaw: They lump together all sorts of heterogeneous activities and call them "education," just as Derek Bok lumped together both teaching and research in extolling "our universities." No one doubts that the development of hybrid corn through agricultural research or the development of a polio vaccine through medical research have been of enormous value to the human race. That does not mean that the tendentious mumbo-jumbo of "deconstructionism" in literature or the propaganda courses which are spreading increasingly through the undergraduate curriculum are a contribution to American society or to the world.

The influx of foreign students is likewise by no means unequivocal in its implications. Vast numbers of people choose to come to the United States, whether legally or illegally, as tourists or as permanent residents. That foreign students should be like other people in wanting to come to the United States is hardly decisive evidence as to the quality of American colleges—which is what is principally being criticized—especially since nearly half of all foreign students come to the U.S. for postgraduate study.[69] Moreover, it cannot be assumed automatically that those who come to go to college are seeking the best education in the world.

The largest number of foreign students in any American academic institution in 1989–90—more than 5,000—went to Miami-Dade Community College,[70] a respectable institution but hardly where one would go for world-class scholarship. Among colleges with undergraduates from more than a hundred countries, the California State University in Los Angeles—definitely not to be confused with U.C.L.A.—led the way with students from 120 countries.[71] In percentage terms, among the institutions where more than 10 percent of the students are foreign are Cogswell College in San Francisco, an institution of little renown, despite its auspicious location, and such Washington, D.C. institutions as Mount Vernon College and Southeastern University[72]—both little known, even among Washingtonians.

This is not to say that foreign students go only to lesser-known or lower-quality American colleges and universities. Foreigners are of course even more heterogeneous than Americans, since they come from everywhere on the planet except the United States. Many foreign students in fact go to leading American colleges and universities. More than 2,200 were enrolled at Harvard in 1989–90, for example, though that was still less than half as many as were enrolled at Miami-Dade Community College.[73] In short, the argument that large influxes of foreign students are evidence of the high quality of American colleges and universities will not stand up under scrutiny.

There is no need to challenge the claim that American academic research is among the most highly regarded anywhere. Harvard Dean Henry Rosovsky made a more complete statement when he claimed, "fully two thirds to three quarters of the best universities in the world are located in the United States" and at the same time admitted, "we also are home to a large share of the world's worst colleges and universities."[74] Elsewhere he clarified this point by noting that the top American universities he was referring to were "about 50 to 100 institutions"[75]—out of more than 3,000. The *lumping together* of all kinds of institutions, courses, and programs, at all kinds of levels of quality—ranging down to some of the worst in the world—is what make both impressionistic and statistical assessments of the value of "education" in general so meaningless and misleading. Moreover, however much American research universities predominate internationally, that is not to say that their associated—indeed, subsidiary—colleges are providing high-quality education for undergraduates.

There is yet another side to the question of the influx of foreign students and the high quality of leading American research universities. Both phenomena are especially prominent at the postgraduate level. As of 1989, just over one-fourth of all doctorates awarded at American universities were awarded to foreigners.[76] The more difficult and demanding the academic standards of the field, generally the higher the percentage of the Ph.D.s which went to foreigners. In mathematics and engineering, half or more of all the Ph.D.s awarded at American universities have been earned by foreigners.[77] In the much easier—not to say trivial—field of education, Americans have their highest representation among doctoral recipients, 83 percent.[78]

Over the past two decades, in every field surveyed by the Council of Graduate Schools, the proportion of graduate degrees in the United States going to Americans has declined.[79] In mathematics the change has been especially dramatic. In 1977, just under 20 percent of all Ph.D.s in mathematics in the United States were received by foreigners. But a decade later that proportion had more than doubled to 44 percent.[80] The number of Ph.D.s in mathematics earned by Americans declined absolutely, by 39 percent.[81] As a *New York Times* news account revealed, there was a reason for such trends:

Recognition is growing that many American students cannot make the grade in the demanding graduate and postgraduate levels because they have not received adequate training and motivation, especially in the sciences, from kindergarten through college.

"Our graduate schools are extremely attractive internationally," said Peter D. Syverson, director of information services for the Council of Graduate Schools, a national organization. "We get terrific applications from abroad, but not the same level and quality from American students."[82]

This declining representation of American college graduates among the recipients of postgraduate degrees in the United States cannot be blamed on reduced financial support. On the contrary, during the two decades when Americans were receiving a declining proportion of postgraduate degrees, across fields, expenditures on higher education were generally rising. These expenditures were rising not only absolutely, but even as a percentage of a growing Gross National Product (GNP). By 1987, almost twice as high a percentage of GNP went to higher education as in 1960.[83] As elsewhere in education, money has never been the crucial factor.

To such plain and damning facts, defenders of the educational establishment such as Derek Bok can only reply with the misdirection of a magician: When critics denounce American college teaching, respond with praise of American university research. When critics condemn colleges for selling out to threats by ideologues, point out that there is not as much violence as during the 1960s. When criticized for racial double standards, point to statistics showing more "diversity." When criticized for the prostitution of the classroom to propaganda, reply that students are resistant to propaganda.[84]

None of the "vehement" critics who have so "savagely" attacked universities, in Derek Bok's words,[85] has said that there should be *no* education at the university level, any more than critics of American education in general have said that we should abolish it all and become an illiterate society. The specific criticisms which they have made are precisely what Bok and other defenders of academia refuse to confront, but instead seek refuge in large generalities about the contributions of universities in general. Their evasions are perhaps more telling than the critics' attacks.

Money and Sanctimony

Nothing inspires such sanctimonious replies to critics as discussions of money.

When a federal investigation of Stanford University turned up all sorts of questionable items charged to government grants—including depreciation on a yacht and part of the cost of University President Donald Kennedy's $17,000 wedding reception[86]—President Kennedy replied that he would eliminate "expenses that are easily subject to public misunderstanding" and would examine "especially carefully" anything "that smacks of entertainment." By the time he said this, Stanford was already under investigation by the Office of Naval Research, the General Accounting Office, and a Congressional subcommittee.[87] According to Kennedy, Stanford was now "reexamining our policies in an effort to avoid any confusion that might result."[88] This picture of innocent misunderstandings and a confused public was somewhat undermined, however, by the fact that one of Stanford's own officials had previously been in demand as a speaker at other institutions, explaining to them how to extract more money from government grants.[89] Its credibility was further reduced when the investigation of Stanford led other colleges and universities to begin suddenly returning money to the government.

Harvard withdrew about half a million dollars in research grant claims.[90] So did Cal Tech.[91] M.I.T. agreed to pay back $731,000,[92] Duke University discovered "inadvertent errors" in its charges to the government, and Cornell and Dartmouth likewise scaled back their claims. Among the items charged to the taxpayers as research expenses by academic institutions were country club memberships by Cal Tech,[93] jewelry and the salary of a cook for the president of M.I.T.; opera tickets, Christmas cards, and airfare to Grand Cayman Island for the president of the University of Pittsburgh and his wife; chartered airplane flights by the president of Cornell;[94] and travel and entertainment expenses for the president of Dartmouth, as well as more

than $50,000 in legal expenses growing out of a lawsuit with
The Dartmouth Review.[95] Brazen loftiness has not been a tactic
confined to Donald Kennedy or to Stanford, but has been a
common response to disclosures of their own generosity to
themselves at other academic institutions as well.

Equally sanctimonious have been the responses of colleges
under federal investigation for collusion in setting their tuitions. President William R. Cotter of Colby College, for example, admitted that there were "agreements among colleges to
offer a student who has been admitted to two or more of the
colleges, financial-aid packages that require virtually identical
family contributions." However, he considered it to be "in the
public interest" for colleges to "estimate more accurately the
ability of students' families to contribute to their education
costs." Even the students apparently benefit, in this cheery
scenario, for the academic cartel "aims to increase students'
freedom to choose colleges on the basis of the most appropriate
academic program, not the cost to the family." Otherwise
"many families would find the already difficult task of choosing
a college distorted by the varied grant offers."[96]

Similar altruism could be claimed by any monopoly or cartel engaged in price-fixing, for uniform prices relieve all customers of price-shopping, giving them more "freedom" to
choose goods and services on non-price criteria. Yet no one
would take such sanctimony seriously, coming from a commercial business under investigation for anti-trust law violations. It is not the uniformity of price, as such, that is the key
issue. What matters is the *level* of prices at which this uniformity is achieved. That level is almost certain to be higher than
it would be in the absence of collusion. President Cotter in fact
backed into such an admission when he said:

> If colleges were required to assess student's need independ-
> ently, we might be dragged into a "bidding war" for the best
> students—making conservative estimates of the amounts
> their families could contribute and then beefing up their aid
> packages. The principle of need-based aid would be eroded.[97]

There is only a semantic difference between "need-based
aid," as used here, and "charging what the traffic will bear."
This is especially clear when "need" applies across a wide range
of family incomes, including some incomes more than double

the national average. Likewise, there is only a semantic difference between "being dragged into a bidding war" and the ordinary competition of a free market.

Others have tried to justify price discrimination in tuition by a Robin Hood theory that it is good for the rich to subsidize the poor.[98] That theory might have been plausible years ago, when genuinely poor students received scholarships based on genuine scholarship. The same reasoning hardly applies today at schools where most of the students receive "financial aid"— that is, where they pay tuition on a sliding scale—and it is largely unrelated to their academic performance. Moreover, the Robin Hood theory conflicts with another favorite theme of colleges, that tuition covers only part of the cost of education. Harvard's dean of admissions prefers this latter assertion:

> . . . it is important to point out that every student at Harvard-Radcliffe receives a substantial subsidy, since the tuition charged does not cover the full cost of an undergraduate education. The more affluent families paying the "full" tuition charge pay for only about one-half of the true costs.[99]

The impossibility of determining the average cost of a joint product has already been noted in Chapter 5. The impossibility of determining the "true" or "full" cost of an undergraduate education should be especially clear at Harvard, where the faculty engaged in more than $169 million worth of scientific research and development activity alone in 1987.[100] Any apportionment of the costs of a professor who engages in both teaching and research is necessarily arbitrary, as is any apportionment of the $37 million spent annually on the Harvard library system,[101] or the costs of buildings and grounds, and other huge expenditures for the multiple activities of the university. An admissions director who imagines that he can predict future "leaders" among 18-year-olds may also imagine that he can determine the "true cost" of an undergraduate education. But, if he can perform these two feats, he should be able to relax afterwards by walking on water.

Sometimes the sanctimony of academics when it comes to money is more simple and direct. When Texas legislators proposed trimming the budget of the University of Texas system, the chancellor of that system wrote in *The Dallas Morning News*:

Lawmakers contemplating cuts in higher education funding should have to look Tommy Blair in the eye and tell him, "Sorry, son, we just didn't want to spend the money it takes to help you get the education you could have gotten at Harvard or Stanford or MIT."[102]

This sanctimony assumes that money spent on the University of Texas goes to teaching rather than research. But the University of Texas already spends, on the Austin campus alone, virtually the same amount of money on scientific research and development as Harvard does.[103] To think that more money for the university system translates into better undergraduate education is a faith which passeth all understanding. As at other research universities, it is at least equally likely that a *reduction* in research money would benefit undergraduate teaching.

Tenure

No feature of academic life is defended more fiercely than tenure. It too generates much sanctimony—and little sense of any need for evidence or analysis behind assertions.

Academic tenure has been said to promote the pursuit of truth by "a professoriate that is free to seek, discover, teach, and publish without interference."[104] However, the claim that tenure is necessary to promote free expression flies in the face of the experience of many "think tanks," which have no tenure but which have produced some of the most controversial writings of our times, including fundamental challenges to the orthodoxy pervading academic social science departments. By contrast, leading academic scholars like Stephan Thernstrom at Harvard and Reynolds Farley at the University of Michigan, who have devoted a career to the study of racial and ethnic groups, have simply abandoned the teaching of the subject in college, rather than continue to be targets of ideological intolerance and harassment on campus. No other major contemporary American institution has the kind of intolerance for free expression which has spawned the phrase "politically correct" in academia. Yet it is academia which has tenure.

Like much else in the academic world, tenure has been depicted as a product of public demands:

> Outsiders will have confidence in the research and output of a faculty only if they believe in the independence of its authors; students will study with faculty only if they believe in the independence of their teachers; and private donors and government agencies will support the ongoing activities of the faculty only if they believe in the independence and openness of their inquiry.[105]

Tenure is thus a "response to this wide range of pressures brought to bear on the university."[106] All this was said in a publication of a think tank—a kind of organization which lacks tenure and which has been spreading rapidly, as its output has been widely accepted by the public and has attracted financial support from "private donors and government agencies."

The radical divergence of academic opinion from public opinion in general in no way negates the conformity *within* academia. Nor are academics noted for courage in voicing what differences of opinion do exist. When Professor Bernard Davis of the Harvard Medical School publicly questioned double standards for some black students, he received "hundreds of private expressions of support from colleagues, at the school and elsewhere," though he charitably noted, "it would have taken a great deal of courage to offer any public support."[107] Any academic who has challenged any fundamental aspect of the prevailing orthodoxy will be familiar with the phenomenon of "private support" from colleagues. At the very least, academic tenure has yet to demonstrate that it produces any more courage or diversity of views than exists in professions without tenure.

Much discussion of the merits of tenure focuses on the benefits it provides to those who get it. By this kind of reasoning, one could justify monarchy on grounds that it benefits kings. The real test of tenure, as of monarchy, is how it performs *as a system* serving public purposes. The tenure system, as it exists in American four-year colleges and universities, entails a Draconian "up or out" decision and confers general academic governing power on tenured professors. The ramifications of this whole set of practices are many.

One claim for tenure is that it promotes collegiality.[108] However, a study based on hundreds of interviews at dozens of colleges across the United States[109] found that, on many campuses, junior untenured faculty had "isolated" themselves in order to meet "the overwhelming pressure to produce and publish," to get tenure before the dreaded "up or out" decision was at hand.[110] This same study also found "a general pall of uncertainty and injustice" among untenured faculty who were "living in a state of nagging anxiety about their future status."[111] What was unjust was that the younger, untenured faculty were often better qualified than the tenured professors who would be judging them. Dean Henry Rosovsky of Harvard referred to "the conviction of some non-tenured younger faculty members that they are smarter and more qualified than the old bastards who deny them promotion."[112] In many places, this conviction is shared by others[113] but tenure prevents anybody from doing much about it. Whatever the merits of older and younger faculty, isolation and resentment are not collegiality.

Where collegialilty does exist, as among the tenured elites, it readily lends itself to log-rolling, making the maintenance of institutional standards and the protection of other interests—those of students, taxpayers, or the larger society—much more difficult.

The sheer inefficiency of governance by large numbers of unaccountable faculty members is yet another hidden cost of tenure. Tenured faculty members are not entirely employees, but at least quasi-managers, except that they are not a management who can be either fired from within or taken over by outsiders, as in business. Moreover, tenure does not make them live with the consequences of their decisions, as the commitment is entirely one way. The departure of a tenured professor for greener pastures is without either legal constraint or social stigma.

It would be hard to conceive an institutional arrangement with more potential for irresponsibility. More of that potential has been realized in recent decades, as vast sums of research money have turned many senior professors into grant entrepreneurs, to whom a given academic institution is simply a place to have an office, pending a better offer elsewhere, and as ideological passions have led other faculty members to see education as simply a continuation of politics by other means.

Tenure reduces the ability of a college or university to assert its own institutional mission or responsibilities to students, parents, or the public, as against such self-indulgent professors.

Ideological Double Standards

One of the best books written in defense of the academic es-tablishment—*The University: An Owner's Manual* by Henry Rosovsky—handles the whole issue of ideological double stan-dards on campus in the best way possible strategically, by not mentioning the issue at all. Like the silence of the dog which did not bark while a crime was being committed, in a famous Sherlock Holmes story, the silence of Dean Rosovsky is itself an important clue. Derek Bok's attempt to dismiss the issue in his book, *Beyond the Ivory Tower*, is much less effective. While President Bok wrote that universities "have a critical interest in preserving free expression,"[114] his reference to "the brief period in the late 1960s" when the militant left "threatened to push all opposition aside" depicts the dangers from that quarter as long past. He observes complacently "how grossly the radicals overestimated their power."[115]

Derek Bok's picture of a left-wing takeover danger long past on campus is a view widely promoted by defenders of the ac-ademic establishment. Superficial comparisons with the mag-nitude of disruption and violence on campus during the 1960s might well suggest that there is no comparable level of turmoil today. However, much of that calm is the calm of surrender. Bok's own institution, Harvard, is a classic example. By allow-ing disruptions and thugs on the left to harass and assault visiting speakers with impunity, thereby discouraging other potential speakers with views abhorrent to the left from ap-pearing on campus, Harvard undoubtedly has succeeded in minimizing the total amount of violence and negative publicity it has had to endure. But this is a *confirmation* of the power of those using storm trooper tactics, rather than a sign that they "overestimated" that power. Bok's claim that "the principles of academic freedom are now widely accepted"[116] is not true even on his own campus, unless all he means by "acceptance" is lip service.

As one of Harvard's giants of the past, J. A. Schumpeter,

once said: "Power wins, not by being used, but by being there." Left-wing storm trooper power has won on elite campuses all across the country. There are organized, nationwide campus groups who openly proclaim their intention to prevent speakers with views they abhor from being able to talk at colleges or universities.[117] Their members include faculty as well as students.

Ideological double standards have become so common in the academic world that any criticism of them is treated as an attack on the particular groups receiving the benefits. Those who criticize double standards for minorities are almost certain to be labeled "racist" while those who criticize double standards for homosexuals will automatically be labeled "homophobic" and those who criticize double standards for radical feminists will be labelled "sexist."

Another trivializing tactic is to respond to any criticism of academic politicization by claiming that education is *already* politicized, so that it is hypocritical to object when someone else's politics become influential. These are not arguments but word games. The facts are blatant that scholarly associations which had never taken a stand on political controversies before, throughout their history, have collectively become shrill partisans on many political issues in recent times, that free speech on ideological issues has been stifled by violence and/or administrative punishment on many campuses, that ideological questions once considered taboo in employment interviews are often used as litmus tests for academic appointments. The list could go on and on.

It is a true but trivial statement that no individual or institution has ever been 100 percent free of political or ideological views or 100 percent free of some influence of those views on their choices of words or deeds. But this is like saying that Abraham Lincoln and Adolf Hitler were both imperfect human beings. It is true in itself, but more than a little misleading. That defenders of contemporary academic trends so frequently resort to misdirection and trivialization does more to establish the substantive bankruptcy of their positions than the worst their critics could do.

Stung by media attention to "political correctness" on campus, many academics and their media allies have struck back by either denying its existence or by equating "political correctness" with the holding of particular social and political views, rather than the suppressing of opposing views through double standards.

Defenders of "political correctness" almost invariably evade the heart of the criticisms against it—namely, that it is an imposition of ideological conformity. Instead, defenders proclaim the merits of their particular ideology or its social goals. Those merits and those goals are things which might well be debated in the marketplace of ideas, but the charge against "political correctness" is precisely that it is antithetical to the marketplace of ideas. The very rhetoric of "politically correct" zealots betrays the fact that they are not seeking an open debate between opposing viewpoints, but rather an institutional process by which they "raise the consciousness" of others, give others "awareness" or "sensitivity," or otherwise engage in one-way enlightenment of the benighted. Everything from "residential education" programs to automatic deductions of students' "contributions" to the Naderite P.I.R.G.s shows the weight of academic institutions being put behind one particular ideological vision.

This is done, not simply at the expense of other viewpoints, but more fundamentally at the expense of the educational process itself, as more and more courses and programs are set up to lead students to ideologically defined conclusions—whether about the environment, race, sex, or other topics—rather than to develop their own ability to think for themselves, and to subject all arguments to the various kinds of systematic analysis known as disciplines. One symptom of this fundamental shift in the purpose of education is the zest for so-called "interdisciplinary" studies, where this means in practice *non-disciplinary* studies—studies which require no mastery of the analytical methods of science, economics, logic, statistical analysis, or other encumbrances to "exciting" ideological discussions.

What is routinely passed over in silence by defenders of "political correctness" is the institutionalization of ideological conformity, not only through propaganda courses—increasingly required—but also through active suppression of alternative viewpoints via cultural *Gauleiters* in the dormitories, restrictive speech codes, and administrative toleration of storm trooper tactics against outside speakers who seek to bring alternative viewpoints to campus. These issues are almost never confronted by defenders of "political correctness."

Race

Among critics' charges against American colleges and universities is that they have engaged in preferential admissions policies to fill racial quotas. Here again, the education establishment's response has been tactical rather than substantive.

President James Duderstadt of the University of Michigan, for example, gave a typical academic response on the issue of racial quotas in admissions: "There is no quota system at the U-M." He added, "We've never had quotas." At the same time, he said, "We seek a student body composition that is reflective of the national composition."[118] Such a distinction without a difference has been typical of the utter unreality of so much that has been said and done as regards the racial policies of American colleges and universities.

"At Stanford, we don't have a double standard with regard to admissions," that school's alumni have been told.[119] However, race and ethnicity of minority students are "taken into account and may give them an edge over other outstanding candidates." The distinction between an "edge" and a "double standard" can also be a distinction without a difference, depending on how big the "edge" is—and it is precisely this which Stanford refuses to reveal, despite the other statistics it issues on all sorts of other aspects of its students, including minority students. At the University of Virginia, an official likewise denied that they would admit a black student "just for a number." However, while fewer than half the Asian applicants were accepted, more than two thirds of the black applicants were accepted—even though the Asians admitted had SAT scores averaging 180 points higher than that of blacks.[120]

One of the most remarkable counter-attacks against critics of preferential admissions policies for minorities has been the claim that these critics are hypocritical for not criticizing preferential admissions policies for alumni children and other groups admitted on non-meritocratic grounds.[121] An Amherst professor made the charge even broader, accusing the critics of believing in some kind of prior perfection—the Camelot or

Eden argument already noted in other contexts—leading to "fantasies of unconditional individual accomplishment" as a basis for their "critiques of affirmative action." This professor then launched into a list of special privileges in general, such as "the deduction of mortgage interest" from taxable income, "insider trading," and many other "special advantages" underlying "many Americans' individual achievement and comforts."[122]

These might be telling arguments *if critics had been saying that minority students were benefitted too much.* Yet, for more than twenty years, critics of racial double standards have been arguing just the opposite—that preferential admissions are *damaging* to minority students. Whether preferential admissions policies are also damaging to privileged alumni children is obviously not an issue of comparable social importance, partly because the privileged are in a better position to look out for themselves. As for the Camelot and Eden arguments— if one took them seriously, it would mean that no criticism of any policy on any subject could ever be made, except on the assumption of prior perfection, which no one believes in.

If believers in racial double standards wish to argue that these are in fact a net benefit to minority students, and do no substantial harm to the colleges and universities, then they are of course free to take on the formidable task of trying to make that case. Their misleading characterizations of the critics, and especially their suppression of hard evidence, suggest that they are not about to take on such a task. They find it far easier to argue on the basis of rhetoric and dogmas.

Dogmas about a need for racial "role models" on the faculty or a "critical mass" of minority students on campus, as a prerequisite for their academic success, are confidently asserted and unquestioningly accepted, with evidence being neither asked nor given. So are other dogmas about a need for special racial or ethnic enclaves to cushion minority students from the culture shock of encountering an alien, white, middle-class environment on campus. On some elite college campuses, where this kind of doctrine is most prevalent, a majority of the black students have come from middle-class, racially integrated neighborhoods and have attended predominantly white high schools. Yet the creation of separatist enclaves and the expansion of minority mini-establishments on campus is defended by speaking of these native-born, English-speaking, middle-class Americans as being from a radically different culture, almost as if they were fresh off the boat from Africa.

At Harvard, for example, 70 percent of the black under-graduates have parents who are in professional or managerial occupations.[123] At Cornell, a report labeled "not intended for public consumption" revealed that more minority students came from suburbs than from cities—in one year, twice as many.[124] A study of black students at Stanford found that two-thirds came from predominantly white high schools.[125] Nationwide, less than 2 percent of all college students come from completely non-white high schools, even though blacks alone are nearly 10 percent of these college students. Altogether, nearly 16 percent of all college students are non-white, while only 7 percent of college students come from schools which are either completely non-white or mostly non-white.[126] A majority of non-white college students therefore comes from predominantly white high schools. In short, the separate racial and ethnic enclaves on many college campuses are the first segregation experienced by many minority students.

The campus minority mini-establishment's self-interest in having a segregated and alienated racial enclave is obvious, but what makes this possible is that so many others unthinkingly accept what is said from this quarter as if it were disinterested "expertise."

If there were any interest in checking the "role models" and "critical mass" dogmas against facts, one way would be to look at the academic achievements of minority students in the era before either of these factors was present. Those black or other minority students who attended predominantly white colleges in the era before there were any minority "role models" on the faculty, and when the small numbers of minority students never approached a "critical mass," showed no signs of having been less successful academically than the minority students of today. A study of black students who graduated from an elite university in the 1950s found that their grades were closer to the school average than the grades of black students who graduated in the 1980s.[127] In an earlier period, during which 34 graduates of all-black Dunbar High School in Washington, D.C., went on to Amherst College over the years, 7 of these 34 became Phi Beta Kappas. Seven of the 12 who went to Williams

College during the same era also became Phi Beta Kappas.[128]

Very similar stories could be told of other racial or ethnic groups from the same era who had neither "role models" nor a "critical mass"—second-generation Asian students on the west coast and second-generation Jewish students on the east coast being prime examples. It was a little over half a century ago when the first black professor was hired by a major university, the University of Chicago—and this was just a few years after the first Jewish professor achieved tenure at Columbia University. The likelihood that a Japanese American student would ever see a professor of his own racial background was even less than for blacks and Jews. None of this produced the academic disasters so common in colleges and universities today. If evidence rather than dogmas were the test, it would be easier to argue that the minority students of those days were more successful. If incentives rather than hopes were the focus, it would be easy to see why: They were not enough of a constituency for anyone to mobilize them politically and create distracting agendas.

Today's economic differences and lifestyle differences between black or Hispanic students and their white classmates may in some cases be quite real, but no more so than such differences were among students from various backgrounds in times past, or between many Vietnamese students and their classmates today. These differences were not as academically or socially traumatic as those among black or Hispanic students today because these other groups—including black students on white campuses in an earlier era—did not have to contend with the handicaps growing out of preferential admissions: (1) academic mismatching and (2) the creation of a minority mini-establishment to complement the mismatched students with substandard faculty, leading them in nonintellectual directions.

Nowhere has the moral bankruptcy of academia been more blatant than in its racial policies, which have managed simultaneously to damage every racial or ethnic group involved—with the worst damage being done to blacks, the supposedly most favored beneficiaries. White applicants may be denied admission to some colleges, in favor of less qualified blacks but, with three-quarters of black students failing to graduate nationwide, this "favor" to blacks is much more damaging than forcing a white student to go to his second-choice college. A graduate of a second-choice college still ends up far better off than someone who failed to graduate from a more prestigious institution.

Academic double standards may be resented by white students, but their principal victims are black students. Not even "affirmative grading" is ultimately a favor to black students, who suffer needlessly longer, until the honest grades they get convince them that they are not going to make it. Academic double standards are like certain medical procedures which do nothing to cure the disease, but simply prolong the suffering of a terminal patient. Both white and black students may end up embittered by this situation—and justifiably so. They are, after all, inexperienced young people to whom college officials have a responsibility.

This is only one of many responsibilities which academics have abdicated, in pursuit of the fashions of the moment or the path of least resistance, with the costs being borne by others.

CHAPTER 11

Bankruptcy

THE BRUTAL REALITY is that the American system of education is bankrupt. Allowed to continue as it is, it will absorb ever more vast resources, without any appreciable improvement in the quality of its output, which is already falling behind world standards. Its educational failures cannot be justified, or even mitigated, by its many non-academic social goals, such as the psychological well-being of students, harmony among racial, ethnic, or other social groups, the prevention of teen-age pregnancy, or the like. It has not merely failed in these areas but has been counterproductive.

This is not a blanket condemnation of every aspect of American education. Even an enterprise in bankruptcy often has valuable assets. Both the assets and the liabilities of our educational system need to be assessed, to see what can be salvaged from the debacle and reorganized into a viable enterprise.

ASSETS AND LIABILITIES

The greatest assets of American education are its postgraduate institutions, especially in the sciences, mathematics, and medicine—all justly renowned around the world—and the enormous generosity of the American people which makes this renown possible. The abundance of resources made available for research, not only in these fields but also in economics, history, and other fields, provides American scholars with decisive advantages over their counterparts in other countries. However, to turn from scholarship to teaching, and from postgraduate education to that in most colleges, and still more so in the elementary and secondary schools, is to turn from the assets to the liabilities.

One symptom of the deficiencies of American colleges is the declining ability of their graduates to compete with foreign students for places in the postgraduate institutions of the United States. This inability to compete is most glaring in such intellectually demanding areas as doctoral programs in mathematics and engineering, where American students have in recent years become a minority in their own country. Only 40 percent of the Ph.D.s in engineering awarded in the United States in 1990 went to Americans.[1]

In elementary and secondary education, the lag of American school children behind their counterparts in other countries has become a widely known disgrace. What is not so widely understood is that this lag is greatest in *thinking* skills, rather than in mere information or even in the application of mathematical recipes, as distinguished from multi-step analysis.[2] *Johnny can't think.* That is the bottom line that makes American education bankrupt.

That bankruptcy is both in institutions and in attitudes. The two go together. Attitudes wholly antithetical to the intellectual development of students flourish in elementary and secondary schools across the country, and are gaining more and more of a foothold in even our elite colleges. The institutional protection of tenure insulates such attitudes from accountability for their consequences. It is not merely that sweeping fads come and go in the schools and colleges, leaving all sorts of educational wreckage in their wake. What is more fundamentally harmful is the enduring attitude of self-indulgence among ~~educators behind such reckless~~ experiments. It is not enough to discover, *seriatim* and *ex post*, the deficiencies and disasters of particular educational fads, unless it leads to ~~institutional changes~~ restricting the self-indulgence of educators.

In education, as elsewhere, perpetual self-indulgence and divorce from reality are often results ~~of being over-indulged~~ by others. These others include legislators, both in the states and ~~in Washington, who pour ever~~ more billions of tax dollars down ~~a bottomless pit to demonstrate their "commitment" to "ed-~~ ~~ucation," without requiring~~ even the most rudimentary accountability for *results*. College trustees who ~~rubber-stamp the~~ expediency-minded policies of smooth-talking ~~college presi-~~ dents, and alumni who contribute money in utter disregard of what is being done with it, are also among those who ~~over-~~ ~~indulge academics. Media~~ coverage of academia is indulgent to the point of gullibility, as reporters hang on every word of professors and college presidents, in a way they would never listen uncritically to businessmen, generals, or politicians. Even law-enforcement agencies are skittish about prosecuting academic institutions, though it would be hard to think of a more unconscionable "conspiracy in restraint of trade" than the National Collegiate Athletic Association.

The assets and liabilities of American education are ~~atti-~~ ~~tudinal, as well as institutional. One of its chief assets—the~~ public's generosity to a fault—can also become a liability when it becomes a blank-check subsidy of spoiled-brat attitudes on the part of educators. One small but significant symptom of such attitudes are the many claims by educators that the 1980s were "a decade of greed," when in fact Americans' voluntary donations to all sorts of philanthropic causes rose steeply during that decade to unprecedented heights—with education being one of the principal beneficiaries, as government support to education rose nearly 29 percent in real terms and voluntary contributions to higher education reached record heights.[3] As of 1983, there were also 40,000 "partnerships" between businesses and schools, in which the business donated goods, services, money, or all three. Five years later, the number of such arrangements had increased to 140,000.[4]

Back in the 1970s, when public disenchantment with the demonstrable decline in the performance of public schools led to resistance to new demands for teacher pay increases and other school expenditures, this resistance to spending was one of the few things to get the education establishment's attention and lead to a few modest improvements. Yet even a knowledgeable and intelligent journalist could refer to the tax revolt in the 1970s as having "devastated many school systems."[5] One of the few rises in test scores occurred after one of the few declines in the real income of teachers.[6] That is hardly devastation. If anything, it was confirmation that educators had been over-indulged and needed to be reminded that the taxpayers' patience was not unlimited. As public generosity resumed during the 1980s, the rise in test scores leveled off, and in 1988 they began a new decline, with the verbal SAT hitting an all time low in 1991.[7]

Schools

The institutional assets of American public schools are largely financial, while their liabilities are both institutional and attitudinal. Per-pupil expenditures in the United States are more than $5,000 per year[8]—which is to say, more than $100,000 per year for a class of 20 students. American expenditures on education top those in Japan, whether measured absolutely, per-pupil, or as a percentage of Gross National Product. The money is there. The results are not.

Part of the reason for American educational deterioration is that much of this money never reaches the classroom. A study of educational expenditures in New York City found that less than $2,000 reached the classroom out of more than $6,000 spent per pupil. The same was true in Milwaukee, where less than half the money even reached the school.[9] Educational bureaucracies, both at boards of education and in the schools, absorb much of the money spent to educate students. One of the reasons why private schools are able to educate students better, while spending far less money per pupil, is that private schools have far less administrative overhead.

The biggest liability of the American public school system is the legal requirement that education courses be taken by people who seek careers as tenured teachers. These courses are almost unanimously condemned—by scholars who have studied them, teachers who have taken them, and anyone else with the misfortune to have encountered them. The crucial importance of these courses, and the irreparable damage they do, is not because of what they teach or do not teach. It is because they are the filter through which the flow of teachers must pass. Mediocrity and incompetence flow freely through these filters, but they filter out many high-ability people, who refuse to subject themselves to the inanity of education courses, which are the laughing stock of many universities. One of the great advantages of the private schools is that they do not have to rely on getting their teachers from such sources.

Mere defects in the quality of education courses are not, by themselves, what produce such poisonous effects on American education. Most college students studying to become high school teachers take only about one-fifth of their courses in education, and even though students training to become elementary school teachers take about two-fifths of their courses in education, that still leaves a majority of their courses in other fields.[10] It is the effect of education courses in repelling high-ability people, and attracting people of meagre intellectual ability, which is crucial.

By their virtual monopoly of the credentialing process, schools and departments of education determine the calibre of people who enter the teaching profession—and the inadequacies of those people determine the upper limit of the quality of American education. Just as it is not the mere failure of education courses to provide adequate training that is crucial to the low intellectual quality of teachers, but rather the perverse filtering function these courses perform, so it is not the low academic skills of these teachers which are so damaging in the schools, but rather the historically demonstrable and pervasive tendency of teachers and administrators alike to seek *non-academic* roles and functions for themselves and the schools.

Such recent trends as "affective education," "multiculturalism" and "environmental studies" are only the latest in a long series of non-academic subjects promoted in the public schools by the National Education Association and kindred groups and movements throughout this century.[11] In the ongoing tug-of-war between the education establishment and outside critics, the education establishment has been consistently pulling in non-intellectual directions. These are the directions in which non-intellectual people can be expected to pull. Intellectual activity in academic subjects can hardly be a happy memory for people who were consistently in the bottom half of their classes in high school and college.

The painful shallowness of education courses is nothing new. Critics have denounced them throughout their history in this century—to no avail. Similarly, the spread of non-intellectual subjects in the public schools, and the watering-down of academic subjects, have both proceeded virtually unchecked for more than half a century. Even when educational reformers of the 1980s were successful in getting academic requirements written into law, those laws were often effectively nullified in the educational establishment by simply re-naming non-academic courses or teaching existing academic courses at a lower level to accommodate the broader spectrum of students now taking them.

In short, the educational establishment has been very effective in blocking or deflecting attempts to raise the intellectual content and level of American education. Nowhere has it been more successful than in blocking all efforts to end the monopoly of schools and departments of education as gate-keepers of the teaching profession. The consequences of this success include sacrificing the education of more than 40 million American school children to the jobs of less than 40,000 professors of education.[12] That is sacrificing the education of more than one thousand youngsters to save one education professor's job.

The second largest institutional liability of the public school system in the United States is tenure. While the calibre of people entering the teaching profession is the key limiting factor on the quality of education possible in the public schools, the tenure and seniority system reduces the incentives to reach even these limits. *There is simply no institutional pay-off to being a good teacher.* Pay and promotion depend on such things as seniority and additional education-course credits amassed during the summers, neither of which has any demonstrable correlation with better teaching. Some individuals may indeed become outstanding teachers for individual reasons, but there is no *institutional* reason to become a good teacher, when serving time is what is rewarded. As none other than the president of the American Federation of Teachers put it:

People are paid for coming in the morning and leaving at night, and for saying "Good morning" in the morning and "Good afternoon" in the afternoon and never confusing the two.[13]

Yet another major liability of the American school system is the multitude of regulations and externally imposed requirements which snarl the educational system in red tape and tie the hands of those who actually do the teaching. In part this grows out of a justifiable suspicion of educators and a desire to make education "teacher-proof." The magnitude of this external micro-management is hard to imagine for anyone who has not seen, for example, the several volumes of the Education Code for California, or similar minute regulations in other states. Congress has piled on top of this a mass of federal regulations, governing everything from athletics to foreign languages and fire extinguishers, and courts have produced an alarming number of precedents making it risky and costly for a school to expel students for even the most flagrant misconduct.

While these many attempts at micro-management impose large costs and constraints on public school systems, they are often very ineffective as a way to monitor educational effectiveness, as measured by actual results. Any attempt at serious educational reform must, at the outset, recognize the utter futility of micro-management of processes as a means of improving educational outcomes.

To these institutional liabilities must be added liabilities in the attitudes of educators, politicians, parents, and the general public. Whatever the lofty rhetoric of the educational establishment, their actions clearly and consistently demonstrate their view of the school system as a place whose primary purpose is to provide employment for teachers and administrators, with students being a means to that end. Students are also treated as guinea pigs for social experiments and as targets for propaganda for world-saving causes (though if emotionalized superficiality could save the world, it would have been saved long ago). The desires of parents or the public to put the education of the students ahead of the career ambitions, or the psychological, ideological, or ego satisfactions of educators, are treated tactically as obstacles to be circumvented.

Among the external influences on educational policy, labor unions have historically been prominent in promoting laws extending the number of years that students must be kept in school—and out of the job market, where they would otherwise compete with the unions' members. In short, students are to be warehoused in the public schools, for the benefit of others. Some parents also want students warehoused for a certain number of hours a day, as a baby-sitting service. Here too, the educational needs of the students are considered secondary, at best.

Politicians, the media, and the public too often want educational goals and results expressed in simple terms, even when those terms distort reality beyond recognition. Perennial focus on "the dropout problem" is a classic example. Reformers and the establishment alike express alarm at whatever percentage of high school students fail to stay on to graduation. Yet, clearly, every single person in the whole society drops out of education at some point. Otherwise, everyone would go on to get a Ph.D. and spend the rest of his life as a post-doctoral fellow on campus. The term "drop-out," like so many other buzzwords, serves as an evasion of the need to address specifics—in this case, why it is better or worse for some people to terminate their education at different times.

Many of those who drop out have already ceased to be serious students, if they ever were, and while in school not only absorb resources that are wasted on them, but also generate disorder, disruption, intimidation, and violence that jeopardize the education of others. If one is concerned with education, rather than with body count, there is a very serious question as to whether, or how much, public policy should be geared to reducing drop-out statistics. Yet, as long as those statistics remain politically potent, all sorts of ways will be found to keep students in school, regardless of what that means in terms of the education (or even physical safety) of other students.

Once again, the generosity of the American public is apparent in campaigns to reduce drop-out rates. Literally millions of dollars have been contributed in a single city, not only from the public treasury but also from private donations, to try to reduce the drop-out rates in New York and Boston, for example. Often enough, these campaigns fail, even in statistical terms, as well as in terms of getting some meaningful education to those who drop out. The "alternative schools" set up for drop-outs or potential drop-outs are widely recognized as dumping grounds,[14] ways of meeting politically defined goals in a politically expedient way.

Like so many labels put on people, the label "drop-out" describes a transient observation as if it were an eternal fact. A statistical survey by the U.S. Department of Education showed that nearly half of all the drop-outs surveyed later returned to complete their high school education within four years of their originally scheduled graduation—and an additional 12 percent were still working toward graduation.[15] Altogether, nearly three-fifths resumed their education later. The experience of trying to earn a living with inadequate education no doubt had an influence, both in their return to school and in the attitudes with which they regarded education afterwards. But that experience could only be acquired outside of school. Forcing them to remain in school, or enticing them to remain in school with pseudo-education, would have denied them that experience.

The politicized hysteria to which both the educational system and the political system are so vulnerable has created a dropout "crisis" at a time when a record high percentage of American youngsters complete high school. As of 1940, only one-fourth of young adults in the United States had completed high school. By 1970, this had climbed to just over half. During the 1980s, when hysteria about drop-outs became rampant, more than four-fifths of all high school students—black and white—graduated.[16]

Colleges and Universities

In addition to postgraduate institutions unsurpassed anywhere in the world, American higher education still has many small liberal arts colleges where the education of undergraduates remains the central purpose. As noted in Chapter 5, many of these small colleges are more effective educationally than more renowned research universities. For these colleges, as well as for the large universities, the generosity of the American public is simply unrivalled. In no other country can so many private institutions of higher learning survive on private support. Australia, for example, is still struggling to establish its first private university, which is treated in the media there as a far-out experiment. By contrast, a number of American colleges receive contributions annually from at least half of all their living alumni—and dead alumni often contribute in their wills. Voluntary contributions to higher education from alumni, foundations, corporations, and others totaled nearly $10 billion in 1989–90, about one-fourth of this coming from alumni.[17] In addition, endowments built up from past contributions exceeded one billion dollars in each of a dozen academic institutions in 1990, led by Harvard with an endowment of more than four and a half billion dollars.[18] In addition to this private generosity, the federal government in academic year 1987–88 contributed nearly $15 billion in appropriations, grants, and contracts, while state governments contributed more than $33 billion.[19]

Among the leading institutional liabilities of American colleges and universities are tenure and faculty self-governance. While tenure in the academic world is not as destructive of incentives as it is in the public schools, because academic tenure is not combined with lock-step pay and promotion based on the mere passage of time, academic tenure is made more pernicious than it needs to be by being combined with faculty self-governance and the up-or-out system of promotion. The temptation to log-rolling is very strong among colleagues who must regard each other as "facts of life" for years to come. More fundamentally, it is the wholly unaccountable nature of faculty self governance which makes it so dangerous—and so vulnerable to strident groups, threatening to make life unpleasant on campus for all who oppose their demands.

While the faculty as a whole will suffer if their decisions drive the college or university into financial straits, that is a very weak incentive or constraint for an individual faculty member pushing an individual project. This is one of the inherent problems of collectivized decision-making by unaccountable individuals, whether in an academic setting or a political setting, here or overseas. Yet seldom, if ever, is collectivized decision-making so utterly unaccountable as among college and university professors.

Elected officials in democratic countries can be defeated for re-election or even recalled during their terms of office. In totalitarian countries, they are purged. Among business decision-makers, red ink can destroy even the biggest corporations in a relatively short time, if the situation is not turned around, and even a failure to make the most of profit opportunities can attract hostile takeover bids or a stockholder revolt that ends in heads rolling in the executive suites. Yet absolutely nothing prevents a tenured professor from promoting or voting for disastrous institutional policies for years—or decades—on end.

It would be considered a gross violation of "academic freedom" to fire anyone because the policies he supported in faculty meetings over the years have led to a drastic decline in the college or university's academic standing or financial viability. In virtually no other institution anywhere is there such a blank check for irresponsibility.

Given the degree of insulation from accountability, the degree of self-indulgence found among academics can hardly be surprising. Where else do people protest events outside their institutions by refusing to carry out the duties for which they are paid? Yet it has been common at leading elite institutions for professors to cancel classes to protest decisions made in Washington concerning foreign policy or military action. Moreover, these self-awarded additional days of paid vacation are often treated as some kind of sacrifice to a cause.

In recent times, there has been a progressively more politicized, esoteric, and self-indulgent set of tendencies in academia, diluting and polluting academic endeavors with trendy ideological movements like "deconstructionism" in literature and "critical legal studies" in the law schools—to name just two. These symbolize the new scholasticism, with its inbred, self-congratulatory nihilism and its abdication of traditional responsibilities of training the young in fundamental intellectual disciplines, rather than in the ideological fashions of the day. In addition to these signs of decadence in traditional fields, there have been developing new, so-called "interdisciplinary" fields like feminist studies, ethnic studies, peace studies, and other semi-academic endeavors, more or less frankly propagandistic and politically activist, and less restrained by disciplinary canons still persisting and resisting complete politicization of the social sciences and humanities.

Not all self-indulgence is ideological. The sacrifice of teaching for research has long been a scandal at the large universities, and a growing emphasis on seeking research grants has spread the research ethos even to the small liberal arts colleges. The role of research in putting a professor's qualifications to a stronger test than the applause of sophomores is not to be denied. However, the *amount* of the research output required for this useful purpose falls far short of the research output required by the competitive pressures of individuals and institutions, all engaged in the zero-sum game of pursuing prestige and all typically financed in their mutually cancelling efforts by the taxpayers' money.

RE-ORGANIZATION

The most important thing to re-organize about education is our own thinking about it. Our purpose cannot be to project yet another Utopia as to what teaching methods are best, what educational goals are the loftiest, or what kind of end-product would represent the student of our dreams. We need to begin instead by facing up to the debacle in which we find ourselves, so as to understand not only the institutional and attitudinal factors behind the failures of the educational system, but also the factors behind its successes in thwarting repeated attempts at fundamental reform. We need to face the harsh reality of the kind of people we are dealing with, the kind of bitter fight we can expect from them if we try to disturb their turf and perks—and the bleak future of our children if we don't.

Despite the lofty rhetoric which is as much a part of the educational world as the cap and gown, we must face up to what educators have actually done, as distinguished from what they have said:

1. They have taken our money, betrayed our trust, failed our children, and then lied about the failures with inflated grades and pretty words.

2. They have used our children as guinea pigs for experiments, targets for propaganda, and warm bodies to be moved here and there to mix and match for racial balance, pad enrollments in foreign-language programs mislabeled "bilingual," or just to be warehoused until labor unions are willing to let them enter the job market.

3. They have proclaimed their special concern for minority students, while placing those students into those colleges where they are most likely to fail.

4. They have proclaimed their dedication to freedom of ideas and the quest for truth, while turning educational institutions into bastions of dogma and the most intolerant institutions in American society.

5. They have presumed to be the conscience of society and to teach ethics to others, while shamelessly exploiting college athletes, overcharging the government, organizing price-fixing cartels, and leaving the teaching of undergraduates to graduate student assistants and junior and part-time faculty, while the tenured faculty pursue research and its rewards.

All this says something, not only about educators, but also about the rest of us, who let them get away with such things. At the very least, it says something about the kind of institutional insulation which protects misfeasance and malfeasance from detection and correction. No reforms which leave that institutional insulation intact are likely to escape the fate of innumerable previous reforms, which have either been nullified or turned to the further advantage of the education establishment.

If there is any lesson in the continuing deterioration of American educational standards, despite a growing inflow of money and an escalating proliferation of rules, it must at the very least be that (1) money is not the bottleneck preventing higher educational quality and (2) micro-managing procedures in no way ensures better educational results. The task is not specific prescription but institutional changes to enable results to be monitored and accountability to become a reality in the schools and in the colleges and universities.

Once it is clearly understood that changing an educational establishment which is experienced, skilled, resourceful, and unscrupulous in defense of its territory[20] is going to be a bitter battle the question can then be squarely faced as to what the advantages and disadvantages are on each side in the struggles that are sure to follow. For reformers to have any hope of success, it is necessary *but not sufficient* to mobilize enough political muscle to win decisive votes in state legislatures and in

Congress, over the determined opposition of the National Education Association, the National School Boards Association, and many other vocal, organized, well-financed, and influential members of the educational establishment. It can be done. It has been done. But it is not sufficient.

Even after reformers have mobilized enough political support to defeat the education establishment, whether in Washington or in state legislatures, they are much like a nation which has advantages of firepower over its enemy, but lacks enough troops and staying power for a long war of attrition. If reform legislation is set forth as general principles which must later be given specific interpretation and implemented by state education departments, district superintendents, and school principals, then this is a war of attrition which the educational establishment is almost certain to win. For the reformers to win, they must mobilize their superior firepower for decisive assaults on strategic objectives. This means, first of all, that they must be clear in their own minds as to what these strategic objectives are, whether in the school system or in the colleges and universities.

Schools

The first strategic objective in the battle for educational quality in the public schools must be destroying the monopoly of credentialing held by schools and academic departments of education. This battle has already been fought once, apparently won when alternative credentialing processes were created, and yet lost in the wars of attrition that followed, as those teachers acquiring credentials through alternative processes have turned out to be no more than one percent of those still being credentialed by taking education courses.[21]

It is hard to see how this monopoly can be destroyed, once and for all, as long as such courses remain as sources of employment, tenure, and raises for teachers. It would be worth a considerable amount of money to buy out the existing professors teaching teacher-training courses and close down such courses, departments, and schools permanently. Early-retirement bonuses and research grants in lieu of salaries for teaching could be among the strategies used to help get rid of this key factor in the low quality of American public school education. There would probably need to be a stick as well as a carrot—a fixed date, after which education courses would lose their legal status as determinants of employment, tenure, and pay raises.

Those who wish to take such courses would remain free to take them and employers who wish to give them weight in choosing among job applicants would likewise remain free to do so. However, the almost unanimous condemnation of such courses suggests that few would survive without the legal monopoly. Alternative programs of teaching training might well spring up, but they would have to be very different to survive in free competition.

Another strategic objective is the abolition of tenure. Here again is an institution which must be destroyed, even if existing possessors of tenure must be compensated or saved by a "grandfather clause." But if the institution of tenure is not destroyed—if some compromise simply makes terminations easier, for example—then this sets the stage for a war of attrition which the educational establishment is sure to win, as terminations gradually grow more complex and more difficult again, after the reformers have turned their attention elsewhere.

A third crucial institutional objective is accountability. Although the word has been used before, the reality would represent a revolution in American public school education. Discussions of educational institutions at all levels are dominated by input variables and process variables—for example, statistics on expenditures, numbers of students being processed, numbers of embossed pieces of paper issued to those students on completion of particular programs. Qualitative measures of the educational results remain all too rare. The educational establishment has a long—and successful—history of opposing and thwarting virtually all attempts to measure educational results. Even when testing and publication of the results have been mandated by law, schools and boards of education have used their power to choose the tests in such a way that the great majority of jurisdictions end up "above average."[22]

Any serious attempt at monitoring results must take the choice of test out of the hands of those who are being monitored. One nationwide test would be ideal, if only to forestall confu-

sion as how different states and districts compare, and to
foreclose the chicanery possible when different tests have been
normed on different populations. Not only must the test itself
be outside the control of the education establishment; the results must also be monitored outside the establishment, and
the consequences be determined elsewhere as well.

Some form of parental choice among schools is essential to
provide numerous independent monitors. Despite campaigns
of disparagement of parents by educators, where parents and
educators differ sharply the parents tend to favor more academic programs and fewer non-academic fads like "affective
education," "multiculturalism," and the like. Strict academic
schools tend to have waiting lists of students whose parents
are trying to get them out of trendy schools. No doubt there
are some parents who lack the knowledge, the interest, or even
the sense of responsibility to make good choices. But the children of such parents would be no worse off than under the
current public school system. They would simply not reap the
benefits of educational reform. To say that any particular reform is no panacea is to say what must be true of anything
human. To object to reforms on such grounds is to say that
there can be no reform.

College and Universities

Accountability is the most important strategic objective to be
achieved in colleges and universities, as it is in the public
schools, and tenure is a key obstacle to that accountability in
academia, as elsewhere. Moreover, the wedding of tenure to an
up-or-out system of promotion, and to faculty self-governance,
add to the difficulties of making academic institutions accountable for the quality of education of undergraduates.

While the up-or-out system of promotion is a vast improvement over the time-and-credentials method of awarding tenure
and pay raises in the public schools, it often promotes the sacrificing of teaching for research from the very beginning of a
new faculty member's career. The claim that tenure is essential
to academic freedom is belied by the experience of think tanks
staffed by scholars very similar to professors—people whose
writings are at least as non-conformist and controversial as

those of tenured faculty members. The belief that tenure simply cannot be gotten rid of is belied by the experience of Britain, where it has been gotten rid of.

Stability of employment is not without its benefits, to the institution as well as to the individual. Other organizations recognize that with multi-year contracts or with customs which accomplish the same thing informally. There is no reason why colleges and universities could not extend their current practice of offering multi-year contracts from the junior faculty to the senior faculty, varying the length of these contracts according to the individual and the financial commitments of the institution. Many current faculty abuses, including gross neglect of students, reflect an arrogance and irresponsibility to which iron-clad job security is the institutional foundation. That institutional foundation needs to be destroyed.

Faculty self-governance is also not without its benefits, but the costs are enormous. This self-governance covers many things and not all of them are bad, by any means. At the core of its meaning is the idea that only scholars are competent to judge scholarship within their respective fields. This is undoubtedly true where those fields are genuine disciplines—structures of intellectual principles—such as mathematics or chemistry, rather than mish-mashes of subject matter, spiced with ideology and activism, like too many "interdisciplinary" ethnic, peace, feminist, or other "studies." However, the more fundamental division is not between various academic departments, but between policy-making in individual academic fields and college-wide or university-wide policy-making.

That chemistry professors should control the curriculum in chemistry is one thing. That they should vote on whether the college or university should permit R.O.T.C., or invest its endowment according to financial or ideological criteria, are issues on which expertise in chemistry is not germane, much less decisive. Yet all sorts of institutional decisions have become— *de facto*, if not *de jure*—subject to faculty "self-governance." In many cases, it is no longer self-governance, but the making of institutional policy decisions by professors who are insulated from accountability for the consequences. Administrators can at least be held accountable, in the sense that they can be removed as administrators, even if they still have tenure as faculty members.

The present system of so-called faculty self-governance reduces the accountability of administrators, as well as faculty. College presidents, provosts, and deans are not without means of influencing faculty decisions, beginning with how issues are framed, decisions timed, and information selectively released. Yet the administrators can plead "faculty self-governance" when the trustees, the public, or the legislators are upset with some policy promoted by those administrators and voted on by the faculty. Unlike Robert Burns, professors often see academia as an island, enjoying a sort of extra-territoriality which permits it to offer sanctuary and which makes the calling of police to quell riots a kind of violation of something sacred. Unaccountability breeds unreality as well as irresponsibility.

Accountability to the outside world must be maintained institutionally, for the sake of the internal sense of reality in academia itself. Otherwise, it is all too easy for academics to degenerate into self-indulgence at others' expense, including indulgence in self-flattering illusions. Just as outside forces have been instrumental in occasionally bringing public schools back to some sense of reality, and to their mission of teaching academic skills, so outside influences have moderated some of the worst excesses of "political correctness" and extravagant spending in academia. Trustees, alumni, and legislators need to bring to bear the rights of those who are supporting the academic enterprise with their money, as well as the rights of the students for whom these schools exist.

As in the public schools, the key to effective monitoring is some independent source of information. If trustees, alumni, or legislators know only what academic administrators tell them, then those controlling knowledge can nullify the power of those to whom they are formally accountable. The answer is not micro-management but independent information. The crucial role of information is well understood by academic administrators themselves, and is attested to by many embarrassing revelations, often with devastating consequences when academic dirty linen is aired in public and comes to the attention of legislators and lawyers.

While a board of trustees cannot micro-manage a college or university, it can certainly equip itself with the institutional means of receiving different views from individual students and faculty members critical of existing policies and practices.

Whether this is done by hiring its own full-time ombudsman or inspector general, or by other means, the board of trustees can open its eyes institutionally, if it chooses. The governor of a state can certainly establish an inspector general for education, reporting directly to the governor on the public schools and the state universities, and a state legislature can certainly create a mini-General Accounting Office for education.

An alumni association can at least subscribe to alternative student newspapers, to hear something other than what the college administrators feed them in the melange of public-relations handouts which constitute the typical alumni magazine. Merely by encouraging student and faculty groups to send to the alumni association any material they wish to have considered for distribution to those on the alumni mailing list, an alumni association can open its eyes to a world it may never have suspected existed.

For both trustees and alumni, the equipping of themselves institutionally with alternative sources of information may well increase the candor and reliability of the information they receive from official sources.

CONCLUSIONS

All the ingredients for a successful educational system already exist in the United States—some of the leading scholars in the world in numerous fields, masses of college-educated people capable of teaching in the public schools, and a public whose willingness to provide financial support for education has far outstripped educators' willingness to buckle down to the task of teaching academic skills to the next generation. The problems are fundamentally institutional. Changing those institutions is the key to changing behavior and attitudes too long insulated from accountability.

The political task is enormous, but no more so than the task of others before who have made vast changes in the social landscape of the United States, or who created this country in the first place. The stakes today are our children's future—and nothing should be more worthy of the effort.

NOTES

EPIGRAPH

The National Commission on Excellence in Education, *A Nation at Risk: The Full Account* (Cambridge, Massachusetts: U.S.A. Research, 1984), p. 13.

CHAPTER 1: DECLINE, DECEPTION, AND DOGMAS

1. Ernest L. Boyer, *High School: A Report on Secondary Education in America* (New York: Harper & Row, 1983), pp. 23, 25, 32.
2. Faith Keenan, "8th-Grade Students No Math Whizzes," *San Francisco Examiner*, June 6, 1991, p. A22.
3. Cooperative Institutional Research Program, *The American Freshman: National Norms for Fall 1989* (Los Angeles: The Higher Education Research Institution, University of California at Los Angeles, 1989), p. 6.
4. Cooperative Institutional Research Program, *The American Freshman: National Norms for Fall 1990* (Los Angeles: Higher Education Research Institution, University of California at Los Angeles, 1990), p. 43.
5. Matt Freeman, "Rise in Grades Attributed to Better, Concerned Students," *U. The National College Newspaper*, October 1988, p. 27.
6. Seth Leopold, "Are Grades Inflated Here?" *Chicago Maroon* (University of Chicago), October 4, 1988, p. 3. According to David Riesman, "only a few institutions, such as the outstanding women's colleges and the college of the University of Chicago, maintained the older norms." David Riesman, *On Higher Education: The Academic Enterprise in an Era of Rising Consumerism* (San Francisco: Jossy-Bass Publishers, 1980).
7. Paul Hollander, *Anti-Americanism: Critiques at Home and Abroad,*

1965–1990 (New York: Oxford University Press, 1992), p. 203.

8. Peter Scalet, "G.P.A., Work Load Contribute in Determining Academic Rigor," *College Reporter* (Franklin & Marshall College), October 2, 1989, p. 1.

9. Computed from Chris Gilleland, "Academic Dishonesty," *The Critic* (North Carolina State University), p. 14.

10. "Education Openers," *Wall Street Journal*, Supplement, February 9, 1990, p. R5.

11. Curtis C. McKnight, et al., *The Underachieving Curriculum: Assessing U.S. School Mathematics from an International Perspective* (Chicago: Stripes Publishing Co., 1987), pp. 18, 20, 22, 24, 40.

12. Diane Ravitch and Chester E. Finn, Jr., *What Do Our 17-Year-Olds Know?* (New York: Harper & Row, 1987), pp. 53, 62.

13. Joyce D. Stern and Mary Frase Williams, editors, *The Condition of Education: A Statistical Report*, 1986 Edition (Washington, D.C.: Center for Education Statistics, 1986), p. 36.

14. Susan Dodge, "Average Score on Verbal Section of '89–90 SAT Drops to Lowest Level Since 1980; Math Score Unchanged," *Chronicle of Higher Education*, September 5, 1990, p. A33.

15. Karen DeWitt, "Verbal Scores Hit New Low in Scholastic Aptitude Tests," *New York Times*, August 27, 1991, pp. 1ff.

16. Archie E. Lapointe, Nancy A. Mead, and Gary W. Philips, *A World of Difference: An International Assessment of Mathematics and Science* (Princeton: Educational Testing Service, 1989), p. 38.

17. Diane Ravitch, *The Schools We Deserve: Reflections on the Educational Crises of Our Time* (New York: Basic Books, Inc., 1985), p. 8.

18. Ben Stein, "Ben Stein's High School Diary," *Los Angeles*, December 1986, p. 178.

19. Carl Rogers, *Freedom to Learn for the 80's* (Columbus: Charles E. Merrill Publishing Company, 1983), p. 3.

20. *Ibid.*, p. 2.

21. *Ibid.*, p. 3.

22. *Ibid.*, p. 20.

23. Ben Stein, "Ben Stein's High School Diary," *Los Angeles*, December 1986, p. 178.

24. Diane Ravitch and Chester E. Finn, Jr., *What Do Our 17-Year-Olds Know?*, p. 13.

25. The Carnegie Foundation for Advancement of Teaching, *The Condition of the Professoriate: Attitudes and Trends, 1989* (Princeton: Princeton University Press, 1989), pp. 19, 23, 27.

26. *Ibid.*, p. 22.

27. The Carnegie Foundation for the Advancement of Teaching, *Campus Life: In Search of Community* (Princeton, 1990), p. 10.

28. Susan Dodge, "Poorer Preparation for College Found in 25-Year Study of Freshmen," *The Chronicle of Higher Education*, November 20, 1991, p. A39.
29. Bill Richards, "Wanting Workers," *The Wall Street Journal*, Supplement, February 9, 1990, p. R10.
30. Sam Ginn, "Time to Get Down to Business on the Reform of Education," *San Francisco Chronicle*, August 19, 1991, p. B3.
31. John Hood, "When Business 'Adopts' Schools: Spare the Rod, Spoil the Child," *Policy Analysis* (Cato Institute), June 5, 1991, p. 3.
32. Steven O'Brien, "The Reshaping of History: Marketers vs. Authors," *Curriculum Review*, September 1988, p. 11.
33. Stanley W. Lindberg, editor, *The Annotated McGuffey Selections from the McGuffey Eclectic Readers, 1836–1920* (New York: Van Nostrand, 1976), pp. 19, 20.
34. *Ibid.*, pp. 71, 125, 167.
35. Harvey C. Minnich, editor, *Old Favorites from the McGuffey Readers* (New York: American Book Co., 1936), pp. 154, 167, 247.
36. Stanley W. Lindberg, editor, *The Annotated McGuffey*, p. xv.
37. Avis Carlson, *Small Wonder . . . Long Gone: A Family Record of an Era* (Evanston: The Schori Press, 1975), p. 83.
38. John E. Chubb and Terry M. Moe, *Politics, Markets & American Schools* (Washington, D.C.: The Brookings Institution, 1990), pp. 105–111.
39. Joyce D. Stern and Mary Frase Williams, editors, *The Condition of Education* (1986), p. 36.
40. James Cass and Max Birnbaum, *Comparative Guide to American Colleges* (New York: Harper and Row, 1965), pp. 67, 79, 91, 112, 149, 422, 457, 462, 472, 478, 658, 682; James Cass and Max Birnbaum, *Comparative Guide to American Colleges*, Twelfth Edition, (New York: Harper & Row, 1985), pp. 51, 60, 77, 93, 126, 358, 384, 387, 394, 399, 538, 558.
41. Diane Ravitch, *The Schools We Deserve*, p. 48.
42. Curtis C. McKnight et al., *The Underachieving Curriculum*, p. 17.
43. Ernest L. Boyer, *High School*, pp. 38–39.
44. U.S. Department of Education, *What Works: Research About Teaching and Learning* (Washington, D.C.: Government Printing Office, 1987), p. 28.
45. *News from the College Board*, for release August 27, 1991, p. 5. This is quite clear as regards blacks and Mexican Americans. Puerto Rican SATs had a small gain in composite scores, their verbal scores having declined 3 points and their mathematical scores having risen 5 points.
46. Paul T. Hill, Gail E. Foster, Tamar Gendler, *High Schools with*

Character (Santa Monica: The RAND Corporation, 1990), p. 32; Susan Chira, "Where Children Learn How to Learn: Inner City Pupils in Catholic Schools," *New York Times*, November 20, 1991, p. A14; Joe Davidson, "Private Schools for Black Pupils are Flourishing," *Wall Street Journal*, April 15, 1987, p. 37; Stuart Steers, "The Catholic Schools' Black Students," *This World*, December 23, 1990, pp. 8 ff. See also Gary Putka, "Education Reformers Have New Respect for Catholic Schools," *Wall Street Journal*, March 28, 1991, pp. 1 ff.

47. Paul T. Hill et al., *High Schools with Character*, p. 2.
48. *Ibid.*, pp. 2, 14–56. See also Thomas Sowell, "Patterns of Black Excellence," *The Public Interest*, Spring 1976, pp. 47–50.
49. "State Education Statistics," (Wall Chart), U.S. Department of Education, February 1986.
50. John E. Chubb and Terry M. Moe, *Politics, Markets, and America's Schools*, p. 126.
51. "The Myth Debunked—Spending Not the Cure-All for Schools," *Education Update* (Heritage Foundation), Fall 1990, p. 1.
52. Peter Brimelow, "Are We Spending Too Much on Education?" *Forbes*, December 29, 1986, p. 75.
53. Chester E. Finn, Jr., *We Must Take Charge: Our Schools and Our Future* (New York: The Free Press, 1991), p. 36.
54. Curtis C. McKnight et al., *The Underachieving Curriculum*, pp. 56, 57.
55. National Center for Educational Statistics, *Digest of Education Statistics: 1988* (Washington, D.C.: U.S. Government Printing Office, 1988), p. 39.
56. Lewis J. Perlman, "The 'Acanemia' Deception," Hudson Institution Briefing Paper, No. 120, May 1990, p. 3.
57. *Ibid.*, pp. 5–6.
58. Jacques Barzun, *Teacher in America* (Indianapolis: Liberty Press, 1981 [originally 1945]), p. 37.
59. Ernest L. Boyer, *College: The Undergraduate Experience in America* (New York: Harper & Row, 1987), p. 121.
60. *Ibid.*, p. 128.
61. Howard R. Bowen and Jack H. Schuster, *American Professors: A National Resource Imperilled* (New York: Oxford University Press, 1986), p. 73.
62. Charles J. Sykes, *Profscam: Professors Are the Demise of Higher Education* (Washington, D.C.: Regnery Gateway, 1988), p. 24.
63. *Ibid.*, p. 40.
64. The Editors of the Chronicle of Higher Education, *Almanac of Higher Education 1989–1990* (Chicago: University of Chicago Press, 1989), p. 54.

65. James Cass and Max Birnbaum, *Comparative Guide to American Colleges* (New York: Harper & Row, 1989), p. 280.
66. The Carnegie Foundation for Advancement of Teaching, *The Condition of the Professoriate*, p. 48.
67. Pearl Evans, *Hidden Dangers in the Classroom* (Petaluma, California: Small Helm Press, 1990), pp. 41–42.
68. Charles H. Hartman, *Driver Education in Schools* (Washington: Automatize Safety Foundation, 1968).
69. "The 1991–92 Resolutions of the National Education Association," *NEA Today*, September 1991, pp. 16, 24, 25.
70. Herbert I. London, *Armageddon in the Classroom: An Examination of Nuclear Education* (Lanham, Maryland: University Press of America, 1987), pp. 2–3.
71. Tupper Hull, "S.F. Pupils Send Lawmakers Bitter Hate Mail on Prop. 98," *San Francisco Examiner*, May 5, 1991, p. B1.
72. Quoted in Herbert I. London, *Armageddon in the Classroom: An Examination of Nuclear Education*, p. 3.
73. "The Derisory Tower," *New Republic*, February 18, 1991, p. 5.
74. Eugene D. Genovese, "Heresy Yes—Sensitivity, No," *New Republic*, April 15, 1991, pp. 30, 35.
75. Herbert I. London, *Armageddon in the Classroom*, pp. vii–viii.

CHAPTER 2: IMPAIRED FACULTIES

1. Geraldine Jonçich Clifford and James W. Guthrie, *Ed School: A Brief for Professional Education* (Chicago: University of Chicago Press, 1988), p. 18.
2. *Ibid.*, pp. 20–21.
3. Thomas Toch, *In the Name of Excellence: The Struggle to Reform the Nation's Schools, Why It's Failing, and What Should Be Done* (New York: Oxford University Press, 1991), p. 138.
4. Dennis A. Williams, "Teachers Are in Trouble," *Newsweek*, April 27, 1981, pp. 79, 81.
5. Computed from U.S. Department of Education, *Digest of Education Statistics: 1990* (Washington, D.C.: Department of Education, 1991), p. 11.
6. See, for example, Martin Mayer, *The Schools* (Garden City, N.Y.: Doubleday & Co., Inc., 1963), p. 465; James Conant, *The Education of American Teachers* (New York: McGraw-Hill Book Company, Inc., 1963), pp. 1–2.
7. Martin Mayer, *The Schools*, p. 465.
8. Geraldine Jonçich Clifford and James W. Guthrie, *Ed School*, p. 137.

9. Professor X, *This Beats Working for a Living* (New Rochelle, N.Y.: Arlington House, 1973), p. 108.

10. Geraldine Jonçich Clifford and James W. Guthrie, *Ed School*, p. 141; Sue Berryman, *Who Will Do Science?* (New York: The Rockefeller Foundation, 1983), pp. 74–75.

11. W. Timothy Weaver, *America's Teacher Quality Problem: Alternatives for Reform* (New York: Praeger Publishers, 1983), pp. 39–58, 163–173; Ernest Boyer, *High School: A Report on Secondary Education in America* (New York: Harper & Row, 1983), pp. 171–72.

12. William Whyte, *The Organization Man* (New York: Simon & Schuster, 1956), p. 83.

13. W. Timothy Weaver, *America's Teacher Quality Problem: Alternatives for Reform* (New York: Praeger Publishers, 1983), p. 163.

14. Sue Berryman, *Who Will Do Science?*, pp. 74–75.

15. William H. Whyte, *The Organization Man*, p. 83.

16. Martin Mayer, *The Schools*, p. 466.

17. *Ibid.*, p. 467.

18. Geraldine Jonçich Clifford and James W. Guthrie, *Ed School*, pp. 32, 34.

19. W. Timothy Weaver, *America's Teacher Quality Problem*, p. 62.

20. *Ibid.*

21. *Ibid.*, p. 63; Ernest Boyer, *High School*, p. 172.

22. Edwin M. Bridges, *The Incompetent Teacher: The Challenge and the Response* (Philadelphia: The Falmer Press, 1986), p. 2.

23. John E. Chubb and Terry M. Moe, *Politics, Markets, and American Schools* (Washington, D.C.: The Brookings Institution, 1990), p. 3.

24. Geraldine Jonçich Clifford and James W. Guthrie, *Ed School*, p. 20.

25. *Ibid.*, p. 25.

26. *Ibid.*, p. 15.

27. "Education at Last," *Stanford Daily*, November 1, 1989, p. 4.

28. See, for example, Geraldine Jonçich Clifford and James W. Guthrie, *Ed School*, pp. 47–153.

29. Diane Ravitch, "Scapegoating the Teachers," *The New Republic*, November 7, 1983, p. 27.

30. Edwin M. Bridges, *The Incompetent Teacher*, pp. 21–23.

31. *Ibid.*, p. 33.

32. *Ibid.*, p. 41.

33. *Ibid.*, p. 38.

34. *Ibid.*

35. *Ibid.*

36. *Ibid.*, p. 40.
37. *Ibid.*, p. 31.
38. Thomas Toch, *In the Name of Excellence*, pp. 46–54, 100–110. See also Diane Ravitch, *The Troubled Crusade* (New York: Basic Books, 1983), Chapter 2.
39. Thomas Toch, *In the Name of Excellence*, p. 50.

CHAPTER 3: CLASSROOM BRAINWASHING

1. *Child Abuse in the Classroom*, edited by Phyllis Schlafly (Westchester, Il.: Crossway Books, 1988), p. 190.
2. *Ibid.*, p. 321.
3. W. R. Coulson, *"Helping Youth Decide:* 'When the Fox Preaches, Beware the Geese,' " *New York State Journal of Medicine*, July 1985, p. 357.
4. *Child Abuse in the Classroom*, edited by Phyllis Schlafly, pp. 401–402.
5. William Sargant, *Battle for the Mind* (Garden City, N.Y.: Doubleday & Co., Inc., 1957), p. 163.
6. *Child Abuse in the Classroom*, edited by Phyllis Schlafly, pp. 68, 403.
7. *Ibid.*, p. 308.
8. *Ibid.*, p. 260.
9. *Ibid.*, p. 368.
10. *Ibid.*, pp. 236, 283.
11. *Ibid.*, pp. 63, 262.
12. *Ibid.*, p. 295.
13. *Ibid.*, pp. 130, 176.
14. Ruth Engs, S. Eugene Barnes, and Molly Wanta, *Health Games Students Play: Creative Strategies for Health Education* (Dubuque, Iowa: Kendall/Hunt Publishing Co., 1975), pp. 47–48.
15. Loren B. Bensley, Jr., *Death Education as a Learning Experience* (Washington, D.C.: ERIC Clearinghouse on Teacher Education, 1975), pp. 8–9.
16. David W. Berg and George G. Daugherty, *Perspectives on Death: Student Activity Book*, copyrighted 1972 by authors, *passim*.
17. *Child Abuse in the Classroom*, edited by Phillis Schlafly, p. 85.
18. *Ibid.*, pp. 210–211.
19. *Ibid.*, p. 464.
20. *Ibid.*, p. 211.
21. *Ibid.*, pp. 210–211.
22. *Ibid.*, p. 215.
23. *Ibid.*, p. 339.
24. *Ibid.*, p. 413.

25. *Ibid.*, pp. 72, 155, 223.
26. *Ibid.*, p. 44.
27. Jacquelin Kasun, "Sex Education: The Hidden Agenda," *The World & I*, September 1989, p. 103.
28. *Child Abuse in the Classroom*, edited by Phyllis Schlafly, p. 148.
29. Thomas Sowell, "Visions of War and Peace," *Encounter*, December 1987, pp. 40–49.
30. Thomas Sowell, *A Conflict of Visions* (New York: William Morrow and Co., 1987), pp. 143–146.
31. Herbert I. London, *Armageddon in the Classroom: An Examination of Nuclear Education* (Lanham, Md.: University Press of America, 1987), p. vii.
32. *Ibid.*, p. xiii.
33. *Child Abuse in the Classroom*, edited by Phyllis Schlafly, p. 101.
34. *Ibid.*, p. 153.
35. *Ibid.*, pp. 170, 204, 260, 283, 428.
36. *Ibid.*, p. 264.
37. *Ibid.*, p. 417.
38. William Sargant, *Battle for the Mind*, p. 189.
39. Richard Crossman et al., *The God That Failed* (New York: Bantam Books, 1949), pp. 140–141.
40. *Child Abuse in the Classroom*, edited by Phyllis Schlafly, p. 46.
41. *Ibid.*, pp. 65–66.
42. *Ibid.*, p. 245.
43. *Ibid.*, pp. 61, 83, 260, 398.
44. *Ibid.*, pp. 99. See also pp. 323, 61, 248.
45. Liu, Shaw-tong, *Out of Red China* (New York: Duell, Sloan and Pearce, 1953), p. 11.
46. William Sargant, *Battle for the Mind*, p. 166.
47. George Orwell, *1984* (London: Secker & Warburg, 1949).
48. *Child Abuse in the Classroom*, edited by Phyllis Schlafly, p. 103.
49. *Ibid.*, pp. 103, 110, 112–113, 151, 227, 245, 269–270, 279, 301–302, 322, 388, 429.
50. *Ibid.*, pp. 110, 112, 227, 270, 279.
51. *Ibid.*, p. 245.
52. *Ibid.*, p. 302.
53. *Ibid.*, pp. 103, 269–270, 321–322.
54. Ruth Engs et al., *Health Game Students Play*, p. 2.
55. Sidney B. Simon, Leland W. Howe, and Howard Kirschenbaum, *Values Clarification: A Handbook of Practical Strategies for Teachers and Students* (New York: Hart Publishing Co., Inc., 1972), p. 139.
56. *Ibid.*, p. 141.
57. *Ibid.*, p. 160.

58. *Ibid.*, p. 181.
59. *Ibid.*, p. 205.
60. *Ibid.*, pp. 143, 146, 148, 149, 153, 154, 155.
61. *Ibid.*, p. 179.
62. *Ibid.*, p. 180.
63. *Ibid.*, p. 181.
64. *Ibid.*, p. 181.
65. *Ibid.*, p. 180.
66. *Child Abuse in the Classroom*, edited by Phyllis Schlafly, p. 223.
67. *Ibid.*, p. 223.
68. Richard Crossman et al., *The God That Failed*, pp. 140–141.
69. Richard Crossman et al., *The God That Failed*, pp. 140–141.
70. Lucy S. Dawidowicz, "How They Teach the Holocaust," *Commentary Magazine*, December 1990, pp. 25–32.
71. Jacquelin Kasun, *The War on Population*, p. 103; *Child Abuse in the Classroom*, edited by Phyllis Schlafly, p. 148.
72. Ruth Engs et al., *Health Games Students Play*, 48.
73. Sidney B. Simon et al., *Values Clarification*, pp. 255–256.
74. Ruth Bell et al., *Changing Bodies, Changing Lives*, Revised and updated (New York: Random House, 1987), p. 3.
75. *Ibid.*, p. 6.
76. *Ibid.*, p. 68.
77. *Ibid.*, p. 78.
78. *Ibid.*, p. 4.
79. *Ibid.*, p. 9.
80. *Ibid.*, p. 43.
81. *Ibid.*, p. 48.
82. *Ibid.*, p. 51.
83. *Ibid.*, p. 57.
84. Testimony before the U.S. Department of Education, quoted in *Child Abuse in the Classroom*, edited by Phyllis Schlafly, p. 57.
85. *Ibid.*, p. 64.
86. *Ibid.*, p. 244.
87. *Ibid.*, p. 261.
88. *Ibid.*, p. 277.
89. *Ibid.*, pp. 61, 99, 248, 398, 418.
90. Alvyn M. Freed, *T.A. for Tots* (Sacramento: Jalmar Press, Inc., 1976), pp. 21–22.
91. *Ibid.*, p. 100.
92. Linus Wright, "Sex Education: How to Respond," *The World & I*, September 1989, pp. 506–507.
93. *Ibid.*, p. 509.
94. *Ibid.*, p. 515.
95. *Child Abuse in the Classroom*, edited by Phyllis Schlafly, p. 53.

96. Ruth Bell et al., *Changing Bodies, Changing Lives*, p. 61.
97. Gary F. Kelly, *Learning About Sex: The Contemporary Guide for Young Adults* (New York: Barron's Educational Series, Inc., 1987), p. 73.
98. *Ibid.*, pp. 3–4.
99. *Ibid.*, p. 51.
100. *Ibid.*, p. 57.
101. *Ibid.*, p. 61.
102. *Ibid.*, p. 99.
103. *Ibid.*, p. 50.
104. *Ibid.*, p. 85.
105. Ruth Bell et al., *Changing Bodies, Changing Lives*, p. 42.
106. *Ibid.*, pp. 45, 65.
107. *Ibid.*, p. 61.
108. *Ibid.*, p. 70.
109. *Ibid.*, p. 67.
110. *Ibid.*, p. 50.
111. *Ibid.*, p. 52.
112. *Ibid.*, p. 59.
113. *Ibid.*, p. 59.
114. *Ibid.*, p. 61.
115. *A Gifted and Talented Curriculum Handbook for Science in the Intermediate Grades of Lee County's Department of Exceptional Children* (Sanford, N.C.: Lee County Schools, 1981), p. 16.
116. Carl Rogers, *Freedom to Learn for the 80's* (Columbus, Ohio: Charles E. Merrill Publishing Company, 1983), p. 131.
117. Sidney B. Simon et al., *Values Clarification*, p. 177.
118. *Ibid.*, p. 268.
119. Carl Rogers, *Freedom to Learn for the 80's*, p. 127.
120. *Quest International Resource Catalog, 1990–91* application blank included.
121. *Ibid.*, pp. 21, 22.
122. *Ibid.*, p. 7.
123. *Ibid.*, p. 4.
124. John J. Dunphy, "A Religion for a New Age," *Humanist*, January/February 1983, p. 26.
125. Carl Rogers, *Freedom to Learn for the 80's*, p. 269.
126. *Ibid.*, p. 260.
127. William E. Dannemeyer, "The New Sex Education: Homosexuality," *The World & I*, September 1989, pp. 521–541.
128. Jacqueline Kasun, "Sex Education: The Hidden Agenda," *The World & I*, September 1989, p. 488.
129. See, for example, Thomas Sowell, *The Economics and Politics of Race: An International Perspective* (New York: William Mor-

row, 1983), pp. 208–213; Julian Simon, *The Ultimate Resource* (Princeton: Princeton University Press, 1981).

130. Jacqueline Kasun, *The War Against Population* (San Francisco: Ignatius Press, 1988), pp. 95–97.

131. Lynda Carl Frankenstein, "Man: A Course of Study—A Case Study of Diffusion in Oregon," Ph.D. dissertation, School of Education, Stanford University, 1977, pp. 82–83.

132. *Ibid.*, p. 85.

133. *Ibid.*, p. 148.

134. For example: "To educate for values is to provide opportunities for students to choose between competing values and live with the consequences of their choice," Michael Silver, *Values Education* (Washington, D.C.: National Education Association, 1976), p. 7.

135. See, for example, Thomas Toch, *In the Name of Excellence: The Struggle to Reform the Nation's Schools, Why It's Failing, and What Should Be Done* (New York: Oxford University Press, 1991), p. 52.

136. Abraham Maslow, *The Farther Reaches of Human Nature* (New York: Viking Press, 1971), p. 151.

137. Maury Smith, *A Practical Guide to Value Clarification* (La Jolla, Calif.: University Associates, Inc., 1977), p. vii.

138. Jacqueline Kasun, "Sex Education: The Hidden Agenda," *The World & I*, September 1989, p. 495.

139. Jacqueline Kasun, *The War Against Population*, pp. 142, 144.

140. Dinah Richards, *Has Sex Education Failed Our Teenagers?* (Pomona, Calif.: Focus on the Family Publishing), 1990, p. 6.

141. Jacqueline Kasun, *The War Against Population*, p. 144.

142. Dinah Richards, *Has Sex Education Failed Our Teenagers?*, p. 7.

143. *Ibid.*, p. 42.

144. *Ibid.*, p. 41.

145. Jacqueline Kasun, *The War Against Population*, p. 144.

146. Lawrence A. Bailis and William R. Kennedy, "Effects of a Death Education Program Upon Secondary School Students," *Journal of Educational Research*, Vol. 71, No. 5 (1977), p. 65.

147. Fergus M. Borderich, "Mortal Fears," *The Atlantic*, February 1988, p. 32. See also *Ibid.*, pp. 30, 31.

148. "QUEST: Internal Memorandum Reveals More Drug Use after Skills for Adolescence," Research Council on Ethnopsychology, San Diego, California; Frederick Johnson, "Psychologist Renounces Quest Theory," *Topeka Capital-Journal*, September 25, 1990, p. 1a.

149. *Child Abuse in the Classroom*, edited by Phyllis Schlafly, p. 53.

150. *Ibid.*, p. 273.

151. *Ibid.*, p. 351.

152. See, for example, *Baboons*, Vol. 5 of *Man: A Course of Study* (Cambridge, Mass.: Education Development Center, Inc., 1969).

153. Ruth Bell et al., *Changing Bodies, Changing Lives*, p. 49.

CHAPTER 4: ASSORTED DOGMAS

1. See, for example, William J. Bennett, *Our Children and Our Country: Improving America's Schools and Affirming the Common Culture* (New York: Simon and Schuster, 1988), pp. 193–201.

2. The Report of the New York State Social Studies Review and Development Committee, *One Nation, Many Peoples: A Declaration of Cultural Interdependence*, June 1991, p. vii.

3. Rosalie Pedalino Porter, *Forked Tongue: The Politics of Bilingual Education* (New York: Basic Books, Inc., 1990), pp. 33, 123–124, 186.

4. Rosalie Pedalino Porter, "Language Choice for Latino Students," *The Public Interest*, Fall 1991, p. 60.

5. Sally Peterson, "A Practicing Teacher's Views on Bilingual Education: The Need for Reform," *Learning in Two Languages: From Conflict to Consensus in the Reorganization of Schools*, edited by Gary Imhoff (New Brunswick, N.J.: Transaction Publishers, 1990), pp. 246–247.

6. The Report of the New York State Social Studies Review and Development Committee, *One Nation, Many Peoples: A Declaration of Cultural Interdependence*, June 1991, p. ix.

7. *Ibid.*, p. 13.

8. *Murder in the Playground: The Burnage Report* (London: Longsight Press, 1989), pp. 173, 211.

9. *Ibid.*, p. 337. See also, pp. 355–356, 400–401.

10. *Ibid.*, pp. 175–176, 180–181, 197.

11. Brian Bullivant, *The Pluralist Dilemma in Education: Six Case Studies* (Sydney: George Allen & Unwin, 1981), p. 219.

12. See Laurel Shaper Walters, "American Dreamers Learn the Lingo," *Christian Science Monitor*, November 5, 1990, p. 12; Rosalie Pedalino Porter, "The Disabling Power of Ideology: Challenging the Basic Assumptions of Bilingual Education," *Learning in Two Languages: From Conflict to Consensus in the Reorganization of Schools*, edited by Gary Imhoff (New Brunswick, N.J.: Transaction Publishers, 1990), p. 22.

13. Rosalie Pedalino Porter, "Language Trap: No English, No Future," *Washington Post*, April 22, 1990, p. B3.

14. Diana Walsh, "S.F.'s Bilingual Bombshell, *San Francisco Examiner*, May 19, 1991, p. A-1.

15. Peter Schmidt, "Blacks' Assignment to Bilingual Classes in S.F. is Criticized," *Education Week*, June 12, 1991, p. 13. Bilingual education programs have also sometimes been used as dumping grounds for problem teachers. See Rosalie Pedalino Porter, *Forked Tongue*, p. 29.

16. Diana Walsh, "S.F.'s Bilingual Bombshell," *San Francisco Examiner*, May 19, 1991, p. A-18.

17. Keith Baker and Christine Rossell, "An Implementation Problem: Specifying the Target Group for Bilingual Education," *Education Policy*, Vol. 1, No. 2 (1987), pp. 262–263.

18. Linda Chavez, *Out of the Barrio: Toward a New Politics of Hispanic Assimilation* (New York: Basic Books, 1991), p. 37.

19. Rosalie Pedalino Porter, *Forked Tongue*, p. 21.

20. Heidi Dulay and Marina Burt, "The Relative Proficiency of Limited English Proficient Students," *Current Issues in Bilingual Education*, edited by James E. Alatis (Washington, D.C.: Georgetown University Press, 1980), p. 183.

21. Linda Chavez, *Out of the Barrio*, p. 20.

22. Keith Baker and Christine Rossell, "An Implementation Problem: Specifying the Target Group for Bilingual Education," *Education Policy*, Vol. 1, No. 2 (1987), p. 263.

23. Rosalie Pedalino Porter, *Forked Tongue*, p. 34.

24. Joan Keefe, "Bilingual Education: Costly, Unproductive," *Christian Science Monitor*, August 1985, p. 16. See also Sally Peterson, "A Practicing Teacher's Views on Bilingual Education: The Need for Reform," *Learning in Two Languages*, edited by Gary Imhoff, p. 244; Rosalie Pedalino Porter, *Forked Tongue*, p. 6.

25. Linda Chavez, *Out of the Barrio*, p. 29. See also Rosalie Pedalino Porter, *Forked Tongue*, p. 33.

26. Rosalie Pedalino Porter, "The Disabling Power of Ideology: Challenging the Basic Assumptions of Bilingual Education," *Learning in Two Languages*, edited by Gary Imhoff, p. 34.

27. Rosalie Pedalino Porter, *Forked Tongue*, p. 35.

28. Sally Peterson, "A Practicing Teacher's Views on Bilingual Education: The Need for Reform," *Learning in Two Languages*, edited by Gary Imhoff, pp. 246–247.

29. Linda Chavez, *Out of Barrio*, pp. 15–16.

30. Rosalie Pedalino Porter, *Forked Tongue*, pp. 39, 42–58.

31. Richard Bernstein, "A War of Words," *New York Times Magazine*, October 14, 1990, p. 53.

32. Sally Peterson, "A Practicing Teacher's Views on Bilingual Education: The Need for Reform," *Learning in Two Languages*, edited by Gary Imhoff, p. 252.

33. Rosalie Pedalino Porter, *Forked Tongue*, p. 27.
34. Hugh Davis Graham, *American Liberalism and Language Policy: Should Liberals Support Official English?* (Washington, D.C.: U.S. English, 1990), pp. 18, 20.
35. Edward B. Fiske, "One Language or Two?" *New York Times*, Section 12: *Education: Fall Survey*, November 10, 1985, p. 45.
36. Walter McManus, William Gould, and Finis Welch, "Earnings of Hispanic Men: The Role of English Language Performance," *Journal of Labor Economics*, April 1983, pp. 101–130.
37. James A. Banks, "Fostering Language and Cultural Literacy in the Schools," *Learning in Two Languages*, edited by Gary Imhoff, p. 11.
38. See Robert N. Kearney, *Communalism and Language in the Politics of Ceylon* (Durham, N.C.: Duke University Press, 1967).
39. *Ibid.*, pp. 2, 11, 12.
40. Linda Chavez, *Out of the Barrio*, p. 134.
41. Sally Peterson, "A Practicing Teacher's Views on Bilingual Education: The Need for Reform," *Learning in Two Languages*, edited by Gary Imhoff, pp. 252, 254.
42. Del Stover, "The New Racism," *American School Board Journal*, June 1990, p. 14.
43. *Ibid.*, p. 17.
44. *Murder in the Playground*, p. 112.
45. *Ibid.*, pp. 299–300.
46. *Ibid.*, p. 112.
47. *Ibid.*, p. 178.
48. *Ibid.*, pp. 135–136.
49. See *Ibid.*, pp. 18, 144.
50. *Ibid.*, p. 196.
51. *Ibid.*, pp. 323–325.
52. *Ibid.*, p. 144.
53. *Ibid.*, p. 324.
54. *Ibid.*
55. Maria Kruglik, "Working Toward Textbook Realism: Is 'Multiculturalism' Going Too Far?" *Curriculum Review*, April 1990, p. 3.
56. *Ibid.*
57. *Ibid.*
58. *Ibid.*, p. 4.
59. Robert T. Reilly, "Making Standard Textbooks Relevant," *Curriculum Review*, March 1989, p. 4.
60. Diana Walsh, "Integration Efforts Fail Outside of Class," *San Francisco Examiner*, March 26, 1991, p. 1.

61. *Ibid.*, p. A-12.
62. Carl Rogers, *Freedom to Learn for the 80's* (Columbus, Ohio: Charles E. Merrill Publishing Co., 1983), p. 137.
63. *Ibid.*, p. 136.
64. *Ibid.*, pp. 18–19.
65. *Ibid.*, p. 288.
66. Robert Klitgaard, *Elitism and Meritocracy in Developing Countries: Selection Policies for Higher Education* (Baltimore: Johns Hopkins University Press, 1986), pp. 15–21.
67. *Ibid.*, p. 25.
68. *Ibid.*, p. 29.
69. *Ibid.*, pp. 21–23.
70. Herbert I. London, *Armageddon in the Classroom: An Examination of Nuclear Education* (Lanham, Md: University Press of America, 1987), pp. 2–3.
71. Tupper Hill, "S.F. Pupils Send Lawmakers Bitter Hate Mail on Prop. 98," *San Francisco Examiner*, May 5, 1991, p. B1.
72. Memorandum, May 15, 1991, from Bill Honig to "All County and District Superintendents."
73. Tupper Hill, "S.F. Pupils Send Lawmakers Bitter Hate Mail on Prop. 98." *San Francisco Examiner*, May 5, 1991, p. B4.
74. Mary Gibson Hundley, *The Dunbar Story (1870–1955)* (New York: Vantage Press, 1965); Thomas Sowell, "Black Excellence: The Case of Dunbar High School," *The Public Interest*, Spring 1974, pp. 1–21.
75. Thomas Sowell, "Patterns of Black Excellence," *The Public Interest*, Spring 1976, p. 42.
76. David G. Savage, "L.A. School Drop 'F' Grade for Youngsters," *Los Angeles Times*, March 18, 1986, p. A1.
77. Thomas Toch, *In the Name of Excellence: The Struggle to Reform the Nation's Schools, Why It's Failing, and What Should Be Done* (New York: Oxford University Press, 1991), pp. 48–49.
78. *Ibid.*, pp. 102–107.

CHAPTER 5: DAMAGING ADMISSIONS

1. David O. Levine, *The American College and the Culture of Aspiration, 1915–1940* (Ithaca: Cornell University, 1986), p. 139.
2. *Ibid.*, p. 140.
3. E. J. Kahn, Jr., *Harvard: Through Change and Through Storm* (New York: W. W. Norton & Co., Inc., 1969), p. 31.
4. *Ibid.*, p. 33.
5. Robert Klitgaard, *Choosing Elites* (New York: Basic Books, 1985), p. 31.

6. See advertisement for Dean of Admissions, Middlebury College, *The Chronicle of Higher Education* November 21, 1990, p. B44.

7. Duncan C. Murdoch, "Harvey Mudd College," *50 College Admission Directors Speak to Parents*, edited by Sanova F. McGowan and Sara M. McGinty (San Diego: Harcourt Brace Jovanovich, Publishers, 1988), p. 49.

8. James W. Schmotter, "Colleges Have Themselves to Blame for the Influence of Journalistic Rankings of Their Quality," *The Chronicle of Higher Education*, August 16, 1990, p. A40.

9. William R. Fitzsimmons, "Risky Business," *Harvard Magazine*, January–February 1991, p. 27.

10. Robin Wilson, "As Competition for Students Increases, Admissions Officers Face Dismissal If They Don't 'Win and Keep on Winning,'" *The Chronicle of Higher Education*, October 31, 1990, p. 1.

11. *Ibid.*

12. "Median Salaries of College and University Administrators, 1989–90," *The Chronicle of Higher Education: Almanac*, September 5, 1990, p. 22.

13. *Ibid.*, p. A36.

14. Julie L. Nicklin, "Liberal Arts Colleges Face Up to Cost-Saving Measures but Fear Their Character May be Affected by the Cuts," *The Chronicle of Higher Education*, January 30, 1991, p. A25.

15. Loren Pope, *Looking Beyond the Ivy League: Finding the College That's Right for You* (New York: Penguin Books, 1990), p. 26.

16. Robert A. Service, "Marketing College Publications for Today's Students," *Journal of College Admissions*, Winter 1990, p. 26. This motto is repeated at the end of the article. *Ibid.*, p. 28.

17. *Ibid.*, p. 27.

18. *Ibid.*, p. 28.

19. William R. Fitzsimmons, "Risky Business," *Harvard Magazine*, January–February 1991, p. 26.

20. David Riesman, *On Higher Education: The Academic Enterprise in an Era of Rising Student Consumerism* (San Francisco: Jossey-Bass Publishers), p. 110.

21. Tom Fishgrund, editor, *Fishgrund's Insider Guide to the Top 25 Colleges* (Atlanta: Platinum Press, 1989), p. xv.

22. "The Admissions Game," *America's Best Colleges 1990* (Washington, D.C.: U.S. News & World Report, 1989), p. 44.

23. Deidre Camody, "Colleges' S.A.T. Lists Can Be Creative Works," *New York Times*, November 23, 1987, p. B10.

24. B. Ann Wright, "The Rating Game," *College Board Review*, Winter 1990–91, p. 16.

25. George J. Stigler, *The Intellectual and the Market Place and Other Essays* (Glencoe, Ill.: The Free Press, 1963), p. 91.
26. Peter Rapalus, "Class of '94 Most Ethnically Diverse Ever," Stanford University *Campus Report*, April 11, 1990, p. 1, 6.
27. Loren Pope, *Looking Beyond the Ivy League: Finding the College That's Right for You*, pp. 125–126.
28. Carol H. Fuller, "Ph.D. Recipients: Where Did They Go to College?" *Change*, November–December, 1986, p. 43.
29. Loren Pope, *Looking Beyond the Ivy League*, p. 115.
30. David Boroff, *Campus USA* (New York: Harper & Row, 1961), p. 192.
31. Loren Pope, *Looking Beyond the Ivy League*, p. 33.
32. Howard R. Bowen, *The Costs of Higher Education: How Much Do Colleges and Universities Spend Per Student and How Much Should They Spend?* (San Francisco: Jossey-Bass Publishers, 1980), p. 119.
33. Letter from Olin Robison to David Gergen, July 10, 1987.
34. "Rankings of Universities' Reputations and Number of Faculty Publications," *New York Times*, January 17, 1983, p. 9.
35. "Getting Back to Basics," *America's Best Colleges 1991* (Washington, D.C.: U.S. News & World Report, 1990), p. 6.
36. "National Snapshot: Top Producers of Ph.D.'s" *The Chronicle of Higher Education: Almanac*, September 1, 1988, p. 34.
37. Robert J. Morse, "Behind the Rankings," *America's Best Colleges*, 1991, p. 9.
38. "To determine a school's over all rank, data for each of the five key attributes . . . were converted to percentiles. This was done by assigning the highest raw score for any attribute or sub-attribute a 100 percent value and determining all the other percentile scores as a percentage of that top score." "Best Big Universities," *Ibid*, p. 17. According to this procedure, if there were a hundred institutions and the fourth from the top scored 85 percent of the score of the top institution, it would be at the 85th "percentile"—while by anyone else's definition it would be at the 95th percentile. The same misuse of the term appeared in the previous year's edition, "What's Behind the Rankings," *America's Best Colleges 1990*, p. 11.
39. "Best Small Colleges," *America's Best Colleges 1991*, p. 21.
40. "Regional Liberal Arts," *Ibid.*, p. 38.
41. *America's Best Colleges, 1988*, p. 28.
42. Scott White, "The Myth of the American Dream: Whatever Happened to Honesty in College Admission?" *Journal of College Admissions*, Fall 1989, p. 30.
43. Jean Evangelauf, "Cost," *The Chronicle of Higher Education*, Au-

gust 16, 1989, p. A1; Jean Evangelauf, "Fees Rise, More Slowly This Year, But Surpass Inflation Rate Again," *The Chronicle of Higher Education*, October 3, 1990, pp. A1, 36, 42.

44. Thomas DeLoughry, "Education Secretary Calls on Colleges to Hold Down Costs," *The Chronicle of Higher Education*, December 5, 1990, p. A26.

45. "Range of 1990–91 Tuition at Four-Year Colleges," *The Chronicle of Higher Education*, October 3, 1990, p. A36.

46. *Ibid.*

47. National Center for Education Statistics, *Digest of Education Statistics: 1990* (Washington, D.C.: U.S. Department of Education, 1991), p. 168.

48. *Dartmouth: General Information Bulletin 1988–89*, p. 46.

49. Karen Grassmuck, "Big Increases in Academic Support Staffs Prompt Growing Concerns on Campus," *The Chronicle of Higher Education*, March 28, 1990, pp. A1, A23.

50. Eric Krock, "Administration Spending Skyrockets," *Stanford Review*, October 15, 1989, p. 4.

51. Gregory Nagler, "Spring Opening for Chile," *The Stanford Daily*, October 3, 1989, p. 1.

52. David Riesman, *On Higher Education*, p. 338.

53. "Controversy over Spending Practices Does Not End When President Quits," *The Chronicle of Higher Education*, July 11, 1990, p. A20.

54. Jeff Gottlieb, "Stanford Billed Taxpayers for Flowers, Probes Discover," *San Jose Mercury News*, December 14, 1990, p. A1.

55. David Dietz, "U.S. Funds Used for Wedding," *San Francisco Chronicle*, February 15, 1991, p. A2.

56. "Some Dynamic Aspects of Academic Careers: The Urgent Need to Match Aspirations with Compensation," *Academe*, March–April 1990, p. 5.

57. Alex Steinberg, "Vassar's Tuition Continues to Skyrocket," *Vassar Spectator*, September 1989, p. 9.

58. Howard R. Bowen, *The Costs of Higher Education*, p. 227. See also pp. 15–19.

59. *Ibid.*, p. xii.

60. Julie L. Nicklin, "Liberal Arts Colleges Face Up to Cost-Saving Measures but Fear Their Character May be Affected by the Cuts," *The Chronicle of Higher Education*, January 30, 1991, p. A26.

61. Liz McMilley, "To Boost Quality and Cut Costs, Oregon State University Adopts a Customer-Oriented Approach to Campus Services," *The Chronicle of Higher Education*, February 6, 1991, p. A27.

62. Joseph Berger, "College Officials Defend Sharply Rising Tuition," *New York Times*, March 23, 1988, p. 18.
63. Robin Wilson, "Undergraduates at Large Universities Found to Be Increasingly Dissatisfied," *The Chronicle of Higher Education*, January 9, 1991, p. A38.
64. "New Math," *The Dartmouth Review*, March 8, 1989, p. 4.
65. Gary Putka, "Do Colleges Collude on Financial Aid?" *The Wall Street Journal*, May 2, 1989, p. B1.
66. Gary Putka, "Colleges Cancel Aid Meetings Under Scrutiny," *The Wall Street Journal*, March 12, 1991, p. B1.
67. James Cass and Max Birnbaum, *Comparative Guide to American Colleges*, 14th edition (New York: Harper & Row Publishers, 1989), pp. 240, 492.
68. William R. Fitzsimmons, "Risky Business," *Harvard Magazine*, January–February 1991, p. 29.
69. *The Marquette Investment* (Milwaukee: Marquette University Office of Admissions, undated), p. 7.
70. Karen Kaplan, "Tuition Will Rise 8.3%," *The Tech* (M.I.T.), March 5, 1991, p. 1.
71. Kareen Khan, "Affording Brown," *Brown Daily Herald*, March 13, 1990, p. 1.
72. Howard R. Bowen, *The Costs of Higher Education*, p. 15.
73. Computed from table in Gary Putka, "Elite Private Colleges Routinely Share Plans for Raising Tuition," *The Wall Street Journal*, September 5, 1989, p. A1.
74. *Ibid.*, p. A11.
75. Gary Putka, "Do Colleges Collude on Financial Aid?" *The Wall Street Journal*, May 2, 1989, p. B1.
76. *This is Amherst* (Amherst: Amherst College Admissions Office, undated), p. 23.
77. *Stanford Undergraduate University Admissions* (Stanford: Stanford University, 1987), unpaged.
78. *Bulletin of Duke University, 1987–88* (Durham, N.C.: Duke University, undated), p. 44.
79. "Fitzsimmons Answers Questions on Admissions and Financial Aid," *Harvard Alumni Gazette*, February 1990, p. 5.
80. *Ibid.*
81. Jacques Barzun, *Teacher in America* (Indianapolis: Liberty Press, 1981), p. 269.
82. "Incomplete," *New York Times*, March 3, 1991, p. E7.
83. Darrell Tarasewicz, "Study: MIT Rejects Some Top Academic Achievers," *The Tech*, December 2, 1988, p. 1.
84. *Ibid.*, pp. 1, 13.

85. Lawrence Feinberg, "Harvard: The Best, Not the Brightest?" *Washington Post Book World*, November 19, 1989, p. R13.
86. Robert Klitgaard, *Choosing Elites*, pp. 23–26.
87. *Ibid.*, p. 30.
88. *Ibid.*, p. 31.
89. Quoted in Lawrence Feinberg, "Harvard: The Best, Not the Brightest?" *Washington Post Book World*, November 19, 1989, p. R13.
90. Robert Klitgaard, *Choosing Elites*, p. 133.
91. *Ibid.*, pp. 132–153.
92. David Riesman, *On Higher Education*, p. 237.
93. Dave Bianco, "Number of Applications Drops Again," *Stanford Daily*, February 9, 1990, p. 1.
94. David O. Levine, *The American College and the Culture of Aspiration, 1915–1940*, pp. 141–142.
95. *Ibid.*, pp. 137–139, *passim*; James Crouse and Dale Trusheim, *The Case Against the SAT* (Chicago: University of Chicago Press, 1988), p. 17.
96. David O. Levine, *The American College and the Culture of Aspiration, 1915–1940*, pp. 31, 32.
97. U.S. Bureau of the Census, *Historical Statistics of the United States, Colonial Times to 1970* (Washington, D.C.: U.S. Government Printing Office, 1975), p. 383.
98. James Crouse and Dale Trusheim, *The Case Against SAT*, p. 35.
99. Robert Klitgaard, *Choosing Elites*, pp. 104–115; Stanley Sue and Jennifer Abe, *Predictors of Academic Achievement Among Asian Students and White Students* (New York: College Entrance Examination Board, 1988), p. 1; Robert A. Gordon and Eileen E. Rudert, "Bad News Concerning IQ Tests," *Sociology of Education*, July 1979, p. 176; Frank L. Schmidt and John E. Hunter, "Employment Testing," *American Psychologist*, October 1981, p. 1131; Arthur R. Jensen, "Section of Minority Students in Higher Education," *University of Toledo Law Review*, Spring-Summer 1970, pp. 440, 443; Donald A. Rock, "Motivation, Moderators, and Test Bias," *ibid.*, pp. 536, 537; Ronald L. Flaughter, *Testing Practices, Minority Groups and Higher Education: A Review and Discussion of the Research* (Princeton: Educational Testing Service, 1970), p. 11; Arthur A. Jensen, *Bias in Mental Testing* (New York: The Free Press, 1980), pp. 479–490.
100. Stanley Sue and Jennifer Abe, *Predictors of Academic Achievement Among Asian Students and White Students*, p. 1.
101. See Thomas Sowell, "New Light on Black I.Q.," *New York Times Magazine*, March 27, 1977, pp. 57ff.

102. Carl Brigham, *A Study of American Intelligence* (Princeton: Princeton University Press, 1923), p. 190.

103. Rudolph Pinter, *Intelligence Testing: Methods and Results* (New York: Henry Holt and Co., 1931), p. 453; Ernest van den Haag, *The Jewish Mystique* (New York: Stein and Day, Publishers, 1969), pp. 21–22.

104. Robert Klitgaard, *Elitism and Meritocracy in Developing Countries* (Baltimore: The Johns Hopkins University Press, 1986), pp. 70–95.

105. *Ibid.*, pp. 118–121.

106. David Karen, "Who Gets into Harvard? Selection and Exclusion at an Elite College," Ph.D. dissertation in Sociology, Harvard 1985, pp. 139, 158a.

107. Robert Klitgaard, *Elitism and Meritocracy in Developing Countries: Selection Policies for Higher Education*, pp. 101–104.

CHAPTER 6: "NEW RACISM" AND OLD DOGMATISM

1. Fred M. Hechinger, "On Campus, the Political Pendulum Swings Again," *The New York Times*, September 22, 1987, p. C5.

2. Christina Salvin, "Takaki on Target," *City on a Hill* (University of California at Santa Cruz), January 25, 1990, p. 11.

3. Constance Casey and Renee Koury, "The Walls of Ivy," *San Jose Mercury News*, *West* magazine section, February 17, 1991, p. 12.

4. Shelby Steele, "The Recoloring of Campus Life," *Harper's Magazine*, February 1989, p. 47.

5. Lisa Birnbach with Annette Geldzahler, *Lisa Birnbach's New and Improved College Book* (New York: Prentice-Hall Press, 1990), p. 283.

6. U.S. Bureau of the Census, *Historical Statistics of the United States: Colonial Times to 1970* (Washington, D.C.: U.S. Government Printing Office, 1975), Part 1, p. 380.

7. G. Franklin Edwards, editor, *E. Franklin Frazier on Race Relations* (Chicago: The University of Chicago Press, 1968), p. 54.

8. See, for example, Derek Bok, *Beyond the Ivory Tower* (Cambridge, Mass.: Harvard University Press, 1982), pp. 100–101.

9. See, for example, *Presidential Nomination to the Civil Rights Commission: Hearings before the Committee on the Judiciary, United States Senate*, Ninety-eighth Congress, First Session, July 13 and 26, 1983 (Washington, D.C.: U.S. Government Printing Office, 1984), pp. 10, 11–12, 28–29, 53, 374–375, 383, 486.

10. Clyde W. Summers, "Admission Policies of Labor Unions," *Quarterly Journal of Economics*, November 1946, pp. 66–107.

11. Clyde W. Summers, "Preferential Admissions: An Unreal So-

lution to a Real Problem," *University of Toledo Law Review*, Spring/Summer, 1970, p. 381.

12. *Ibid.*, p. 377.
13. *Ibid.*, p. 380.
14. *Ibid.*, p. 384.
15. *Ibid.*
16. *Ibid.*, p. 385.
17. *Ibid.*, p. 393.
18. *Ibid.*, p. 395.
19. *Ibid.*, pp. 395–396.
20. *Ibid.*, p. 397.
21. *Ibid.*, pp. 398–400.
22. Macklin Fleming and Louis Pollak, "An Exchange of Letters: The Black Quota at Yale Law School," *The Public Interest*, Spring 1970, p. 44.
23. *Ibid.*, p. 45.
24. *Ibid.*
25. *Ibid.*, pp. 45–46.
26. *Ibid.*, p. 46.
27. *Ibid.*
28. *Ibid.*, p. 51.
29. *Ibid.*, p. 52.
30. Clyde W. Summers, "Preferential Admissions: An Unreal Solution to a Real Problem," *University of Toledo Law Review*, Spring/Summer 1970, p. 382.
31. Robert Klitgaard, *Choosing Elites* (New York: Basic Books, Inc., 1985), p. 175.
32. Macklin Fleming and Louis Pollak, "An Exchange of Letters: The Black Quota at Yale Law School," *The Public Interest*, Spring 1970, pp. 50–51.
33. Robert Klitgaard, *Competing Elites*, p. 162.
34. Salim Muwakkil, "Bias in the Bar Exam?" *Student Lawyer*, January 1980, pp. 14ff; Sarai Ribicoff, "California's New Bar Exam Tests Charges of Racial Bias," *American Lawyer*, June 1980, 11–12; "Council Will Study Bar Exam Pass Rates to Gauge Bias," *Bar Leader*, May–June 1991, pp. 7, 21.
35. James Alan McPherson, "The Black Law Student: A Problem of Fidelities," *The Atlantic*, April 1970, p. 99.
36. Derrick Bell, "Black Students in White Law Schools: The Ordeal and the Opportunity," *University of Toledo Law Review*, Spring/Summer 1970, pp. 551–553.
37. Thomas Sowell, "Colleges Are Skipping Over Competent Blacks to Admit 'Authentic' Ghetto Types," *New York Times Magazine*, December 13, 1970, p. 49.

38. Leonard Ramist and Solomon Arbeiter, *Profiles, College-Bound Seniors, 1985* (New York: College Entrance Examination Board, 1986), pp. 32, 52, 62, 72.

39. David Karen, "Who Gets into Harvard? Selection and Exclusion at an Elite College," Ph.D. dissertation in Sociology, Harvard University, 1985, p. 433.

40. "Affirmative Action Report to the Senate of the Academic Council of Stanford University," *Stanford University Campus Report*, February 22, 1989, p. 13.

41. Peter Rapalus, "Class of 1994 Most Ethnically Diverse Ever," *Stanford University Campus Report*, April 11, 1990, p. 6.

42. Leonard Ramist and Solomon Arbeiter, *Profiles, College-Bound Seniors, 1985*, p. 42.

43. Geoff Henley, "Unequal Justice Under Law School," *The Daily Texan* (University of Texas-Austin), April 3, 1991, p. 4.

44. Timothy Maguire, "Admissions Apartheid," *Law Weekly* (Georgetown University), April 8, 1991, p. 5.

45. Robin Wilson, "Article Critical of Black Students' Qualifications Rails Georgetown U. Law Center," *The Chronicle of Higher Education*, April 24, 1991, pp. A33, A.35.

46. Arthur Hu, "Minorities Need More Support," *The Tech* (M.I.T.), March 7, 1987, p. 8.

47. Janice C. Simpson, "Black College Students Are Viewed as Victims of a Subtle Racism," *Wall Street Journal*, April 3, 1987, p. 1. Black students were also less likely to be invited to join informal student study groups, which are an important way of coping with difficult courses. However, a black student with an A average was invited to join such groups, suggesting that race alone is not the problem. *Ibid.*, p. 18.

48. John H. Bunzel, "Affirmative Action Admissions: How it 'Works' at Berkeley," *The Public Interest*, Fall 1988, p. 124, 125.

49. *Ibid.*, p. 124.

50. *Ibid.*, pp. 123, 125.

51. *Ibid.*, p. 118.

52. Memorandum of September 7, 1982 from Director, Admissions Liaison Office, addressed: "Dear Liaison Officer," p. 2.

53. Edward Fiske, *The Best Buys in College Education* (New York: Times Books, 1987), p. 408.

54. Charles J. Sykes, *The Hollow Men: Politics and Corruption in Higher Education* (Washington, D.C.: Regnery Gateway, 1990), p. 47n.

55. Steven Mays, "Racism in University Admissions," *Texas Review*, March 1989, p. 6.

56. See, for example, "Affirmative Action Report to the Senate of

the Academic Council of Stanford University," *Stanford University Campus Report*, February 22, 1989, pp. 13–18.

57. *Final Report of the University Committee on Minority Issues* (Stanford: Stanford University, 1989), p. 59.

58. The minority LSAT score of 36 falls at the 75th percentile. See, for example, Sally F. Golfarb, *Inside the Law Schools: A Guide for Students by Students*, fourth edition (New York: E.P. Dutton, 1986), p. 49.

59. "A Numbers Game at Georgetown Law," *New York Times*, April 18, 1991, p. A24.

60. Clarence Page, "Test Scores Aren't All that Counts," *San Jose Mercury News*, April 30, 1991, p. 7B.

61. See, for example, "Black Students are Dropping Out Because of Racism," *The Chicago Maroon* (University of Chicago), October 11, 1988, p. 5.

62. Dinesh D'Souza, "Sins of Admissions," *New Republic*, February 18, 1991, p. 33.

63. Shelby Steele, *The Content of Our Character: A New Vision of Race in America* (New York: St. Martin's Press, 1990), p. 138.

64. Oscar F. Porter, *Undergraduate Completion and Persistence at Four-Year Colleges and Universities: Detailed Findings* (Washington, D.C.: National Institute of Independent Colleges and Universities, 1990), p. 13.

65. See, for example, data cited in Barry Beckham, *The Black Student's Guide to Colleges*, second edition (Providence: Beckham House Publishers, Inc., 1984), pp. 58, 64, 67, 72, 74, 84, 103, 105, 122, 126, 132, 136, 142, 156, 159, 169, 172, 199, 213, 219, 222, 231, 237, 265, 271, 274, 280, 283, 289, 296, 306, 312, 326, 331, 340, 346, 349, 360, 363, 368, 371, 376, 382, 385, 387, 406, 409, 418, 424, 431, 445, 458, 460, 469, 481, 484, 486.

66. Oscar F. Porter, *Undergraduate Completion and Persistence at Four-Year Colleges and Universities*, p. 13.

67. See, for example, David Riesman, *On Higher Education: The Academic Enterprise in an Era of Rising Student Consumerism* (San Francisco: Jossey-Bass Publishers, 1980), p. 80–81.

68. John H. Bunzel, *Race Relations on Campus: Stanford Students Speak* (Stanford: Stanford Alumni Association, 1992), pp. 91–92.

69. Bernard D. Davis, *Storm Over Biology: Essays on Science, Sentiment and Public Policy* (Buffalo: Prometheus Books, 1986), p. 172.

70. *Ibid.*, p. 169.

71. Kent G. Mommsen, "Black Ph.D.s in the Academic Market Place," *Journal of Higher Education*, April 1974, p. 253.

72. American Council on Education, *Minorities in Higher Education* (Washington, D.C.: American Council on Education, 1987), p. 21.
73. "Degrees Conferred by Racial and Ethnic Groups, 1986–87," *The Chronicle of Higher Education: Almanac*, September 5, 1990, p. 15.
74. "Universities Awarded Record Number of Doctorates Last Year; Foreign Students Thought to Account for Much of the Increase," *The Chronicle of Higher Education*, April 25, 1990, p. A1.
75. Dinesh D'Souza, *Illiberal Education*, p. 170.
76. Thomas Sowell, *Education: Assumptions vs. History* (Stanford: The Hoover Institution Press, 1986), p. 81.
77. See, for example, Wlliam Moore, Jr., and Lonnie H. Wagstaff, *Black Educators in White Colleges* (San Francisco: Jossey-Bass Publishers, 1974), pp. 130–313, 198.
78. Lisa James et al., editors, *Student Course Guide, Spring 1987* (Princeton: Princeton University, 1988), p. 3.
79. "Afro-American Students: Slip Sliding Away," *The Confidential Guide: Courses at Harvard-Radcliffe 1988–89* (Cambridge, Mass.: The Harvard Crimson, Inc., 1988), p. 78.
80. *The Confidential Guide: Courses at Harvard-Radcliffe, 1987–88* (Cambridge, Mass.: The Harvard Crimson, Inc., 1987), p. 73.
81. David Riesman, *On Higher Education*, p. 97.
82. Bayard Rustin, "Introduction," *Black Studies: Myths and Realities*, edited by Bayard Rustin (New York: A. Philip Randolph Fund, 1969), p. 6.
83. Roy Wilkins, "The Case Against Separatism: 'Black Jim Crow,' " *Ibid.*, pp. 38, 39.
84. Pamela Moreland and Johnson Johnson, "Black Studies Program under Scrutiny in Grade-Selling Scandal," *Los Angeles Times*, May 31, 1988, Part II, p. 6.
85. David Riesman, *On Higher Education*, p. 250.
86. Henry Louis Gates, Jr., "Academe Must Give Black-Studies Program Their Due," *The Chronicle of Higher Education*, September 20, 1989, p. A56.
87. Gregory Lewis, "S.F. State Fight Over Who'll Control Black Politics Class," *San Francisco Examiner*, September 17, 1990, p. A4.
88. Jake Jones, "Minorities at Carleton: Beware of Becoming 'Happy Campers,' " *The Carletonian*, February 17, 1989, p. 5.
89. This is an old pattern. See Thomas Sowell, "Colleges Are Skipping Over Competent Blacks to Admit 'Authentic' Ghetto Types," *New York Times Magazine*, December 13, 1970, pp. 40, 49.
90. Bernard D. Davis, *Storm over Biology*, pp. 174, 190.

91. Michelle N. K. Collison, "Ivy League Black Students Urged to Commit Themselves to Improving the Lot of Those Who Are Less Fortunate," *The Chronicle of Higher Education*, February 15, 1989, p. A31.

92. Ken Emerson, "When Legal Titans Clash," *New York Times Magazine*, April 22, 1990, pp. 63, 66.

93. Randall L. Kennedy, "Racial Critiques of Legal Academia," *Harvard Law Review*, June 1989, p. 1746n.

94. Quoted in Abigail Thernstrom, "On the scarcity of Black Professors," *Commentary*, July 1990, p. 22.

95. "Brest: The Incident May Have Led to Something Positive," *Stanford University Campus Report*, December 2, 1987, p. 15.

96. Derrick Bell, "The Price and Pain of Racial Perspective," *Stanford Law School Journal*, May 9, 1986, p. 5.

97. Quoted in Randall L. Kennedy, "Racial Critiques of Legal Academia," *Harvard Law Review*, June 1989, p. 1776.

98. *Ibid.*, p. 1771.

99. *Ibid.*, p. 1773.

100. Richard Delgado, "Racism in Legal Academe: White Professors Should Step Aside," *San Francisco Banner Daily Journal*, February 27, 1990, p. 4.

101. *Ibid.*

102. Charles Horner, Patty Pyott, and Steven B. Loux, editors, *The Common-Sense Guide to American Colleges 1991–1992* (Washington, D.C.: The Madison Center for Educational Affairs, 1991), pp. 63–64.

103. Dinesh D'Souza, *Illiberal Education*, pp. 9–10.

104. "Masked Student Incident at Otero Sparks University Probe," *Stanford University Campus Report*, May 25, 1988, p. 8.

105. Bill King, "BSU Chair Attacks Student Ignorance, Passivity and Racism," *The Stanford Daily*, June 2, 1988, p. 6.

106. "Hypocrite of the Month," *Vassar Spectator*, April/May 1988, p. 7.

107. Dinesh D'Sousa, *Illiberal Education*, p. 10; Jamie Hoare, "*Vassar Spectator* Slapped with Gag Order," *Dartmouth Review*, October 5, 1988, p. 8.

108. "Rich Radicals, Poor Conservatives," *Michigan Review* (University of Michigan), March 1990, p. 4.

109. Irfan Khawaja, "Qualms About Carmichael," *The Princeton Tory*, February 1990, p. 24. At Dartmouth, during ceremonies honoring Martin Luther King, Jr., the master of the ceremonies referred to "the fascist state of Israel." John H. Sutter, "Deformation of a Dream," *Dartmouth Review* January 25, 1989, p. 7.

110. "Anti-Semites at Columbia," *New York Post*, January 26, 1991, p. 16.

111. Gregory Lewis, "S.F. State Fight Over Who'll Control Black Politics Class," *San Francisco Examiner*, September 17, 1990, p. A4; Carl Irving, "Furor at UC over 'Racist' Course," *San Francisco Examiner*, November 25, 1990, pp. 1ff; Joseph Berger, "Professors' Theories on Race Stir Turmoil at City College," *New York Times*, April 20, 1990, p. B1.

112. David Rossie, "SUNY Offers A Lesson in Mobocracy," *Press and Sun Bulletin*, March 31, 1991, p. 2. See also Carol Innerst, "Black Activists Disrupt Lecture," *Washington Times*, April 2, 1991, p. A5; "Return of the Storm Troopers," *The Wall Street Journal*, April 10, 1991, p. A22.

113. Matt Corman, "Two Brown Students Harassed By Drunk Assailants on Hope St.," *Brown Daily Herald*, February 9, 1990, p. 1.

114. Marian Raab, "Attack on Students Investigated," *The Badger Herald* (University of Wisconsin, Madison), January 29, 1990, p. 1.

115. ". . . students at Columbia held a strike, at Northwestern they disrupt classes, at Berkeley they conducted sit-ins, at Cornell they chose to carry guns. The choice is up to Mr. Chace and the Board of Trustees." A document from black sit-in protesters said that they had engaged in "a peaceful protest, perhaps for the last time." *The Wesleyan Argus*, February 6, 1990, p. 11. An earlier statement was in a similar vein: "Demands imply action. We must act by means necessary to achieve our goals." *The Wesleyan Argus*, October 18, 1989, p. 1. Later, in speaking of the unknown firebomber or firebombers, one of these activists said, "it is not their fault that they were forced to resort to violence." *The Wesleyan Argus*, April 17, 1990. A letter to the student newspaper from a student identified as an African-American major said of the bombing: "No one should mistake this action for anything but an attempt to communicate," an attempt "as legitimate as picketing or signing petitions." Michael Reinke and Brian Needleman, "Bombing Represented as Effort to Communicate," *The Wesleyan Argus*, April 13, 1990, p. 3.

116. Chris Kenedi and Alex Navarro, "Chace Hopeful, Not Afraid After Bombing," *The Wesleyan Argus*, April 10, 1990, p. 1. While the Wesleyan Student Assembly voted to condemn the bombing—not unanimously, but by an 8 to 2 vote—another group of students refused to condemn it, and instead criticized the university, which they said was "being allowed by the public to

revel in self-pity and ignore major issues on campus." Dina Kaplan, "100 Students Meet Press, Show Concern for Bombing Response," *The Wesleyan Argus*, April 17, 1990, p. 1. "The WSA [Wesleyan Student Assembly] passed a resolution, by an 8–2 vote, condemning the fire-bombing . . ." Chris Kenedi and Alex Navarro, "Chace Hopeful, Not Afraid After Bombing," *The Wesleyan Argus*, April 10, 1990, p. 7. One Wesleyan student responded to criticism of the bombing by saying, "there is no progress without a struggle." *The Wesleyan Argus*, April 10, 1990, p. 3.

117. "Racism on Campus," *Christian Science Monitor*, June 14, 1988, p. 17.
118. Jeffrey Hart, "The Poison of Affirmative Action," *The Dartmouth Review*, October 11, 1989, p. 10.
119. Dinesh D'Souza, *Illiberal Education*, p. 38.
120. Dinesh D'Souza, "Sins of Admissions," *New Republic*, February 18, 1991, p. 33.
121. Allan C. Brownfeld, "Affirmative Action: The New Racism?" *Campus Report from Accuracy in Academia*, July/August 1990, p. 7.
122. James McCutcheon, "Filling Quotas in the Admissions Dept.," *The Dartmouth Review*, October 11, 1989, p. 6.
123. "Conservative Student Journalist Wins Free Speech Lawsuit," *Campus Report from Accuracy in Academia*, May 1989, pp. 1ff. The article which cost the student his job at California State University (Northridge) is also reprinted in this issue: James Taranto, "At UCLA, 'Sensitivity' Means Violence and Censorship," *ibid.*, p. 5.
124. Cartoon reprinted in *Time*, May 7, 1990, p. 106.
125. Memorandum, June 1, 1990, addressed "To Whom It May Concern."
126. The false analogy to Hillel and Newman clubs has been made by many, including Troy Duster, "Understanding Self-Segregation on the Campuses," *The Chronicle of Higher Education*, September 25, 1991, p. B1.
127. Lisa Birnbach, *Lisa Birnbach's New & Improved College Book* (New York: Prentice-Hall Press, 1990), p. 327.
128. Mark Mathabane, "The Blight of Black Racism," *New York Times*, August 23, 1989, p. A19.
129. Keith Lee, "Discrimination of a Different Color," *The Carletonian*, September 30, 1988, p. 5.
130. Harmeet Dhillon, "Apartheid at Dartmouth," *The Dartmouth Review*, February 10, 1988, p. 13.

131. *Ibid.*
132. Joan Walsh, "School Colors," *San Francisco Chronicle/Examiner, This World* section, February 4, 1990, p. 9.
133. "Calendar," *Stanford University Campus Report,* June 13, 1990, p. 24.
134. Allan Bloom, *The Closing of the American Mind* (New York: Simon and Schuster, 1987), p. 316.
135. Kenneth B. Clark, "Letter of Resignation from Board of Directors of Antioch College," *Black Studies: Myths & Realities,* edited by Bayard Rustin (New York: A. Philip Randolph Educational Fund, 1969), p. 34.
136. Jeffrey Hart, "Selective Concern for Student Safety," *The Dartmouth Review,* December 7, 1988, p. 12.
137. "Chicanos Allege Harassment," *Stanford Review,* February 26, 1990, p. 2; Daryl Josefer, "Student Affairs Unresponsive, Some Chicanos Allege," *Ibid.,* pp. 3, 15.
138. Jesse Luna, "MEChA Doesn't Represent Concerns of Community," *The Stanford Daily,* March, 1990, p. 4.
139. Denise K. Magner, "Minority Students on Both Black, White Campuses Found to Feel Alienation," *The Chronicle of Higher Education,* January 9, 1991, p. 2.
140. Mike Rogoway, "Dr. Charles King to Speak," *Whitman College Pioneer,* October 12, 1989, p. 1.
141. *Ibid.*
142. See, for example, Stephen Goode, "Selling Diversity: Harmony Gurus on Campus," *Insight,* November 25, 1991, pp. 12 ff.
143. Robert Detlefsen, "White Like Me," *New Republic,* April 10, 1989, p. 20.
144. Anne Yeoman, "Racism Within," *Inside Tulane* (published by the Office of University Relations, Tulane University), March 1990, pp. 1–2.
145. Jeff Rosen, "Hate Mail," *New Republic,* February 18, 1991, p. 20.
146. Robert R. Detlefsen, "White Like Me," *New Republic,* April 10, 1989, pp. 18–19.
147. Jean Chrisensen, "Racism Workshop Emotion," *The Daily Cardinal* (University of Wisconsin-Madison), March 12, 1990, p. 1.
148. See, for example, Jeff Rosen, "Hate Mail," *New Republic,* February 18, 1991, p. 20; Jacob Weisberg, "Thin Skins," *ibid.,* p. 23.
149. Jacob Weisberg, "Thin Skins," *New Republic,* February 18, 1991, pp. 22, 23.
150. Keith E. Whittington, "Crusading Against Racism at UT," *Texas Review,* October 1987, p. 1.

151. Peter Miskech, "The Freshman Guide to Diversity," *Michigan Review*, September 1989, p. 12.
152. David Edwards, "Censorship in the Name of the 'Politically Correct,'" *University Review of Texas*, February 1991, p. 5.
153. D. L. Cavicke, "Legal Briefs: From the Law School," *Stanford Review*, January 8, 1990, p. 11.
154. *The Virginia Advocate* (University of Virginia) December 1990.
155. "Letters: Racism Against Whites Spreading Across University," *The Stanford Daily*, April 2, 1990, p. 4.
156. Jacob Weisberg, "Thin Skins," *New Republic*, February 18, 1991, p. 23.
157. Thomas Short, "Selective Intolerance in the University," *The Dartmouth Review*, January 25, 1989, p. 10.
158. "A Mass Exodus" *The Bryn Mawr & Haverford News*, November 18, 1988, p. 8.
159. "Bonner Questioned," *ibid.*, November 11, 1988, p. 10. The article to which this letter responded was Robert Lee Bonner, Jr., "Bonner Describes Minorities' Up-hill Battle," *ibid.*, November 4, 1988, p. 6.
160. Quoted in Constance Casey and Renee Koury, "The Walls of Ivy," *San Jose Mercury News, West* Magazine Section, February 17, 1991, p. 15.
161. "Racism on Campus," *The Christian Science Monitor*, June 14, 1988, p. 17.
162. *Campus Report from Accuracy in Academia*, January 1989, p. 3.
163. "Racism on Campus," *The Christian Science Monitor*, June 14, 1988, p. 17; Dinesh D'Souza, *Illiberal Education*, p. 135.
164. Charles S. Farrell, "Black Students Seen Facing 'New Racism' on Many Campuses," *The Chronicle of Higher Education*, January 27, 1988, p. A1.
165. *Ibid.*, p. A36.
166. Constance Casey and Renee Koury, "The Walls of Ivy." *San Jose Mercury News, West* Magazine Section, February 17, 1991, p. 14; "Letters to the Sun," *The Cornell Daily Sun*, February 27, 1990, p. 4.
167. Letter, *Dartmouth Review*, November 22, 1989, p. 2.
168. Constance Casey and Renee Koury, "The Walls of Ivy." *San Jose Mercury News, West* Magazine Section, February 17, 1991, p. 14.
169. "Letters to the Sun," *The Cornell Daily Sun*, February 27, 1990, p. 4.
170. John H. Bunzel, "Black and White at Stanford," *The Public Interest*, Fall 1991, p. 7.

171. Charles S. Farrell, "Black Students Seen Facing 'New Racism' on Many Campuses," *The Chronicle of Higher Education*, January 27, 1988, p. A36.
172. Stephen Goode, "On the Outs Over Who Gets In," *Insight*, October 9, 1989, p. 9.
173. Charles S. Farrell, "Black Students Seen Facing 'New Racism' on Many Campuses," *The Chronicle of Higher Education*, January 27, 1988, p. A36.
174. Philip G. Altbach, "The Racial Dilemma in American Higher Education," *The Racial Crisis in American Higher Education*, edited by Philip G. Altbach and Kofi Lomotey (Albany: State University of New York Press, 1991), p. 7.
175. "1988 Enrollment by Race at 3,100 Institutions of Higher Education," *The Chronicle of Higher Education*, April 11, 1990, pp. A38, A41.
176. "Winners and Losers," *Campus Report from Accuracy in Academia*, April 1987, p. 6.
177. Loren Pope, *Looking Beyond the Ivy League* (New York: Penguin Books, 1990), p. 159.
178. Troy Duster, "Understanding Self-Segregation on Campus," *The Chronicle of Higher Education*, September 25, 1991, p. B1.
179. "1988 Enrollment by Race at 3,100 Institutions of Higher Education," *The Chronicle of Higher Education*, April 11, 1990 pp. A38–A46, *passim*.
180. Quoted in Constance Casey and Renee Koury, "The Walls of Ivy," *San Jose Mercury News, West* Magazine Section, February 17, 1991, p. 16.

CHAPTER 7: IDEOLOGICAL DOUBLE STANDARDS

1. Caleb Nelson, "McCarthyism Revisited: How Harvard Stifles Free Speech," *Harvard Salient*, October 1986, pp. 4ff; Caleb Nelson, "Welcome to the Company of Educated Men and Women," *Harvard Salient*, Commencement 1987, pp. 66ff.
2. "Free Speech at Harvard?" *Campus Report from Accuracy in Academia*, November 1987, pp. 1, 4.
3. Lisa J. Goodall, "Forum Debates Policy on Speech Harassment," *The Harvard Crimson*, December 3, 1987, p. 1.
4. Robert Brundage, "Placing Pennies Over Principles," *Harvard Salient*, April 1987, p. 7.
5. Caleb Nelson, "McCarthyism Revisited: How Harvard Stifles Free Speech," *Harvard Salient*, October 1986, p. 5.
6. Les Corba III, *Appeasing the Censors: A Special Report on Campus*

Free Speech Abuses (Washington, D.C.: Accuracy in Academia, Inc., no date), pp. 8–15, *passim.*

7. Natalie and Gerald Sirkin, "Saving Education," *Stanford Review*, January 14, 1991, p. 3.

8. Dinesh D'Souza, *Illiberal Education: The Politics of Race and Sex on Campus* (New York: The Free Press, 1991), pp. 148–151, 194–197.

9. Carl Irving, "Furor at UC over 'Racist' Course," *San Francisco Examiner*, September 17, 1990, p. A4.

10. Frank H. T. Rhodes, "The Student Decides," *America's Best Colleges and Professional Schools* (Washington, D.C.: U.S. News & World Report, 1987), p. 42.

11. See Sandra F. MacGowan and Sarah M. McGinty, editors, *50 College Admissions Directors Speak to Parents* (San Diego: Harcourt Brace Jovanovich, Publishers, 1988), p. 43.

12. *Ibid.*, p. 16.

13. Kathleen O'Toole, "Dr. Ruth Stirs up Storm with Views on Student Sexual Mores," *Stanford University Campus Report*, November 16, 1986, p. 8.

14. Alice Supton, "Dr. Ruth's Logic Just Doesn't Wash," *The Stanford Daily*, November 13, 1986, p. 4.

15. Uprising, "Debate Must Rise to a Higher Level," *The Stanford Daily*, November 18, 1986, p. 4.

16. Elaine Riggs, "Dr. Ruth Draws Critics," *The Stanford Daily*, November 13, 1986, p. 1.

17. Judy David, Karen Gulick and Eileen McManus, "Acquaintance Rape is No Fad," *The Stanford Daily*, November 24, 1986, p. 4.

18. Charlie Goren, "Do Students Really Agree with Dr. Ruth?" *The Stanford Daily*, November 13, 1986, p. 3.

19. Frank Stoddard, "Dr. Ruth's Advice Bad, Chauvinistic," *The Stanford Daily*, November 18, 1986, p. 4.

20. Gretchen Eliot, "Westheimer Was Misunderstood," *The Stanford Daily*, November 18, 1986, p. 4.

21. Megan Swezey, "Talk Raised Issues," *The Stanford Daily*, November 18, 1986, p. 4.

22. Amy Chamberlain, "Women's Studies: Women's Center Pushing NU to keep Up with the Times," *Daily Northwestern*, April 25, 1990, p. 3.

23. Michelle Guido, "Sexuality Class: A Squeamish Look at the Wild Side of Sex," *Golden Gater*, November 12, 1987, p. 1; *idem.*, "Bestiality Films: The Controversy Continues," *Golden Gater*, November 17, 1987, p. 1.

24. "SAFE SEX EXPLORER'S ACTION PACKED STARTER KIT

HANDBOOK," (no date, no place of publication, 1986), p. 1.
25. *Ibid.*, p. 2.
26. The Stanford AIDS Educational Project Presents the 1989 Third Annual Condom Rating Contest, front page.
27. Baie Netzer, "Campus Launches Condom Week," *The Stanford Daily*, February 17, 1987, pp. 1, 2.
28. *The Trail* (University of Puget Sound), February 10, 1988, p. 16.
29. Beverly Conant Sloane, *Partners in Health* (New York: Charles E. Merrill Publishing Co., 1986), p. 8.
30. *Ibid.*, p. 10.
31. *Ibid.*
32. Congressman William Dannemeyer, *Shadow in the Land: Homosexuality in America* (San Francisco: Ignatius Press, 1989), pp. 24–39.
33. "Yalie Punished for Posters," *Campus Report from Accuracy in Academia*, July 1986, p. 1.
34. Ronald J. Gramieri, "The Politics of Punishment," *Harvard Salient*, November 1987, p. 4.
35. "Heterosexuals Rally for Rights," *Campus Report from Accuracy in Academia*, June 1990, p. 5.
36. James M. Klein, "Where Have All the Flowers Gone?" *Wesleyan Review*, May 1990, p. 17.
37. Michele Paige, "Vermont Frat Bars Gay Student," *Brown Herald*, March 16, 1990, p. 3.
38. Mark Silver, "Homophobic Slurs Discovered," *The Amherst Student*, February 28, 1990, p. 1.
39. "Heterosexuals Rally for Rights," *Campus Report from Accuracy in Academia*, pp. 1, 5.
40. *Ibid.*, p. 5.
41. "Gay Graffitti," *Cornell Review*, April 26, 1990, p. 2.
42. Doug McLellan, "A Very Public 'ORGASM,' " *Harvard Salient*, November 1990, p. 4.
43. Amy Lundy, "Area Universities Named as Gay Meeting Places," *The Hoya* (Georgetown University), February 23, 1990, p. 1; Brian Wheeler, "Book Lists 3 Campus Sites for Homosexual Activity," *Ibid.*
44. Michael Koretzky, "Sex in Men's Bathrooms Worries Gay Activists," *U.: The National College Newspaper*, September 1989.
45. "Lavatory Love," *Dartmouth Review*, October 4, 1989, p. 5; Chris Reid, "Lauinger Battles 'Perverts,' " *The Hoya* (Georgetown University), October 3, 1989, p. 1; "Sexual Deviance at UCSD," *California Review*, May 1989, p. 4.
46. "Two Men, One a SJS Prof, Cited at 'Cruising' Restroom," *San Jose Mercury News*, April 20, 1991, p. 4B.

47. *Stanford Daily*, March 7, 1990, p. 6.
48. Daryl Joseffer, "Homosexual Harassment," *Stanford Review*, October 29, 1990, p. 3.
49. Jill Sporleder, "Coed by Bed," *The Stanford Daily*, March 5, 1990, p. 1; Marie Bui, "Burbank Students Try Out Different Kind of Lifestyle," *Ibid*, February 13, 1991, p. 1.
50. "Basic Training," *The Stanford Daily*, December 5, 1990, p. 1.
51. "Mandated Sensitivity," *Campus*, Winter 1991, p. 12.
52. Andrew Zappala, "Free Speech Violations: A Sampling," *Campus*, Fall 1990, p. 6.
53. Mary Ann Campo, "Abortion and the Brown Student," *Brown Daily Herald*, March 2, 1990, p. 1.
54. "Officials Struggle to Curb Unplanned Pregnancies," *U. The National College Newspaper*, February 1991, p. 12.
55. "Campus Pregnancy: A Lesson Unlearned," *U. The National College Newspaper*, February 1991, p. 13.
56. "Multiculturism," *The Cavalier Daily*, April 5, 1990, p. 2.
57. Robert Vega, "In Defense of Free Speech," *The Wesleyan Review* (Wesleyan University), December 1989, p. 10.
58. Jonathan Bunce, "Race Relations Face Double Standards," *Northwestern Review*, February 9, 1990, p. 3.
59. Benjamin Hart, Jr., *Poisoned Ivy* (New York: Stein and Day, 1983), pp. 240–241.
60. *Ibid.*, pp. 60–65.
61. *Ibid.*, p. 68.
62. James B. Meigs, "College Papers Do the Right-Wing Thing," *Rolling Stone*, October 5, 1989, p. 152.
63. Benjamin Hart, *Poisoned Ivy*, pp. 152–153, 155–163.
64. *Ibid.*, pp. 161, 168–169, 171, 173.
65. Charles J. Sykes, *The Hollow Men: Politics and Corruption in Higher Education* (Washington, D.C.: Regenery Gateway, 1990), p. 241.
66. Benjamin Hart, Jr., *Poisoned Ivy*, pp. 220–223.
67. James McCutcheon, "Freshman Railroaded by COS," *Dartmouth Review*, January 24, 1990, p. 7.
68. While this judgement is inevitably subjective, anyone can make his own subjective judgement by reading the essay, which was reproduced in the *Dartmouth Review*. Kieran Shields, "Reader's Court: You Decide Baker's Guilt," *Dartmouth Review*, March 17, 1990, pp. 10, 12.
69. William F. Buckley, "Dartmouth Rides Again," *Dartmouth Review*, February 28, 1990, p. 7.
70. See, for example, Hugh Restall, "College Rescinds Baker Suspension," *Dartmouth Review*, April 4, 1990, p. 7; Andrew Baker,

"Andrew Baker Set His Record Straight," *Dartmouth Review*, April 24, 1991, p. 8; Robert Fogelin, "Sedgwick Acted Properly in Baker Case," *The Dartmouth*, April 19, 1990, p. 4; Jeffrey Hart, "Baker Was Not the One Acting Without Honor," *The Dartmouth*, April 24, 1990, p. 4; James Wright, "Sedgwick Has Been Victim of Vicious Attacks," *The Dartmouth*, May 1, 1990, p. 4; Jeffrey Hart, "Wright's Response to Baker-Sedgwick Defends an Egregious Wrong," *The Dartmouth*, May 3, 1990, p. 4.

71. "Text of Kennedy's Decision in Mosher Dismissal Case," *Stanford University Campus Report*, October 2, 1985, p. 9.

72. *Ibid.*

73. *Ibid.*, p. 11.

74. *Ibid.*, pp. 11, 12.

75. *Ibid.*, pp. 12, 13, 15, 16.

76. *Ibid.*, pp. 12, 13, 14.

77. *Ibid.*, p. 12.

78. *Ibid.*

79. *Ibid.*

80. *Ibid.*, p. 13.

81. *Ibid.*, p. 12.

82. Jerry Adler et al., "Taking Offense," *Newsweek*, December 24, 1990, p. 48.

83. Jeffrey Hart, "Selective Concern for Student Safety," *Dartmouth Review*, December 7, 1988, p. 12.

84. Thorstein Veblen, *The Higher Learning in America: A Memorandum on the Conduct of Universities by Business Men* (New York: Sagamore Press, Inc., 1957), p. 69.

85. Charles Krauthammer, "Political Correctness Meets Patriotism," *Campus Report from Accuracy in Academia*, March 1991, pp. 7, 8.

86. Joseph E. Gehring, Jr., "The Crisis in the University," *Cornell Review*, February 28, 1991, pp. 6ff.

87. Martin Kaste, "MPIRG's Organization and Politics Examined," *The Carletonian*, September 30, 1988, p. 1.

88. Jenny Choo, "Goodbye, CalPIRG?" *Redwood Review*, October 3, 1990, p. 2.

89. Tony Abboud and Katherine Cooper, "Organization has Potential for Everybody: Mailing was Unfounded," *The Carletonian*, September 23, 1988, p. 5.

90. Jenny Choo, "Goodbye, CalPIRG?" *Redwood Review*, October 3, 1990, p. 2.

91. Darrell McKignen, "Special Funding Mechanism is Not Fair or Legitimate," *The Carletonian*, September 23, 1988, p. 5.

92. Elizabeth Brinkley, "MassPIRG Funding Re-Examined," *Wellesley News*, September 22, 1988, p. 1.
93. *Ibid.*
94. Elizabeth Brinkley, "MassPIRG Loses, Defeated by 9 Votes," *Wellesley News*, April 20, 1989, p. 1.
95. *Ibid.*, pp. 1, 3.
96. Jenny Choo, "Goodbye CalPIRG? UC Regents Eliminate the Negative Check-off System," *Redwood Review* (University of California at Santa Cruz), October 3, 1990, p. 2.
97. *Harvard Salient*, December 1990, p. 11.
98. Marcus Mabry, "A View from the Front: My Life as a Member of the PC Patrol," *Newsweek*, December 24, 1990, p. 55.
99. Art Macum, "Grad Theme House Called Apathetic," *The Stanford Daily*, February 15, 1991, p. 1.
100. *Ibid.*, p. 10.
101. Dinesh D'Souza, *Illiberal Education*, p. 217.
102. James High, "Beware, the Thought Police," *Redwood Review*, October 3, 1990, p. 11.
103. "Deane Baker Discusses the U-M, Himself," *Michigan Review*, November 1990, p. 8.
104. Marcus Mabry, "A View from the Front: My Life as a Member of the PC Patrol," *Newsweek*, December 24, 1990, p. 55.
105. Dinesh D'Souza, *Illiberal Education*, p. 239.
106. Marcus Mabry, "A View from the Front: My Life as a Member of the PC Patrol," *Newsweek*, December 24, 1990, p. 55.
107. Scott Heller, "Reeling from Harsh Attacks, Educators Weigh How to Respond to 'Politically Correct' Label," *Chronicle of Higher Education*, June 12, 1991, p. A16.
108. "Political Correctness," *The Stanford Daily*, May 1991, p. 4.
109. Michael Kinsley, "P.C.B.S.," *The New Republic*, May 20, 1991, p. 8.
110. Scott Heller, "Reeling from Harsh Attacks, Educators Weigh How to Respond to 'Politically Correct' Label," *Chronicle of Higher Education*, June 12, 1991, p. A16; "Mr. Bush and the Freedom to Hurt," *The New York Times*, May 12, 1991, Section E, p. 16.
111. Former CBS news executive Fred Friendly posed the issue as whether a white student should be allowed to say to a black student: "You niggers stink. I don't know why we ever let you in here. I wish your kind would all get out of here." Eleni Kirkas and Eden Quainton, "Panel Debates Free Speech," *The Stanford Daily*, April 11, 1991, p. 1. The pervasive straining to find "covert racism" at campuses across the country should

alone be enough to suggest that this kind of grossness is hardly the issue.

112. The earlier standard dates from 1896; the later from June 1990.
113. Andrew Zappala, "Free Speech Violations: A Sampling," *Campus*, Fall 1990, p. 6.
114. Scott Heller, "Reeling from Harsh Attacks, Educators Weigh How to Respond to 'Politically Correct' Label," *Chronicle of Higher Education*, June 12, 1991, p. A16.

CHAPTER 8: TEACHING AND PREACHING

1. Professor X, *This Beats Working for a Living: The Dark Secrets of a College Professor* (New Rochelle, N.Y.: Arlington House, 1973), p. 18.
2. See, for example, Jonathan Eisenberg, "Emphasis on Teaching, Streamlining," *The Stanford Daily*, April 6, 1990, p. 1; Christine Moll, "Shalala: University to Focus on Undergrads," *The Badger Herald* (University of Wisconsin), February 8, 1990, pp. 1, 3.
3. "Can't Fire Professor for Ethical Lapses, Rutgers Told," *The Chronicle of Higher Education*, August 15, 1990, p. A2.
4. Mary Madison, "Suicide Suspected in Cox Death," *Peninsula Times Tribune*, January 28, 1978, p. 1; "Carolyn Lougee Named First Recipient of Allan V. Cox Medal," *Stanford University Campus Report*, June 17, 1987, p. 26.
5. Robin Wilson, "Widespread Complaints: Undergraduates at Large Universities Found to Be Increasingly Dissatisfied," *The Chronicle of Higher Education*, January 9, 1991, p. A38.
6. Tom Jehn, Ellen Liebner, and Mario Orlovich, "Forum Reveals College Dilemma: Larger Classes, Smaller Faculty," *Chicago Maroon* (University of Chicago), May 31, 1988, p. 2.
7. Adam Lisberg, "Why College Professors Are Not There," *Chicago Maroon* (University of Chicago), May 5, 1989, p. 1.
8. David Hood, "*Profscam* at UNC," *The Carolina Critic*, September 1989, p. 26.
9. Robin Wilson, "Widespread Complaints: Undergraduates at Large Universities Found to be Increasingly Dissatisfied," *The Chronicle of Higher Education*, Jan. 9, 1991, p. A38.
10. *Ibid.*, p. A1.
11. *Ibid.*, p. A38.
12. Lucia Kendall, "Davidson College Needs to Hire More Professors," *The Davidsonian*, January 15, 1988, p. 15; Caroline Worlock, "Registration Problems Plague Freshmen," *The Carle-*

tonian, November 11, 1988, p. 1; "Workload Woes," *The Wellesley News,* February 14, 1990, p. 2.

13. Jason DeParle and Liza Munday, "Why Higher Education is Neither," *The Washington Monthly,* October 1989, p. 31.
14. Wendy Kahn, "Crowded Classes," *Daily Brown Herald,* April 16, 1990, p. 1.
15. Robin Wilson, "Widespread Complaints: Undergraduates at Large Universities Found to Be Increasingly Dissatisfied," *The Chronicle of Higher Education,* January 9, 1991, p. A38.
16. *Ibid.*
17. David J. Powell, "LSA's Road to Insanity," *Michigan Review* (University of Michigan), December 1990, p. 1.
18. Linda D'Angelo, "Whittaker Denies Wolfe Tenure," *The Tech* (M.I.T.), March 11, 1990, pp. 1, 15.
19. Scott Heller, "Teaching Award: Aid to Tenure or Kiss of Death?" *The Chronicle of Higher Education,* March 16, 1988, p. A14.
20. "Is Good Teaching, Valued? Biology Students Wonder," *Stanford University Campus Report* (Stanford University), April 25, 1990, p. 9.
21. Scott Heller, "Teaching Award: Aid to Tenure or Kiss of Death?" *The Chronicle of Higher Education,* March 16, 1988, p. A14.
22. *Ibid.*
23. Eric Hirsch, "Good Teaching Leads to Tenure Trouble," *Columbia Daily Spectator,* February 6, 1989, p. 3.
24. Jeffrey S. Nordhaus, "Brinkley Decides to Take Tenured Post at CUNY," *Harvard Crimson,* November 2, 1987, p. 1.
25. Committee on Undergraduate Education, *CUE Course Evaluation Guide, 1987–88* (Cambridge, Mass.: Harvard University, 1987), p. 658.
26. "Ameliorate Advising System," *Columbia Daily Spectator,* March 3, 1989, p. 3.
27. "Dear Adviser," *The Cavalier Daily* (University of Virginia), April 26, 1990, p. 2.
28. "Senior Survey," *Stanford University Campus Report,* November 16, 1988, p. 10.
29. David Riesman, *On Higher Education: The Academic Enterprise in an Era of Rising Student Consumerism* (San Francisco: Jossey-Bass, 1980), p. 258.
30. "Guilty! Guilty! Guilty!," *The Confidential Guide: Courses at Harvard-Radcliffe 1990–91* (Cambridge, Mass.: The Harvard Crimson, Inc., 1990), p. 66.
31. *Ibid.*
32. "History of the Earth," *The Confidential Guide: Courses at Har-*

vard Radcliffe 1987–88 (Cambridge, Mass.: The Harvard Crimson Inc., 1987), p. 63.

33. *Ibid.*
34. "TR Rates the Professors: The Excellent, the Mediocre, and the Atrocious," *Texas Review*, September 1987, p. 7.
35. "Student Hits Porn Lecture," *Campus Report from Accuracy in Academia*, December 1985, p. 2.
36. "The Best and the Bogus," *Northwestern Review*, November 17, 1989, p. 5.
37. "What Am I in For?" *California Review of Berkeley*, November 1989, p. 9.
38. *Student Course Guide, Spring 1987* (Princeton: USG Committee on Academics, 1987), pp. 32, 33, 34, 44, 75.
39. *Teacher-Course Evaluation Book 1986* (Durham, N.C.: Duke University Publications Board, 1986), p. 7.
40. *Ibid.*, p. 16.
41. Committee on Undergraduate Education, *CUE Course Evaluation Guide, 1987–88*, p. 658.
42. David Hood, *"Profscam* at UNC," *The Carolina Critic*, September 1989, p. 30.
43. "Evaluation of Psychology 060," mimeographed, unpaged, and undated.
44. *Student Course Evaluations 1987–88* (Chicago: University of Chicago Dean's Student Advisory Committee), pp. P-15, P-22.
45. Robin Wilson, "Widespread Complaints: Undergraduates at Large Universities Found to Be Increasingly Dissatisfied," *The Chronicle of Higher Education*, January 9, 1991, p. A38.
46. Scott Heller, "Teaching Award: Aid to Tenure or Kiss of Death?" *The Chronicle of Higher Education*, March 16, 1988, p. A14.
47. "TA's May Learn English," *The Johns Hopkins News-Letter*, February 9, 1990, p. 2.
48. "The Beautiful . . . And the Damned," *Dartmouth Review*, September 15, 1989, p. 8.
49. "Prof. Mark Reader Won't Talk," *AIA Report* (Accuracy in Academia), November 1985, unpaged.
50. Todd D. Harbour, "Philpott's Class a Study of Distraction," *Texas Review*, February 1987, pp. 1, 12.
51. Bill Dillon, "The Professor as Politician," *Harvard Salient*, December 1987, p. 11.
52. "U Mass to Begin Teaching Diversity," *Campus Report from Accuracy in Academia*, January 1991, p. 1.
53. George F. Will, "Radical English," *The Washington Post*, September 16, 1990, p. B7.

54. Agnes Sagan, "A Look at the Course Book and the Courses' Books," *Cornell Review*, September 1989, p. 3.
55. Jeff Muir, "The Pea Plant—Sandinista Connection," *Michigan Review*, December 1990, p. 10.
56. "And They Call It 'Education'," *Campus Report from Accuracy in Academia*, October 1987, p. 1.
57. *Ibid.*, p. 4.
58. Christopher Baldwin, "Bill Cole in His Own Words—Sound and Fury, Signifying Nothing," *Dartmouth Review*, February 24, 1988, p. 5.
59. *The Confidential Guide: Courses at Harvard-Radcliffe 1987–88*, p. 169.
60. "Violent Views and Tender Grades," *Campus Report from Accuracy in Academia*, March 1987, pp. 1, 5.
61. "Campus Briefs: Prof Criticized for 'Points for Protest,' " *Campus Report from Accuracy in Academia*, July/August 1990, p. 3.
62. See, for example, "Marxist Professors: Winning Votes and Minds," *Campus Report from Accuracy in Academia*, December 1987, p. 4.
63. Economics 357K Syllabus, The University of Texas at Austin, Fall 1985, page 3.
64. "Good Profs, Bad Profs—Students Rate the Faculty," *Campus Report from Accuracy in Academia*, October 1987, p. 4.
65. "Anti-Military Bias Offends Vet," *Campus Report from Accuracy in Academia*, February 1988, p. 1.
66. Jeff Muir, "The Pea Plant—Sandinista Connection," *The Michigan Review*, December 1990, p. 10.
67. "First Muzzled, Then Jailed," *Campus Report from Accuracy in Academia*, April 1986, pp. 1, 5.
68. "TR Rates the Professors: The Excellent, the Mediocre, and the Atrocious," *Texas Review*, September 1987, p. 6.
69. *Ibid.*, p. 8.
70. Gerald Davis, "Departing Seniors Award University High Marks," *Stanford University Campus Report* (Stanford University), April 25, 1990, p. 6.
71. *Student Course Evaluations 1987–88* (University of Chicago), pp. P-16, P-26.
72. *Ibid.*, p. S-18.
73. *Ibid.*, p. S-22.
74. *Ibid.*, p. S-28.
75. *Ibid.*, p. S-34.
76. *Ibid.*, p. S-41.
77. *Ibid.*, p. S-57.

78. *Teacher-Course Evaluation Book 1986* (Durham, N.C.: Duke University Publications Board, 1986), 21, 22, 23.
79. *Ibid.*, pp. 59, 60, 61.
80. "Rating the Faculty," *California Review*, June 1991, p. 12.
81. "The Best and the Bogus," *Northwestern Review*, November 17, 1989, p. 5.
82. "What Am I in For?" *California Review of Berkeley*, November 1989, pp. 8, 9.
83. Committee on Undergraduate Education, *CUE Course Evaluation Guide, 1987–88*, pp. 124, 185, 198, 246, 275, 323, 365.
84. Henry Rosovsky, *The University: An Owner's Manual* (New York: W. W. Norton & Co., 1990), p. 91. See also J. H. Hexter, "Publish or Perish—A Defense," *The Public Interest*, Fall 1969, pp. 66–67.
85. "Ameliorate Advising System," *Columbia Daily Spectator*, March 3, 1989, p. 3.
86. Natalie and Gerald Sirkin, "Saving Education," *Stanford Review*, January 14, 1991, p. 3.
87. "The Graduate," *Life*, August 1987, p. 25.
88. William F. Buckley, Jr., "Introduction," *The National Review College Guide: America's 50 Top Liberal Arts Schools* (New York: The National Review, Inc., 1991), p. vii.
89. Letter from Professor Arthur Jaffe, Chairman, Department of Mathematics, Harvard University, November 25, 1987.
90. See, for example, Page Smith, *Killing the Spirit: Higher Education in America* (New York: The Viking Press, 1990), Chapter 1, 13; Carolyn J. Mooney, "Efforts to Cut Amount of 'Trivial' Scholarship Win New Backing from Many Academics," *The Chronicle of Higher Education*, May 22, 1991, p. A1.
91. Carolyn J. Mooney, "Professors Feel Conflict Between Roles in Teaching and Research, Say Students Are Badly Prepared," *The Chronicle of Higher Education*, May 8, 1991, p. A15.
92. "Change Trendlines," *Change*, May/June 1991, pp. 25, 26.
93. David Riesman, *On Higher Education*, p. 20. For similar attitudes among the scientists, see Charles J. Sykes, *The Hollow Men* (Washington, D.C.: Regnery Gateway, 1990), p. 149.
94. Ellen W. Schrecker, *No Ivory Tower: McCarthyism and the Universities* (New York: Oxford University Press, 1986), p. 18.
95. Martin J. Finkelstein, *The American Academic Profession: A Synthesis of Social Scientific Inquiry since World War II* (Columbus: Ohio State University Press, 1984), p. 75.
96. Jacques Barzun, *Teacher in America* (Indianapolis: Liberty Press, 1981), p. 259.
97. Robert Nisbet, "The Future of Tenure," *On Learning and Change*,

edited by the editors of *Change* Magazine (New Rochelle: *Change* Magazine, 1973), p. 47.

98. Andrew Oldenquist, "Tenure: Academe's Peculiar Institution," *Morality, Responsibility, and the University: Studies in Academic Ethics*, edited by Steven M. Cahn (Philadelphia: Temple University Press, 1990), p. 57.

99. As just one example, Dr. Peter Duignan of the Hoover Institution has authored or co-authored a number of works on Africa which have been praised in scholarly journals around the world over a period of a quarter of a century, but he has never been on the faculty of any college or university. At a time when recognized authorities who are liberal professors are being forced out of ideologically sensitive courses on race and ethnicity for not being far enough to the left—Stephan Thernstrom at Harvard and Reynolds Farley at Michigan being liberals—there is little or no prospect of many conservative scholars being hired to contribute to the "diversity" so loudly proclaimed and so little in evidence intellectually.

100. *Sarah Lawrence College, 1988–98*, p. 73.

101. *Whittier College Catalogue of Courses, 1990–92*, pp. 108–110.

102. Adam Smith, *An Inquiry into the Nature and Causes of the Wealth of Nations* (New York: The Modern Library, 1937), p. 718.

103. Jacques Barzun, *Teacher in America*, p. 283.

104. *Ibid.*, p. 263.

CHAPTER 9: ATHLETIC SUPPORT

1. "Athletics Revenues and Expenditures of NCAA Institutions," *The Chronicle of Higher Education*, December 5, 1990, p. A36.

2. "This Season's Bowl Games," *The Chronicle of Higher Education*, December 12, 1990, p. A25.

3. "Share of NCAA Basketball Money for Conferences in Division I, 1990–91," *The Chronicle of Higher Education*, October 31, 1990, p. A37.

4. "Median Salaries of College and University Administrators, 1989–90," *The Chronicle of Higher Education: Almanac*, September 5, p. 22; "Average Faculty Salaries, 1989–90," *Ibid.*, p. 23.

5. Murray Sperber, *College Sports Inc.: The Athletic Department vs. The University* (New York: Henry Holt and Co., 1990), p. 149.

6. *Ibid.*, p. 88.

7. *Ibid.*, pp. 16, 102.

8. *Ibid.*, p. 117.

9. *Ibid.*, pp. 124–125.
10. *Ibid.*, pp. 131–135.
11. *Ibid.*, p. 15.
12. "Athletic Revenues and Expenditures of NCAA Institutions," *The Chronicle of Higher Education*, December 5, 1990, p. A36.
13. Murray Sperber, *College Sports Inc.*, pp. 2–3.
14. "Of Steroids and Scholarships: Eli Commish Talks to Spec," *Columbia Daily Spectator*, February 8, 1989, p. 5.
15. Murray Sperber, *College Sports Inc.*, pp. 85–89.
16. *Ibid.*, p. 89.
17. Douglas Lederman, "Top Sports Programs' Costs Found to Outrun Inflation," *The Chronicle of Higher Education*, December 5, 1990, p. A36.
18. "Athletic Revenues and Expenditures of NCAA Institutions," *The Chronicle of Higher Education*, December 5, 1990, p. A36.
19. "Rankings of Universities' Reputations and Number of Faculty Publications," *New York Times*, January 17, 1983, p. 9.
20. Murray Sperber, *College Sports Inc.*, pp. 70–81.
21. *Ibid.*, p. 73.
22. Peter Rapalus, "Scholar-Athlete Standards Affirmed," *Stanford University Campus Report*, January 16, 1991, p. 8.
23. Tim Hevly, "Whitman Skiers No. 1," *The Whitman College Pioneer*, March 10, 1988, p. 1.
24. Rich Thomas, "Koger Honored by NCAA," *Bryn Mawr/Haverford News*, September 23, 1988, p. 16.
25. Jill Daniels, "Athletic Scholarships Determined by Need," *The Stanford Daily*, November 2, 1989, p. 1.
26. Murray Sperber, *College Sports Inc.*, pp. 100–102.
27. *Ibid.*, pp. 211–213.
28. "Choosing the Class of 1983," *Time*, April 9, 1979, p. 73; Penny Hollander Feldman, "Recruiting an Elite: Admission to Harvard," Ph.D. dissertation, Department of Government, Harvard University, May 1975, pp. 96–97.
29. Murray Sperber, *College Sports Inc.*, pp. 252–253.
30. Harry Edwards, "The Black 'Dumb Jock': An American Tragedy," *College Board Review*, Spring 1984, p. 9.
31. Douglas Lederman, "Black Athletes Who Entered Colleges in Mid-80s Had Much Weaker Records Than Whites, Study Finds," *The Chronicle of Higher Education*, July 10, 1991, p. A30.
32. *Studies of Intercollegiate Athletics Report No. 1: Summary Results from the 1987–88 National Study of Intercollegiate Athletes* (Washington, D.C.: American Institutes for Research, 1988), p. 8.
33. Murray Sperber, *College Sports Inc.*, pp. 302–303.

34. Douglas Lederman, *Chronicle of Higher Education*, January 30, 1991, p. A33.
35. "Contemporary Middle East," *The Confidential Guide: Courses at Harvard-Radcliffe 1987–1988* (Cambridge, Mass.: The Harvard Crimson, Inc., 1987), pp. 30, 49, 92.
36. Murray Sperber, *College Sports Inc.*, p. 277.
37. *Ibid.*, pp. 277–278.
38. "Freedman was There," *Dartmouth Review*, May 3, 1989, p. 6.
39. Murray Sperber, *College Sports Inc.*, p. 282.
40. Douglas Lederman, "North Carolina Board Adopts University-Wide Reforms After Study Finds Abuses in N.C. State Basketball," *The Chronicle of Higher Education*, September 6, 1989, p. A32.
41. Sue Collins, "The High Price of Honesty," *NEA Today*, October 1990, p. 15.
42. Fred Girard and Norman Sinclair, "Teachers Say They're Pressured to Pass Students," *Detroit News*, April 6, 1987, pp. 1ff.
43. Murray Sperber, *College Sports Inc.*, p. 291.
44. "Graduation Rates of Athletes and Other Students in Division I Colleges," *The Chronicle of Higher Education*, March 27, 1991, p. A39.
45. *Ibid.*, pp. A41–A43.
46. *Ibid.*, p. A43.
47. *Stanford Sports Quarterly*, Winter 1990, pp. 7, 11, 14, 16.
48. Raymie E. McKerrow and Norinne Hilchey Daly, "Student-Athletes in Search of Balance," *Phi Kappa Phi Journal*, Fall 1990, p. 43.
49. Murray Sperber, *College Sports Inc.*, pp. 264–265.
50. *Ibid.*, pp. 272–274.

CHAPTER 10: THE EMPIRE STRIKES BACK

1. Mary Hatwood Futrell, "Report of the President," National Education Association of the United States, *Proceedings of the Sixty-Eighth Representative Assembly*, July 2–5, 1989 (Washington, D.C.: National Education Association, 1990), p. 7.
2. Thomas Toch, *In the Name of Excellence: The Struggle to Reform the Nation's Schools, Why It's Failing, and What Should Be Done* (New York: Oxford University Press, 1991), p. 152.
3. *The World Almanac and Book of Facts 1991* (New York: Pharos Books, 1990), p. 207.
4. The Editors of the Chronicle of Higher Education, *The Almanac*

of Higher Education 1989–90 (Chicago: University of Chicago Press, 1989), pp. 24–25.

5. *Ibid.*, p. 50.

6. Thomas Toch, *In the Name of Excellence*, p. 115.

7. *Ibid.*, p. 154.

8. Scott Jaschik, "To Win More Money from State Legislatures, Colleges Find They Must Use the 'T-Word,' " *Chronicle of Higher Education*, April 27, 1988, p. A25.

9. Anne Lowrey Bailey, "President of United Negro College Fund Denounces Corporate Practice of Specifying a Grant's Purpose," *Chronicle of Higher Education*, April 20, 1988, pp. A37–A38.

10. Quoted in John Searle, "The Storm over the University," *New York Review of Books*, December 6, 1990, p. 35.

11. "Bok Focuses on Criticisms of Higher Education," *Harvard Alumni Gazette*, June 1990, p. 6.

12. Amy Parker, "First Annual Convocation Held," *The Johns Hopkins News-Letter*, September 14, 1990, p. 1.

13. Edward B. Jenkinson, *Student Privacy in the Classroom* (Bloomington, Ind.: Phi Delta Kappa Educational Foundation, 1990), p. 9.

14. Francis Oakley, "Despite Its Critics, Undergraduate Education Is a Success," *The Chronicle of Higher Education*, March 14, 1990, p. A52.

15. Karen J. Winkler, "Organization of American Historians Back Teaching of Non-Western Culture and Diversity in Schools," *The Chronicle of Higher Education*, February 6, 1991, p. A5; Henry Rosovsky, *The University: An Owner's Manual* (New York: W. W. Norton & Co., 1990), pp. 297–298.

16. "Freedman Speaks at Harvard," *Dartmouth Review*, January 2, 1991, p. 5.

17. "Learning to Love the PC Canon," *Newsweek*, December 24, 1990, p. 50.

18. "Teaching Your Children," *Forbes*, November 11, 1991, p. 20.

19. *News from the College Board*, for release August 27, 1991, p. 5.

20. Thomas Toch, *In the Name of Excellence*, pp. 44–56.

21. Lynda Carl Frankenstein, "*Man: A Course of Study*—A Case Study of Diffusion in Oregon," Ph.D. dissertation, School of Education, Stanford University, 1977, pp. 82–83.

22. Peter B. Dow, "MACOS Revisited: A Commentary on the Most Frequently Asked Questions About *Man: A Course of Study*," *Social Education*, October 1975, p. 389.

23. Congressman John B. Conlan, "MACOS: The Push for a National Curriculum," *Social Education*, October 1975, p. 390.

24. Ruth C. Engs, S. Eugene Barnes, and Molly Wanta, *Health Games Students Play: Creative Strategies for Health Education* (Dubuque, Iowa: Kendall/Hunt Publishing Co., 1975), p. 48.

25. *Ibid.*, p. 47.

26. See, for examples, Stanley W. Lindberg, editor, *The Annotated McGuffey: Selections from the McGuffey Eclectic Reacers 1836–1920* (New York: Van Nostrand Reinhold Co., 1976), p. 357, where the index lists four lines of page citations under the entry for death.

27. *Ibid.*, p. 203.

28. *Ibid.*, p. 204.

29. Ruth Engs, S. Eugene Barnes, and Molly Wanta, *Health Games Students Play*, p. 47.

30. Daniel Leviton, "Response to a Closet Death Educator," *Curriculum Review*, September 1989, p. 6.

31. Jacquelin Kasun, "Sex Education: The Hidden Agenda," *The World & I*, September 1989, p. 111.

32. Pearl Evans, *Hidden Damages in the Classroom* (Petaluma, Calif.: Small Helm Press, 1950), p. 10.

33. *Quest*, pp. 85–86.

34. *Child Abuse in the Classroom*, edited by Phyllis Schlafly (Westchester, Ill.: Crossway Books, 1988), p. 285.

35. *Ibid.*, pp. 286–287.

36. *Ibid.*, pp. 211–213.

37. *Murder in the Playground: The Burnage Report* (London: Longsight Press, 1989), pp. 175–176, 181, 196, 197, 207–208, 210–211, 218.

38. *Child Abuse in the Classroom*, p. 240.

39. *Ibid.*, pp. 413–414.

40. *Ibid.*, p. 306.

41. Bill Youngblood, "Here's Why Parental Choice for Public Schools is Nonsense," *Peninsula Times Tribune*, March 14, 1991, p. B-7.

42. American Federation of Teachers President Albert Shanker, quoted in "Nine Phoney Assertions About School Choice: Answering the Critics," *Backgrounder*, No. 852, September 13, 1991 (The Heritage Foundation), p. 7.

43. *Ibid.*, p. 6.

44. See, for example, Joe Nathen, "The Rhetoric and the Reality of Expanding Educational Choices," *Phi Delta Kappan*, March 1985, p. 477.

45. *Ibid.*

46. Stuart Steers, "The Catholic Schools' Black Students," *This World*, December 23, 1990, p. 8.

47. "Skimming the Cream Off Schools," *New York Times*, July 25, 1991, p. A16.
48. James S. Coleman, Thomas Hoffer, and Sally Kilgore, *High School Achievement: Public, Catholic, and Private Schools Compared* (New York: Basic Books, Inc., 1982), p. 194.
49. *Ibid.*, p. 144.
50. Stuart Steers, "The Catholic Schools' Black Students," *This World*, December 23, 1990, p. 9.
51. Stefanie Weiss, "Open Enrollment Plans," *NEA Today*, May/June 1990, p. 3.
52. "Bok Focuses on Criticisms of Higher Education," *Harvard Alumni Gazette*, June 1990, p. 5.
53. Ansley A. Abraham, *Racial Issues on Campus: How Students View Them* (Atlanta: Southern Regional Education Board, 1990), p. 24.
54. Derek Bok, *Beyond the Ivory Tower: Social Responsibilities of the Modern University* (Cambridge, Mass.: Harvard University Press, 1982), p. 52; Henry Rosovsky, *The University*, p. 296.
55. The Editors of the Chronicle of Higher Education, *The Almanac of Higher Education 1989–90*, p. 36.
56. Congressional Budget Office, *Student Aid and the Cost of Postsecondary Education* (Washington, D.C.: Congressional Budget Office, 1990), pp. xx–xxiv, 12–13, 105–106.
57. Chester E. Finn, Jr., "Consumers Need A 'No-Frills University' to Turn the Higher-Education Marketplace Upside Down," *The Chronicle of Higher Education*, October 26, 1988, p. B1.
58. Harold Howe II, "At $60 a day, College is a Bargain: A Room, 3 Meals, Myriad Activities, and an Education," *The Chronicle of Higher Education*, May 9, 1988, p. B1.
59. Thomas M. Burton, "Some Small Colleges Survived by Lining Up Very Needy 'Students,' " *The Wall Street Journal*, December 14, 1990, pp. 1ff.
60. See, for example, "Survey of Financial Aid to Minority Students, 1990–91: Results Compiled by the American Council on Education," September 13, 1991 (mimeographed).
61. *The Red and Blue* (University of Pennsylvania), October 1989, p. 5.
62. "Loss of Advertising," *The Red and Blue* (University of Pennsylvania), November 1989, unpaged.
63. Andrea Lamberti, "Report Raises Concerns, *The Tech* (M.I.T.), December 7, 1990, p. 1.
64. Dinesh D'Souza, *Illiberal Education: The Politics of Race and Sex on Campus* (New York: Free Press, 1991), p. 9.
65. Derek Bok, *Beyond the Ivory Tower*, p. 103.

66. "President James Duderstadt," *The Michigan Review* (University of Michigan), September 1988, p. 10.
67. Derek Bok, "What's Wrong with Our Universities," *Harvard Magazine*, May–June 1990, p. 44.
68. Many of these studies are summarized and re-examined by Larry L. Leslie and Paul T. Brinkmay, *The Economic Value of Higher Education* (New York: Macmillan Publishing Co., 1988), though ignoring the scholarly literature which suggests that much of what is attributed to education, as such, may in fact be due to sorting people by ability and persistence—a process which could be performed more cheaply than spending years in expensive institutions.
69. Robin Wilson, "Foreign Students in U.S. Reach a Record 386,000," *The Chronicle of Higher Education*, November 28, 1990, p. A36.
70. "Fact File: Foreign Students in U.S. Institutions, 1989–90," *The Chronicle of Higher Education*, November 28, 1990, p. A36.
71. *Peterson's National College Databank* (Princeton: Peterson's Guides, Inc., 1987), p. 42.
72. *Ibid.*, pp. 54–55.
73. "Institutions Enrolling the Most Foreign Students, 1988–89," *The Chronicle of Higher Education*, September 5, 1990, p. 19.
74. Henry Rosovsky, *The University*, p. 29.
75. "A Conversation with Henry Rosovsky," *Harvard Gazette*, February 16, 1990, p. 6.
76. Anthony DePalma, "Foreigners Flood U.S. Graduate Schools," *The New York Times*, November 29, 1990, p. A1.
77. *Ibid.*, p. A14; "Characteristics of Recipients of Doctorates 1988," *The Chronicle of Higher Education*, September 5, 1990, p. 18.
78. "Characteristics of Recipients of Doctorates 1988," *The Chronicle of Higher Education*, September 5, 1990, p. 18.
79. Anthony De Palma, "Foreigners Flood U.S. Graduate Schools," *New York Times*, November 29, 1990, p. A14.
80. National Center for Educational Statistics, *The Condition of Education 1990* (Washington, D.C.: U.S. Government Printing Office, 1990), p. 64.
81. *Ibid.*, p. 158.
82. Anthony De Palma, "Foreigners Flood U.S. Graduate Schools," *New York Times*, November 29, 1990, p. A14.
83. National Center for Educational Statistics, *The Condition of Education 1990*, Vol. 2 (Washington, D.C.: U.S. Government Printing Office, 1990), p. 86.
84. "Young people are too independent and exposed to too many points of view on and off the campus to be manipulated for very

long by what they hear and do not hear in the seminar room or the lecture hall." Derek Bok, *The President's Report, 1989–1990, Harvard University*, p. 12.

85. Derek Bok, "What's Wrong with our Universities," *Harvard Magazine*, May–June 1990, pp. 44, 47.

86. David Dietz, "U.S. Funds Used for Wedding," *San Francisco Chronicle*, February 15, 1991, p. A2.

87. John Wagner, "University May Retreat on Costs," *The Stanford Daily*, January 14, 1991, p. 1.

88. "Kennedy Sees No Evidence of Wrongdoing on Cost Recovery," *Stanford University Campus Report*, January 9, 1991, pp. 14, 15.

89. Jeff Gottlieb, "U.S. Probe of Stanford May Cost Other Schools," *San Jose Mercury News*, January 22, 1991, pp. 1A, 6A.

90. "Harvard Withdraws $500,000 of Overhead," *The Stanford University Campus Report*, April 10, 1991, p. 4.

91. Colleen Cordes, "Angry Lawmakers Grill Stanford's Kennedy on Research Cost," *The Chronicle of Higher Education*, March 20, 1991, p. A27.

92. Katherine Shim, "M.I.T. to Pay back Government $731,000," *The Tech* (M.I.T.), April 26, 1991, p. 1.

93. Colleen Cordes, "Angry Lawmakers Grill Stanford's Kennedy on Research Cost," *The Chronicle of Higher Education*, March 20, 1991, p. A27.

94. Colleen Cordes, "As Congress Fumes, More Universities Withdraw Overhead Charges," *The Chronicle of Higher Education*, May 8, 1991, p. A21.

95. Hugo Restall, "Dartmouth Accused of Abusing Grants," *The Dartmouth Review*, May 15, 1991, p. 7.

96. William R. Cotter, "Colleges' Efforts to Rationalize the Financial-Aid System Should Not Be Treated as Violations of Antitrust Laws," *The Chronicle of Higher Education*, September 6, 1989, pp. B1, B2.

97. *Ibid.*, p. B2.

98. Joseph Berger, "College Officials Defend Sharply Rising Tuition," *New York Times*, March 23, 1988, p. 18.

99. "Fitzsimmons Answers Questions on Admissions and Financial Aid," *Harvard Alumni Gazette*, February 1990, p. 26.

100. The Editors of the Chronicle of Higher Education, *The Almanac of Higher Education 1989–90* (Chicago: University of Chicago Press, 1989), p. 54.

101. *Ibid.*, p. 57.

102. Hans Mark, "Now is No Time to Shortchange Higher Learning," *Dallas Morning News*, December 30, 1990, p. 4.

103. The Editors of the Chronicle of Higher Education, *The Almanac of Higher Education 1989–90*, p. 54.

104. Howard R. Bowen and Jack H. Schuster, *American Professors: A National Resource Imperilled* (New York: Oxford University Press, 1986), p. 235.

105. Richard A. Epstein and Saunders MacLane, "Keep Mandatory Retirement for Tenured Faculty," *Regulation*, Spring 1991, p. 87.

106. *Ibid.*

107. Bernard D. Davis, *Storm over Biology* (Buffalo, N.Y.: Prometheus Books, 1986), p. 179.

108. See, for example, Andrew Oldenquist, "Tenure: Academe's Peculiar Institution," *Morality, Responsibility, and the University: Studies in Academic Ethics*, edited by Steven M. Cahn (Philadelphia: Temple University Press, 1990), p. 65.

109. Howard R. Bowen and Jack H. Schuster, *American Professors*, p. v.

110. *Ibid.*, p. 147.

111. *Ibid.*, pp. 45, 46.

112. Henry Rosovsky, *The University*, p. 177.

113. Howard R. Bowen and Jack H. Shuster, *American Professors*, pp. 148–150.

114. Derek Bok, *Beyond the Ivory Tower*, p. 20.

115. *Ibid.*, p. 22.

116. *Ibid.*, p. 24.

117. Les Csorba II, *Appeasing the Censors: A Special Report on Campus Free Speech Abuses* (Washington, D.C.: Accuracy in Academia, undated), pp. 20–26.

118. "The Dude's Been Called Worse," *Michigan Review*, March 1990, p. 9.

119. Kathleen O'Toole, "Alumni Ask About Racial Issues," *Stanford Observer*, January–February 1990, p. 10.

120. Kimberly Naahielua, "Admitting Goals," *The Virginia Advocate* (University of Virginia), April 1991, p. 7.

121. See, for example, John Larew, "Why are Droves of Unqualified, Unprepared Kids Getting into Our Top Colleges? Because Their Dads Are Alumni?" *The Washington Monthly*, June 1991, pp. 10–14.

122. Benjamin DeMott, "Legally Sanctioned Special Advantages Are a Way of Life in the United States," *The Chronicle of Higher Education*, February 27, 1991, p. A40.

123. Paul Hollander, *Anti-Americanism*, p. 209.

124. Davidson Goldin, "Report Says Suburban Minorities At Cornell

Outnumber Urbanites," *Cornell Daily Sun*, March 13, 1990, p. 3.

125. John H. Bunzel, "Living Together: Ethnic Theme Houses at Stanford," *The Stanford Magazine*, Summer 1985, p. 54.

126. "This Year's College Freshmen: Attitudes and Characteristics," *The Chronicle of Higher Education*, January 30, 1991, p. A30.

127. Claude M. Steele, "Race and the Schooling of Black Americans," *Atlantic Monthly*, April 1992, p. 78.

128. Mary Gibson Hundley, *The Dunbar Story (1870–1955)* (New York: Vantage Press, 1965), pp. 75–78.

CHAPTER 11: BANKRUPTCY

1. National Science Foundation, *Selected Data on Science and Engineering Doctorate Awards: 1990* (Washington, D.C.: U.S. Government Printing Office, 1991).

2. Archie E. Lapointe, Nancy A. Mead, and Gary W. Phillips, *A World of Differences: An International Assessment of Mathematics and Science* (Princeton: Educational Testing Service, 1989), pp. 10–11.

3. Chester E. Finn, Jr., *We Must Take Charge: Our Schools and Our Future* (New York: The Free Press, 1991), p. 36.

4. John Hood, "When Business 'Adopts' Schools: Spare the Rod, Spoil the Child," *Policy Analysis* (Cato Institute), June 5, 1991, p. 5.

5. Thomas Toch, *In the Name of Excellence: The Struggle to Reform the Nation's Schools, Why It's Failing, and What Should Be Done* (New York: Oxford University Press, 1991), p. 5.

6. Joyce D. Stern and Mary Frase Williams, *The Condition of Education: A Statistical Report*, 1986 Edition (Washington, D.C.: Center for Education Statistics, 1986), pp. 36, 69.

7. Karen De Witt, "Verbal Scores Hit New Low in Scholastic Aptitude Tests," *New York Times*, August 27, 1991, p. A16.

8. Chester E. Finn, Jr., *We Must Take Charge*, p. 36.

9. "The Myth Debunked—Spending Not the Cure-All for Schools," *Education Update*, Vol. 13, No. 4 (Fall 1990), p. 1.

10. Diane Ravitch, "Scapegoating the Teachers," *New Republic*, November 7, 1983, p. 28.

11. Thomas Toch, *In the Name of Excellence*, pp. 44–55.

12. "Public Schools Enroll 41.5 Million," *NEA Today*, October 1991, p. 8; Thomas Toch, *In the Name of Excellence*, p. 158.

13. Mary Ann Seawell, "Union Leader Shanker Urges 'Market' Approach to Bringing About Major Changes in Education," *Stanford University Campus Report*, January 3, 1990, p. 5.

14. Thomas Toch, *In the Name of Excellence*, pp. 240, 270–271.

15. "High School Dropouts: How Much of a Crisis?" *Backgrounder* (The Heritage Foundation), No. 781 (August 3, 1990), p. 9.
16. *Ibid.*, p. 5.
17. "Sources of Voluntary Support for Higher Education, 1989–90," *Chronicle of Higher Education: Almanac*, August 28, 1991, p. 35.
18. "College and University Endowments Over $60 Million, 1990," *ibid.*, p. 36.
19. "Revenues and Expenditures of College and Universities, 1987–88," *ibid.*, p. 35.
20. Anyone who doubts this is referred to Thomas Toch, *In the Name of Excellence*, pp. 151–193.
21. Chester E. Finn, Jr., *We Must Take Charge*, p. 195.
22. *Ibid.*, pp. 100–104; Thomas Toch, *In the Name of Excellence*, pp. 205–232.

INDEX